THE COLLECTED LETTERS OF
JOHN MILLINGTON SYNGE

VOLUME ONE

1871–1907

THE COLLECTED
LETTERS OF
JOHN MILLINGTON
SYNGE

EDITED BY

ANN SADDLEMYER

VOLUME ONE

1871 – 1907

CLARENDON PRESS · OXFORD

1983

Oxford University Press, Walton Street, Oxford OX2 6DP
London Glasgow New York Toronto
Delhi Bombay Calcutta Madras Karachi
Kuala Lumpur Singapore Hong Kong Tokyo
Nairobi Dar es Salaam Cape Town
Melbourne Auckland
and associated companies in
Beirut Berlin Ibadan Mexico City Nicosia

Oxford is a trade mark of Oxford University Press

Published in the United States
by Oxford University Press, New York

British Library Cataloguing in Publication Data
Synge, J. M.
The collected letters of John Millington Synge
Vol. 1: 1871–1907
1. Synge, J. M. — Correspondence
I. Title   II. Saddlemyer, Ann
822'.912   PR5535
ISBN 0-19-812678-6

Library of Congress Cataloging in Publication Data
Synge, J. M. (John Millington), 1871–1909.
The collected letters of John Millington Synge.
Includes index.
1. Synge, J. M. (John Millington), 1871–1909 — Correspondence.
2. Dramatists, Irish — 20th century — Correspondence.
I. Saddlemyer, Ann.   II. Title.
PR5533.A44 1983   822'.912 [B]   82-14535
ISBN 0-19-812678-6 (v. 1)

Typeset by Hope Services, Abingdon
and printed in Great Britain
at the University Press, Oxford
by Eric Buckley
Printer to the University

For my mother and father

CONTENTS

ILLUSTRATIONS

in the text

INTRODUCTION

IT is possible, from the many word pictures left us by his friends and admirers, to tease out a fairly consistent portrait of John Synge as he impressed his contemporaries.

He was a strong, well-built man, muscular, with broad shoulders, standing five feet eight or nine inches tall and carrying his large, finely shaped head upright. His thick, dishevelled hair was dark chestnut in colour, and the cleanly shaven rectangular jaw was decorated with a thick heavy moustache and a small tuft of hair on his chin, protecting lips that trembled with nervous intensity and quiet humour. 'Synge's face reminds me of Gorki with a touch of Nietzsche. Later in life he may develop a resemblance to Balzac,' the artist Charles Ricketts noted in his diary. The nervous and virile face was pale beneath his summer tan, the cheeks rather drawn through constant illness; it was not a handsome face, but singularly expressive and sometimes almost sad. His light hazel eyes, at once smoky and kindling, gazed directly and frankly.

He did not look like a poet at first glance. He dressed simply, in plain brown clothes, with a celluloid collar and tie, a soft hat and overcoat with a cape, thick home-knitted stockings in heavy walking boots. His voice was guttural and quick, almost foreign-sounding, with a kind of lively bitterness in it, and he had a curious laugh, a pulsating whistle between his teeth, the smile at the same time ironic and sympathetic. Most friends agreed that John Butler Yeats's drawing in *Samhain*, 1904, was the man himself.

His was a strange, alluring personality, unaffected yet confident; he was a simple man of courtesy and sensitivity, conducting himself with charm and good manners; on first meeting mild, perhaps slightly shy. He was not talkative, 'but one saw something deep in him,' Arthur Symons recalled. Once engaged, he was open and welcoming, his conversation holding the charm of absolute sincerity and insight. 'He never deceived himself nor anybody else, and yet he had the enthusiasm of the poet,' especially when he spoke of the west of Ireland. He was 'the best companion', 'the best of all "observers" '. 'Of all men he was the easiest to live with or to talk to. Most times he was listening, but when he talked in his hasty and rapid utterance, everyone listened and gave way.' 'I never heard him say a brilliant thing. He said shrewd things.' 'He was a scholar, precise in his phrases, perhaps even a little formal in conversation, but always frank in his opinions'; 'an excellent critic with clear and definite ideas', 'his criticisms usually terse'. 'His talk was best when it was about life and the ways of life.' 'He liked people to talk to him. He liked to know the colours of people's minds. He liked to be amused. His merriest talk was like playing catch with an apple of banter, which one afterwards ate and forgot.' J. B. Yeats wrote immediately after his death, 'Morally he was one of the most fastidious men I ever met, at once too sensitive and too proud and passionate ever to stoop for a moment to any kind of action that would be unworthy.' Some time later John Masefield summed up his responses: 'He eschewed all things that threatened his complete frugal independence and thereby the integrity of his mind.' 'His place was outside the circle, gravely watching, gravely summing up, with a brilliant malice, the fools and wise ones inside.'[1]

It did not take long for this arresting figure to pass into mythology and become the quasi-romantic, innocent and naïve primitive of poetry and memoirs. Masefield reluctantly admitted that Synge had read — but passionately disliked — the writers of the 1890s. W. B. Yeats strongly denied any hint of decadence in those early Paris years, insisting that his friend had read Racine only, and never the writings of his own time. Stephen MacKenna went so far as to call into question any facility Synge had with languages whatsoever, and destroyed with green ink and scissors such lively expressions of distaste or criticism as would mar the perfect statue of this 'most perfect companion'.

What would Synge, the man who so exulted in extremes and violent passions, who hated even the smell of a lie, have thought of such emasculation? 'Your uncle John', Samuel Synge wrote to his daughter, 'did not care to read books of history, but preferred to read the original letters or records concerned if possible.'[2] And this is perhaps the strongest justification — if any is required — for the

---

[1] This description is a collage of details and impressions from the following sources: Sara Allgood's reminiscences, unpublished, Berg Collection, New York Public Library; James H. Cousins and Margaret E. Cousins, *We Two Together* (Madras, 1950), 50; Louis Esson, 'J. M. Synge', *Fellowship* (Melbourne), VII, 9 (April 1921), 138–41; Anatole LeBraz to Maurice Bourgeois, 23 Feb 1913; Stephen MacKenna, unpublished notes in National Library of Ireland (forthcoming 1983, in *Irish University Review*); John Masefield, *John M. Synge, A Few Personal Recollections* (Letchworth, 1916); Karel Mušek, trans. O. F. Bablet, *Notes and Queries*, 21 Sept 1946, 124; Charles Ricketts, *Self-Portrait*, ed. Cecil Lewis (1939), 104, 127; Arthur Symons, 'John Synge', unpublished manuscript (1914), University of Florida, Gainesville; Alfred Wareing, 'The Abbey Theatre's First Invasion of Britain', unpublished lecture (1938), Berg Collection, New York Public Library; Jack B. Yeats, letter to the Editor, *Evening Sun* (New York), 20 July 1909; John Butler Yeats, letter to the Editor, *Evening Sun* (New York), 3 Apr 1909; John Butler Yeats, 'Synge and the Irish', *Essays Irish and American* (Dublin, 1918), 51–61; W. B. Yeats, letter to the Editor, *The Nation*, 10 Apr 1909, 54.
[2] Samuel Synge, *Letters to My Daughter* (Dublin, 1932), 121.

publication of his collected letters. He kept copies of his own business correspondence and letters from friends throughout his life; he preserved practically every draft of his works; although intensely private, he even retained his early commonplace books and pocket diaries, until the pressure of daily activities in the theatre made such reminders unnecessary. And, it should be remembered, he published the letters of his Aran friends.

We are not, alas, so fortunate in *his* correspondents. Little survives from the years before 1903, and what there is, is sporadic. Despite years of research, I have been unable to turn up any of his letters to friends in Germany, France, or Italy during the years of travel on the Continent. I am grateful to Synge himself, that earnest young student of languages, for having kept fair copies of them in his notebooks, so that the first 28 letters — in German, French, and Italian — preserve some of the flavour of his years of travel and study abroad. Unhappily his brothers, to whom Mrs Synge sent lengthy descriptions of his experiences, saved her letters but not his. And so we are dependent on the brief summaries she confided to her own diaries.

In this and in many other ways, John Synge owed much to his mother. Solitary as a child, too sickly even to attend school regularly with his three older brothers, he ranged outward into the country around Dublin from a tight family centre. When a friend presented him with an 'extraordinary' in 1888, he cycled further afield (frequently to Enniskerry and back, a distance of some twenty miles, before lunch). But he returned always to a household where although there was little outward expression of affection, a tacit assumption of unity and caring prevailed. The pattern would be repeated throughout his life; even after making his first journey abroad, at twenty-two years of age, he never really left home.

Synge's nephew Edward Stephens has perceptively remarked that even after her 'headstrong' son rejected his mother's strict Evangelical teaching, her training in 'private judgement and the pursuit of truth' and her insistence on the avoidance of public controversy fortified him in his slow private preparation. Austere but kindly, she could only watch and care:

This is Johnnie's birthday. I can hardly fancy he is 17. I have been looking back to the time he was born. I was so dreadfully delicate and he, poor child was the same . . . . I see no signs of spiritual life in my poor Johnnie; there may be some, but it is not visible to my eyes. He is very reserved and shut up on the subject and if I say any thing to him he never answers me, so I don't know in the least the state of his mind — it is a trying state, *very* trying. I long so to be able to see behind that close reserve, but I can only wait and pray and hope.[3]

---

[3] *My Uncle John: Edward Stephens's Life of J. M. Synge*, ed. Andrew Carpenter (1974), 42.

Her favourite maxim, 'Be ye in the world but separate from the world', could aptly describe her son's demeanour not only then, but for the rest of his life.

Mother and son shared other qualities. She too loved nature, and looked forward eagerly each summer to the months in Wicklow. When he studied the violin, she accompanied him on the piano. Seeking always to understand his choices in life, even if she could not fully sympathize with them, she arranged first for him to study music in Germany, later to concentrate on languages in Paris and Italy. Against her better judgement she pleaded her son's suit to Cherrie Matheson. And she knew before he confessed it of his love for Molly Allgood; although other details worried her — Molly was not only a Roman Catholic but an actress, and neither John nor the girl had any money. She would not have been surprised at her son's choice of such a young bride; had she not herself married happily, at seventeen, a man fourteen years her senior?

What she could not conceive of, nor hope to comprehend, was her son's determination to be a man of letters, and within a nationalist movement to boot. For hers was a 'Unionist Club',[4] and its rules demanded not only inner morality — John's she never doubted — but outward piety and an income matching the state of grace. She wrote to Samuel, her missionary son,

He says I am to tell Robert to get old George Borrow's Book of travels or as it is called 'The Bible in Spain' .. . . . I am thankful among all the queer literature he gathers up that he gets some good books among them . . . .

I heard from Johnnie on Sunday his letters are getting shorter each week he says nothing. I don't think he likes the advice I gave him to try to earn money by writing what will sell and not that high flown stuff that so few can appreciate![5]

Not even with the assurances of his cousin Emily Synge — one of the few members of his family to whom Synge could speak openly — that Yeats had altered his complete disbelief in any spiritual existence, comforting though that might be,[6] could she express any confidence in her son's new-found friends:

I asked him in one letter how he could be mixed up with nationalists, and he said I was not to think he is a rebel, but he thinks Ireland will come to her own in years to come when socialistic ideas spread in England, but he does not at all

---

[4] The title Synge gave to an unfinished article (TCD) on the Anglo-Irish professional class to which his family belonged.
[5] Letters to Samuel Synge, 21 Nov 1899 and 30 Jan 1900 (TCD).
[6] Recollections by E. M. Stephens (TCD). One wonders whether Mrs Synge would have taken any comfort in her son's careful preservation of a correspondence in the *Daily Telegraph*, 'Do We Believe?', or another cutting from the *Irish Times* concerning memory in protoplasm (both TCD).

approve of fighting for freedom. He thinks things will change by degrees in the world and there will be equality and no more grinding down of the poor.[7]

With a suggestion of enjoyment, she wrote in her diary of his 'great fight over the [Boer] war' with her sister Harriet.[8] But she would not have been amused by this defence of his friendship with Maud Gonne: 'A radical is a person who wants change root and branch, and I'm proud to be a radical.'[9]

After several years' experience on the Continent, Synge wrote in his notebook,

In friendship a man approves of the conception that his friends form of him and tends to become it. Hence at last the intercourse is between A's conception of B and B's conception of A. Which is the reason why many friendships with women especially develop a man. I mean the conceptions which are formed by the whole being not the character we might give a person in speaking even to ourselves a portrait not a specification. (TCD)

Ever the student of literature, human nature, and most especially of himself, Synge's remarks are particularly apt concerning his own development. When we look over the list of recipients of the letters rescued from oblivion, and the names of those whose letters he himself preserved, it is striking how few are men, how many women. When one analyses, for example, his correspondence with Stephen MacKenna, it is clear from Synge's letters that he is playing a role established during those early Paris years when the two innocent boulevardiers supported each other's interests, ambitions, and secret dreams; his language is rich with double — sometimes triple — meanings, relying on shared reading and cultural experience; it is redolent of bygone raillery and resposed confidence; it swaggers. Yet it stops short of full confession, trusting more to the passionate exchange of ideas than to the revelation of inner emotions. From MacKenna's reminiscences and letters we gain confirmation of Synge's love for and technical knowledge of paintings, drawings, and prints, explaining the frequent visits to the Louvre dutifully noted in his pocket diaries of the 1890s; of his continuing interest in — but reluctance to commit himself to — spiritualist thought; of his need for the renewal brought by solitude and nature. MacKenna's knowledge of Synge's intense nationalism and hatred of English imperialism places in more accurate perspective the letters from Rome reporting on political disturbances. And MacKenna himself perhaps most accurately summed up their relationship in the inscription

---

[7] Quoted by David H. Greene and Edward M. Stephens, *J. M. Synge 1871-1909* (New York, 1959), 63.
[8] Diary, 25 May 1900 (TCD).
[9] A conversation recalled by E. M. Stephens in his unpublished MS, 'The Life of J. M. Synge' (TCD).

written on the copy of FitzGerald's translation of the *Rubáiyat of Omar Khayyám* enclosed with a letter of 15 June 1900:

To the Loyal and Sympathetic camarade J. M. Synge — this minisculous gifteen in memory of delightful talks and walks and of gladnesses and sorrows, minisculous too, shared in unclouded friendliness in the Quartier Latin 1899–1900.

STEPHEN MACKENNA[10]

We do not know the character of Synge's friendship with Georges Roeder, a young family man in a wholesale business who collected stamps and did some translating; judging from Roeder's replies, the letters remained on a friendly, informative, but not too personal basis, nor were they frequent. Similarly with Albert Cugnier, the young Breton student introduced by the von Eicken sisters, who writes banteringly from French Guinea of Synge's silence. A greater loss is the correspondence with Henri Lebeau, for obviously Synge trusted this friend's literary judgement, and wrote often of his career in the theatre and his artistic progress. In all probability, these letters contained the most complete exposition of his dramatic theory. But as he was later to admit to Molly Allgood, he did not really know Lebeau very well.

With women, on the other hand, as we can see from his letters to Valeska von Eicken, Thérèse Beydon, Rosie Calthrop — even those to the formidable Sarah Purser — we do indeed find more of 'the whole being'. Masefield was to write, 'When I turn over my memories of him, it seems that his grave courtesy was only gay when he was talking to women. His talk to women had a lightness and charm.'[11]

Apart from Cherrie Matheson's brief quotations, we have no record of those conversations. With her Synge talked of subjects which constantly crop up in letters from Lily Capps, the American student he met in Rome; Maria Zdanowska, the Polish art student with whom he regularly visited museums in Paris; Hope Rea, the English art historian with whom he continued to meet and correspond throughout his life; Edie Harmar and Madeline Kerr, Mrs Synge's visitors in Wicklow;[12] Margaret Hardon, the American art student with whom he fell in love.[13] They talked of politics, the quality of friendship, religion, belief and unbelief, spiritualism and

---

[10] This book is now in the possession of Dr Andrew Carpenter, Dublin.

[11] *John M. Synge*, 9.

[12] Thérèse Beydon may well have been referring to these two when she wrote, 'I am so glad that those three young ladies in the country have proved a distraction for you, especially the one 30 years old with whom you can discuss things' (TCD).

[13] Margaret Hardon was evidently a very forthright, as well as charming, young woman, judging from the outspokenness of an article, 'In the Quartier Latin, The Truth About the American Girl's Life', *Boston Evening Transcript*, 22 May 1899, 8: 'She will be disappointed in her first view of the Quartier and must put up with many inconveniences, but if she is of the right stamina she will succeed.'

mysticism, relationships between men and women, books, life, and, of course, art. One longs especially for a glimpse of his relationship with the two women within his own family circle who were responsive to his needs and ambitions: his cousin Florence Ross, herself an artist (appropriately in a house run by deaconesses), whose shared childhood he describes in his autobiographies;[14] and 'Cousin Emily', of Uplands near Castle Kevin, aunt of the etcher Edward Synge and somewhat suspect because of her liberal leanings and love of animals.

Both Emily Synge and Florence Ross approved of the theatre, much to Mrs Synge's disappointment, and thus provided for John the one link between home and artistic activity. Although his relationship with his mother remained as firmly based as ever, the demands of theatre business and an increasing interest in the young actress Molly Allgood took him away from summers in Wicklow and even, for two short periods, from Mrs Synge's household. But he could still delight in Wicklow with Molly at his side, and companionship with Yeats and Lady Gregory provided the pattern for which his long European apprenticeship had prepared him. Uneasy though the relationship between Synge and his fellow directors of the Abbey Theatre might be at times — for, ironically, they too disapproved of his intimacy with an actress — it was founded on a common desire for the establishment of a true kingdom of art on this specific earth, for which new commandments must be established and a new temple erected. The theatre brought also new friendships, and, above all, the knowledge that he was needed. Here were fellow craftsmen whom he could respect, who spoke his language, and in turn recognized him. They included not only writers — though these were accorded chief place — but performers, designers, translators, publishers, and (occasionally) critics. Together they made living in Ireland and writing for Ireland worth while.

But his colleagues in the Abbey Theatre did not understand him either, no matter how much more approachable and charming they found him than Yeats or Lady Gregory. Or, rather, they liked the man but could not stomach the work — and found difficulty reconciling the two. Lady Gregory respected his genius, but mistook his reluctance to become involved in public quarrels (a trait he shared with his family) for weakness of spirit, his single-minded devotion to the development of self, for mere vanity. And Yeats felt comfortable with Synge only after his death, when, despite the genuineness of his sense of loss, he was able to engrave an image more nearly fitting his own pantheon.

---

[14] J. M. Synge, *Prose*, ed. Alan Price (1966), 6–9; see also the memories of women quoted from a notebook written about 1899, 110 n.

The theatre brought Synge not only creative fulfillment, but the promise of his ideal love. Molly Allgood (whose stage name was 'Maire O'Neill') was beautiful, with a natural — almost animal — grace and charm, and her instinctive approach to her art was marked by an honesty of feeling which he valued above all.[15] In his letters to Molly, Synge comes full circle, bringing together all the strands of personality, training, and habit we find being formed in his early years: that passion for truth and trust and hatred of anything remotely resembling deception; the desire to be 'of the world but separate from the world'; comradeship in the arts. With Molly at his side among the natural splendours of the Irish countryside, both responding to the hierarchy of their moods and passions, the completed personality was realizable at last. The significance of his signature, 'Your old Tramp', extends far beyond the role of the lyrical wandering stranger who frees Nora Burke from the shadows of the glen.[16]

These letters of 1906 and 1907 also echo early drafts of his first completed play, *When the Moon Has Set*, begun in notebook jottings when he first embarked on his journey to the Continent:

'If you love a woman subdue her. You will not love a woman it is not lawful to love. No man of our blood has ever been unlawful. If you live in the country live with the country and find a woman who will understand with you the mysteries of growth and life. Let her know as you will know the two twilights and the quietness of the night. Neglect nothing, for God is in the earth and not above it.'

'The world is an orchestra where every living thing plays one entry and then gives his place to another. We must be careful to play all the notes . . . . Every passion will unite in new discords resolving in what are to us inconceivable harmonies.'

'Every life is a symphony. It is this cosmic element in the person which gives all personal art, and all sincere life, and all passionate love a share in the dignity of the world.'[17]

---

[15] Molly was able later to express in words her approach to acting: 'An actor or actress must have one essential quality, he or she must be an actor at heart. One must feel one is an actor within. Otherwise how can you *feel* your part? . . . Just as Delacroix revelled in the background of organ-music while painting in Saint Sulpice in Paris, so likewise must the sincere actor *feel* the moving power of his words in his heart, that same power, that verbal motivating music which finds *expression* in utterance by the lips.' (Quoted by Sean O'Mahony Rahilly, 'Synge and the Early Days of the Abbey', *Irish Press*, 21 Apr 1949.) Yeats wrote to Lady Gregory of Molly's performance in his *Deirdre* in 1911, 'I am beginning to think that Miss O'Neill will be a great tragic actress. The scenes between her and Mrs Emery are wonderful things — everyone else is blotted out. Mrs Emery thinks her finer than Mrs Campbell because of her natural emotion.' (Joseph Hone, *W. B. Yeats 1865-1939* [1962], 252.)
[16] See ' "A Share in the Dignity of the World": J. M. Synge's Aesthetic Theory', *The World of W. B. Yeats*, ed. Robin Skelton and Ann Saddlemyer (Seattle, 1967), 207-19, and 'Art, Nature, and "The Prepared Personality", A Reading of *The Aran Islands* and Related Writings', *Sunshine and the Moon's Delight*, ed. S. B. Bushrui (Gerrards Cross, 1972), 107-20.
[17] J. M. Synge, *Plays* Book I, ed. Ann Saddlemyer (1968), 164, 176.

Appropriately, this first volume of his letters ends with the ca-
cophony accompanying *The Playboy of the Western World* behind
him, the plaintive notes of a lengthy illness silenced, as Synge and
Molly prepare for a well-deserved rest among the harmonies of
Wicklow.

During the 1920s Edward Hutchinson Synge planned, apparently,
to include his uncle's letters in a new edition of the works. Thanks
to his interest, copies of Synge's correspondence with Karel Mušek,
James Paterson, and M. J. Nolan are among the Synge papers now in
the Library of Trinity College, Dublin. Unfortunately a severe break-
down prevented Edward Hutchinson Synge from carrying out his
plan and at this time he appears to have destroyed the letters of
Synge's which Cherrie Matheson sent him from South Africa.[18] The
1932 edition of Synge's plays contains only a few observations from
one of his notebooks and 'A Letter to a Young Man'.

In 1924 Dr Max Meyerfeld published some of Synge's letters in
the *Yale Review*, n.s. XIII (July 1924), 690–709, and in 1964 I published some of his letters to Stephen MacKenna in the *Massachusetts
Review*, V (Winter 1964), 279–96, but neither of these collections is
complete. *Some Letters and Documents of J. M. Synge*, comprising
nine letters, drafts of two poems, a publisher's contract, and an
anonymous criticism written after Synge's death, from the collection
of Lawrence Wilson, were published by the Redpath Press, McGill
University Library, in 1959; these papers are now in the Trinity
College, Dublin, Library. Fragments from his letters appear in Lady
Gregory's memoirs and in the Greene and Stephens biography.

Three collections of letters edited by me have previously been
published: *Some Letters of John M. Synge to Lady Gregory and
W. B. Yeats* (Dublin: Cuala Press, 1971), since incorporated in
*Theatre Business, The Correspondence of the First Abbey Theatre
Directors* (Gerrards Cross: Colin Smythe, and University Park, Pa.:
Pennsylvania State University Press, 1982), and *Letters to Molly,
John Millington Synge to Maire O'Neill* (Cambridge, Mass.: Belknap
Press of Harvard University Press, 1971). I have been able to correct
transcriptions, dates and references in all these earlier publications. In
doing so, I have been greatly assisted by access to the Synge papers in
the possession of the Stephens family and in Trinity College, Dublin,
Library, especially Synge's own diaries and those of Mrs Kathleen
Synge and the complete text of Edward Stephens's 'Life', and to the
complete Joseph Holloway diaries and other relevant manuscript collections in the National Library of Ireland. Certain published works

[18] See Ronald Ayling, 'Synge's First Love: Some South African Aspects', *Modern Drama*,
February 1964, 450–60.

have been invaluable, especially the two biographies, by Maurice Bourgeois, *John Millington Synge and the Irish Theatre*, (1913), and by David H. Greene and Edward M. Stephens, as well as Andrew Carpenter's edition of Stephens's 'Life', Samuel Synge's *Letters to my Daughter*, and the first three volumes of *The Modern Irish Drama*, documentary histories compiled by Robert Hogan and James Kilroy (Dublin, 1975–8).

All letters have been transcribed from the originals where these still exist; sometimes copies also exist in other collections and these have been compared. (The originals of the photographic copies now in the National Library of Ireland are in the possession of Patrick Synge-Hutchinson.) Despite Synge's disclaimer to Molly that he made few mistakes in his letters, grammatical and spelling errors are prevalent and have been reproduced, with editorial emendations and additions provided only where absolutely necessary, in square brackets ([   ]). Where it has been possible to decipher passages struck out either by Synge or by MacKenna, these have been incorporated within angle brackets (〈 〉). Synge's underlining is rendered as follows: a word underlined once is set in italics; twice, in small capitals; more than twice, in small capitals underlined. Occasional words in Gaelic have been transliterated. Letters in languages other than English are given in the original, each with a translation which attempts to preserve the flavour of Synge's original.

Ann Saddlemyer

Victoria College
University of Toronto
June 1982

CHRONOLOGY
EDMUND JOHN MILLINGTON SYNGE
1871–1909

1871	16 Apr	Born, youngest child of John Hatch and Kathleen (Traill) Synge, at 2 Newtown Villas, Rathfarnham, Dublin.
1872	13 Apr	John Hatch Synge dies of smallpox.
	Summer	Mrs Synge moves to 4 Orwell Park, Rathgar, Dublin, next door to her mother, Mrs Anne Traill.
c. 1881		Irregular attendance at Mr Harrick's Classical and English School, 4 Upper Leeson Street, Dublin.
c. 1884		Irregular attendance for one year at Aravon House, Bray School.
1884–8		Private tutoring at home three times a week; regular Bible classes at Zion Church, Rathgar, supplemented by Mrs Synge.
c. 1885		First reads Darwin, and begins to doubt his mother's Evangelical theology.
1885	December	Joins the newly established Dublin Naturalists' Field Club.
1887	13 Oct	First violin lesson with Patrick J. Griffith, Dublin.
1888	18 June	Passes entrance examinations for Trinity College, Dublin.
1889	February	Attends first lectures at Trinity College where his tutor is his mother's cousin, Anthony Traill.
	November	Enrols in Royal Irish Academy of Music for classes in violin, musical theory, and composition.
	December	Informs his mother that he will no longer attend church, except during summers in County Wicklow.
1890	October	Following the death of her mother, Mrs Synge rents 31 Crosthwaite Park, Kingstown, next door to her daughter, Mrs Annie Stephens.
	Autumn	Takes third class in Little Go examinations at Trinity College; is certified by Royal Irish Academy of Music for advanced study in counterpoint with Sir Robert Stewart.
1891	January–March	Joins student orchestra at Academy; plays in first concert at Antient Concert Rooms, Dublin.
	Summer	Begins to study German privately.
	Autumn	Studies Hebrew and Irish at Trinity College.

1891	December	His cousin Florence Ross joins Mrs Synge's household after her mother's death.
1892	16 Mar	Awarded scholarship and medal in counterpoint at Academy.
	June	Takes first place in examinations in Hebrew and Irish at Trinity College.
	20 July–15 Sept	With Mrs Synge at Castle Kevin, Co. Wicklow.
	15 Dec	Awarded second class B.A. from Trinity College.
1893	28 Feb	Canvasses for anti-Home Rule petition.
	17 Apr	Arranges and publicizes piano recital by his cousin Mary Synge at Antient Concert Rooms, Dublin.
	Spring	His sonnet 'Glencullen' published in *Kottabos*, Trinity College.
	7–30 June	Resumes study of German with Herr Wespendorf.
	1–24 July	With Mrs Synge at Avonmore, Co. Wicklow.
	26 July	Leaves for London.
	29 July–21 Jan 1894	Lodges with von Eickens, Oberwerth, near Koblenz, Germany, while studying music.
1894	22 Jan–1 June	Lodges with Frau Süsser, Hanger Ring 16, Würzburg, while studying violin and piano.
	20–27 Mar	Holiday with von Eickens in Koblenz, returning by way of Frankfurt.
	April–May	Begins to write his first play (uncompleted), and turns from study of music to literature.
	1–12 June	Visits von Eickens in Koblenz.
	14 June	Returns to Dublin.
	3 July–5 Sept	With Mrs Synge at Castle Kevin, Wicklow, where Cherrie Matheson spends two weeks from 28 July as sketching companion for Florence Ross.
	30 Oct	Returns to Koblenz by way of London.
	3 Nov–31 Dec	Lodges with von Eickens while studying German and French.
1895	2 Jan	Lodges with M. Arbeau, 94 rue Lafayette, Paris X^e. Joins the Société Fraternelle d'Étudiants Protestants.
	10 Feb	Death of his aunt Jane Synge who leaves him a legacy of £500.
	1 Apr	Lodges with M. Peter, 2 rue Léopold-Robert, Paris XIVe.
	25 Apr	Enrols at Sorbonne in courses in modern French literature with A. E. Faguet and medieval literature with Petit de Julleville; starts course in general and comparative phonetics with Paul Passy at the École Pratique des Hautes-Études.
	3 June	Begins exchange of language lessons with Thérèse Beydon.

1895	28 June	Leaves Paris for Dublin by way of London.
	6 July–5 Sept	With Mrs Synge in Wicklow (Lough Dan, 5–31 July; Castle Kevin, 31 July–5 Sept); refuses to attend church.
	11 Nov	First lesson in Italian with Signor Morosini, Dublin.
1896	2 Jan	Leaves Kingstown for Paris by way of London.
	3 Jan–3 Feb	At Hôtel Corneille, 5 rue Corneille, Paris VIe. Italian lessons with Dr Meli.
	5 Feb–30 Apr	Studies art and Italian in Rome (5–7 Feb, Hotel Continental; 7–17 Feb, Pension Hayden; 17 Feb–30 Apr, lodges with Signor Conte Polloni, 73 via Aureliana). Sends reports to *Irish Times*.
	1 May–1 June	Studies in Florence; meets Maria Zdanowska and Hope Rea.
	3–29 June	At Hôtel de l'Univers, 9 rue Gay-Lussac, Paris V^e.
	9 June	Writes to Cherrie Matheson proposing marriage; is rejected.
	30 June–14 Sept	With Mrs Synge at Castle Kevin, Wicklow.
	21 Oct	His brother Samuel Synge leaves for China.
	26 Oct	Leaves Dublin for Paris by way of London.
	29 Oct–29 Dec	At Hôtel Corneille, Paris VIe. Meets Stephen MacKenna. Takes courses at Sorbonne on Petrarch with Emile Gebhart, on La Fontaine with Faguet, and on French literature with Petit de Julleville. Studies socialism, and joins an English debating society.
	21 Dec	Meets William Butler Yeats.
	29 Dec	Lodges again with M. Peter, 2 rue Léopold-Robert, XIVe.
1897	1 Jan	Present with Yeats at inaugural committee meeting of the Association Irlandaise at Maud Gonne's.
	6 Apr	Resigns from Association Irlandaise; studies spiritualism.
	13 May	Leaves Paris for Dublin by way of London.
	25 June–31 Aug	With Mrs Synge in Wicklow (Castle Kevin, 25 June–31 July; Casino, Avondale, August).
	11 Dec	Undergoes operation to remove swollen gland in his neck; writes about experience, 'Under Ether'.
1898	19 Jan	Leaves Dublin for Paris by way of London.
	23 Jan–22 Apr	At Hôtel St Malo, 2 rue d'Odessa, XIVe. Begins novel on nurses (unfinished). Meets Richard Best.
	18 Feb	Enrols at Sorbonne in course by d'Arbois de Jubainville on Irish and Homeric civilizations.
	2 Apr	Meets Margaret Hardon.
	22 Apr	Leaves Paris for Dublin.

1898	10 May–25 June	Visits Aran Islands for first time (10–24 May, Atlantic Hotel, Kilronan, Aranmore; 24 May–9 June, with Patrick McDonagh, Inishmaan; 9–25 June, Kilronan).
	27–29 June	Guest of Lady Gregory at Coole, with Yeats; visits Edward Martyn.
	2 July–2 Sept	With Mrs Synge at Castle Kevin.
	November	'A Story from Inishmaan' in *New Ireland Review* (Dublin).
	14 Nov	Leaves Dublin for Paris by way of London.
	18 Nov	Takes over Richard Best's room at 90 rue d'Assas, VIe, his permanent address in Paris until 1903; begins studying Breton.
1899	28 Jan	'Anatole Le Braz. A Breton Writer' in *Daily Express* (Dublin).
	3–16 Apr	Visits Quimper, Brittany.
	7 May	Leaves Paris for Dublin by way of London.
	12 May	Attends Irish Literary Theatre production of Yeats's *The Countess Cathleen* in Antient Concert Rooms, Dublin.
	1 June–5 Sept	With Mrs Synge at Castle Kevin.
	9 Sept	To Galway on way to Aran; visits Martin McDonagh.
	12 Sept–7 Oct	On Inishmaan, except for few final days on Inishmore.
	3 Nov	Leaves Dublin for Paris.
1900	22 Mar	'A Celtic Theatre' in *Freeman's Journal* (Dublin).
	23 May	Leaves Paris for Dublin.
	1 June–30 Aug	With Mrs Synge at Castle Kevin, where Rosie Calthrop is her guest.
	15 Sept–14 Oct	On Inishmaan except for a few days on Inishere.
	17 Oct	Returns to Kingstown from Galway.
	1 Nov	Returns to Paris.
1901	April	'The Last Fortress of the Celt' in *The Gael* (New York).
	6 May	Returns to Dublin.
	4 June–6 Sept	With Mrs Synge at Castle Kevin.
	14–20 Sept	With Lady Gregory and Yeats at Coole.
	21 Sept–19 Oct	On Aran (Inishmaan 21–30 Sept; Inishere 1–19 Oct).
	21 Oct	Attends Irish Literary Theatre production of Yeats's and Moore's *Diarmuid and Grania* and Hyde's *Casadh an tSugáin* at Gaiety Theatre, Dublin.
	26 Nov	Leaves Dublin for Paris by way of London with MS of *The Aran Islands*.

1902	14 Feb	Enrols at Sorbonne in course in Old Irish by d'Arbois de Jubainville.
	15 Mar	'La Vieille Littérature irlandaise' in *L'Européen* (Paris).
	April	Begins writing verse plays.
	17 May	Returns to Dublin from Paris.
	31 May	'Le Mouvement intellectuel irlandais' in *L'Européen*.
	7 June	Review of Lady Gregory's *Cuchulain of Muirthemne* in *The Speaker* (London).
	21 July–6 Sept	With Mrs Synge at Tomrilands, Co. Wicklow.
	6 Sept	'The Old and New in Ireland' in *The Academy and Literature* (London).
	8–13 Oct	With Lady Gregory and Yeats at Coole; shows them *Riders to the Sea* and *In the Shadow of the Glen*.
	14 Oct–8 Nov	On Inishere.
	23 Nov	Cherrie Matheson marries Kenneth Houghton.
	? 4 Dec	Sees W. G. Fay's company for the first time performing *The Laying of the Foundations*, *The Pot of Broth*, *Eilís agus an Bhean Déirce*, and *The Racing Lug* at Camden Street Hall, Dublin.
1903	9 Jan	Leaves Dublin for London.
	12 Jan	Lodges at 4 Handel Street, Russell Square; is introduced by Yeats and Lady Gregory to John Masefield, G. K. Chesterton, Arthur Symons, Pamela Colman Smith, and others.
	6–13 Mar	Crosses to Paris to give up his room at 90 rue d'Assas; spends time with James Joyce.
	18 Mar	Leaves London for Dublin.
	April	'An Autumn Night in the Hills' in *The Gael*.
	23 May	Completes one-act play, *When the Moon Has Set*.
	? June	'A Dream of Inishmaan' in *The Green Sheaf* (London).
	28 Aug–19 Sept	Lodges with Philly Harris, Mountain Stage, Glenbeigh, Co. Kerry.
	October	*Riders to the Sea* published in *Samhain* (Dublin).
	8–10 Oct	*In the Shadow of the Glen* produced, with *The King's Threshold*, by W. G. Fay's Irish National Theatre Society at Molesworth Hall.
1904	25–27 Feb	*Riders to the Sea*, with AE's *Deirdre*, produced by Irish National Theatre Society at Molesworth Hall.
	26 Feb–8 Mar	Ill in bed.
	March	'A Dream of Inishmaan' in *The Gael*.
	24 Mar	Leaves for London with players; stays at 4 Handel Street.

1904	26 Mar	*The Shadow of the Glen* and *Riders to the Sea* performed at matinée, Royalty Theatre, London.
	2 Apr	Review of d'Arbois de Jubainville's *The Irish Mythological Cycle*, translated by Richard Best, in *The Speaker*.
	30 Apr	Leaves London for Dublin.
	16–31 July	At Coole helping Lady Gregory revise her *Kincora*.
	1 Aug–1 Sept	With Philly Harris at Mountain Stage, Co. Kerry.
	17 Sept–1 Oct	Bicycles through North Mayo instead of returning to Aran.
	10 Oct	Lodges with Mrs Stewart, 15 Maxwell Road, Rathgar.
	31 Oct	Present with John Quinn from New York at first rehearsal in new Abbey Theatre.
	December	*The Shadow of the Glen* published in *Samhain* and privately published by John Quinn in New York.
	27 Dec	Opening of the Abbey Theatre; revival of *The Shadow of the Glen* on the 28th.
1905	24 Jan	'An Impression of Aran' in *Manchester Guardian*.
	4–11 Feb	*The Well of the Saints* produced; Molly Allgood has a walk-on part.
	7 Feb	John Quinn copyrights *The Well of the Saints* in New York simultaneously with publication of theatre edition by Maunsel & Co. (Dublin).
	11 Feb	Letter to *United Irishman* over renewed controversy concerning *The Shadow of the Glen*.
	13 Feb	George Moore writes to the *Irish Times* praising *The Well of the Saints*.
	15 Feb	Moves back to Crosthwaite Park; 'The Oppression of the Hills' in *Manchester Guardian*.
	8 May	*The Shadow of the Glen* and *Riders to the Sea* published in Vigo edition by Elkin Mathews, London.
	3 June–3 July	Tours the Congested Districts of west of Ireland with Jack B. Yeats for *Manchester Guardian*; publishes 12 articles.
	7 Aug–16 Sept	Visits West Kerry (William Long, Ballyferriter), the Blasket Islands (Shawn Keane, 13–?27 Aug), and Mountain Stage.
	16–20 Sept	Attends policy meeting at Coole with Yeats, Lady Gregory.
	22 Sept	Company votes to become a limited company with Yeats, Lady Gregory, and JMS as directors; JMS, George Russell, and Fred Ryan authorized to draw up rules.

1905	20 Nov–12 Dec	In England, staying first with Edward Synge at Byfleet, Surrey. Company on tour 23–30 Nov to Oxford, Cambridge, and London; JMS joins them at Cambridge. In London, stays at Kenilworth Hotel from 26 Nov; meets Charles Ricketts and Charles Shannon.
1906	12 Jan	Max Meyerfeld's translation of *The Well of the Saints* performed at Deutsches Theater in Berlin.
	6 Feb	Lodges at 57 Rathgar Road.
	7 Feb	Karel Mušek's translation of *The Shadow of the Glen* performed at the Inchover Theatre in Prague.
	26–27 Feb	Accompanies players to Wexford; first public indication of his attachment to Molly Allgood.
	17 Mar	Accompanies players to Dundalk.
	23–30 Apr	Accompanies players on tour to Manchester, Liverpool, and Leeds.
	15 May	Accompanies players to Dundalk.
	26 May–9 July	Accompanies players on extensive tour to Cardiff, Glasgow, Aberdeen, Newcastle, Edinburgh, and Hull.
	9 July	Moves with Mrs Synge to Glendalough House, Glenageary, Kingstown.
	17–18 July	Joins Yeats, Lady Gregory, and W. G. Fay for policy meeting at Coole.
	24 July–4 Aug	Entertains Karel Mušek in Dublin.
	25 Aug–12 Sept	With Philly Harris, Mountain Stage, Kerry.
	Autumn	'The Vagrants of Wicklow' in *The Shanachie* (Dublin).
	30 Nov–14 Dec	Visits cousin Edward Synge in Byfleet, Surrey.
1907	26 Jan	First performance of *The Playboy of the Western World*, to unruly audiences for a week; theatre edition published by Maunsel.
	4 Feb–11 Mar	Ill at mother's home; Molly visits regularly.
	6 Mar	*The Playboy* copyrighted by John Quinn in New York.
	March	'The People of the Glens' in *The Shanachie*.
	?28 April	*The Aran Islands* published by Maunsel and Elkin Mathews.
	9 May	'At a Wicklow Fair. The Place and the People' in *Manchester Guardian*.
	11 May–17 June	Company on tour to Glasgow, Cambridge, Birmingham, Oxford, and London, performing *The Playboy* in Cambridge, Oxford, and London.
	30 May	Leaves Dublin to visit Jack Yeats in Devon before joining company in London on 8 June; stays at 4 Handel Street.
	17 June	Returns to Dublin with players.

1907	Summer	'In West Kerry' in *The Shanachie*.
	28 June–28 July	In Glencree, Molly also except for 11–23 July.
	1 July	'A Landlord's Garden in County Wicklow' in *Manchester Guardian*.
	22 Aug	*The Shadow of the Glen* produced at National Theatre, Prague.
	13–26 Sept	In Elpis Nursing Home for removal of swollen glands in neck.
	Autumn	'In West Kerry. The Blasket Islands' in *The Shanachie*.
	12–16 Oct	Visits Kerry, asthma attack forces return to Kingstown.
	Winter	'In West Kerry. To Puck Fair' in *The Shanachie*.
	23 Dec	*The Tinker's Wedding* published by Maunsel.
1908	13 Jan	The Fays resign from company.
	24 Jan	'Good Pictures in Dublin. The New Municipal Gallery' in *Manchester Guardian*.
	2 Feb	Takes rooms at 47 York Road, Rathmines, in preparation for marriage to Molly.
	26 Feb	Directs Lady Gregory's translation of Sudermann's *Teja*.
	4 Apr	Directs Lady Gregory's translation of Molière, *The Rogueries of Scapin*.
	30 Apr–6 July	To Elpis Nursing Home for abdominal operation 5 May; inoperable tumour discovered.
	14 May	Revised version of *The Well of the Saints* performed, with costumes and setting designed by Charles Ricketts; Molly playing Molly Byrne.
	6 July–13 Aug	Convalesces at his sister's home, Silchester House, Kingstown.
	6 Oct	Leaves Dublin for Koblenz by way of London.
	8 Oct–5 Nov	With the von Eickens, Koblenz.
	26 Oct	Mrs Synge dies.
	10 Dec	'In Wicklow. On the Road' in *Manchester Guardian*.
1909	2 Feb	Enters Elpis Nursing Home.
	24 Mar	Dies.
	5 June	*Poems and Translations* published by Cuala Press, Dublin.
1910	13 Jan	*Deirdre of the Sorrows* at Abbey Theatre, with Molly as Deirdre.
	5 July	*Deirdre of the Sorrows* published by Cuala Press.
	22 Nov	*The Works of John M. Synge*, 4 vols., published by Maunsel.

ACKNOWLEDGEMENTS

IN addition to those institutions and individuals listed at p. xxix under Manuscript Sources, the members of the Synge family especially deserve my gratitude for the assistance and encouragement they have constantly given me. The late Mrs Lilo Stephens, executor of the J. M. Synge estate after the death of her husband, Synge's nephew and biographer E. M. Stephens, over the years provided me not only with information, introductions and material, but most generous of all, an enduring friendship and a home in Dublin. Her family, Denis Synge Stephens QC, Edward Brandon Stephens FRCS, and Mrs Ann Porter, have continued to offer every assistance possible. Miss Edith Synge and Mr John Samuel Synge, children of the Revd Samuel Synge, have also been generous and active in their support. It has been a privilege to have been associated with them all for more than twenty years.

An edition such as this, so long in gestation, draws upon the strength and resources of so many people that it is impossible to name them all; I hope a general acknowledgement here will be taken in the genuine spirit with which it is offered. Certain individuals have done me specific service, in particular the translators: Dr Paul Botheroyd, who translated Synge's draft letters in German from transcriptions made from his nearly illegible 'old German' script by Mrs Friderun Barrow and Mr Andreas Weiland; Professor David Nolan, who transcribed and translated the Italian letters; Professor Gérard LeBlanc, who translated the letters in French; Dr Declan Kiberd and Professor Kevin B. Nowlan, who translated the letter in Irish.

The staffs of the Library of Trinity College, Dublin, the National Library of Ireland, and the John P. Robarts Research Library in the University of Toronto have been helpful, courteous, and patient.

And, finally, my thanks to the following for their willing assistance: Miss Constance Babington Smith, Professor Karl Beckson, Mr John Bell, Sir Basil Blackwell, Professor Brian Boydell, Professor Francis John Byrne, Dr Andrew Carpenter, Miss Catharine Carver, Mr Seamus Cashman, Professor Joan Coldwell, Dr Thomas Conroy, Professor Adele Dalsimer, Mr John Doyle, Professor Janet Egleson Dunleavy, Mr Stephen Fay, Professor Richard Finneran, the late Mr James Gallagher and Mrs Patricia Gallagher, the late Professor David Greene, Father Aubrey Gwynn SJ, Professor Joyce Hemlow, Miss Tanis Hinchcliffe, Professor Robert Hogan, Mr Thomas Kabdebo (of the University Library of Manchester), Dr John Kelly, Mrs Marianne Kirchgassner, Ms Pia Kleber, Professor Heinz Kosok, Professor R. G. Lawrence, the late Mrs Sybil LeBrocquy, Professor J. B. Lyons (Librarian of the Royal College of Surgeons in Ireland), Mr Alf MacLochlainn (Director of the National Library of Ireland), Miss Heather McCallum (Head of the Theatre Division, Metropolitan Toronto Library), Dr Peggy Miller, Dr Christopher Murray, Professor Desmond Neill, Mr Maurice F. Neville, Professor Johann Norstedt, Mr William O'Sullivan (Curator of Manuscripts, Trinity

Acknowledgements

College, Dublin, Library), Professor Patrick Rafroidi, Dean John Rea, Professor B. L. Reid, Professor Laure Rièse, Mrs J. E. Robinson (Librarian of Keble College, Oxford), Professor Joseph Ronsley, Professor Arthur Sheps, Mr Theo J. Snoddy, Mr Colin Smythe, Mr F. M. Sutherland (Librarian of the British Medical Association), Dr Lola Szladits (Curator of the Berg Collection, New York Public Library), Mrs Faith White, Mrs Maírin Woods, Dr Carol Wootton, Dr James Hardon Wright, Mr Kenneth R. Wright. A Canada Council Research Fellowship assisted me in the early years of research.

A. S.

LIST OF ABBREVIATIONS

AND MANUSCRIPT SOURCES

JMS = J. M. Synge

The following abbreviations and short forms are used in the description and provenance given at the foot of each letter, together with a record of its previous publication:

MS	autograph original or copy
TS	typescript original
copy	transcribed by another hand; original unavailable
draft	rough draft retained by JMS among his papers
photo	transcribed from photostatic copy

MANUSCRIPT SOURCES

Institutions

Beinecke	Beinecke Rare Book and Manuscript Library, Yale University
Berg	The Henry W. and Albert A. Berg Collection of the New York Public Library, Astor, Lenox and Tilden Foundations
Columbia	The Libraries, Columbia University in the City of New York
Kansas	University of Kansas Special Collections
Lilly	Lilly Library, Indiana University
Lockwood	Lockwood Memorial Library, State University of New York at Buffalo
NLI	The National Library of Ireland
TCD	Manuscripts Division, Trinity College Library, University of Dublin
Texas	Humanities Research Center, the University of Texas at Austin

Private owners

AS	Ann Saddlemyer
Boydell	Professor Brian Boydell, Dublin
Carpenter	Dr Andrew Carpenter, Dublin
Esposito	the late Signor Mario Esposito, Florence
Farrington	Mrs Doreen Hamilton Synge Farrington, Dublin
Gilvarry	Mr James Gilvarry, New York
Gregory	the late Major Richard Gregory, Budleigh Salterton, Devon
Healy	the late Mr James Healy, New York
Langmuir	Mr Robert Langmuir, The Book Mark, Philadelphia
LMS	the late Mrs L. M. Stephens, Dublin
Pepper	Mr James Pepper, Santa Barbara

Ray	Professor Gordon N. Ray, New York
Skelton	Professor Robin Skelton, Victoria, B.C.
Walker	Dr David Walker, University of New South Wales
Yeats	Mr Michael Yeats and Miss Anne B. Yeats, Dalkey, Co. Dublin

SOURCES OF PREVIOUS PUBLICATION

LM	*Letters to Molly*, ed. Ann Saddlemyer (Cambridge, Mass.: Harvard University Press, 1971)
LMD	*Letters to My Daughter* by the Revd Samuel Synge (Dublin: Talbot Press, 1932)
TB	*Theatre Business. The Correspondence of the first Abbey Theatre Directors: W. B. Yeats, Lady Gregory and J. M. Synge*, ed. Ann Saddlemyer (Gerrards Cross: Colin Smythe / University Park, Pa.: Pennsylvania State University Press, 1982)

Other abbreviations and short forms used in the annotation:

MUJ	*My Uncle John: Edward Stephens's Life of J. M. Synge*, ed. Andrew Carpenter (1974)
Plays	J. M. Synge, *Plays* Book I and Book II (vols. III and IV of the *Collected Works*), ed. Ann Saddlemyer (1968)
Poems	J. M. Synge, *Poems* (vol. I of the *Collected Works*), ed. Robin Skelton (1962)
Prose	J. M. Synge, *Prose* (vol. II of the *Collected Works*), ed. Alan Price (1966)
Stephens MS	E. M. Stephens's unpublished MS, 'The Life of J. M. Synge', in the Library, Trinity College, Dublin

The place of publication for all sources cited is London unless otherwise indicated.

PART ONE
1871–1896

*

Beginnings

Beginnings

Dublin, Koblenz, Würzburg, Paris

*

EDMUND JOHN MILLINGTON SYNGE was born on 16 April 1871 at 2 Newtown Villas in the Dublin suburb of Rathfarnham, the youngest of eight children, three of whom died in infancy. His father, John Hatch Synge (1824–72), a barrister, came from a well-known Wicklow family; his mother, Kathleen Traill Synge (1838–1908), was the daughter of the Protestant rector of Schull in County Cork, a man of great classical scholarship and intense Evangelical zeal. Widowed when her youngest son was only one year old, Mrs Synge moved next door to her widowed mother in Orwell Park in the neighbouring suburb of Rathgar, and here Synge lived until he was twenty.

Left with enough landed income to live quietly but comfortably and provide her sons with a college education, Mrs Synge varied her routine only by taking her family each summer to County Wicklow. John was a sickly child, already suffering from the asthma which would plague him throughout his life. He attended Mr Harrick's Classical and English School in Dublin for a year, about 1881, with his brother Samuel (1867–1951), and was again intermittently at Aravon House, Bray School, in 1884; from 1884 to 1888 his only regular schooling was with a private tutor at home, three times a week.

Although he enjoyed walking and fishing with his older brothers Robert (1858–1943) and Edward (1859–1939), Synge spent most of his childhood with Sam and his cousin Florence Ross (1870–1949), who lived next door. An early notebook shared with Florence records their bird-watching activities; other notes refer to the costs of breeding rabbits with Sam. By the mid-1880s Synge's studies in natural history led him to read Darwin, and this precipitated the rejection of his mother's and grandmother's Evangelical teaching. In 1886 he joined the Dublin Naturalists' Field Club and continued through extensive reading in both natural science and theology his slow evolution away from the social, religious, and political beliefs of his family.

The family circle itself was by this time changing. In 1883 Robert went to Argentina to work on an uncle's ranch; he did not visit Ireland again until 1895. By 1884 Edward was a land agent, first for

the family estates in County Wicklow and later also for other properties in the west of Ireland; he married in 1885. In January 1884
Annie (1863–1944), Synge's only sister, married an ambitious young
solicitor, Henry Francis (Harry) Stephens (1856–1935), and they
became tenants of part of her grandmother's house next door.

In October 1887 Synge began taking violin lessons from Patrick
Griffith of Dublin. During that same winter he became interested in
Irish antiquities, filling the small pocket notebooks he habitually
carried with precise details from his reading and observations on his
explorations of Wicklow and County Dublin. In June 1888 he was
accepted by Trinity College, Dublin, but elected not to attend
lectures until the following February. He enrolled in the Royal
Irish Academy of Music in November 1889 to study the violin,
composition, and musical theory, the latter from Sir Robert Stewart.
In 1890 he scraped through with a third-class result in his first-year
exams at Trinity, and was certified by the Academy to pursue
advanced study in counterpoint.

Meanwhile he moved with his mother to 31 Crosthwaite Park,
Kingstown (now Dun Laoghaire), next door to where her daughter
and son-in-law and their three children were living. Samuel Synge
was preparing for a career as a medical missionary in China. Florence
Ross joined the household in December 1891 after the death of her
mother, but Synge's refusal to attend church services made him even
more solitary. During 1891 and 1892 he divided his time fairly
evenly among his interests in music, languages, and long forays into
the country on foot or bicycle. He joined the student orchestra at
the Academy, playing in several concerts with great enjoyment, and
won prizes in harmony and counterpoint. He studied German on his
own and Hebrew and Irish at Trinity, winning prizes in both. In
December 1892 he was awarded a second-class degree from Trinity
College. But he continued his studies at the Academy, started to
write an opera on Eileen Aruine, and joined the Dublin Junior
Instrumental Club.

In March 1893 Mary Synge (b. 1840), his father's cousin and a
professional musician, visited Dublin. She held a piano recital in the
Antient Concert Rooms for which Synge took charge of publicity
and all practical arrangements; but even more significantly she
persuaded Mrs Synge, who had grave doubts about a career in the
arts, to allow her son to study music in Germany. Synge resumed his
study of German with a private tutor, Herr Wespendorf, and on
25 July 1893 left Dublin to join his elderly cousin in London.

On 29 July they arrived at Oberwerth, an island in the Rhine
near Koblenz where the six von Eicken sisters ran a guest house;
'eighteen ladies in the place,' Synge reported to his mother. Mary

Synge, who had been at Oberwerth before, returned to England on 7 October, but Synge stayed on, studying German literature, taking violin lessons from Konrad Heubner, playing in the local orchestral society, attending concerts, and enjoying the relaxed and expansive atmosphere of the von Eicken household where one of the sisters, Valeska, quickly became his close confidante. On 29 December Mrs Synge confided to her diary, 'I had a long letter from poor Johnnie . . . curious letter attributing his unsociableness to his narrow up-bringing and warning me!'

Despite her misgivings, Synge's mother supported his decision to move to Würzburg, on 22 January 1894, for further musical training. She wrote to Robert in Argentina on 29 January,

I had a long letter from Johnnie on Friday giving a great account of his journey to Würzburg and arriving in the dark about 6 o'clock and trying to find a lodging. [See p. 8, n. 2] . . . The Von Eickens, whom he has just left have been very kind and pleasant, and he feels as if they were his oldest friends instead of his *newest*! What a pity that, when thrown among strangers, we only show ourselves as amiable and agreeable and taking everything in good part — while at home we show ourselves sometimes in a very unpleasant aspect, and temper often spoils our comfort, and certainly the comfort of those we live with. Poor Johnnie forgets this, and I won't remind him. I am glad he is happier than when he was at home, but I am very sorry it was out of my power to make him happy though I did all I could for him. He tells me that he has got complete control over his temper. I hope, when he comes home, he may continue on calm and unruffled poor boy. (TCD)

In Würzburg Synge began studying the piano, but his diaries for April and May 1894 also record attempts to write poetry and a play in German, and the usual long walks in the countryside. He returned twice to Oberwerth, first for Easter, when he returned to Würzburg by way of Frankfurt to visit the birthplace of Goethe, whose works he was studying, and again on his way back to Ireland. By the time he arrived in Dublin on 14 June 1894, he had transferred his allegiance from music to languages.

During that summer he again joined his mother in County Wick-low, where for two weeks from 28 July a neighbour in Crosthwaite Park, Cherrie Matheson, joined them as sketching companion for Florence Ross. Evidently Synge had already confided his interest in Cherrie to Valeska, who had dubbed her 'the Holy One' because of her strict Plymouth Brethren upbringing. Now he fell in love, delaying his departure for the Continent until 30 October.

Once again, however, he made careful preparation for his studies, deciding to further his knowledge of languages not at a German university, as he had first intended, but in Paris. From 3 November to 31 December 1894 he stayed at Oberwerth, studying German with Valeska and French with a friend of the von Eickens, Mlle Mansaca.

On 1 January 1895, armed with addresses and information provided by his German friends, he arrived in Paris. Introduced by Pastor Jean Monnier, he joined the Société Fraternelle d'Étudiants Protestants, and soon his life took on the pattern it was to have for the next seven years: formal lectures at the Sorbonne and the École Pratique des Hautes-Études; outings with students with whom he exchanged language lessons, some of whom became firm friends (Edward Denny, Albert Cugnier, Otto Boehrig, Morik Dalmigere, Paul Messin, Thérèse Beydon, Georges Roeder); long walks in the countryside surrounding Paris; regular visits to art exhibitions and the Louvre (where, according to Cherrie, he once found a young man sobbing on the floor, overwhelmed by the beauty of the statue of Venus de Milo); efforts at journalism, describing public events in France for Irish readers.

Some of the articles sent to the *Irish Times* during these years seem to have been accepted and published anonymously, but more and more Synge turned towards the serious study of literature. His first creative endeavour, proudly preserved by his Aunt Jane Synge for whom he had written it in 1881, had been a juvenile satire, 'Poem on my Ant'. A Wordworthian poem, 'A Mountain Creed', had been rejected by the *Irish Monthly* in 1892; a sonnet, 'Glencullen', received publication in the Trinity College magazine *Kottabos* in 1893. When he returned to Dublin on 28 June 1895, he was at last confident of the life he wanted: he would be a writer.

The summer of 1895 was spent once again in Wicklow; but Florence had left to join her brother in Tonga and Synge did not see Cherrie (whom he referred to in his diaries as 'Scherma') until their return to Crosthwaite Park in September. His interest in her painting (she exhibited water-colours at the Paris Salon in the 1890s) provided opportunities for him to accompany her to art exhibitions in Dublin during November, and on 31 December he had his photograph taken for her before he returned to Paris. Perhaps influenced by Lafcadio Hearn, his brother-in-law Harry Stephens's cousin, for a time he contemplated going to Japan and went so far as to commission Sam, who was embarking for China, to make enquiries about work as an interpreter on liners to the Far East. But instead he decided to prepare for a trip to Italy, taking lessons in Italian from Signor Morosini throughout November and December.

From 3 January to 3 February 1896 he stayed at the Hôtel Corneille in Paris, renewing acquaintances and making new ones, especially Dr James Cree, another Dubliner; studying French with Thérèse Beydon and Italian with Dr Eustachio Meli; and attending the theatre. Armed with letters of introduction from Cherrie, he travelled to Rome and remained there until 30 April. He enrolled in

literature courses at the Collegio Romano, studied Italian with his
landlord, Count Polloni, and made friends among the art students.
Once again he tried his hand at newspaper reporting, this time of
the riots and demonstrations over the failure of the Italian invasion
of Abyssinia. He then spent the month of May in Florence, where he
made friends with Maria Antoinette Zdanowska, a Polish student of
sculpture and a devout Roman Catholic whom he was to meet often
in Paris, and Hope Rea (b. 1860), an English art historian and theosophist, with whom he was to correspond for the rest of his life.

Back in Paris in June, at the Hôtel de l'Univers, he was writing
long letters to Cherrie. None of these have survived, but she described
them many years later as 'closely written in a small, pointed hand,
and often misspelt. Sometimes he began a word in the middle, as
if he were thinking much faster than he could write.' ('John Synge
as I Knew Him', *Irish Statesman*, 5 July 1924) On 3 June, he proposed marriage by letter to Cherrie. Her refusal arrived on 17 June,
but Synge pursued his courtship for at least two more years, even
persuading his reluctant mother to speak on his behalf the following
October. On 29 June 1896 he left for Ireland, immediately joining his
mother in County Wicklow. On 21 July he received a sympathetic
letter from Thérèse Beydon, commenting, 'I quite understand it
must be difficult for you to go about and even that sometimes you
have no wish to do so.'

Cherrie evidently continued to visit his mother, and even allowed
Synge to accompany her to hear the music in the Dublin cathedrals,
but when he stopped in London to visit Hope Rea on 27 and 28
October life was already taking another turn. 'He has gone back to
Paris to study Socialism,' Mrs Synge wrote to Samuel, 'and he wants
to do good, and for that possibility he is giving up everything. He
says he is not selfish or egotistical but quite the reverse. In fact
he writes the most utter folly.' (TCD)

Once more installed at the Hôtel Corneille, he pursued his usual
activities, exchanging language lessons, writing (and apparently
occasionally publishing anonymously) articles for the *Irish Times*,
paying regular visits to the Louvre and the theatre, enrolling at the
Sorbonne for courses on Petrarch (with Emile Gebhart), on La
Fontaine (with Emile Faguet), and on French literature (with Petit
de Julleville), and reading extensively not only on socialism, but
Thomas à Kempis. He saw James Cree frequently and it is likely
through this fellow Dubliner that he met Stephen MacKenna and, on
21 December 1896, William Butler Yeats.

To THE VON EICKEN FAMILY[1]

[c/o Frau Süsser, Hanger Ring 16, Würzburg][2]
[? 2 February 1894]

. . . um sie zu treffen, nicht wissen Sie weil ich so besonders wünschte dass ich sie sehen möchte, aber weil ich sehr neugierig war ob sie Nachricht aus der lieben Insel hätte.[3] Nach einer halben Stunde kam die Kleine (als die Leute hier sie nennen) und erzählt mir dass sie nichts Neues aus Oberw. gehört hätte, ich war im Begriff meine Zähne zu über meinen unfruchtbaren Zeitverderb, aber Gott sei Dank erinnerte ich mich zur Zeit wie schlecht meine armen Zähne waren und so that ich es nur im Geist. Jetzt die Tischgesellschaft ist ein bisschen irischer geworden[4] Einmal als ich allein bei Tisch mit dem jüngeren Herrn war, fing ich an mit ihm zu sprechen, und nun so oft wie wir allein sind, schwatzen wir ganz freundlich zusammen. Er ist ein jüngerer Arzt aus Norddeutschland, und hat in Berlin und Leipzig studiert. Er ist aber ein furchtbar neugieriger Kerl und zuerst war meine arme Einbildungskraft ganz ungut nach Tisch aber jetzt glücklicherweise habe ich einen Schutz gefunden, zum Beispiel, vorgestern fing er wie gewöhnlich an und fragte mich wie viele Einwohner in Belfast leben. „100,000," oder vielleicht „300,000" antwortete ich gerade wie es mir im Kopf kam. Dann fing ich auf den Punkt an „Wie viele tollen Männer giebt es in Würzburg" er dacht fleissig und gab mir eine lange Antwort da fragte ich, wie viele tolle Frauen dann Kinder und so weiter solang wie die kleinste Spur von Neugierigkeit in seinem armseligen Gesicht schien zu bleiben. Der andere Herr ist Polnisch und manchmal bringt er einen Freund und sie sprechen Polnisch zusammen. Ich habe neulich von einer Englischen Familie gehört die in Deutsch leben wollte, und erzähte ich ihnen von dem Oberwerthischen Himmelchen aber ich weiss nicht was . . .[5]

MS fragment (draft), TCD

1 Six von Eicken sisters ran the family guest house at No. 8 Oberwerth, near Koblenz: Emma (see p. 11); Claire, who travelled widely on the Continent, seems to have had some kind of teaching position in Redhill, Surrey, England, and visited JMS in Dublin during the autumn of 1903; Hedwig, who also spent some time in Redhill; Maria; Thekla; and JMS's confidante, Valeska (see p. 10).
2 JMS had sent his mother an account of finding this lodging, after a search, as she reported to her son Robert on 29 Jan 1894:
He was directed to one, but could not find it until a man kindly led him to it,

and then he had to go up 4 flights of stairs in pitch darkness. Then he could not find the bell (the houses are all built in flats, and he had to go to the top flat). So he pawed about the door and at last the proprietor heard him and came and opened the door. She is 'Frau Susser' by name and he struck a bargain with her and took a room at 26/— a month, which he thinks is very cheap. He seems to have only one room and says it is a very good one and has a nice view of the hills and trees and has country air, but the bed is a truly German bed! — a mattress, 2 pillows, one sheet and feather bed 4 ft. 6 in. long! He seems to think more of the loss of the sheet!   (TCD)

3 Nellie Wrigton (?), a music student and friend of the von Eickens, had also recently moved to Würzburg; on 25 Jan 1894 both Emma and Claire had written, in separate letters (TCD), apparently in reply to an earlier letter from JMS, warning him of visiting a lady, especially when she was in lodgings.

4 An entry in JMS's diary (TCD) for 25 Jan 1894 reads, 'subscribed in Railway Hotel for a month'.

5 (Translation)
. . . to meet her, not because I wanted to see her particularly, but because I was very curious to hear if she had news from the beloved island. After half an hour the 'little girl', as people call her here, came to tell me that she had heard nothing new from Oberw. I was just going to [gnash] my teeth because of such futile waste of time but thank God I remembered in time how bad my poor teeth were so I only did it in spirit. The company at table is slightly more Irish. Once when I was alone at table with the young gentleman, I started to talk to him and now we chat together in quite a friendly way. He is a youngish doctor from North Germany, who has studied in Berlin and Leipzig. He is a terribly curious fellow. At first my imagination was quite exhausted after dinner but now fortunately I have found a way of defending myself. For instance, at table yesterday he started again as usual and asked me what the population of Belfast was — "100,000", or perhaps "300,000"? I replied with anything that came into my head and began from there "How many mad men are there in Würzburg?" He thought about it industriously and gave me a long reply then I asked him, how many mad women are there mad children and so on as long as the smallest trace of curiosity remained in his wretched face. The other gentleman is Polish and sometimes he brings a friend and they speak Polish together. I heard recently of an English family who wanted to live in Germany and I told them about the little Heaven in Oberwerth but I don't know what [they have done] . . .

To A GERMAN BOOKSELLER

[Würzburg. ? Early February 1894]

Da ich während meines vorjährigen Aufenthalts in Coblenz Gelgenheit hatte in Irher Handlung Büchner zu kaufen so möchte ich Sie bitten mir die folgenden Werke zu schicken.[1] Da ich nicht weiss wie viel das Postgeld betragen wird kann ich noch nicht bezahlen, aber ich werde das Geld sogleich schicken, wenn ich die Bücher bekomme.

Wenn es Ihnen lieber ist können Sie mir vorher die Summe mittheilen wonach ich Ihnen das Geld sofort senden werde.[2]

MS (draft), TCD

¹ No list of books survives; Valeska von Eicken's letters to JMS (TCD) and entries in his diary refer to his reading works by Goethe, Lessing, Schiller, Heine, and Ibsen's plays in German.

² (Translation)

As I had the opportunity of buying books in your shop during my stay in Koblenz last year I should like to ask you to send me the following works. As I do not know how much the postage will be I cannot pay yet but I will send the money as soon as I receive the books.

If you would prefer it you can inform me of the sum and I will then send the money at once.

To VALESKA VON EICKEN¹

[Würzburg. *c.* 7 March 1894]

Viel Dank für die angenehme Störung² die am Freitag morgen ankam, und welcher ich jetzt gans bequem antworten kann da das Wetter heute nicht angenehm für eine Spazierengang ist. Ich glaube der andere Brief, den ich an Sie schreib war eine durchaus alberne lächerliche abgeschmackte Epistle, aber freilich war ich denn ein paar Woche furchtbar sentimental. Ferner, verstehen Sie, da ich immer solche artige vernünftige Briefen an Irland schreiben muss ist es mir sehr angenehm wenn ich einmal, wie jetzt gerade aus dem Kopf (aber viel mehr Herzen) Tollheiten und Thorheiten aller Arten ganz unvorsichtig und formlos schwatzen kann. Ich habe Frln [Wrigton] nur einmal seit ich schreib gesprochen und zwar war das am letzten Dienstag. Ich hatte sie zweimal bei Frau Ritter³ besucht aber sie war nicht zu Hause, so am Dienstag da das Dienstmädchen mir erzählte dass sie in der Musikschule sei ging ich zwischen Ludwigstr. und die Musikschule auf und ab⁴

MS fragment (draft), TCD

¹ One of the youngest of the 'cloistered maidens' of Oberwerth, Valeska von Eicken (1863–*c.* 1940) became JMS's German teacher; she nicknamed him 'Holy Moses' after his favourite expression, and Cherrie Matheson, his despairing love for whom he confided to her, 'the Holy One'. Although she travelled occasionally to visit family and friends in Germany and Holland, she maintained the guest house at Oberwerth until 1932, finally moving to a Protestant old people's home in Koblenz-Oberwerth in 1937. Despite repeated enquiries, I have been unable to trace any of JMS's letters to her other than these drafts in his notebook, but it is evident from Valeska's letters to him (TCD) that he corresponded with her until his death.

² A reference to her letter of 1 Mar 1894 (TCD) which begins (in German), 'Probably a little disturbance in your lonely life . . . will do you good.'

³ Hermann Ritter (1849–1926) taught the viola and musical history at the Würzburg Music School; since Nellie Wrigton (?) was now boarding with her teacher, it was proper for JMS to call upon her.

⁴ (Translation)

Many thanks for the pleasant disturbance which came on Friday morning and which I can answer at my ease as the weather is not pleasant for a walk. I think that the other letter which I wrote to you was a thoroughly silly, absurd, tasteless epistle, but I have been terribly sentimental for a few weeks. Further you must understand that I have to write such well-behaved, sensible letters to Ireland I find it very pleasant just as I am doing now to be able to talk straight out of my head (or rather heart) about all kinds of silly and foolish things without caution and quite informally. I have seen Miss [Wrigton] only once since I wrote and that was last Tuesday. I had called on her twice at Mrs Ritter's but she was not at home, so on Tuesday as the maid told me that she was in the Music School I went up and down between the Ludwigstr. and the Music School

To EMMA VON EICKEN[1]

[Würzburg. ? 2 April 1894]

Seit meiner Rückkehr[2] habe ich keine angenehme Zeit zugebracht als ich einen schlimmen Husten bekommen habe, ich weiss nicht wie oder wo Auch habe ich die traurige Nachricht aus Irland gehört dass mein alter geliebter Harmonie Lehrer[3] am Osternsamstag nachmittag an einem Schlag gestorben ist, und freilich mit ihm ist der klugste irische Musiker und einer von den freundlichsten und angenehmsten Männern dieses Jahrhunderts von uns gegangen In den letztigen Jahren war er freilich kein strenger Lehrer aber doch hatte er durchaus mehr Genie als Heubener und van Zeyl zusammen.[4] Am Ostermontag starb noch ein alter Bekannter von uns und eine alte Freundin die vermalige Lehrerin meiner Mutter[5] ist todkrank gewesen.

Am Freitag früh als ich erwachte fand ich den grossen Postboten neben meinem Bett, ich war es lässt sich denken, ein bisschen erstaunt aber er holte ganz ruhig eine Feder und ich schreib meinen Namen in seinem Buch dann aber musste ich aufstehen um Trinkgeld zu holen, und der Kerl sah furchtbar amusiert aus als er sah dass ich in Strümpfen schlief, jedoch sagte er nichts weiteres als zu fragen wie viel meine Uhr kostet welches ich eine . . .[6]

MS fragment (draft), TCD

[1] Emma von Eicken (1847–1921), the oldest of the sisters, and responsible for the guest house accounts. JMS enclosed 26 marks with this letter.

[2] JMS had spent the Easter holiday (20–7 Mar) in Koblenz, returning by way of Frankfurt on 28 March.

[3] Sir Robert Prescott Stewart (1825–94), Irish organist, conductor, and respected teacher, with whom JMS studied at the Royal Irish Academy of Music from 1889 to 1893. He was Professor at Trinity College, and taught at the Royal Irish Academy from 1872, the year he was knighted. From 1873 he was conductor of the Dublin Philharmonic, and edited the *Irish Hymnal* (1876); among his compositions are two cantatas.

[4] Konrad Heubner (1860–1905), composer and director of the Koblenz Conservatory of Music, with whom JMS studied counterpoint from mid-September

to the end of December 1893; Herr von Zeyl, a Würzburg friend of the von Eickens, gave JMS piano lessons from February to May 1894.

5   Miss Osborne, Mrs Synge's old governess.

6   (Translation)

Since my return I have not had a pleasant time as I got a bad cough, I do not know how or where. Moreover I have had sad news from Ireland that my beloved old harmony teacher died on Easter Saturday afternoon from a stroke, and with him the cleverest Irish musician and one of the kindest and pleasantest of men of this century has gone from us. In recent years it is true he was not a strict teacher but yet he had definitely more genius than Heubener and van Zeyl together. On Easter Monday another old acquaintance of ours died and an old friend my mother's former teacher has been terribly ill.

On Friday morning when I woke up I found the big postman by my bed. As you can imagine, I was a little surprised but he quietly fetched a pen and I wrote my name in his book but then I had to get up to find him a tip, and the fellow seemed greatly amused when he saw that I slept in stockings, however he did not say anything except to ask me how much my watch cost which I . . .

To EMMA VON EICKEN

[Würzburg. *c.* 7 April 1894]

Besten Dank für Ihre Karte, und das Briefchen gestern kam.[1] Es thut mir zwar leid dass ich Sie so lange ohne Nachricht liess, und ich weiss kaum, wie es geschah, ich sass stundenlang in der Ecke und hustete ohne zu bemerken wie die Zeit vorbei ging und wissen Sie, die Tage hier gleichen sich etwas nur, dass ich eine Stunde am Samstag habe und Sauerkraut am Donnerstag; übrigens ist es mir eben flach langweilig, u.s.w.

Es fängt jetzt an, mir etwas besser zu gehen, und zwar zur rechten Zeit da ich so steif und schmerzend geworden war vom Husten dass ich mich nicht mehr der ausserordentlichen Herrlichkeit meines jetzigen Lebens erfreuen konnte, welches ich ganz entsetzlich schade fand . . . .[2]

MS fragment (draft), TCD

1   Emma had sent a postcard on 2 Apr 1894 asking for news, adding, 'I am worried in case letter with contents may have been lost or that something happened to you on the journey.' Apparently JMS's previous letter 'with contents' (26 marks) crossed with her postcard, for she wrote again on 5 Apr 1894 to thank him for the money. (Both TCD)

2   (Translation)

Many thanks for your card and the short letter which came yesterday. I am indeed very sorry to have left you so long without news, I do not know how it happened, I sat for hours in the corner and coughed without noticing how the time passed and you know, the days here are much the same except that I have one class on Saturday and sauerkraut for lunch on Thursday; otherwise I find it all terribly boring, etc.

I am now beginning to get better, and just at the right time, as I had become so stiff and the coughing gave me such pains that I was unable to enjoy the extraordinary splendour of my present life, a thing which I found a quite terrible shame . . .

To [? VALESKA VON EICKEN]

[Würzburg. *c.* 20 April 1894]

Besten Dank für Ihren Brief und die damit gesandte gute Wünsche[1] Seit meinem letzten Schreiben nach Oberwerth ist nichts Merkwürdiges in Würzburg geschehen, ausser dass wegen des warmes staubiges Wetters die Leute nun viel mehr Bier trinken und werden dadurch recht wohl betrunken. Ich kann nicht leugnen dass er mir freit [zu] sehen dass diese Deutschen ist ebenso sündlich wie der Irischer als ich freilich immer geglaubt habe. Die ganze Gegend hat sich während [des letzten] Monat auf eine ganz unglaubliche Weise geändert . . .[2]

Am Mittwoch abend fand ich einen grossen Buchenwald nach dem Süden zu dessen bessere Bekanntschaft ich bald zu machen hoffe aber er liegt mehr wie eine Stunde von der Stadt.

Meine Tischgesellschaft ist nach und nach gewachsen und zählt jetzt 8 alte Mediziner sondern der Floh.[3] Ich kenne alle aber ich spreche nicht weil das Gespräch stets in medizinischen [? Sätzchen] aufheilt, welche ich nicht leicht verstehe und wovon ich nichts sagen kann. Auch ist es mir, wie gesagt, unendlich schwer so ganz leise sowohl als deutlich zu sprechen wie man leider im Hotel sprechen muss.

Während der Woche habe ich leider keine Zeit für längen Spaziergänge aber täglich bringe ich die herrlichen Abendstuden unter den Bergen zu. In einer halben Stunde von meiner Wohnung kann ich Würzburg nicht mehr hören allenfalls sehen aber schaue hinunter in ein herrliches Thal worin in einem Kranze von blühenden Apfelbäumen ein Dörfchen liegt dessen rothen Dächer im Vor[der]grund mit schwarzen Tannenwälder dahinter unter dem Licht der sinkenden Sonne unglaublich schön aussehen[4]

MS fragments (drafts), TCD

[1] On 15 Apr 1894 Valeska wrote (TCD) wishing him a happy birthday the next day.

[2] One fragment ends here, but appears to belong with the fragment following.

[3] Evidently Valeska's nickname for the inquisitive young doctor described above, p. 8.

[4] (Translation)

Many thanks for your letter and the good wishes sent with it. Since my last letter to Oberwerth nothing extraordinary has happened in Würzburg, except that because of the warm and dusty weather people seem to drink much more beer and are therefore frequently drunk. I don't deny I am delighted to see that Germans sin just as the Irish do a fact which I always believed. During the last month the country round has become amazingly beautiful . . .

On Wednesday evening I found a large beechwood towards the south, of which I hope to make better acquaintance soon but it is more than an hour from the town.

My company at table is growing gradually and now numbers 8 old medical men apart from the Flea. I know all of them but I don't talk because they talk to one another about medical [matters] which I find it difficult to understand and about which I have nothing much to say. As I have said, I find it terribly difficult to speak in a low and distinct voice as one must in a hotel.

During the week I have no time for long walks but every day I spend the beautiful evening hours in the hills. Half an hour away from my lodging I can neither hear Würzburg nor see it any longer but look down into a splendid valley in which within a wreath of blossoming apple trees there is a small village the red roofs of which in the foreground look incredibly beautiful with the black fir trees behind them in the light of the setting sun

To VALESKA VON EICKEN

[Castle Kevin, Co. Wicklow]
[28 ? July 1894[1]]

Liebes Frln Valewska

Ich glaube Sie haben Ihren Geburts Tag nächste Woche so muss ich Ihnen alle gute Wünschen dazu senden und hoffe ich dass er viel lustiger wie im vorigen Jahre sein wird. Gestern mittag schickte ich Ihnen zwei kleine Faren die hoffentlich die Reise gut machen, und Ihr schreckliches Klima vertragen werden Sie sind Royal flowering Ferns (Osmunda Regalis) eine sehr prachtvoll und berühmigte Art, und waschen bei uns mehr wie ein Meter hoch. Pflanzen Sie sie wo sie nicht zu viel Sonne schein kriegen werden aber sonst, wenn es Ihnen lieber ist in den heissen Stunden sitzen Sie dabei und schützen Sie sie mit Ihrem Regen Schirm und derweilen denken an was Sie mir . . . Ich brauche kaum zu sagen dass sie Wasser sehr lieb haben

Nun muss ich Ihnen für Ihren Brief[2] danken den ich den Abend da wir Dublin verlassen empfangen habe, und bitte ich Sie mein Tuch wie Sie sagen zu behalten bis eine Gelegenheit sich anbietet es zu schichen. Jetzt sind wir, wie Sie oben lesen können, auf dem Lande und genossen wir die Herrlichkeiten dieser Gegenden von morgens früh bis tief in der Nacht. Ich will nicht leugnen dass ich ein bisschen ängstlich war ob ich die irische Schönheit wieder so wundervoll finden würde wie ich sie so oft beschrieben habe und auf Ehre versichere ich dass ich *überrascht* und *erstaunt* mit ihrem erhabenen

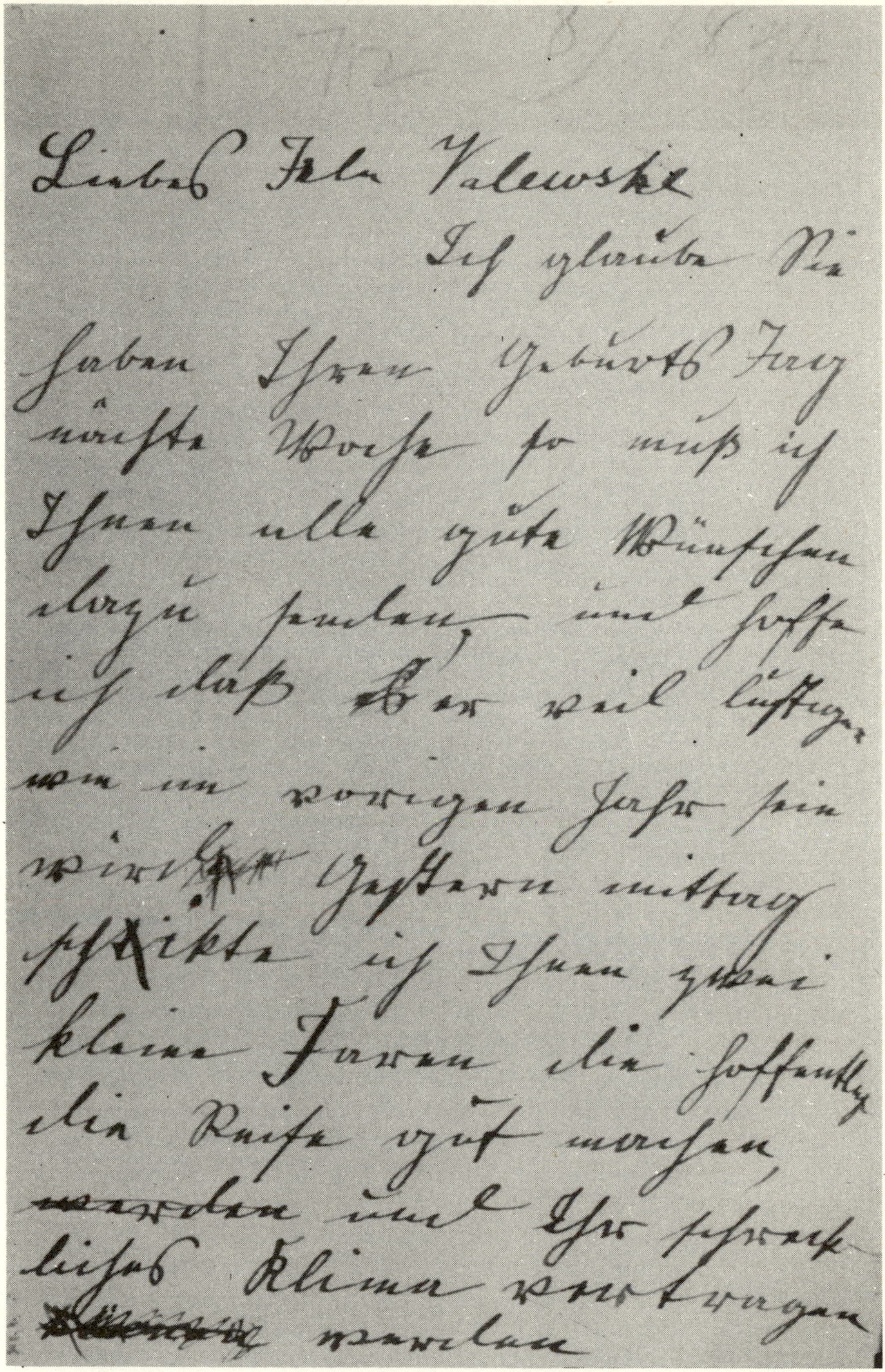
Liebes Frln Valeska
Ich glaube Sie
haben Ihren Geburtstag
nächste Woche so muß ich
Ihnen alle gute Wünschen
abzusenden und hoffe
ich daß Sie viel lustiger
wie im vorigen Jahre sein
wird. Gestern mittag
schickte ich Ihnen zwei
kleine Farne die hoffentlich
die Reise gut machen
~~werden~~ und Ihr schwäch-
liches Klima vertragen
~~[illegible]~~ werden

To Valeska von Eicken, 28 ? July 1894

Pracht [bin]. In einigen Hinsichten ist meine Zeit bis jetzt nicht . . .[3]

MS fragments (drafts), TCD

[1] Although at some other time JMS marked this draft '8/1894', he referred
in his diary for 27 July to sending Osmunda to Valeska, whose birthday appears
to have been in early August.

[2] JMS left for Castle Kevin with his mother on 3 July; Valeska's letter of
25 June 1894 (TCD) mentions the ferns and asks him, 'Have you made up your
mind as to whether you are going to return to Germany to attend a university?
What a pity that your Holy One is just now absent from that damp Ireland.'

[3] (Translation)
Dear Miss Valewska,
   I think it is your birthday next week so I must send you all best wishes
and I hope that it will be much merrier than it was last year. Yesterday I
sent you two small ferns which I hope will travel well and will stand up to
your horrible climate They are Royal flowering ferns (Osmunda Regalis) a
very beautiful and famous variety and here they grow more than a metre in
height. Plant them where they will not get too much sun or if you prefer you
can sit by them in the heat of the day and protect them with your umbrella
and think of what you . . . me . . . I need hardly to say that they like water
very much indeed
   Now I must thank you for your letter which I received the evening before
we left Dublin. Please keep my scarf as you say until there is an opportunity
to send it. We are now in the country, as you can see from the above, and are
enjoying the delights of this area from morning till late at night. I will not
deny that I was a bit anxious as to whether I would find the beauty of
Ireland as wonderful as I have often described and I assure you on my honour
that I am *amazed* and *surprised* by its sublime splendour. In some respects my
time up to now has not . . .

To VALESKA VON EICKEN

c/o Mons Arbeau | 94 Rue Lafayette | Paris [X^e][1]
16/1/95

Liebe Gorse
   'Kennst du das Land wo die gelb Gorsen blühn?'[2] Nein, Sie kennen
es leider doch nicht, dieser herrliche Blumen haben Sie nie gesehen.
Es sind wirklich gar prachtvoll anzusehen die Farbe ist so entzückend
warm . . . so gemütlich, und sie duften so schön dass wenn die
Seligen im Himmel es nur riechen könnten, würden sie in dem
Augenblick noch einmal so selig werden. Manchmal in meiner ver-
flossenen Jugend wurde ich angereizt diese Blumen zu pflücken um
sie nach Hause mit mir zu bringen, aber liebster Himmel da fand ich
dass sie lauter Dornen waren wenn man ihnen zu nah kommt, so war
ich genötigt mich ruhig auf den kalten Fels hin zu setzen und wie der
fromme Lineus[3] dem lieben Gott zu danken dass er so viele Herrlichkeit in der Welt erschaffen habe. Es erinnert mich an eine hübsche
Gesichte die meine Mutter mir oft vorlas als ich noch ein kleiner

artiger Knabe war und in einem Stühlchen zu ihren Füssen sass, nämlich die Geschichte des heiligen Moses als er vor dem brennenden Busch in Aufregung stand und bemerkte wie es brannte und brannte ohne im geringsten verbrannt zu werden, er soll auch vor lauter Verehrung seine Schuen ausgezogen haben aber das kann ich nicht thun da ich meine Strümpfe noch nicht gestopft habe.

Gorse hat noch eine schöne Eigenschaft die hier erwähnt werden muss, nämlich hübsche Blumen sind immer daran zu finden, das ganze Jahr durch kann man sich darüber freuen wenn alles sonst kalt aussieht und kühl und öde in der Welt ist. Der Gedanke ist mir durch den Kopf gegangen dass diese Eigenschaft in diesem Winter ausgestorben sei und will ich bald an den Floh[4] schreiben um mich zu erkundigen ob das wirklich der Fall sei.

Aber nun nach so viel symbolische Träumerei muss ich Ihnen recht sehr danken für Ihren langen Brief,[5] der gestern Abend um 9 Uhr ankam ich setzte mich sofort in meinen grossen Stuhl um es bequem lesen zu können, und als ich meine Uhr das nachste Mal aus der Tasche zog, war es schon durch 12 Uhr; 3 ganze Stunden hatte [ich] ohne zu bemerken darüber geträumt ohne einmal aufzustehen! Dann ging ich zu Bett und in der Nacht träumt ich immer weiter und weiter, endlich auf folgende Weise. Ich stand vor einem grossen Eisberg auf dessen Spitze wuchs der herrlichste Gorsebush, ich wollte hinauf klettern um die Herrlichkeit der Blumen näher ansehen zu können und die Duft davon zu geniessen, aber es [war] alles so glatt so unbarmherzig kalt und glatt dass es nach meiner Ansich gar nicht gelingen würde. Da bemerkte ich erst einige kleine blaue Blümchen die ganz wunderschön aus dem [Eis] blickte. Es waren Vergissmeinnicht! Wo sie wachsen war es nicht mehr glatt und da konnte [ich] klettern und klettern bis ich ganz in der Nähe der herrlichen Gorse ges[ti]egen war. Aber dann hörte die Vergissmeinnicht auf und als ich den letzten Strauch überspringen wollte, da fiel ich und fiel bis ich in.grossen Schrecken aufwachte.

Cugnier besuchte mich letzten Donnerstag um sein Paket zu holen, und ich gehe zu ihm morgen Nachmittag. Sie fragen wie er mir gefällt, nun ja er war sehr liebenswürdig und erzähte mir wie stark er sei, wie ausgezeichnet er reiten könne, und versicherte mich seine deut[sch]e Aussprach bei weitem besser wie die meinige sei, dass kann wohl sein aber in dem Fall hätte ich neulich . . . meine ganze Aufmerksamkeit dazu widmen sollen. Demungeachtet war er wirklich sehr freundlich gegen mich, über Oberwerth haben wir nur wenig gesagt, ich hatte gar keine Lust mit einem Fremden über Sie zu reden noch ihn reden zu hören; so . . . mit einigen herrlichen Worten lassen wir die Sache in Ruhe, und scherzten auf eine freiere Weise über Jumbo.[6] Ich bin noch nicht nach Versailles gegangen so habe ich Monsieur Paul M. noch nicht besucht . . . Ich weiss nicht ob [ich] die anderen besuchen werde, ich glaube nicht.[7]

Als ich Ihren Brief zum ersten Mal las kam es mir vor dass mein letzter Brief verloren gegangen [sein] muss, am zweiten Lesen glaubte ich eine versteckte Anspielung zu etwas . . . in der letzten Zeile des P.Ss zu erkennen. Nachher erinnerte ich mich, dass ich in eben diesen die Bemerkungen über Ihr Englisch gemacht hatte So haben Sie es doch bekommen! Haben Sie es nicht lesen können? [Dass Sie das Englische üben sollten,][8] muss ich Ihnen völlig beistimmen. Ich brauche nicht zu sagen dass es mir nur Freude macht die Sachen zu korrigieren. Zuerst müssen Sie wissen dass in der englischen Schreibart dankt man immer am Anfang auf irgend eine artige Weise wenn man einen langen Brief bekommen hat. Ihre andern Fehler werde ich im P.S. erklären, um den Inhalt meines Brief der so intere[ssant] wie nur möglich sein sollte, nichts zu schaden

Sie fragen also, ob Sie meine Briefe Ihrer Schwester mittheilen dürfen. Schon lange müssen Sie wissen dass wenn Sie etwas wirklich wollen ich dagegen nichts haben kann. Aber ehe Sie sich so was zu thun beschliessen, denken Sie nochmals was dadurch gerüstet werden würde. Ein Brief wird immer geschrieben für den, der ihn liest es macht nichts wessen Name darauf stehen möge. Die Menschen sind im ganzen so ähnlich dass [wenn auch hier wählt und sagt der] und zwei Briefe wenn sie zu derselben Zeit geschrieben [wurden] wird man diese Briefe sehr ähnlich finden Also wenn Sie so was thun, werde ich an Sie nie wieder schreiben können. Briefe an eine Familie sind eine ganz andere Sache, wozu ich freilich keine Vorliebe habe. Es kommt gar nicht darauf an dass man die Familie gern hat. Wenn ich an meine Mutter schreibe so sind die Briefe für sie nicht für die anderen, so ist es mit mir immer. Kennen Sie die schöne Ausserung von Bacon, one doubleth a joy when one imparts it to a friend, and a sorrow loseth half its pain. Leider werde ich Sie wahrscheinlich eine Zeit von jetzt an selten sehen und dann für kurze Zeit und Sie wollen dass ich ihnen inzwischen nur nichts als dumme Aufsätze übers Wetter schreiben! Es hätte mich gewundert als ich jünger war. Doch, doch, thun Sie nur wie es in Wirklichkeit angefangen ist genieren Sie sich nicht meinetwegen[9]

MS fragment (draft), TCD

---

[1] Albert Cugnier (see p. 21), a friend of the von Eickens, at their request had arranged JMS's first lodgings in Paris. They were probably those referred to by Cherrie Matheson in her memoir: 'Though he had hardships I don't think he minded them much; they were all more or less of an adventure. He said the weather was bitterly cold, so he used to stay in bed to keep warm. It was the only way. Also he said his landlady's servant warned him not to eat the meat,

and told him it was cat's meat. That amused him very much.' (*Irish Statesman*, 5 July 1924)

2 An adaptation of the first line of Mignon's song, 'Kennst du das Land, wo die Zitronen blühn' (Knowest thou the land where the lemons blossom?), from Bk. III, ch. 1 of Goethe's novel *Wilhelm Meisters Lehrjahre*. 'Gorse' was JMS's nickname for Valeska.

3 Linnaeus (1707–78), the Swedish botanist who introduced the classification of plants into genus and species.

4 His medical acquaintance in Würzburg; see above, p. 13.

5 Encouraged by a letter of 4 Jan 1895 which assures him of her lasting friendship, JMS apparently began his reply with the informal 'Liebe Valeska'; her response, begun 11 Jan and continued on the 14th, chastises him for this 'slip of the pen'. (Both letters, TCD)

6 A giant elephant purchased amidst great controversy from the London Zoological Gardens in 1882 and exhibited until its death in 1885 by the Barnum and Bailey Circus in the United States.

7 A letter from Valeska of 10 Mar 1895 (TCD) again enquires whether he has yet visited Paul M[essin] of Versailles, Monsieur Bouffe, d'Ussell and Madame Maniel, all friends of the von Eickens; JMS's diary mentions only Paul Messin (see p. 22).

8 Words in square brackets here and elsewhere in the German text are supplied by the translators.

9 (Translation)
Dear Gorse

'Knowest thou the land where the yellow gorse blossom?' No, unfortunately you do not know it, you have never seen these lovely flowers. They are really so wonderful to look at the colour is so delightfully warm . . . so charming, and they smell so beautiful that if the blessed in Heaven could smell it, they would at once feel even more blessedly happy. Sometimes in my past youth I was tempted to pluck these flowers to take them home with me, but good Heavens I found they were full of thorns if you get too near to them, so I was forced to sit down quietly on the cold rock and like the pious Lineus to thank dear God for having created so many splendours in this world. It reminds me of the pretty story that my mother used to tell me when I was still a little boy and sat at her feet in a little chair, that is the story of how the Holy Moses stood in excitement before the burning bush and saw how it burned without being burnt in the least, he is stated to have taken off his shoes in reverence but I cannot do that because I have not yet darned my socks.

Gorse has another fine quality which has to be mentioned here, that is pretty flowers can always be found on it, you can take delight in it all the year round when everything else in the world looks cold and is cool and desolate. It has occurred to me that this property may have ceased to exist this winter and I shall soon write to the Flea to enquire whether this is really the case.

But now after so much symbolic dreaming I must thank you very much for your long letter, which arrived yesterday evening at 9 o'clock I immediately sat down in my armchair to be able to read it comfortably and the next time I took out my watch from my pocket it was long past 12 o'clock; [I] had been dreaming over it for a full three hours without getting up once! Then I went to bed and then I dreamt on and on, eternally in the following fashion. I was standing in front of a great iceberg on the top of which there was the most glorious gorse bush. I wanted to climb up to be able to took more closely at the splendour of the flowers and to enjoy their scent, but it [was] all so smooth so mercilessly cold and slippery that it seemed that I could not succeed at all. Only then did I notice some little blue flowers which were peeking out of the [ice] beautifully. They were forget-me-nots! Where they were growing it was not slippery any longer and I could climb and climb until I had climbed quite near the lovely gorse. But then the forget-me-nots disappeared and when I wanted to jump over the last bush, I fell and fell until I woke up in a great fright.

Cugnier visited me last Thursday to collect his parcel, and I am going to him tomorrow afternoon. You ask how I like him, well he was very kind and told me how strong he was, how excellently he could ride, and assured me that his German pronunciation was far better than mine, that may well be true but if so I . . . should have devoted all my attention to it recently. Apart from that he was really very friendly towards me, we did not say much about Oberwerth, I did not want to talk about you with a stranger nor to hear him talk about you, so . . . after a few fine words we let the matter pass, and joked more freely about Jumbo. I have not been to Versailles yet so have not yet visited Monsieur Paul M. . . . I do not know whether [I] will visit the others, I think not.

When I first read your letter I thought that my last letter must have got lost, on the second reading I thought I recognized a hidden allusion to something in . . . the last line of my P.S. Afterwards I remembered that I had made a remark about your English there. So you got it after all! Couldn't you read it? I fully agree with you [that you ought to practice your English]. I need not say that it is a pleasure for me to correct the things. First of all you must realize that in English letter-writing we always say thank you at the beginning for having received a long letter. I will explain your other mistakes in the P.S., so as not to disturb the contents of my letter which is intended to be as interesting as possible

You ask whether you may tell your sister about my letters. You ought to have realized long ago that if you really want something I cannot have anything against it. But before you decide to do anything like that consider once again what might be set in motion by it. A letter is always written for the person who reads it, it doesn't matter whose name is on it. Human beings are on the whole so similar that even if [one is writing to two different recipients and one writes] two letters at the same time, one will find these letters very similar. So if you do anything like that, I shall never be able to write to you again. Letters to a family are something quite different that I have no liking for. It does not matter whether one likes the family. When I write to my mother my letters are for her and not for the others, that's how I feel about it. Do you know the beautiful quotation from Bacon, one doubleth a joy when one imparts it to a friend, and a sorrow loseth half its pain. Unfortunately I shall see you very little for a time and even then only briefly and in the meantime you want me to write you stupid essays about the weather! It would have surprised me when I was younger. Oh yes, continue as you started out don't mind me

To [? MADAME CUGNIER][1]

[Paris X^e. ? Early February 1895]

Je vous remercie beaucoup de votre aimable invitation pour Jeudi prochain.

Cela me fera un grand plaisir d'aller déjeuner chez vous, et je m'y rendrai au jour indiqué . . . .

Agréez Madame, l'assurance de mes sentiments les plus distingués, . . .[2]

MS fragment (draft), TCD

1 JMS's diary refers to visits 'chez Cugnier' throughout the next five years. Albert Cugnier and his mother may have been responsible for introducing JMS to, among others, the Protestant pastor, Jean Monnier.

2 (Translation)

Thank you very much for your kind invitation for next Thursday. I shall be delighted to go and have lunch with you and I shall present myself at your house on the appointed day.

Believe me, Madame, yours sincerely, . . .

To [?ALBERT CUGNIER][1]

[c/o Mme Peter, 2 rue Léopold-Robert, Paris XIVe][2]

[? Early May 1895]

Il y a déja longtemps que je n'ai pas eu de vos nouvelles. J'espère que vous allez bien malgré les changement du temps, car il faut bien le dire, je les trouve épouvantables. Dans un mois, environ, je reviendrai en Irlande, pour y passer l'été avec ma famille.

S'il fait beau temps j'irai probablement par le bateau du Havre à Liverpool et puis avec un autre de Liverpool à Dublin, afin d'éviter le voyage toujours assez ennuyeux à travers l'Angleterre.

C'est bien dommage qu'il n'existe pas un service des bateaux entre la France et l'Irlande.[3]

MS fragment (draft), TCD

1 Albert Cugnier was one of the first friends JMS made in Paris; they continued to correspond after Cugnier joined the Colonial Service in French Guinea in 1901, but there is no further trace of him after 1904. According to Maurice Bourgeois (*John Millington Synge and the Irish Theatre* [1913], 47), JMS helped Cugnier translate Wilde's *Intentions* into French.

2 JMS lodged with the Peters, 2 rue Léopold-Robert, from 1 Apr 1895.

3 (Translation)

I have not heard from you for quite a long time. I hope you are doing well in spite of the changes in the weather which, I must say, I find dreadful. In about a month's time, I shall go back to Ireland and spend the summer with my family.

If the weather is fine, I shall probably sail from Le Havre to Liverpool, then from Liverpool to Dublin in order to avoid the journey through England which is always rather dull.

It's a pity there is no direct line between France and Ireland.

To [? MORIK DALMIGERE][1]

[Paris XIVe. *c*. 10 June 1895]

Je regrette de ne pas avoir pu aller vous aider hier après midi. J'avais un rendez-vous avec un M. Allemand.[2]

Dimanche dernier je voulais aller à la rue Nationale mais j'étais invité à aller dejeuner chez M[essin] à Versailles³

J'espere que rien ne m'empêchera Dimanch prochain d'être des vôtres.⁴

MS fragment (draft), TCD

1 Among his papers JMS preserved a visiting card (TCD), 'Morik Dalmigere stud. phil.u.iur. 11 rue de Vaugirard', annotated by his friend Edward Denny (see p. 23, n. 2): 'Will gladly change lessons with you. Is usually in Club every day. This is No. 1.' According to his diary, JMS met regularly with Dalmigere from 10 Apr 1895, six days after he joined the Société Fraternelle d'Étudiants Protestants, 46 rue de Vaugirard, until he left for Dublin. His diary for 16 June (a Sunday) reads, 'l'après-midi a la rue Nationale, joué avec les petits garçons.' There is no other reference among his papers to the rue Nationale, and so despite the confusion over addresses, Dalmigere seems the most likely recipient of this letter.

2 Probably Otto Boehrig, another student he met at the club. JMS's diary for 9 June 1895 records, 'au Grand Prix'.

3 The family of Paul Messin, a friend of the von Eickens studying medicine in Paris, lived in Versailles; according to his diary JMS went there on Sunday, 2 June.

4 (Translation)

I wish I could have gone and helped you yesterday. I had to meet a German gentleman.

Last Sunday I wanted to go to the rue Nationale but I was invited to lunch at the M[essins] in Versailles

I hope nothing will prevent me from joining you next Sunday.

To [THÉRÈSE BEYDON]¹

[Paris XIVᵉ. *c*. 13 June 1895]

Aujourd'hui je n'ai pas eu beaucoup de temps pour travailler.

D'abord je me suis levé assez tard; et puis après le café j'ai copié mes exercices français dans un livre que je garde dans ce but. Au milieu de ce travail j'étais chassé par la bonne qui voulais faire ma chambre. Alors je suis allé au cercle dans la rue V[augirard] pour y lire les journaux. J'ai trouvé M. D[enny] dans la salle de lecture, et je lui ai démandé s'il avait reçu la lettre que je lui ai ecrite l'autre jour. Il m'a dit que Non!

Qelque temps après en pensant à cela je me suis rapelé que j'ai mis 9 Bd. St. M[ichel] sur l'enveloppe au lie de mettre 109,² par consequent ma lettre est perdue.

Au reste j'en suis content puisque je sais maintenant combien j'y avais fait de fautes.

J'ai été forcé de partir, à mon grand regret, avant l'heure fixée pour notre rendez-vous.

Veuillez m'excuser.[3]

MS fragment (draft), TCD

1 Thérèse Beydon, an art teacher at a girls' school and a devout Protestant, began exchanging language lessons with JMS on 3 June 1895; they became fast friends and he frequently visited her family.

2 Edward P. Denny, apparently a fellow Irishman, was one of JMS's first contacts in Paris, again through the students' club; he sent JMS several language students, including Mlle Beydon, and references to him appear in JMS's diary until 1898. Boulevard Saint-Michel was presumably Denny's professional address; his visiting card (TCD) lists 54 rue de Vaugirard and, later that year, 3 rue Casimir Delavigne.

3 (Translation)

I haven't had much time for work today.

First I got up fairly late, then after drinking my coffee, I copied my French exercises in a book I keep for this purpose. As I was at it, I was turned out by the maid who wanted to tidy the room. Then I went to the club in the rue V[augirard] to read the newspapers. I met Mr D[enny] in the reading room and asked him if he had received the letter I'd written him a few days before. He told me he hadn't.

Shortly after, on thinking it over, I remembered I'd written 9 Bd. St. M[ichel] on the envelope instead of 109. My letter must have got lost.

At any rate, I'm rather glad of it, as I know now what a number of mistakes I'd made in it.

Much to my regret I had to leave before the time appointed for our meeting.

I beg you to forgive me.

To PAUL PASSY[1]

[Paris XIVe. 22 June 1895]

Hier après midi en sortant de votre cours je voulais vous démander une attestation pour avoir suivi vos cou[r]s pendant le semestre. Il y avait tant de monde qu'il m'a été impossible de vos aborder et maintenant si vous voulez avoir le bonté de m'excuser je voudrais vous prier de me l'envoyer.[2]

Au bas de cette lettre vous trouverez mon adresse en Irlande et si vous desiriez quelque information à propos du Celtique ou de notre accent je vous prie de vous adresser à moi.[3]

MS fragment (draft), TCD

1 Paul Edouard Passy (1859–1940), phonetician, assistant director of the École des Hautes-Études, founder of the International Phonetic Association and chief originator of its phonetic alphabet; he was editor of *Le Maître phonetique* 1889–1940, and author of *Les Sons du français* (1887), *Dictionnaire phonetique de la langue français* (with H. Michaelis, 1897), and *International French-English and English-French Dictionary* (with G. Hempl, 1904).

JMS apparently had a letter of introduction to Passy, for he went to his home at 92 rue de Longchamp on 25 Feb 1895 and received a list of addresses from him. He attended Passy's course in general and comparative phonetics at the École des Hautes-Études every Wednesday and Friday from 26 Apr to 21 June 1895, and his diary for 25 June notes, 'a Neuilly pour voir P. Passy'. Among his papers he preserved a copy of Passy's phonetic alphabet, dated July 1894 (TCD).

2 A certification of JMS's regular attendance at his course, signed by Passy and dated 26 June 1895, is in TCD.

3 (Translation)

Yesterday afternoon at the end of your lecture I wanted to ask you for a certificate of attendance for this semester. There were so many people that I was not able to speak to you. If you would be so kind as to excuse my boldness, may I presume to ask you to send me the certificate.

You'll find my address in Ireland at the end of this letter and if you need any information about the Celtic language or about our accent, I am at your disposal.

To [? MADAME BEYDON][1]

[Paris XIVe. *c*. 23 June 1895]

Je regrette de ne pas pouvoir aller vous voir avant mon départ, qui est fixé pour Vendredi prochain. Depuis la dernière fois que je vous ai vue j'été si occupé à la Sorbonne[2] et si pris aussi par mes preparatifs de voyage que je ne sais guère comment le temps a passé. Je ne suis pas encore sur (de l'époque à laquelle je pourrai revenir) quand je pourrai revenir à Paris mais dès mon retour je me fera le plaisir d'aller vous voir.

Ayez le bonté de faire me compliments à Mesdemoiselles vos filles et croyez je vous priè à etc.[3]

MS fragment (draft), TCD

1 The mother of Thérèse Beydon, who kept a small boarding house in Paris at 11 rue des Saints-Pères.

2 JMS also received certificates of attendance (TCD) from Auguste Emile Faguet (1847–1916), dated 20 June 1895, for his course in French literature; Louis Petit de Julleville (1841–1901), dated 27 June, for his lectures on medieval French literature; and from the Dean of the Faculty of the Sorbonne on 28 June 1895.

3 (Translation)

I am sorry I can't go and visit you before my departure which is due to take place next Friday. Since I last saw you, I've been so busy at the Sorbonne and so entirely taken up with preparations for my journey that I hardly know how the time went by. I don't know for sure when I'll be able to come back to Paris but as soon as I'm here again, I'll be glad to go and visit you.

Please remember me kindly to your daughters. I remain etc.

To [?THÉRÈSE BEYDON]

[Paris XIVe. 25 June 1895]

Ce matin je suis sorti dans l'intention d'aller voir l'exposition au Champ de Mars[1] mais chemin faisant je me suis rappelé qu' aujour-dh'hui était le jour chic et n'ayant pas le désir de dépenser 4 francs inutilement je suis revenu sans l'avoir vue.[2]

MS fragment (draft), TCD

[1] JMS's diary for 26 June 1895 reads, 'au Salon Champ de Mars'.
[2] (Translation)
This morning I meant to go and visit the 'Exposition' at the Champ de Mars. But on my way there, I remembered today was the day for the smart set. As I did not wish to spend 4 francs unnecessarily, I came back home without seeing it.

To [?THÉRÈSE BEYDON][1]

[Paris XIVe. *c.* 27 June 1895]

Jusqu' à present je n'ai lu que très peu de poésie française. Le vers le plus ordinaire, l'Alexandrin est pour moi et je crois aussi pour presque tous les lecteurs des races Germanique etrange, raid, et monotone. Je sais bien qu'il y a beaucoup de passages en ce vers qui sont veritablement beaux est artistiques mais pour un long poème je ne ne trouve pas qu'il convient à cause de sa rhyme.

A propos de jugements de cette sorte on admit qu'il est seulement le nation même qui peut en parler avec certitude mais la nation peut se tromper à cause de ses habitudes ou de sa fierté national.

Or en ce cas je cherche les jugement de plusieurs nations sur l'un
. . .[2]

MS fragment (draft), TCD

[1] Perhaps part of an essay set by Mlle Beydon as part of their 'more serious' exchange of language studies.
[2] (Translation)
So far I've read only very little French poetry. For me and, I think, for almost any reader belonging to a foreign Germanic race, its most common metre, the alexandrine, is strange, rigid and monotonous. I know that many passages written in this metre are truly beautiful and artistic but on account of its rhyming I don't think it is convenient for a long poem.
About judgements of this kind it is usually granted that only the nation itself can pass them with some certainty but the nation can be wrong because of its habits or its national pride.
Now in this case I consider the judgements of many nations on one . . .

To MADAME PETER[1]

[31 Crosthwaite Park, Kingstown, Co. Dublin]
[30 June 1895]

Hier au soir je suis arrivé chez moi. Mon voyage a été très agréable
et sans aucun accident

J'ai passé Samedi à Londres et bien que j'étais très pressé j'ai pu
voir le Gallery national l'academie et quelques uns de mes parents.[2]
J'ai reçu plusieurs invitations pour y rester quelque jours, mais
l'envie que j'avais de revoir [Irlande] était trop forte.

En commençant un voyage j'aime beaucoup passer quelque temps
à Londres, mais en revenant je ne puis m'arrêter.

Je crois que j'ai laissé un mouchoir dans le tiroir de me chambre
si vous l'avez trouvé je vous prie de me l'envoyer si cela ne vous
deranger pas.

Je trouve le temps bien meilleur ici que celui que nous avons eu
ce dernier mois à Paris c'est a dire que nous n'avons pas ici des
changement de temperature tous les deux jous d'une chaleur effray-
ante à un froid humide ce que est encore plus désagréable. Après
demain nous partirons pour la campagne; nous avons loué une toute
petite maison au bord d'un lac en Co Wicklow. Nous y resterons
probablement pendant un mois après cela nous irons j'espere plus
loin.[3]

MS fragment (draft), TCD

[1] JMS's landlady in the rue Léopold-Robert, Paris. He remained on friendly
terms with the family, visiting them often, and was to stay there again for four
and a half months in 1897.

[2] Mary Synge (b. 1840), JMS's pianist cousin, lived in London, as did other
Synge relations (see his letter to Isabella Synge, p. 36).

[3] (Translation)

I arrived at home last night after a very pleasant and quite uneventful trip.

I spent Saturday in London and though I was in a hurry, I still had time
to see the National Gallery and the Academy and visit a few of my relatives.
I received many invitations to stay for a few days but I was too anxious to
see [Ireland] again.

At the beginning of a journey I like spending a few days in London but on
the way back I can't stop.

I think I left a handkerchief in a drawer in my room. If you've found it,
please be so kind as to send it to me, if it's not too much trouble.

I find the weather here much better than that we had in Paris this month,
I mean, we haven't got these changes in temperature every second day, from
terrible heat to a damp cold, which is even worse.

The day after tomorrow we shall go to the country. We've rented a small
house on the shore of a lake in County Wicklow. We shall probably stay
there for a month, then I hope we'll go further.

Tó A FRENCH BOOKSELLER

[Kingstown. Early ?July 1895]

Monsieur

Veuillez avoir le bonte de m'envoyer les livres suivants[1]

J'ignore le prix du port, mais je vous enverrai le montant par le retour du courrier.

Si vous aimez mieux ecrivez moi d'abord pour me dire quel serait ce montant et je vous l'enverrai immediatement. Veuillez agreer l'assurance . . .[2]

MS fragment (draft), TCD

[1] No list is enclosed. According to his diary JMS was reading works by Molière, Mérimée, La Fontaine, Chateaubriand, Daudet, and French Positivist tracts, while continuing with Heine and Goethe.

[2] (Translation)
Dear Sir

Will you be so kind as to send me the following books.

I don't know what the postage will be, but I shall pay the amount by return of post.

If you prefer, you can write me first and let me know what it will amount to. I'll send you the money immediately. Yours sincerely . . .

To THÉRÈSE BEYDON

[Kingstown. *c.* 4 July 1895][1]

Je vous prie de m'excuser *pour ne pas vous avoir écrit plus tôt,*[2] j'ai eu tant de choses à faire depuis mon retour, que je n'ai pas eu beaucoup de temps pour le français.

Mon voyage a été à peu près comme je vous l'ai dèja decrit, c'est a dire très agreable, mais excessivement fatigant.

Je n'ai pu aller voir Rouen parce que le jour de mon départ, il m'a fallu attendre jusqu'au soir pour demander l'attestation au doyen.

Alors *je suis parti à 9 heures du soir et à 8 heures Samedi matin je suis arrivé à Londres.* La traversee a été tres calme, mais puisque ceux qui voyagent en 2^ieme class ne peuvent monter sur le pont elle ne m'a pas fait beaucoup de plaisir. Arrivé à Londres j'ai pris une voiture et je suis allé à l'autre gare d'ou partent les trains pour l'Irland.[3] J'y ai laissé mon bagage, et puis je me suis acheté un plan de la ville que je ne connais pas bien encore.

D'abord je suis alle à la Nat. Gall et — c'etait fermé!

Je ne sais si je vous ai dejà dit que partout où je vais je trouve tout fermé à clef, cela ne m'est pas arrivé une ou deux fois mais toujours.

Cependant cette fois-ci cela n'etait rien parce qu'on m'a dit que la porte devait être ouverte dans une heure.

Pour passer ce temp je suis entré dans Westminster, où j'etais bien content de trouver qu'on faisait juste le service du matin, et la musique m'a semblé admirable.

Après cela j'ai vu enfin la Gallery. Pour déjeuner je suis tombé assez drôlement dans un restaurant où tout le monde était français et j'y ai parlé votre langue pour la dernière fois. L'après midi j'ai vu l'Academy (notre salon, vous savez) mais j'etais alors beaucoup trop fatigué pour pouvoir en jouir.

A six heures et demi j'ai quitté Londres. Dans le train je me suis trouvé vis-a-vis d'un jeune Irlandais nous avons commencer à causer et en peu de temps j'ai trouvé que c'etait un garçon que j'avais connu, il y a dix ans dans l'école.[4] Cette decouverte nous a fait beaucoup de plaisir et nous avons causé toute la nuit.

Je vous prie de vouloir faire mes compliments aux vôtres.[5]

MS fragment (corrected draft), TCD

[1] Stephens (MS, TCD) dates this draft somewhat later, but it was most likely written just before JMS left Kingstown to join his mother in Wicklow on 6 July 1895.

[2] Throughout the letter JMS appears to have underlined those passages commented on by Thérèse Beydon (see p. 30, n. 3).

[3] i.e. Euston Station.

[4] Aravon House, Bray School, where JMS spent one year at the age of thirteen. The boy is unidentified.

[5] (Translation)

Please forgive me for being so long in writing. I've had so much to do ever since I arrived that I've had very little time for French.

My journey was about as I've already described, that is, very pleasant but excessively tiring.

I couldn't visit Rouen because on the day of my departure I had to wait until late in the evening to apply to the Dean of the Faculty for the certificate [of attendance].

I left Paris at 9 p.m. and at 8 on Saturday morning I arrived in London. The crossing was very smooth but as second-class passengers are not allowed on deck, I enjoyed it very little. Once in London I hired a cab and went to the station where one takes the train to Ireland. I left my luggage there and I bought a map of the town which I don't know very well.

First I went to the Nat. Gall[ery] and — it was closed!

I can't remember if I've already told you that wherever I go I find everything locked, this I've experienced not once or twice but all the time. Still in this particular case it was not too bad as they told me the door was to open within an hour's time.

To while the time away I entered Westminster [Abbey], where I was glad to discover they were just having morning service, and I found the music marvellous.

Then I saw the [National] Gallery at last. At lunch oddly enough I found myself in a restaurant where everybody was French and I spoke your language for the last time. In the afternoon I saw the Academy (our Salon, as you know) but I was much too tired then to enjoy it.

I left London at 6.30 p.m. On the train I sat opposite a young Irishman we started talking and after a moment I found he was a boy I had known ten years ago, at school. We were very glad when we discovered this and we kept talking all night long.

Please remember me kindly to your family.

To AN UNIDENTIFIED CORRESPONDENT[1]

[Lough Dan, Co. Wicklow][2]
[Mid-July 1895]

Le premier resultat de l'application de Home-Rule en Irlande serait un guere, ou du moins un grand conflit social entre Catholique et Protestant.[3] Les Irlandais sont maintenant si habitués de vivre dans un état d'agiration politique, que la question de la possession du terrain suffirait de bannir toute paix interieure pendant probable-ment plusieurs siècles.

Pour pouvoir introduire sans danger un pareil changement il faut attendre un moment plus tranquille.[4]

MS fragment (draft), TCD

[1] Possibly another exercise prepared for Thérèse Beydon.
[2] Mrs Synge hired Duff House, Lough Dan, near Roundwood, Co. Wicklow, from 5 to 31 July 1895.
[3] When Gladstone was returned to power in 1892, a second Home Rule bill was introduced, which passed the House of Commons on 1 Sept 1893, but was defeated by the House of Lords a week later. Gladstone resigned the following March. JMS had canvassed in February 1893 for an anti-Home Rule petition.
[4] (Translation)
The first effect of the application of Home Rule in Ireland would be a war, or at least a great social conflict between Protestants and Catholics. The Irish have been living in a condition of political unrest for so long that the issue of the ownership of the land would probably be enough to banish internal peace for many centuries.
    To bring in such a change safely, one should wait until a more favourable moment.

To THÉRÈSE BEYDON

Avonmore | Annamoe | Greystones| Co Wicklow[1]
August 1/95[2]

Chère Mademoiselle

Merci bien pour votre lettre et les corrections,[3] je suis étonné de voir comment j'y ai fait de fautes d'inattention, c'est affreux!

Votre anglais n'etait pas mal, je l'aurais compris sans la traduction. Pour exprimer la volonté on dit, '*I wish*,' ou plus souvent '*I want*' etc. 'Than' est seulement employé pour faire la comparaison par ex, more French *than* English. Je n'ai pas expliqué toutes vos fautes s'il y a quelque chose que vous ne puvez comprendre je vous prie de me le dire. Avez-vous fini Little Lord F.?[4]

Cela suffit, je crois, pour la grammaire, maintenant il faut chercher quelque chose de plus amusant.

Depuis le 5 juillet j'ai été à la compagne, jusqu'a hier, tout à fait au bord d'un grand lac, Lough Dan, et maintenant dans une autre maison un peu plus loin. Le paysage tout autour d'ici est admirablement beau, des grandes sombres montagnes à chaque côté, et plus près des lacs et une très jolie rivière. Cependant ce qui est le plus frappant c'est les couleurs, qui, grâce à l'humidité, sont merveilleusement douces et variées. Je passe une grande partie du temps en pêchant à la ligne, et j'ai envoyé beaucoup de pauvres petites truites au ciel, c'est triste, n'est ce pas?

Au reste j'ai lu beaucoup de français Contes par Daudet plusieurs comédies de Molière que j'aime beaucoup, etc. etc.[5]

J'ai trouvé, heureusement, ma famille en bonne santé, ma mère ne sait plus parler français mais elle le peut comprendre assez bien.

Mon frère aîné est arrivé tout bien l'Amérique, il n'est pas de tout changé, pendant les huits ans qu'il a passé la-bas[6]

Si vous écrivez encore à Mr Gourlay,[7] je vous prie de lui remercier pour ses amitiés, et de l'envoyer les miennes. Il me semble bien probable que je reviendrai à Paris, je trouve que Alger est trop loin.[8]

Vous avez très bien mis l'adresse, je espere que je mettrai la vôtre aussi justement.

Est-ce que vous avez lu quelque chose de notres elections qui ont fini l'autre jour, j'y ai voté pour la première fois, bien qu'il m'a fallu voyager dix heures exprès pour cela.[9]

Alors c'est assez pour cette fois n'est pas?

Cordialement a vous
John M Synge[10]

MS (uncorrected), TCD

[1] Mrs Synge moved her household to Avonmore, on the side of Castle Kevin hill, where they remained from 31 July to 5 Sept 1895.

[2] According to JMS's diary, this letter was posted 3 Aug 1895.

[3] A fragment of this letter (undated, TCD) suggests that JMS and Mlle Beydon exchanged 'more serious work' as well as returning each other's letters with corrections. JMS entered the corrected version of his letters of 1 Aug, 10 Sept and 31 Oct 1895 to Mlle Beydon in his notebook (TCD) alongside the drafts to other correspondents printed above.

[4] *Little Lord Fauntleroy*, by Frances Hodgson Burnett, was first published in 1886 and was an immediate popular success.

[5] During the previous month JMS noted in his diary having read Molière's *Le Malade imaginaire*, *Tartuffe*, and *Le Misanthrope*, followed by *Contes du lundi* (1873) by Alphonse Daudet (1840–97)

6 Robert Anthony Synge (1858–1943), an engineer, worked in the Argentine from 1883 to 1900; this was his first visit home in twelve (not eight) years.

7 Among the visiting cards JMS kept (TCD) is one from William R. Gourlay, Linden Lodge, Dowanhill; Mlle Beydon reports (undated, TCD) that 'he is travelling at present in Germany, but will soon be returning to Scotland.' No correspondence with Gourlay has been found, but he and JMS had met by 12 Apr 1895 (perhaps at the students' club), and on JMS's recommendation Gourlay stayed with the von Eickens at Oberwerth in December 1895.

8 There is no further reference to Algiers; Gourlay may have invited JMS to travel there with him.

9 The Liberals were defeated in the general election of 19 July 1895. JMS probably cycled to Kingstown — five hours each way — to vote.

10 (Translation)

Dear Mademoiselle

Thank you for your letter and the corrections, I am surprised at seeing how many mistakes are due to my carelessness, it's simply shocking!

Your English was fairly good, I'd have understood it without your translation. To express volition we say, '*I wish*', or more often '*I want*' etc. 'Than' is only used in comparisons for instance, more French *than* English. I haven't commented upon every mistake. If there's anything you don't understand please let me know. Have you finished Little Lord F.?

Enough about grammar, for the moment, let's look for a more entertaining topic.

Since 5 July I have been in the country, first we were right beside a large lake, Lough Dan, and yesterday we moved to another house a little further away. The landscape all around here is quite wonderful with big dark mountains on every side, and lakes and a very pretty river closer by. What is most striking however is the colours, which, due to the general dampness, are admirably soft and varied. I spend most of my time fishing, and I have already sent many a poor little trout to Heaven, sad, isn't it?

Besides I have been reading a lot of French. Daudet's *Contes*, several plays by Molière whom I like very much, etc. etc.

I was pleased to find my family in good health, my mother can no longer speak French but she can still understand it fairly well.

My elder brother has just returned safe and sound from America, he hasn't changed at all during the eight years he spent there.

If you write to Mr Gourlay again, please thank him for his kind regards and remember me to him. I think it most likely that I shall go back to Paris, Algiers seems too far away.

You addressed your letter quite correctly and I hope I shall make no mistake in addressing mine.

Have you read anything about our elections which came to an end a few days ago? I voted for the first time, even though I had to travel ten hours expressly for this purpose.

That's enough for now isn't it?

Yours sincerely
John M Synge

To THÉRÈSE BEYDON

31 Crosthwaite Park | Kingstown | Dublin | Ireland
Sept 10/95

Chère Mademoiselle

Je suis désolé de vous avoir laissée si longtemps sans une réponse, mais votre lettre est arrivée quelques jours avant notre départ de la compagne et j'ai en tant de choses à faire que je suis sûr que vous m'excuserez. Je vous remercie aussi pour m'avoir envoyé la lettre de Mr Gourley que m'a fait beaucoup de plaisir.

Votre anglais j'ai entièrement compris! Il faut ajouter que j'en suis bien fier! C'est admirable que vous avez fini Little Lord F. maintenant vous verrez en peu de temps que vous avez fait des progrès considérables.

Nous sommes maintenant encore en ville, et je vais tous les jours à Dublin pour y travailler dans la bibliothèque[1] c'y est bien tranquille pendant les vacances et on peut s'endormir agréablement parmi les grandes livres.

Après Paris je trouve Dublin extraordinairement petit, mais si drôle, si naif, si charmant que je l'aime plus que jamais.

J'ai rassemblé beaucoup de drôles petites histoires que je vais vous raconter quand je serrai encore à Paris.

Dans six semaines je partirai probablement pour votre grande ville afin d'être comfortablement installé avant le commencement du semestre. Je viens de lire le 'Philosophe sous les toits' par Silvestre[2] je l'ai trouvé bien amusant. J'espère que vous lisez encore quelque chose d'Anglais, il ne faut pas oublier ce que vous avez appris.

Maintenant il me faut aller à la bibliothèque j'ai tellement sommeil!

Cordialement à vous
John M Synge[3]

MS (uncorrected), TCD

[1] At Trinity College, Dublin.

[2] *Un Philosophe sous les toits* [An 'Attic' Philosopher] by Emile Souvestre (1806–54), essayist, dramatist, novelist, and editor of *La Revue de Paris*, had been honoured by the French Academy as a work 'contributing supremely to morals'.

[3] (Translation)

Dear Mademoiselle

I am so sorry I was so long in answering your letter, but I received it only a few days before we came back from the country and I've had so many things to do since then that I'm confident you will excuse me. Thank you for forwarding Mr Gourley's letter which I was very pleased to read.

I understood everything you wrote in English! I must say I am very proud of it. How marvellous that you finished Little Lord F. now you can see that in a short time you have made considerable progress.

We are back in town and I go to Dublin every day to work in the library. It is a very quiet place during the holidays and one can quite pleasantly go to sleep among all those big books.

After Paris I find Dublin extraordinarily small, but so amusing, so naïve, so charming that I am more fond of it than ever.

I have collected a number of funny little anecdotes which I'll tell you when I'm back in Paris.

I shall probably return to your big city in six weeks' time so that I may get comfortably settled in before the semester begins. I have just finished 'Philosophe sous les Toits' by Silvestre I found it very amusing. I hope you're still reading some English, you must not forget what you've already learnt.

I have to go to the library now I feel so sleepy!

Yours sincerely
John M Synge

To THÉRÈSE BEYDON

Oct 31/95
31 Crosthwaite Park | Kingstown | Dublin

Chère Mademoiselle

Merci bien pour votre lettre.

Vous ne devez etre découragée du tout, l'anglais est beaucoup mieux cette fois; naturellement il y a encore des fautes dans chaque phrase mais la tourure est moins française. Dans ma dernière lettre j'ai voulu dire (si vous vous rappelez) que j'étais fier d'avoir pu comprendre votre anglais (l'autre signification aurait été plus vraie cette fois).[1]

Maintenant je vais vous donner des tristes nouvelles! Je n'irai pas à Paris si tôt que je vous ai dit, j'ai tellement peur de votre hiver![2] J'étudie l'italien maintenant avec un Monsieur de ce pays.[3] Un peu plus tard j'irai à Paris pour quelques semaines, et puis à Italie pour trois mois.

Cela fait, je reviendrai à Paris et y resterai jusque à l'été.

Enfin, si vous voulez continuer nos leçons par correspondance j'en serai rave, mais peut-être vous devez trouver un autre monsieur anglais (c'est dommage qu'il y a si peu d'Irlandais à Paris) jusqu'a mon retour de Italie, si cela serrait possible.

En tout cas je vous remercie pour les bonnes leçons que vous m'avez données, et je vais vous voir aussitôt que je sais arrivé à Paris.

Vous savez que les choses tristes ne sont jamais toutes seules, voici la seconde, l'autre jour en revenant pour diner il a commencé à pleuvoir comme tout, et je me suis mis à courir comme un fou. Cependant le chemin était bien glissant, et quand j'étais à peu près vingt pas de ma porte, tout d'un coup, je suis tombé sur les genoux comme un vieux cheval! Je leur ai fait tout de mal que depuis dix jours je ne puis pas bouger du tout.

On trouve encore deux grands trous dans l'asphalte faits par mes genoux, et un'autre beaucoup plus loin fait par mon pauvre nez!

Cordialement à vous
John M Synge

P.S. Probablement je n'irai pas à Paris avant la fin de cette année.[4]

MS (uncorrected), TCD

¹ In her corrections to his previous letter (p. 31), Mlle Beydon had commented on the ambiguity of the phrase 'j'en suis bien fier' and asked for clarification.

² A more likely reason for postponing his departure was his courtship of Cherrie Matheson (1870–1940), who lived with her Plymouth Brethren family three doors away in Crosthwaite Park. She and JMS first met in Greystones during the 1880s, but they did not become friends until after she stayed in Wicklow in August 1894 as sketching companion to Florence Ross. A talented water-colourist with a cheerful, outgoing personality, she corresponded with JMS from 1894 to 1898 and appears to have encouraged him to go to Italy to study art and the language in 1896. JMS did not leave for Paris until 2 Jan 1896.

³ Francisco Morosini; see below, p. 36.

⁴ (Translation)

Dear Mademoiselle
    Thank you for your letter.
    You must not lose heart by any means. Your English is much better this time; of course there are still a few mistakes in every sentence but the turn of phrase is much less French. In my last letter (if you remember it) I meant I was proud to have been able to understand your English (the other meaning would have been more appropriate this time).
    Now I have some bad news to give you! I shall not go to Paris as early as I told you, I am so afraid of your winter! I am studying Italian now with a gentleman from that country. After that I'll go to Paris for a few weeks, then on to Italy for three months.
    Then, I'll come back to Paris and I'll stay there until summer.
    If you care to go on with our lessons by correspondence I'll be delighted to, but perhaps you'll have to find another English gentleman if you can (a pity there are so few Irishmen in Paris) until I come back from Italy.
    In any case I thank you for the good lessons that you gave me, and I shall come and visit you as soon as I am in Paris again.
    You know that misfortunes never come singly, here is another piece of sad news, the other day it started to rain cats and dogs as I was on my way home for dinner, and I began to run like mad. But the road was very slippery, and when I was only a few steps from my front door, suddenly I fell on my knees like an old nag! I hurt them so badly that for ten days I haven't been able to move at all.
    You could still see two large holes made by my knees in the asphalt, and much further on a smaller one made by my poor nose!

Yours sincerely
John M Synge

P.S. It's not likely that I'll go to Paris until the end of this year.

To THÉRÈSE BEYDON

[c/o Signor Conte Polloni, 73 via Aureliana] Rome¹
[*c.* 23 February 1896]

Je ne sais comment m'excuser de ne pas vous avoir ecrit plus tôt. Je vais vous raconter tout ce que j'ai fait et alors vous verrez que j'ai été bien occupé depuis mon arrivée.

J'ai quitté Paris Lundi matin le 3 Feb. et après un voyage de 45 heures je suis arrivé ici de bonne heure Mecredi matin. Je suis allé pour les deux premièrs jours dans une hôtel où il y avait une foule d'Anglais et d'americains. Le lendemain de mon arrivée je suis alle voir la dame la dame anglaise pour laquelle j'avais une introduction.[2] Je l'ai trouvée bien aimable mais malheureusement elle ne connaissait aucune famille où je pourrais entrer en pension. Cependant il m'a fallu quitter l'Hotel sur le champ parce que j'y ai depensé 40 frns. en deux jours. Alors je suis entré dans une pension anglaise[3] pour dix jours et en même temps j'ai cherché une famille. Au bout de quelques jours avec l'aide de mon amie irlandaise[4] j'ai trouvé cette maison et j'y suis installé depuis six jours. Pendant toute cette derniere semaine j'ai été très enrhumé vous pouvez vous figurer que j'ai été bien malade puisque cela a pu m'empêcher de vous écrire.

Il fait un temps merveilleux ici depuis le commencement de Janvier mais malgré cela presque tout le monde est enrhumé. Dans la journée il fait si chaud et puis a partir de six heures du soir il commence a gêler comme tout. Je suis tout a fait enchanté de Rome même beaucoup plus que je n'ai pensé.[5]

MS fragment (draft), TCD

[1] JMS boarded with Count Polloni from 17 Feb to 30 Apr 1896, in addition taking lessons in Italian with him.
[2] Probably the Mrs Smith to whom he wrote from Paris and who invited him frequently to dinner and Thursday 'at homes' (1896 diary, TCD). She may have recommended him to Count Polloni.
[3] JMS moved from the Hotel Continental on 7 Feb 1896, staying at the Pension Hayden until 17 Feb.
[4] Cherrie Matheson, who was probably also responsible for his introduction to Mrs Smith.
[5] (Translation)

I must apologize for not writing earlier. I'll tell you everything I've been doing and you'll realize how busy I've been since I arrived here.

I left Paris on Monday morning 3 Feb. and after a 45-hour journey I arrived in Rome early on Wednesday. The first two days I found accommodation in a hotel crowded with American and English people. The day after my arrival I visited the English lady to whom I had a letter of introduction. I thought her very kind but unfortunately she didn't know of any family with whom I could room and board. I had to leave my hotel however as I'd spent 40 francs in two days. Then I moved to an English boarding house and went on looking for a family. After a few days with the help of my Irish woman friend I found the house where I've been for six days now. I've had a bad cold since the beginning of this week. You can imagine how unwell I must have been as it kept me from writing to you.

They've had wonderful weather here since the beginning of January. It is so warm in the daytime and from six in the evening it's icy cold. I find Rome even more fascinating than I thought I would.

To FRANCISCO MOROSINI[1]

[Rome. *c.* 15 March 1896]

Egregio Signore

La settimana scorsa le ho mandato alcuni giornali Italiani, perche sono sicuro ch' ella sara contenta di poter leggere più dettagliate notizie sulla crise politica di cui parlano i giornali di Dublino.[2] Io sono a Roma da sei settimane e ho molto lavorato non senza qualche buon esito; ma non so ancora se potro imparare abbastanza durante i tre mesi che passero in Italia secondo la mia prima intenzione.

Forse vi rimarro per più lungo tempo. Roma mi piace molto, piu ancora che io non crediva. Abbiamo avuto un inverno meraviglioso quasi due mesi senza pioggia. Adesso il tempo e un po' variabile, ma e pur tuttavia sempre piacevole.

Spero che lei e la sua famiglia stiano bene. Pregandla di ricordarmi ad essa, le porgo Egregio Signor Professor i miei ben distinti saluti.

Devotissimo suo[3]

MS (draft), TCD

[1] Signor Morosini gave JMS private lessons in Italian from 11 Nov to 19 Dec 1895; one letter from him survives (23 Sept 1902, TCD), written from Anna Mount, Mulgrave Terrace, Kingstown.

[2] JMS's diary for 10 Mar 1896 notes (in German): 'Wrote description about the present situation for newspaper'; the *Irish Times*, 16 Mar 1896, 5, under the heading 'The Demonstrations in Rome (By an Eye-Witness)', describes the demonstrations in Piazza Colonna on 5 Mar, when Prime Minister Francesco Crispi resigned over the failure of his policies in the Italo–Abyssinian war.

[3] (Translation)
Esteemed Sir
    Last week I sent you some Italian newspapers because I am sure that you would like to be able to read more detailed news on the political crisis about which the Dublin newspapers speak. I have been in Rome for six weeks and I have worked a lot with some good results; but I do not know yet if I will be able to learn enough in the three months that I will spend in Italy as was my first intention.
    Perhaps I will remain for a longer period. I like Rome very much, even more than I thought. We have had a marvellous winter, almost two months without rain. The weather is now a little changeable but it is however still pleasant.
    I hope that you and your family are well. Please remember me to it. I have the honour to be, my dear professor,
                                                          Your most devoted servant

To FRANCISCO MOROSINI

[Rome. 24 March 1896]

Traduzione da Courier[1]

Dopo la mia ultima lettera alla quale ella rispose cosi gentilmente

molte cose sono accaduto qui che a noi pajono grande eventi ma de'
quali, credo, si parla poco nel suo paese.

In ogni caso se la storia di Grecia ha qualche interesse per lei io
le mandero il mio diario che e un piccolo quaderno dove ho notato
brevemente le brutture e le buffonerie da me viste.[2] E difficili di
vedere tante cose in cosi breve tempo e in spazio tanto limitato.

E il signor Ch——[3] che si e assunto di farle tenere questo pacco che
ho cigillato io stesso. La prego *di non mostrarlo* a nessuno.[4]

MS fragment (draft), TCD

[1] JMS's diary entry for 24 Mar 1896 notes 'Courier Lettres d'Italie'.
[2] Possibly a disguised reference to political events in Italy, drawing an
analogy with the effect on ancient Athens of its overseas ventures, or to the
contemporary instability of Greek politics stemming at least partly from its
policies towards Turkey.
[3] Perhaps Signor Cagione, whom JMS in his diary mentions having visited
in Rome on 16, 18, and 23 Mar. The diary JMS sends has not been discovered.
[4] (Translation)

[Delivery] by Courier

After my last letter to which you so kindly replied, many things have happened here, which to us seem great events but about which I believe little
is said in your country.

In any case if the history of Greece has some interest for you, I will send
you my diary which is a little copybook in which I have noted in brief the
uglinesses and the buffooneries seen by me. It is difficult to see so many
things in such a short time and in a space so limited.

It is Mr Ch—— who has taken it on himself to keep this package for you
which I myself have sealed. I ask you *not to show it* to anyone.

To THÉRÈSE BEYDON

Florence[1]
[*c.* 29 May 1896]

Enfin j'ai trouvé un moment pour vous écrire! Je ne sais comment
m'excuser, mais comme toujours j'ai été très occupé, tous les jours
j'ai voulu ecrire mais il y a tant de choses à voir et à faire ici que ce
mois a passé comme une songe. Lundi prochain je partirai pour
retourner a Paris. J'y serai Mardi puisque je n'ai pas l'intention de
m'arreter pendant mon voyage. Alors au mois de Juin j'espere avoir
l'occasion de vous raconter tout ce que je n'ai pas raconté dans
mes lettres c'est a dire beaucoup de choses. Je suis ravi de l'Italie, cette
Florence surtout est quelque chose de s[p]lendide, la ville les tab-
leaux, les statues, tous charmants.

Malheureusement je ne puis plus parler français c'est si semblable
a l'italien que je dis toujours le mots italiens quand je veux parler

français. En vous priant de faire mes aux vôtres je vous dis au revoir a bientôt.[2]

MS fragment (draft), TCD

[1] JMS was in Florence, staying at a pensione near the Arno, from 1 May to 1 June 1896.

[2] (Translation)

I have at last found a short moment to write to you. I don't know how to apologize but I've been so busy, every day I meant to write but there are so many things to be seen and done here that this month has passed as in a dream. I'm going back to Paris next Monday. I'll be there on Tuesday since I don't intend to stop on my journey. Therefore I hope to meet you in June and have an opportunity of telling you about all that I couldn't write in my letters, that is, a lot of things. I'm delighted with Italy, particularly with this Florence. It is something splendid, the town itself, the pictures, the statues, all lovely.

Unfortunately I can't speak French any more. It is so much like Italian that I always use Italian words when I want to speak French. Please remember me kindly to all your family. Goodbye for the moment.

To THÉRÈSE BEYDON

[Hôtel de l'Univers, 9 rue Gay-Lussac] Paris [V^e][1]
[c. 10 June 1896]

Il y a quelque jours que je suis arrivé ici. Les trois premiers jours je m'ai pu parler que l'italien. Puis pendant trois jours j'ai été si enrhumé que je n'ai plus pu parler du tout.

Maintenant je parle un melange assez pittoresque de quatre langues. C'est une chose assez drôle je vous assure si vous avez envie de l'entendre je vous prie de me dire quand je pourrai vous trouver chez vous.[2]

MS fragment (draft), TCD

[1] JMS returned to Paris on 3 June 1896, staying at the Hôtel de l'Univers until his departure for Ireland on 29 June.

[2] (Translation)

I've been back here for a few days now. I could speak nothing but Italian on the first three days. Then for the next three, I had such a cold that I couldn't speak at all.

Now I speak a fairly quaint mixture of four languages. It's rather funny to hear I can assure you and if you care to listen to it please tell me when I can come and visit you.

PART TWO
1897 – 1902

*

Return from Exile

Return from Exile

Paris and Dublin

*

On 29 December 1896 Synge returned to lodgings with the Peters in rue Léopold-Robert, where he remained until leaving for Dublin on 13 May 1897. As usual supplementing his university lectures with extensive reading and lessons with Thérèse Beydon, he also joined a weekly debating society, recording in his diary the occasions on which he spoke. But more and more of his time during the first three months of 1897 was devoted to the Association Irlandaise which was established on New Year's Day by Yeats and Maud Gonne, to whom Synge had been introduced on 27 December 1896. Not only was he present at the inaugural meeting but he seems to have been instrumental in drawing up the list of associate members. However, he soon became dubious about Maud Gonne's political methods and resigned from the association, though he attended its weekly meetings until he returned to Ireland that May.

His social activities increased sufficiently for him to write home for his dress suit, but the most important relationship Synge established was with another independent and impoverished Irishman, Stephen MacKenna. The two became fast friends and to MacKenna Synge confided his interests and aspirations with a freedom he felt with nobody else: he became interested in spiritualism, noting in his diary, 'saw manifestations', and MacKenna advised him on spiritualist writings; he began writing a series of impressionistic essays which only MacKenna was allowed to read; together — sometimes with James Cree — they attended lectures on moral action, feminism, the Breton revival.

When he returned to Dublin on 14 May 1897 Synge continued to pursue his revived Irish interests, joining Yeats and Maud Gonne at the Contemporary Club, and meeting George Russell (AE), with whom he attended meetings of the Theosophical Society. Once again he spent the summer in Wicklow; and once again he attempted, without success, a meeting with Cherrie Matheson. To MacKenna, he wrote humorously that his mother's guests made him long for 'a breath of the wickedness of Paris'; to Thérèse Beydon he confided his misery and longing for marriage.

Back in Dublin by 31 August, he delayed returning to Paris because of swollen glands in his neck, the first indication of the Hodgkin's disease which would eventually kill him. He underwent surgery on 11 December and, typically, wrote an essay on his experiences under ether; he also contemplated writing a novel about nurses. On 19 January 1898, drawing £60 of his principal, he left Ireland, wearing a black wig to cover temporary baldness caused by the operation. After two days in London visiting Hope Rea and Yeats, he arrived in Paris and immediately settled into his usual routine, adding to the list of Irish friends Richard Best, introduced by MacKenna. He also met another art student, Margaret Hardon, an American etcher and student of architecture, and by the time he returned to Dublin for the summer, on 27 April, he had half fallen in love with '*la robe verte*', as he referred to her in his diary.

Synge made his first visit to Aran on 10 May 1898, and after two weeks at the Atlantic Hotel on Inishmore, travelled to Inishmaan, where he stayed with Patrick McDonagh, whose son Martin became his tutor. He was 'much pleased with his abode,' Mrs Synge wrote to Samuel on 30 May, 'a room in a cottage inside the kitchen of a house like Mavourneen's [Mrs Rochford, an old farmer's wife, who lived in a long low thatched cottage near Castle Kevin], and he lives on Mackerel and eggs and learns Irish — how wonderfully he accommodates himself to his various surroundings' (*LMD*, 153).

While on Aran Synge and Lady Gregory had eyed each other from a distance but did not speak; through Yeats he was invited to visit Coole Park on his return. He arrived there on 27 June, dined next day with Edward Martyn, and arrived back in Kingstown on 29 June. On 5 July Mrs Synge wrote again to Sam, this time from Castle Kevin where Synge had once more accompanied her,

John has been suffering from asthma while he was on the islands, he had a very small room off the kitchen to live in, and he lived on eggs nearly *raw*, and salt fish and Bacon and highly stewed tea and hot bread, the only good thing he got was a quart of milk in the day — he had the Asthma the first two days after he came and said he was eating too much — however I said he must get accustomed to eat proper food again, and he seems much better now.   (*LMD*, 154)

Mrs Synge returned from the country on 2 September and for the next two months Synge busied himself meeting friends in Dublin and writing 'A Story from Inishmaan', which was published in the November issue of the *New Ireland Review*. He left for Paris on 14 November, again spending two days in London on the way. On 18 November 1898 he entered in his diary, 'Installé Chez moi 90 Rue d'Assas', and this room was to be his permanent address in Paris for the next five years. On 17 December his review of *La Sagesse et la Destinée* by Maurice Maeterlinck appeared in the Dublin *Daily*

Express, and he immediately began an article on the Breton writer Anatole LeBraz, which appeared in the same paper on 28 January 1899.

From 31 January to 16 February 1899, Yeats was in Paris, and Synge met with him frequently. Yeats wrote to Lady Gregory on 14 February, 'I have seen Synge. He is really a most excellent man. He lives in a little room which he has furnished himself. He is his own servant. He works very hard and is learning Breton. He will be a very useful scholar.' (*The Letters of W. B. Yeats*, ed. Allan Wade [1954], 314) Not only did Synge study the language; he went to Quimper from 3 to 16 April with a Breton friend, Dr Piquenard, and once again published the results of his experiences; 'A Celtic Theatre' appeared in the *Freeman's Journal* in the following year (22 March 1900), and to Richard Best he confided his desire to do for Aran what Pierre Loti had done for Brittany. He continued also to see Maud Gonne regularly (cherishing for the rest of his life a signed photograph she gave him that April), the Polish art student he had met in Italy, Maria Zdanowska, and Margaret Hardon.

Despite repeated attacks of influenza and his mother's worried pleas for him to give up his '*room* life', Synge remained in Paris until 8 May 1899, returning to Dublin by way of London. Before going to Castle Kevin with his mother on 1 June, it is likely that he attended the Irish Literary Theatre production of *The Countess Cathleen* by Yeats and *The Heather Field* by Edward Martyn on 12 May. In Wicklow that summer, the household included Edie Harmar, sister to Samuel's wife Mary, with whom he soon developed a firm and lasting friendship; to her he confided not only his artistic aspirations, but his need for proof before he could accept his family's religious beliefs. As usual, he corresponded regularly with Thérèse Beydon in Paris; he also wrote to Margaret Hardon, who gracefully deflected his romantic overtures.

After a second visit to Aran, from 12 September to 7 October 1899, he spent several weeks in Dublin, seeing friends — including Richard Best, who had returned from Paris — and regularly attending meetings of the Contemporary Club, where he had by now met many of Yeats's friends and Dublin's best talkers. On 20 October his brother Robert returned from South America. On 3 November Synge left for Paris. MacKenna was again in Paris and in April 1900 Lady Gregory spent some time there, encouraging Synge to continue his Aran articles and suggesting Jack B. Yeats as a possible illustrator.

He left Paris again on 23 May 1900, remained in Dublin long enough to attend the Gaelic League's music festival, *Feis Coeil*, and to renew acquaintance with Best and others before leaving for Castle Kevin on the 1st of June. Of the three-month stay that year in

County Wicklow, Mrs Synge wrote somewhat defensively to Sam in China, that 'though the rent will be more than I have ever paid for a Summer outing I trust I am not doing wrong in spending it. You see I spend nothing on Johnnie for 6 months, so it is only fair to give him some benefit of the money I would spend on him if he was at home; and he hates Kingstown and does not want to be here at all before we leave.' (*LMD*, 161–2)

In addition to Annie Harmar, another of Sam's sisters-in-law, Mrs Synge had invited a cousin of the Harmars, Rosie L. Calthrop, who immediately established a warm rapport with Synge. His mother later described Rosie to Sam as 'a Cheerful bright little person; very kind and unselfish': 'She seemed to appreciate Johnnie's thoughtfulness and kindness very much! It is a pity he does not show it to me and not only to strangers. He was most attentive to both in little matters I could see, and he was always at their beck and call to walk or ride or escort them anywhere! So no wonder they like him. . . .' (*MUJ*, 136) When Rosie Calthrop left, Edie Harmar joined the summer party. Mrs Synge returned to Kingstown at the end of August.

Synge's third visit to Aran lasted from 15 September to 14 October 1900; except for a few days on Inishere he stayed with the McDonaghs on Inishmaan, and spent two nights in Galway on his way back to Dublin. Mrs Synge wrote to Samuel on 17 October, 'Johnnie wants to be off to Paris, as soon as he can get money . . . . I wish he would give up this foolish Paris craze he would be much better nearer home.' (*LMD*, 168) Synge remained in Ireland long enough to buy a typewriter, on Best's advice, and left for Paris on 31 October.

He was anxious over further enlargement of a gland at the back of his neck, and perhaps because of this his mother received more brief postcards than usual. Cree, Synge's doctor in Paris, prescribed an ointment which only irritated the swelling, and on 25 April 1901 Mrs Synge reported to Samuel,

I had a letter from Johnnie yesterday, a sad one. He says he met a Russian doctor a friend of his, and he strongly advised him to have the glands removed at once, before the summer holidays, and then to take quantities of Cod Liver Oil to try and remove the tendency and get strong before he went away again. Johnnie thinks that is good advice. . . . Poor fellow, how sad, he has let himself run down dreadfully and I cant get him home. He has always some excuse; he says he would rather wait till this house is empty as he is 'worn and weary and disfigured' and he does not want to come home until they [Robert Synge and his family] are all gone! . . . He has written an article for some American magazine which has been accepted, and now he wants to stay in Paris until he is paid for it.   (Stephens MS)

The article was another of his Aran essays, 'The Last Fortress of the Gael', which was published in the April 1901 issue of the New York *Gael*; his mother had paid for the typing. The only other article published during this winter was a review of an Irish edition of the poems of Geoffrey Keating which appeared in the *Speaker* on 8 December 1900.

Synge returned to Ireland on 6 May and throughout that month underwent treatment from his doctor in Dublin, Dr Parsons; by 3 June he was pronounced well enough to join his mother and her party (which once again included Rosie Calthrop) at Castle Kevin.

Before making his fourth trip to Aran, Synge spent from 14 to 20 September 1901 at Coole with Yeats and Lady Gregory, probably showing them his first play, *When the Moon Has Set*, as well as the bulk of his manuscript of *The Aran Islands*. After a night in Galway, he went directly to Inishmaan, dividing his time equally between the McDonaghs on Inishmaan and Inishere; this time he took his violin with him, and stayed until 9 October. Mrs Synge reported to Sam, '[He] is looking well but thin; he spent all his £10 but 18/0d and I asked him if he considered he had got the value for his money and he said, "Yes, *very* good value"' (*LMD*, 169).

On 21 October Synge attended the third and final season of the Irish Literary Theatre, seeing *Diarmuid and Grania* by Yeats and George Moore and, what impressed him far more, the first play in Irish in a professional theatre, *Casadh an Tsugaín* by Douglas Hyde, under the direction of W. G. Fay. On 1 November he was in Dublin again to attend Lady Gregory's 'at home' in honour of an exhibition of paintings by Jack B. Yeats. When he left for Paris on 26 November 1901, he dropped off his Aran manuscript with Grant Richards in London.

The first months of 1902 were beset by influenza and a series of rejections of his book, but he persevered with the Wicklow articles he was writing and in January was commissioned by *L'Européen* to write on Irish literature. Two articles appeared, 'La Vieille Littérature irlandaise' in the March issue and 'Le Mouvement intellectuel irlandais' in May; Thérèse Beydon corrected his French. He also studied Old Irish with d'Arbois de Jubainville at the Sorbonne. But, as Mrs Synge wrote to Samuel, 'he says he wants to keep in with French literature, as after a time he may be able to write for some of the big English papers and that is the only hope of his making any money, and if he comes over and lives in Ireland he will be always a pauper, as there is no chance of getting on in Ireland commercially' (Stephens MS). By now Cree had left Paris, and MacKenna was getting married; Synge's new companion became his cousin Edward Synge, an etcher. He also began work on two verse plays.

He returned to Ireland on 17 May 1902 and immediately tackled two reviews for the *Speaker*: one, of Lady Gregory's *Cuchulain of Muirthemne*, was published on 7 June, and another, of *Donegal Fairy Stories* by Seumas MacManus, appeared on 21 June. This summer Mrs Synge had arranged to go to Tomriland House, an old farmhouse near Castle Kevin; but she became ill and there were repeated postponements before the move finally took place on 21 July. Although he remained in County Wicklow until 6 September, Synge seems to have journeyed to Dublin only rarely; but despite bouts of asthma, he completed his two one-act plays, *Riders to the Sea* and *(In) The Shadow of the Glen*, and started work on a more ambitious comedy, *The Tinker's Wedding*. The summer was productive in less measurable ways, thanks to Mrs Synge's new cook, Ellen, whose hearty laugh and witty exchanges with the workmen in the kitchen below his bedroom he was to recall in the preface to *The Playboy of the Western World*. On 6 September 1902 two more articles appeared: 'The Old and the New in Ireland' (the *Academy and Literature*) and a review of Geoffrey Keating's *History of Ireland* (the *Speaker*).

On his way to Aran for the fifth and what was to be his last time, Synge spent five days, from 8 to 11 October, at Coole, discussing with Yeats and Lady Gregory his plays and the Aran book. By now Willie Fay's group of amateurs had replaced the Irish Literary Theatre and it is likely that during this visit Synge determined to transfer his interest from Paris to London.

He spent from 14 October to 8 November on Inishere without visiting the McDonaghs on Inishmaan. Back in Dublin, however, he renewed an even earlier friendship when he met Claire von Eicken on 14 November. Nine days later Cherrie Matheson, with whom he had been in love and to whom he had proposed in the 1890s, was married. Though her final rejection of him had occurred in May 1898, Synge had continued to unburden himself about her to various correspondents until 1900, when she became engaged to Kenneth Hobart Houghton, a schoolmaster ten years her junior. The Houghtons settled in South Africa after their marriage in 1902; Cherrie's last meeting with Synge was on a visit to Ireland in 1904.

When Synge visited the Camden Street Theatre on 4 December, to see Fay's company perform *The Laying of the Foundations* by F. J. Ryan, *The Pot of Broth* by Yeats and Lady Gregory, and *Eilís agus an Bhean Deírce* by Peadar MacFhionnlaich, it was with increasing confidence that here lay the key to his future. As he turned away from thoughts of a literary career in France, Lady Gregory introduced him to James Joyce, who was seeking assistance in planning his own journey to Paris.

To MAUD GONNE[1]

[2 rue Léopold-Robert, Paris XIVᵉ][2]

[6 April 1897]

Dear Miss Gonne

I am sorry to trouble you again so soon but I have something to say which it seems better to say by letter than in one of our meetings as there the French members might misconstrue our difference of opinion. You already know how widely my theory of regeneration for Ireland differs from yours and most of the other members of the Jeune Irlande. I do not wish to enter the question which of us may be in the right but I think you will not be surprised to hear[3] that I cannot possibly continue to be a member of a society which works on lines such as those laid down for the Irlande Libre.[4] I wish to work in my own way for the cause of Ireland and I shall never be able to do so if I get mixed up with a revolutionary and semi-military movement. I have considered the matter very carefully and I see there is no course open to me but ask you to take my name off your list of members. If you think well I shall be glad to attend your meetings in a purely non-official capacity but that is for you and the comity to decide. As member I should have to henceforth contend every point raised in reference to the journal (wasting your time and creating discussion) but as spectator I can still help you where [and] whenever it is in my power and for the rest keep an uncompromising silence.[5] ⟨Perhaps you will think it better not to have⟩

I shall be leaving Paris for Ireland in a few weeks but I greatly hope to be back here again after the summer.[6]

MS (draft), TCD

[1] The Irish revolutionary Maud Gonne (1865–1953), to whom JMS was introduced on 27 Dec 1896. She was in Paris attempting to establish the Association Irlandaise, a Paris branch of the Young Ireland Society, which JMS joined at the inaugural meeting of 1 Jan 1897. He and she remained friends until her objection to *The Shadow of the Glen* led to her resignation from the Irish National Theatre Society.

[2] JMS was again lodging with the Peters, from 29 Dec 1896 to 13 May 1897.

[3] Written in above: 'learn'.

[4] Maud Gonne's monthly journal *L'Irlande libre*, 'the organ of the Irish colony in Paris', openly advocated hatred of England and the need to free Ireland by any means from economic and political slavery; the journal ran from May 1897 until at least April 1900 (vol. IV, no. 1) and included a wide range of articles.

[5] Although JMS attended weekly meetings until he returned to Dublin in May 1897, a letter from Maud Gonne suggests that his doubts were roused very early. 'Many thanks for your letter,' she wrote on 16 Mar 1897. 'Of course in future your name shall not be published in the reports of our meetings etc.' (TCD)

⁶ Barry Delany, Maud Gonne's secretary, replied for her on 13 Apr 1897 (TCD), responding to a further paragraph asking for the address of W. B. Yeats and [?Seumas O']Connolly.

To LADY GREGORY¹

31 Crosthwaite Park | Kingstown
1/7/98

Dear Lady Gregory

I hope I am not keeping the articles² too long. I have hardly had a moment free since my return and am going on to Co Wicklow³ this evening so my hands are pretty full.

I had a very prosperous journey up from Gort. At Athenry an old Irish speaking wanderer made my acquaintance. He claimed to be the best singer in England, Ireland and America. One night he sang a song in Moate and a friend of his heard the words in Athenry. He was so much struck by the event he had himself examined by one who knew and found that his singing did not come out of his lungs but out of his heart, which is a 'winged heart'!

My Aran photos seem a success I will send you some when I can print them⁴

Sincerely yours
John M Synge

MS, Berg. *TB*, 28

¹ Isabella Augusta Gregory (1852–1932), playwright and essayist and founder with W. B. Yeats (see p. 126) of the Irish Literary Theatre. JMS visited her at Coole Park, Co. Galway, on his return from his first visit to Aran.
² Likely Yeats's publications on Irish folklore, written with the help of Lady Gregory and published in the *New Ireland Review*, which later (November 1898) published JMS's 'A Story from Inishmaan'.
³ Mrs Synge had rented Castle Kevin until 2 Sept.
⁴ On 17 May 1898, while visiting Aran for the first time, JMS purchased a Lancaster hand camera from a fellow visitor on the island; this was a heavy box camera holding twelve quarter-plates which were developed by his nephew, Francis Edmund Stephens (1884–1948). Later JMS owned a Kilto. Fifty-three of his photographs were published in J. M. Synge, *My Wallet of Photographs*, arranged and introduced by Lilo Stephens (Dublin, 1971).

To MARTIN McDONAGH¹

90 rue d'Assas | Paris²
[February 1900]

A Mhartin dílis

Is mór an t-am nach bhfuil litir uait agam, Tá súil agam go bhfuil tú agus do mhuintir go maith na sláinte, Tá mé maith go leor fós, acht tá mórán tinneas ins an tír so anis.

Tháinic mé ar Bhaullen³ trí mhí o shoin agus bhí gala an-mhór ann, an lá sin, agus ba beag nach raibh a long gaile briste ar na ail⁴

Tá go leor leabh Gaeilge agam anis agus mé ag l[éamh] go minic. Nil a fhios agam an bhfuil tú [ag] l[éamh] fór.⁵

MS fragment (draft), TCD

¹ Martin McDonagh ('Michael' of *The Aran Islands*) was the son of the family with whom JMS stayed on Inishmaan and his tutor until he left the islands on 25 June 1898. Martin wrote to JMS on 20 Feb 1899 (TCD) and they continued to correspond after he went later that year to Galway to work. JMS visited him after his stay on Aran in October 1899, and the friendship continued, through letters, after JMS ceased to visit Aran.

² JMS took a room at the top of the house at 90 rue d'Assas, Paris VIᵉ, and, with the help of Richard Best (see p. 85), its previous occupant (who had it from Stephen MacKenna), furnished it himself; it was to be his permanent address in Paris until 1903.

³ Probably an attempt to write 'Boulogne' in Irish, although James Stewart of Copenhagen University transcribes 'ar' as 'as' (from, out of) and suggests instead a hastily written, near-phonetic representation of the ordinary Gaelic name for Dublin, Baile Atha Cliat.

⁴ Mrs Synge noted in her diary (TCD) for 3 Nov 1899, 'A very stormy wet morning, Johnnie went off to Paris by early boat, it blew a hurricane and rain in sheets'; and for 6 Nov 1899, 'I heard from . . . John from Paris very bad voyage and escapes.'

⁵ (Translation)
Dear Martin
     It's a long time since I had a letter from you, I hope that you and your people are in good health, I am quite well still, but there is much disease in this country at present.
     I arrived at Boulogne three months ago and there was a very great gale that day — the steamship was almost wrecked upon the rocks
     I have many Gaelic books now which I often [read].
     I do not know if you [are reading] yet.

To MRS KATHLEEN SYNGE¹

Paris [VIᵉ]
Saturday [7 April 1900]

Thanks for yours, paper, etc. I am glad you had fine weather, it has been warmer over here too the last few days²

J.M.S

MS postcard, TCD

¹ Mrs John Hatch Synge (1830–1908), JMS's mother.

² Mrs Synge reported to her son Samuel (see p. 190) on 21 Nov 1899, 'He has not had any fires in his room and it is getting very cold evidently below

50. He said he had been burning newspapers and raised the temperature several
degrees by that means, and had got it up to 50 which was his normal temp. over
there.' (TCD)

To ROSIE L. CALTHROP[1]

Castle Kevin
[?12 July 1900]

Dear Miss Calthrop
    Many thanks for the cyclometer and tubing. I have no doubt that
it will work admirably though I have not had a ride with it yet.
I am glad to hear that your 'Irish Baby' was mercifully preserved
while travelling by land and sea, please give it a cordial salutation
from its god-father.[2] It is a pity that your big pot so nearly kicked
the bucket but perhaps in its cracked condition it will remind you all
the better of the land of — of Jubilee monuments![3]
    Miss Harmar (No 2)[4] changed her mind at the last moment — dam-
sels always do — and came over on Monday night instead of Monday
morning, so I fear you rose and rushed to Euston all in vain — another
instance of the vanity of early rising!
    The weather over here has been much better for the last few days
and I have had some good rides but today it is raining again and
looks like three days.
    I hope you will keep up your Irish airs they will be useful to sing
to the Irish baby when it looks dismal — though I fear it is not
unlikely that the dead march will be more appropriate before long.
    Did you notice that the little star went round to the East of the
big one as soon as you went away? So you have been playing ostrich
in church — I am horrified! You dont say how your knee survived
the journey I hope it is not the worse. The roads were very bad
coming back the day I left you but I managed to keep afloat. Dont
forget to have your bearings seen to in your back wheel the steadier
your bicycle is the less likely you are to come to grief.
    My people are not at hand to send messages but believe me
very sincerely yours
John M. Synge

MS copy, LMS

    [1] Rosie L. Calthrop (b. 1864), daughter of a clergyman and cousin of Samuel
Synge's wife, first joined Mrs Synge's family party in Wicklow in 1900 with
Annie Harmar (1869–1933), Sam's sister-in-law. At this time mourning the death
of her fiancé, Rosie later married a widower, William Godwin. She returned frequently to Wicklow with Mrs Synge.
    [2] When Rosie bought a large three-legged pot in which to pack the Osmunda

ferns she was taking back to England, JMS teased her about her 'Irish baby'; she retorted by dubbing him its godfather (Stephens MS).

[3] Queen Victoria, whose Jubilee was celebrated in 1897 with a rash of memorabilia, visited Ireland in April 1900.

[4] Edith Harmar (1870-1963), sister of Annie and Samuel Synge's wife Mary, who became another frequent summer visitor, stayed at Castle Kevin from 10 to 30 July 1900. She and JMS became close friends (*MUJ*, 131-2, and *LMD*, 106-13, 157).

To ROSIE L. CALTHROP

Castle Kevin
Monday [? 27 August 1900]

Dear Miss Calthrop

Many thanks for your note but luckily my cyclometer is all right now. I set to work at it soon after Miss Edie H[armar] left us and after prolonged efforts I wore off whatever it was that caught inside. It has been on my bike now for the last three weeks and registered 250 miles which brings me up to about 750 for the season so far. The little tapping worried me a bit at first but I taught it to say Cal-Cal-Cal-throp-throp-throp etc and find it rather sociable. We are very sorry to hear that Miss Edie H has been ill, it is too bad so soon after her holidays. I wonder if you've been biking much. I've been through all the corners of the county this month, pretty fast sometimes yet by comparison alas sadly slow! morally slow I mean. However, I had a few rides by the last moon that were startling enough. I've not often seen anything to equal the reservoir[1] with a full moon and all the hills with just an echo of twilight upside down in it. Next week I ride off into the West for a month on Aran then in October I hope for a last glimpse of the Paris Exhibition.

If doing what you dont like is good for you — as you suggest — you're not made as I am, it spoils my temper and digestion. I dont believe its good for any one, you're giving my beautiful green god-child what she — or he as I believe you call it — doesn't like and observe the result. By the way if you take his photo I'd like a copy please. I've been looking out for a 'sweet little ass' to take for you but I haven't found one yet that looked interesting enough. In fact I've taken very few photos this summer, only a few of the children's dog

Very sincerely yours
John M. Synge

MS copy, LMS

[1] The Vartry reservoir, which supplies Dublin with its drinking water, is an artificial lake in the valley at Roundwood village created by damming Vartry River in Co. Wicklow.

To MRS KATHLEEN SYNGE

[Paris VIe]
Monday [11 March 1901]

Have not time to write a letter. The cold is back but all is going on well. I am going over to see C.[1] in a day or two and will write then

J.M.S.

MS postcard, TCD

[1] Probably Dr James Cree (d. 1906), son of one of the governors of the Academy of Music (where JMS first met him, as a member of the Junior Instrumental Club), and nephew of the antiquarian and nationalist George Coffey. He qualified in medicine at Trinity College in 1892 and settled in Paris about 1895, receiving his MD in 1899, and later serving as physician to the Collège des Irlandais in Paris. During this winter JMS was suffering from a swollen gland in his neck.

To GRANT RICHARDS[1]

90 rue d'Assas | Paris
1.1.02

Grant Richards Esq.

Dear Sir

I received your letter yesterday, and regret that you cannot see your way to bring out the manuscript.[2]

I would be much obliged if you would send it in a plain wrapper — as you kindly suggest — to Fisher Unwin,[3] with the photograghs. The number of the 'Gael', however, which I left with you I would like to have sent to me here, if it is not giving you too much trouble.[4]

Thanking you for consideration you have given the manuscript I remain

Sincerely yours,
J. M. Synge

TS (signed), Ray

[1] Grant Richards (1872–1948), founder of the World's Classics series and publisher of, among others, Bernard Shaw.

[2] i.e. *The Aran Islands*, based on JMS's first four visits to the islands from 1898 to 1901. Richards's letter of 30 Dec 1901 (TCD) stated that the book 'would not secure the sale of seven or eight hundred copies'. Mrs Synge commented on its rejection on these commercial grounds in a letter to Samuel Synge: 'Poor Johnnie! We could all have told him that, but then men like Yeats and the rest get round him and make him think Irish literature and the Celtic language and all these things that they are trying to revive are very important, and, I am

sorry to say, Johnnie seems to believe all they tell him. Now perhaps his eyes are beginning to be opened in that direction.' (Stephens MS)

³ T. Fisher Unwin (1848–1935), publisher who supported the work of unknown young authors in his First Novel Library and the Pseudonym Library (in which W. B. Yeats's *John Sherman and Dhoya* first appeared, in 1891).

⁴ Probably *The Gael* (New York), April 1901, in which JMS's article, 'The Last Fortress of the Celt', had appeared, illustrated by four of his photographs.

To LADY GREGORY

90 rue d'Assas | Paris
Feb. 22 [1902]

Dear Lady Gregory

I dont know what part of Europe you may be in now, but I suppose this will reach you if I send it to Coole. I want to tell you the evil fate of my Aran book and ask your advice. It has been to two publishers, to Grant Richards who was sympathetic, though he refused it as he said it could not be a commercial success, and to Fisher Unwin who was inclined to be scornful.

Now that you have seen the book do you think there would be any chance of Alfred Nutt taking it up?[1] I am afraid he is my only chance but I do not know whether there is any possibility of getting him to bring out a book of the kind at his own expense, as, after all, there is very little folklore in it.

The Inishmain people have forgiven me at last for my indicretions, and I have just had a very kind letter from Mourteen,[2] they are in great trouble as the young wife of Seaghan the elder brother died at Christmas. They do not say whether it was typhus or something else.[3]

I hope you are having a prosperous winter and that you have escaped the influenza. I have had it for nearly two months off and on, and have been able to do nothing.

Very sincerely yours
John M. Synge

P.S. I am working at Jubainville's[4] lectures now, so I shall not forget my Irish this winter. He came to see me the other day to ask me to go and give them the pronunciation of modern Irish, I feel rather a blind guide but I do my best.

MS, Berg. *TB*, 32

¹ Alfred T. Nutt (1856–1910), publisher, folklorist, and Celtic scholar, was joint founder of the Folklore Society in 1878 and the Irish Texts Society in 1898. He wrote to Yeats on 30 June 1902 that although the excellent realism of *The Aran Islands* opened out 'more into the behind the real than does any but

the most first-rate imaginative work', he feared it would not sell, being 'too shapeless, too without beginning or end, too much hung in the air'; urged by Yeats to reconsider, Nutt wrote to JMS on 13 Nov 1902 repeating his doubts about the book's appeal to a sufficiently large public. (Both TCD)

² Martin McDonagh had been offended when JMS published a translation of one of his letters in 'The Last Fortress of the Celt' (see p. 53); however, JMS's visit the previous October had not been marred by ill feeling, and five of Martin's letters, as well as those from other islanders, appear in translation in *The Aran Islands*. (The islanders were also distressed by JMS's suggestion that their tea was kept stewing for five hours.)

³ When JMS arrived on Aran in September 1901 he discovered there was an outbreak of mild typhus at the other end of Inishmaan.

⁴ Henri d'Arbois de Jubainville (1827–1910), first holder of the chair of Celtic Languages and Literature at the Collège de France, whose lectures comparing ancient Irish and Greek cultures (1898) and on Old Irish (1902) JMS attended in Paris. He was director of the *Revue celtique* from 1885, and author of the 12-volume *Cours de littérature celtique* (1883–1902) and *Le Cycle mythologique irlandais et la mythologie celtique* (1884), a translation of which JMS reviewed in the *Speaker* in 1904. D'Arbois de Jubainville treated JMS kindly; in the first of his articles for *L'Européen*, March 1902, JMS paid a handsome tribute to him.

To MRS KATHLEEN SYNGE

Paris
[?27 February 1902]

Thanks for yours which came this morning. It is not ink papers that I want but a *tube of Ink Rolls*.¹ Black. it is 38, or 36 Dame St.

J.M.S.

MS postcard, Boydell

¹ JMS purchased a Blickensdorfer typewriter in 1900 and wrote most of his prose drafts, plays, and poetry directly on it. The type could be changed, and about this time he replaced it with a larger size and changed from a green to black inking pad. A photograph of the machine, which is now in Trinity College, is published in *The Synge Manuscripts in the Library of Trinity College Dublin* (Dublin, 1971).

To MRS KATHLEEN SYNGE

Paris. Sunday [23 March 1902]

Thanks for your which came last night. I hope to hear again *by return*.¹ also I would like to have the affair that came for me from New York² any time during the week. It is coole here now.

J.M.S.

MS postcard, TCD

¹ It was Mrs Synge's practice to send her son half a £5 note at a time, for safety, until his yearly income was used up.

² His article 'The Oppression of the Hills', which was rejected by the New York *Gael.*

To LADY GREGORY

90 rue d'Assas | Paris
Wednesday (night) [?30 April 1902]

Dear Lady Gregory

Very many thanks for your book which [I] received yesterday morning. I have been reading it ever since with intense delight. 'Au fond' I am a somewhat quibbling spirit and I never expect to enjoy a book that I have heard praised beforehand, but in this case I have been altogether carried away.¹ I had no idea the book was going to be so great. What puny pallid stuff most of our modern writing seems beside it! Many of the stories, of course, I have known for a long time, but they seem to gain a new life in the beautiful language you have told them in. There are a very few details that I would like differently managed I will tell you about them, if I may, when I see you again, — but the success of the whole is so triumphant one has not time to think of them.²

I told old Jubainville about what you were doing a few weeks ago, and he was very much interested, but I am afraid he looks at Irish things from a too strictly scholarly point of view to appreciate their literary value as fully as we do.

Thanking you again for the very great pleasure I have had in reading your book I remain

Very sincerely yours
John M Synge

MS, Gregory. *TB*, 35

¹ *Cuchulain of Muirthemne*, published by John Murray in April 1902, was praised by Yeats in his Preface as 'the best that has come out of Ireland in my time'. Lady Gregory later recalled JMS's comment to Yeats that 'he had been amazed to find in it the dialect he had been trying to master' (*Our Irish Theatre* [Gerrards Cross, 1972], 124). She reported to Yeats (Berg) that when her *Gods and Fighting Men* was published in February 1904, JMS acknowledged it with the words, 'Your "Cuchulain" is still a part of my daily bread.'

² JMS's review of the book in the *Speaker*, 7 June 1902 (*Prose*, 367), praised the 'wonderfully simple and powerful language that resembles a good deal the peasant dialect of the west of Ireland' but refuted Yeats's claim that Lady Gregory had 'discovered' the language by citing examples from the *Love Songs of Connacht* (1893) translated by Douglas Hyde (1860–1949; founding president of the Gaelic League and future President of Ireland), and from Yeats himself. JMS also gently took issue with some of the 'arrangement' of stories and

warned that the omission of 'certain barbarous features' provided a 'less archaic aspect than the original texts'.

To STEPHEN MACKENNA[1]

31 Crosthwaite Pk | Kingstown
Thursday [? 12 June 1902]

Dear MacKenna

Your card has just come on from Paris, and considerably relieved my soul — I was beginning to fear you'd forgotten my existence. I arrived here on Whitsunday and on the Tuesday after I went and knocked a curious eager chant on the door of 41 K.D. Street[2] but they told me you had gone so I battered my semelles round Dublin feeling wrath.

I have gathered scattered information about a preoccupied Greek figure that appeared here and there in Dublin but the sum of it does not tell me much. So your fatale day has arrived! Fellicitations and sympathy ó m' ćroidè.[3] I was going to present you with a "Cuchulain of M" as a wedding gift — *entre nous* I had two copies one from Lady G. the other from the Speaker — but I hear you have it already. I thought the gods had put it into my hand with benevolent design, but I suppose they only mocked me in their aimless way.

I am going down to Annamoe next Tuesday for the summer but I intend to come up every week for a day in T.C.D. Library so when the presence of a 3rd is not de trop I will be rejoiced to meet or see you somewhere. The visits to the library are intended to carry me further into the recesses of the Vieil Irlandais which as I told you, I have been working at with Jubainville. After a while we became great palls and he took [me] up often into his room to hunt up hidden roots, or to feed richly and drink champagne with his sons and grandsons. I will tell you about him when we meet.

For the rest I am bankrupter than ever although I have certain hopes from the Speaker. I hope to crush Seumas MacManus in the leaves of the next number,[4] and in [a] little while to vaunt Cuchulain in another.[5] Yeats was sent Seamus but passed it on to me with their permission and then Cuchulain came in afterwards on his own hook. Unfortunately the Speaker looks sick unto death — no adds and thin rotten paper with watery stuff on it. I wish it were possible to get some of the blood I crush from lusty Seamus into their anaemic veins.[6]

I hope you like Cuchulain I nearly kicked Best down his own stair-case with the rage came on me at his abuse of it.[7]

Yes Dublin c'est le pays du rêve Celtique, but the realities are crude. The country round here is wonderful just now, but God help the people — the 'near-Dublin' people surtout. I wont repeat what I said last year.

I heard from Picquenard[8] the other day sending you his greetings. He is engaged to a riche Bretonne 'dans l'éclat de ses 17 printemps'! Cugnier flourishes and carries all before him in la Guinée française. Clamart[9] has been verdant and perfumed and melodious beyond describing. Agonisingly beautiful.

I came in the other day on some people who had just cut down a man who had gone out from Paris and hanged himself with delight. He was as dead as mutton which seemed a mistake "on such a night," but otherwise the fait did not surprise me.[10] Our April and March over there were divine but May was diabolical. Colder than winter with an icy wind howling through the Luxembourg. I have drivelled enough. Write if you can if not, let me see you when you come over.

Tout à vous
J M Synge

summer address

> JMS.
> Tomriland House
> Annamoe
> Co Wicklow

. P.S. My concierge et cie must have rigolé-ed at your card! Do you forget already that they speak French in Paris!

MS, Lilly

1 Stephen MacKenna (1872-1934), journalist for the *New York Herald* (1900-2), the *New York World* (1902-7) and the Dublin *Freeman's Journal* (1908-24), translator of the *Imitation of Christ* by Thomas à Kempis (1896) and the *Enneads* of Plotinus (1908-30), whom JMS met in Paris during the winter of 1896-7. A keen Hellenist, MacKenna joined an international brigade to fight for Greece against Turkey in 1897; a life-long nationalist, he knew Irish well and under the pseudonym 'Martin Daly' wrote *Memories of the Dead* (1916) about the leaders of the 1916 rising. Like JMS he was concerned equally with problems of aesthetics and the conduct of life, and after his friend's death spoke movingly of his 'passion for truth' and 'inherent nationalism'. No earlier letters from JMS to MacKenna survive, but it is clear from MacKenna's side of the correspondence (TCD) that their friendship was very close and their interests ranged widely.

2 In Dublin in 1898, before spending a brief time in New York, MacKenna had shared rooms in Kildare Street with D. J. O'Donoghue (see p. 78).

3 Irish for 'from my heart'. MacKenna married Marie Bray, an American pianist, in London on 11 June 1902.

4 Seumas MacManus (1869-1960), an Irish-born American, published poetry, novels, plays, and essays, but is best known for his series of Irish fairy and folk tales; his autobiography, *The Rocky Road to Dublin*, was published in 1938. JMS's review of his *Donegal Fairy Stories* in the *Speaker*, 21 June 1902 (*Prose*,

376–7), criticized MacManus's style and subject matter, although acknowledging a 'jovial note' which would make the volume popular for children.

   5 See above, p. 55, n. 2.

   6 *The Speaker* (new series) continued to be published until 1907; JMS's last review for it was published on 2 Apr 1904.

   7 Richard Irvine Best.

   8 Dr C. A. Piquenard, with whom JMS had toured Brittany from 3 to 16 Apr 1899, was a fellow Breton and neighbour of Albert Cugnier at Quimper. His enthusiasm for things and persons Celtic led him to write a poem celebrating JMS's visit, 'Aimez votre langue bretonne!', published in *Le Bas-Breton*, October 1899.

   9 A village on the outskirts of Paris where MacKenna lived from 1900 to 1901 and later had a cottage from 1906.

   10 JMS's correspondence with MacKenna abounds in quotations in at least three languages, as well as many puns and allusions such as this to *The Merchant of Venice*, making it difficult to determine whether some of the misspellings may have been deliberate games with languages.

PART THREE
1903–1904

*

Finding a Theatre

Finding a Theatre

Dublin and London

*

SHORTLY after Synge arrived in London on 10 January 1903 he was introduced by Yeats to the literary circle attending his Monday 'at home' in Woburn Buildings, and when Lady Gregory arrived ten days later, she set about with characteristic energy to publicize his plays. He met John Masefield (who lived near Synge's lodgings in Handel Street), Arthur Symons, G. K. Chesterton, Pamela Colman Smith, Florence Farr, and was introduced to editors and publishers. A commission from J. L. Hammond of the *Speaker*, to provide 'an occasional article . . . on Contemporary French Literature', resulted in an article on Loti, Anatole France, and Huysmans, which appeared on 18 April 1903. He also saw the publisher Brimley Johnson about his Aran manuscript.

Finally, encouraged by his mother, Synge crossed over to Paris on 6 March to close out his room in the rue d'Assas. Joyce was also in Paris. They met, according to Herbert Gorman, 'seven or eight times, lunching in the humble bistro-restaurant in the rue Saint-André-des-Arts where a four- or five-course meal could be procured for one franc ten centimes' (*James Joyce* [New York, 1939], 101–2); the two men argued, among other things, about the tragic quality of *Riders to the Sea*, which had just been returned by the *Fortnightly*, despite Arthur Symons's good offices. On 12 March Synge said farewell to Thérèse Beydon and regretfully left Paris the next day for what was to be the last time.

He returned to Ireland on 18 March. His friend MacKenna was now living in Dalkey, but even more important, W. G. Fay's company had accepted *The Shadow of the Glen* for performance that autumn by the Irish National Theatre Society. In April 'An Autumn Night in the Hills' was published in the New York *Gael*. Synge was busy revising *Riders to the Sea* for Fay, and turned once again to his earlier play, *When the Moon Has Set*, reducing it to one act. That summer he did not join his mother in County Wicklow, preferring to remain in touch with rehearsals in Camden Street. From 28 August to 19 September he visited County Kerry for the first time, staying with Philly Harris at Mountain Stage near Glenbeigh on the recommendation of his brother Robert.

Riders to the Sea was published by Yeats in the October issue of
Samhain, and *In the Shadow of the Glen* (the *In* was dropped after
the first season) received its first production on 8 October 1903
in the Molesworth Hall, Dublin, in a double bill alongside Yeats's
The King's Threshold. Even before its opening night, however,
Synge's comedy caused controversy: the *Irish Independent* described
Yeats's and Synge's plays in advance as 'unwholesome productions'.
Dudley Digges, who had been in Fay's company since the beginning,
refused to perform and resigned from the Society, taking Maire
Quinn, his future wife, with him. On opening night the couple
ostentatiously walked out with Maud Gonne, who attacked the
Society in the *United Irishman*, commenting particularly on 'foreign
thoughts and philosophies'.

But the most far-reaching accusations came from the editor of the
United Irishman, Arthur Griffith, who claimed that Synge's play was
'no more Irish than the Decameron . . . a staging of a corrupt version
of that old-world libel on womankind — the "Widow of Ephesus" ',
its inspiration 'the decadent cynicism that passes current in the Latin
Quartier and the London salon for wit'. Both W. B. Yeats and his
father wrote in Synge's defence, but the controversy continued for
several weeks. The plays were repeated on 17 October, and Synge
was elected to membership on the reading committee of the Society.
In this capacity he frequently attended rehearsals, until once again he
succumbed to ill health, which prevented him from seeing the
company's next productions. It is possible that a first draft of his
unfinished farce, 'National Drama', was begun during convalescence;
a more serious attempt, also unfinished, was a poetic drama, 'The
Lady O'Connor', drawn as was *The Shadow of the Glen* from his
Aran notebooks.

Fully recovered by the beginning of 1904, Synge began attending
rehearsals regularly and was at the opening night of the Society's
next productions, *The Shadowy Waters*, *Twenty-Five*, and *The
Townland of Tamney*, on 14-16 January. He flung himself whole-
heartedly into preparations for the staging of *Riders to the Sea*,
writing to Galway for cloth and to his Aran friends for authentic
pampooties. And, despite a severe toothache which was to send him
to bed with a fever for two weeks, he was present to acknowledge
the audience's call for the author at the opening night on 25 February. But once again most of the critics condemned his play: the
Independent grudgingly acknowledged the 'careful treatment of a
simple theme', but felt it 'too dreadfully doleful to please the popular
taste'; the *Irish Times* also found the treatment 'repulsive'. The
United Irishman, while commenting on how the play's 'tragic beauty
powerfully affected the audience', objected to the 'cheap trick' of

introducing the body of a drowned man on stage. 'Chanel' of the *Leader* deplored the atmosphere of the 'dissecting room' but offered some hope for Synge in comparison with George Russell, whose *Deirdre* had been revived as a companion piece to *Riders to the Sea*.

In March 'A Dream of Inishmaan' was published in the New York *Gael*; even more important for Synge, however, was his visit with the players to London, where Stephen Gwynn, secretary of the Irish Literary Society of London, had arranged a second opportunity for the Society to show its wares to a wider public. Synge's two plays were performed at the matinée on 26 March, drawing almost unanimous acclaim, and accolades from the critics William Archer and Max Beerbohm. Synge remained in London until 30 April, once again under Yeats's wing. He met Charles Ricketts, and was commissioned by the editor of the *Academy and Literature* to contribute Irish entries for the unsigned 'Literary Notes' section, which he did regularly for two or three months after he returned to Dublin.

Meanwhile his responsibilities to the Society increased; he was busy reading and revising plays and at Frank Fay's suggestion began a scenario on the 1798 rebellion, but this was coolly received by his colleagues.

On 7 June Samuel Synge and his family returned from China. Ten days later Frank Fay read *The Well of the Saints* to the company. Synge remained in Dublin when his mother left for the country on 22 June, and on 16 July went to Coole for two weeks to assist Lady Gregory with her revisions of *Kincora*. He then travelled to Mountain Stage, staying once again with Philly Harris from 1 August to 1 September. He returned briefly to Dublin to observe rehearsals of his play, intending to pay another visit to Aran. News of an outbreak of typhus on the islands changed his plans, however, and on 17 September he left for Sligo with his bicycle for a two-week tour of North Mayo. By 10 October 1904 he was back rehearsing *Well of the Saints* in Camden Street. In order to be nearer the theatre, he had taken rooms at 15 Maxwell Road, Rathgar, just fifteen minutes by tram from Dublin centre. He remained there until 15 February 1905.

While in Kerry thoughts of his next play were already beginning to take shape in Synge's mind. But he had not entirely given up his plans for literary criticism, and sometime in this year submitted, at the editors' request, an article on Anatole France to the newly established journal *Dana*. According to George Moore in *Hail and Farewell*, the editor, John Eglinton, was distressed by Synge's 'incorrect' writing; no article by Synge appeared.

Despite his increased involvement with the Irish National Theatre Society, Synge remained a solitary, describing himself in a letter to MacKenna in mid-October 1904 (now lost) as 'lonesome and .

uncanny, wandering like an unserviceable ghost'. Perhaps influenced by Yeats, Lady Gregory, and AE (who had also been at Coole in July), he turned once again to psychic explorations. MacKenna replied to another letter, also lost:

I am interested to know that you turn back towards your first moods. You would be of use to me if you would sometimes communicate any opinions you form or proofs you find. It is queer, but I, who am the dogmatist, have only on these things a sympathetically open mind, you the lean and hungry sceptic admit 'their reality'. Of course I see that your 'so-called' is meant to annihilate any spiritualistic or other-worldish deductions from the 'so-called occult phenomena'.

(TCD)

About this time Synge began a review of Fiona Macleod's *The Winged Destiny*, which was published in the *Academy and Literature* on 12 November 1904.

Meanwhile, Miss Annie Horniman's interest in Yeats's dramatic experiments led her to offer the Society a permanent home in the Abbey Theatre. Another prominent supporter of the Society, the American lawyer John Quinn, visited Dublin for the first time this autumn and was present with Synge at the first rehearsal in the new theatre on 31 October. When *The Shadow of the Glen* was published in *Samhain* in December, Quinn arranged for a copyright edition in New York. By the time the Abbey Theatre opened on 27 December 1904, it was clear that Synge was not only considered one of the Society's leading dramatists, but had taken his place alongside Yeats and Lady Gregory as architects of a movement rapidly gaining momentum.

To MRS KATHLEEN SYNGE

c/o Mrs Ward | 4 Handel St | Brunswick Square | London W.C.[1]

[17 January 1903]

My dearest Mother

I was very glad to get your two letters but I did not try the Board-ing House as that was not what I wanted. Board–Residence places abound in this neighbourhood and are fairly respectable and fairly cheap, but I dont think [I] could stand that sort of thing now. You have to have your meals every day with the same set of people you get gradually to destest. This lodging where I am now seems to be satifactory enough. I have a comfortable room at 14/0 including breakfast with bacon-egg, jam, etc which, I think is not excessive. The only drawback is that there is a door into the next room where an individual groans and giggles to himself as if he was off his head. However he is only there at night and I believe he is going away soon so I make the best of him. My living here everything included will come very near two pounds a week, I dont think I can feed even fairly well for less. The Restaurants are not very satisfactory or inviting, but perhaps when I know the place better I will find others that are more what I want. My expenses have been pretty heavy with all my pergrination so I have only £1.5.0. in hand now and my lodging paid up to next *Wednesday*. My landlady seems inclined to be suspicious so I suppose I will have to pay her in advance for a while so I would be obliged if you could send me some money before Wednesday, but I think you had better not send a cheque as I would certainly have all sorts of bother with it.

I was with Yeats on Monday evening and met a good many writers artists etc. He has an At-Home night every Monday and a lot of people seem to go. Lady Gregory I believe is coming over this week.[2]

It has been very cold ever since I came here with continual hard frost, but dry and not unpleasant. The unemployed walk about London in dreary endless procession everyday with collecting boxes. A curious end to their Maefking days and all their decoration and triumph a little while ago![3]

I dont feel as if I could ever tollorate London for more than one season. I am quite interested to see it all for once but compared with Paris it is dear and dirty and dismal to an incredible degree.

I hope Ned and party are not the worse for their move, and that you are keeping well.[4] Please dont forget the money as otherwise I will be left in the lurch. I dont know what would be the best way

of sending it. If you sent half-five-pound notes on *Monday* and
Tuesday it would do very well or you could send P.O.s.

I do not know whether you will get this on tomorrow morning
or in the evening.

Your aff son
John M. Synge

MS, LMS

[1] On nearly all succeeding visits to London, JMS returned to these lodgings,
on a quiet street near the cemetery off Gray's Inn Road.

[2] Yeats had been in London since mid-November 1902; Lady Gregory was
in her flat in Queen Anne Mansions by 20 Jan 1903.

[3] The relief in May 1900 of the siege of Mafeking, which had lasted under
Baden-Powell for seven months, caused riotous rejoicing in London; but the
Boer War had caused further disagreements between JMS and his family (*MUJ*,
152).

[4] JMS's brother Edward (1859-1939) and his family, one of whom — his
nephew Edward Hutchinson Synge (1890-1957), became one of JMS's bene-
ficiaries — had moved to Haddington Terrace, Kingstown, the day after JMS left
for London.

To MRS KATHLEEN SYNGE

4 Handel Street | Brunswick Sq | [London] W.C.
21/I/03

My dearest Mother

I am much obliged for your letters and enclosure.[1] On the whole
I am very much pleased with my quarters, and my neighbour has not
made any more disturbance. I daresay he had taken a glass of something strong the night I heard him so much. They have nailed up a
bit of thick baise over the door, so that I hear nothing, or very little
at present.

I had seen nobody when I wrote to you last, so you need not have
expected me to give you news that did not exist. Yesterday however
I was taken to an editor of a paper that is just starting[2] and found,
curiously enough that he was a great friend of Edward Synge's and
knew the Alecks' also. He seemed to speak of "Doreen" as the most
interesting member of the family. Is it the daughter?[3] I had to rush
off then and do him an article and post it to him at 7 the same
evening, which was a terrible rush as I had to dine with Lady Gregory.
I feel pretty limp today as I was with Yeats on Monday night so that
did not get home either evening till very late, and then did not
sleep.

I have several more editors to see on the papers I have written for
already,[4] but I could not go to them last week as I was uncertain
about my adress. This week Joyce[5] — on his way back to Paris —

[is] going to them all so I will not go round for a few days as it is better not to have too many Irish men turning up at once.

Saturday night was the most extraordinary slippery scene I have ever come across. Roads and pathways sheeted in thin ice so that every body had to creep along in single file in the gutter where there was a sort of grip. Since then we have had continual fog, not bad enough to make it impossible to find one['s] way, but still so bad at 11. this morning that when you wanted to cross the street it was very hard to see what vehicles were coming up, and of course as black as night.

If I could once make my connection with editors I would like to go on to Paris, this place reminds me of the descriptions I have read of people working in coal-mines. I dont believe it can be wholesome. Remember me to Miss C.[6]

Your affec son
John M. Synge

MS, LMS

[1] Mrs Synge sent him £5 on 19 Jan 1903 and the following day.
[2] George R. Sims (1847–1922), journalist, short-story writer, playwright, novelist, social reporter, published two registered numbers of *Men and Women* (24 Dec 1902 and 21 Jan 1903); the regular run of the journal ended 26 Dec 1903 after only 46 issues, and does not appear to have published anything by JMS or Joyce.
[3] Edward Millington Synge (1860–1913), JMS's cousin, was an etcher whom JMS had seen frequently in Paris. The Revd Alexander Hamilton Synge (d. 1872), JMS's uncle, became vicar of St. Peter's, Ipswich, after serving as a missionary on Aran; his eldest son, Alexander, who inherited Glanmore, Co. Wicklow, had a daughter named Doreen (b. 1893).
[4] JMS had published reviews and notes in the *Academy and Literature*, previously edited by C. Lewis Hind and now edited by W. Teignmouth Shore, and in the *Speaker*, formerly edited by R. Barry O'Brien; on 19 Feb 1903 the new editor of the *Speaker*, J. L. Hammond, wrote (TCD) to commission occasional articles on contemporary French literature from him.
[5] James Joyce; see p. 68.
[6] Rosie Calthrop was visiting Mrs Synge while she was alone.

To JAMES JOYCE[1]

90 rue d'Assas [Paris] | Sunday [8 March 1903]

Dear Joyce

Very sorry to have missed you this morning I did not get your card on my way out as there was no one in the 'loge' and I did not expect anything. When I got it at midday it was too late.

Can you meet me tomorrow (Monday) under the Odeon cloisters in front of your door[2] at *10 A.M.*? I will be there.

I am only here for a week as I go back to London on Thursday or Friday.

à demain
J. M. Synge

MS, Beinecke

---

¹ James Joyce (1882-1941), the future novelist and playwright, had been recommended to both Yeats and JMS by Lady Gregory, as a worthy young Irish writer in need of assistance. Joyce had apparently met JMS in Dublin the previous November while he was rounding up contacts and letters of introduction in preparation for his first stay in Paris, where he was to take up medical studies and hoped to make his living as a writer.
² Joyce was staying at the Hôtel Corneille, opposite the Théâtre de l'Odéon.

To JAMES JOYCE

[Paris, 10 or 11 March 1903]

. . . You will say so as it is all the same to me. ——

In Haste ——
Yours faithfully
John M Synge

MS fragment, Beinecke

To LADY GREGORY

31 Crosthwaite Park | Kingstown | Co Dublin
Thursday [26 March 1903]

Dear Lady Gregory

I got back a few days ago from Paris and London, and though I have not much news to give about Joyce I believe I promised to tell you what I saw of him. He seems to be pretty badly off, and is wandering about Paris rather unbrushed and rather indolent, spending his studious moments in the National Library reading Ben Jonson. French literature I understand is beneath him!¹ Still he interested me a good deal and as he is being gradually won over by the charm of French life his time in Paris is not wasted. He talks of coming back to Dublin in the summer to live there on journalism while he does his serious work at his leisure. I cannot think that he will ever be a poet of importance, but his intellect is extraordinarily keen and if he keeps fairly sane he ought to do excellent essay-writing.²

I hope the "Hour-glass" and your play went off well.³ I did not get back in time even to see the reports in the papers. My play came back from the Fortnightly, — "as not suitable for their purposes" and I dont think that Brimley Johnson intends to bring out the

Aran book.[4] I saw him on my way home, but he seemed hopelessly undecided, saying at one minute that he liked it very much, and that it might be a great success, and that he wanted to be in touch with the Irish movement, and then going off in the other direction and fearing that it might fall perfectly flat! Finally he asked me to let him consider it a little longer. Do you know what Fay's company thought of my plays?[5] I have been greatly interested in the "Poets & Dreamers" especially in Raftery and the Ballads.[6]

Yours very sincerely
John M Synge

MS, Berg. *TB*, 40

[1] Joyce had written to Lady Gregory on 21 Dec 1902, 'Paris amuses me very much but I quite understand why there is no poetry in French literature; for to create poetry out of French life is impossible'; by now he had given up any thoughts of medicine as a career and on 20 Mar 1903 wrote to his mother, 'I am at present up to the neck in Aristotle's Metaphysics, and read only him and Ben Jonson' (*Selected Letters of James Joyce*, ed. Richard Ellmann [1975], 11, 19).

[2] In his letters home Joyce proudly reported JMS's comment, 'You have a mind like Spinoza', and Stanislaus Joyce writes that the two 'had many quarrelsome discussions . . . about language, style, poetry, the drama, and literature in general' (*My Brother's Keeper*, ed. Richard Ellmann [1958], 213). Apparently Joyce further goaded JMS to anger by mocking his concern for the Irish language revival. But, although he objected to *Riders to the Sea* as non-Aristotelian, Joyce was sufficiently impressed to quote Maurya's final speeches as examples of the musicality of language, and was later to translate the play into Italian.

[3] Yeats's morality play *The Hour Glass* and Lady Gregory's first comedy, *Twenty-Five*, were produced by the Irish National Theatre Society at the Molesworth Hall on 14 Mar 1903 before JMS returned to Ireland.

[4] Reginald Brimley Johnson (1867–1932), publisher and editor. On 28 Mar 1903 Yeats wrote to Johnson offering to write a preface for *The Aran Islands*, if that would 'make any difference in its prospects, or in the prospect of your taking it', adding, 'I think he will come to something as a writer, I have a strong admiration for his plays especially & expect one of them will soon be played by our little National Theatre Company' (*TB*, 44).

[5] Lady Gregory replied from Coole on 29 Mar 1903, 'I have read the Wicklow play . . . to the 'Company' in Dublin. They were much taken with it, & I shd. think will be sure to act it, but their hands are pretty full just now.' (*TB*, 42) An undated letter from W. G. Fay (see p. 79) states, 'I hear that you are under the impression that we did not accept your "Shadow in the Glen" but that is not so. We have accepted it and it will be ready for you to see a rehearsal in about 3 weeks time. The other play "The Riders to the Sea" the committee thought wanted more speed towards the end, after the body is brought in.' (TCD)

[6] The first of Lady Gregory's folklore books, *Poets and Dreamers*, had just been published by John Murray. The blind poet Raftery (*c.* 1784–1835) was the subject of a play in Irish, *An Posadh* (The Marriage), by herself and Douglas Hyde, which she translated for the volume.

To PADRAIC COLUM[1]

31 Crosthwaite Park | Kingstown
Thursday [3 December 1903]

My dear Colum

I see your play is on tonight[2] so I write you a line to wish you all success. I am very sorry I cannot go in to see it as I am down with influenza on my chest and low fever. Please remember me to the Fays and tell them why I have not been in lately.[3] Possibly I may get in on Saturday night but I fear it is not likely.

With best wishes

Yours sincerely
J. M Synge

MS, Berg

[1] Padraic Colum (1881–1972), poet, playwright, novelist, and folklorist, had been a member of W. G. Fay's Irish National Dramatic Society since January 1902; Fay's refusal to produce his propaganda play, *The Saxon Shillin'*, caused the first rift between the nationalists and those interested in the company as a literary theatre. Two of Colum's plays were produced by the company before further disputes led him in 1905 to join the nationalist seceders. After helping found the *Irish Review* in 1911, Colum settled in the United States. He and his wife Mary (née Molly Maguire) were close friends of James Joyce in Paris in the 1920s.

[2] Colum's play *Broken Soil* was first produced, along with Yeats's *The Hour Glass* and *The Pot of Broth* by Yeats and Lady Gregory, on 3 Dec 1903 at the Molesworth Hall; JMS, as a member of the Society's reading committee, had attended rehearsals throughout October and early November.

[3] Since 19 Nov 1903 JMS had been ill, his lung affected by a severe cold; he did not recover until 7 Dec.

To LADY GREGORY

31 Crosthwaite Park | Kingstown
16.XII.03

My dear Lady Gregory

Many thanks for your note and enclosures, I am delighted to find that there is a prospect of getting the book out at last, and equally grateful for the trouble you have taken with it. I am writing to Masefield today to thank him, and ask him by all means to get Mathews to do as he proposes.[1] Do you think if he brings out the plays in the spring I should add the tinkers?[2] I was getting on well with the blind people till about a month ago when I suddenly got ill with, influenza and a nasty attack on my lung. I am getting better now but I cannot work yet satisfactorily so I hardly know when the play is likely to be finished.[3] There is no use trying to hurry on with a thing of that kind when one is not in the mood.

Colum's play seems to have gone well; the influenza keep me at home the week of the performance but I saw it in rehearsal about a fortnight earlier, didn't altogether like it. It is a great thing that Yeats is doing so well in America,[4] I suppose he will not come home just yet.

Please remember me to your son[5] and believe me with very many thanks

Yours sincerely
J.M.Synge

MS, Berg. *TB*, 48

[1] John Masefield (see p. 72) had written to Lady Gregory praising *The Aran Islands*, and saying that he had taken the book to the publisher Elkin Mathews (see p. 106), who 'would like to do the book next autumn' and might also print the two one-act plays by JMS in his Vigo Cabinet Series in the spring of 1904. (*TB*, 47)

[2] i.e. *The Tinker's Wedding*.

[3] *The Well of the Saints* was not completed to JMS's satisfaction until July 1904; it was first produced on 4 Feb 1905.

[4] W. B. Yeats was making his first lecture tour of the United States and Canada from November 1903 to March 1904.

[5] William Robert Gregory (1881–1918), Lady Gregory's only son, was at this time trying to decide whether to study art in Paris or London; he eventually chose the Slade School of Art in London before going to Paris, and later designed some of the Abbey Theatre productions.

To JOHN MASEFIELD[1]

31 Crosthwaite Park | Kingstown | Co Dublin
17. XII. 03

Dear Masefield

Lady Gregory has let me know of your good offices in speaking well of my Aran MS. to Elkin Mathews and I am infinitely obliged. If he definitly intends to bring it out I do not care whether he does so in the spring or next autumn though I seem to feel that if the I.N. Theatre does my little Aran play[2] in London in the spring, it would make good advertisement for the book if it was ready. However that is a matter for the publisher, I dont really care. Part IV was tacked on the rest rather hastily and I have always suspected that there was too much folklore and ill-digested doggerel running through it, though I had not courage to cut out the erring parts with decision. I hope to go over to London in a month or two, and then we can talk it over, if you have ever a moment to spare, and I will do any pruning that is needed.[3]

You increase my debt of gratitude by proposing to persuade Matthews to bring out my plays in the spring. I would be delighted to have them out in book-form if he can be induced to take them up. How would it be to add the Tinker-play — you remember the one you heard with an abortive wedding and a priest in it — so as to have three peasant plays? What is his shilling series? The tinkers have been re-written since you heard them and are now twice as long (in two acts) and I think many times stronger and wickeder. I have other plays on hand[4] but Heaven knows when they will be finished, as I have been off work for the last month with influenza and a sick lung.

I suppose it is too late to felicitate you on your marriage.[5] I heard of it long ago — in the summer I think — from W.B.Y. but I did not then know where you were. I am glad to see in an 'Add.' to the Green Sheaf, that you have brought out a book of ballads,[6] and I wish them much success.

I hear Yeats is having a great success in America, so I suppose he will not come home just yet.

Thanking you again I remain

Yours very sincerely

John M Synge

MS, Gilvarry

[1] John Masefield (1878–1968), poet and dramatist, had first met JMS in London at Yeats's regular Monday evening 'at home' on 12 Jan 1903; he was present at Lady Gregory's reading of JMS's two one-act plays on 3 Mar 1903 and JMS is 'that friend who used to walk / Home to my lodgings with me, deep in talk' in his poem 'Biography' (1912). After JMS's death he published 'John M. Synge' (*Contemporary Review*, April 1911) and *John M. Synge: A Few Personal Recollections with Biographical Notes* (New York, 1915) and was also responsible for the article on JMS in the *Dictionary of National Biography* (1912).

[2] i.e. *Riders to the Sea.*

[3] Masefield replied the following day (TCD) offering to 'doctor the doggerel'.

[4] Probably *When the Moon Has Set* (rejected three times by his fellow directors) and his two unfinished verse plays, 'A Vernal Play' and 'Luasnad, Capa and Laine' (*Plays* Book I), in addition to *The Well of the Saints.*

[5] Masefield was married to Constance Crommelin in July 1903.

[6] Masefield's *Ballads*, published by Elkin Mathews in 1903, was advertised in the November 1903 issue of *The Green Sheaf*, a hand-coloured periodical edited and published by Pamela Colman Smith and distributed by Elkin Mathews, to which both Masefield and JMS contributed. It ran for thirteen numbers, 1903–4.

To JOHN MASEFIELD

31 Crosthwaite Park | Kingstown | Co Dublin
14/I/04

Dear Masefield

I have at last got a version of the "Tinkers" fairly into shape so I am sending you the three plays. No one has seen the "Tinkers" in their present form so I would be very glad if, you could find time to run your eye over them and let me know your opinion. I feel as if there is some good comedy in them, but it is peculiarly hard to measure one's comic work when one grows weary and sick of it, and I have many misgivings. The Tinkers seem more bulky than the others as I have typed the names *between* instead of at the head of the speeches, perhaps if Mathews does not like the "Tinkers" the other two plays would fill the volume.[1]

"The Shadowy Waters" are to be played tonight in Dublin[2] as I daresay you know. I saw a rehearsal a few days ago and it seemed to promise well — more of course as a recitation than as a play. The excellent company have an extraordinary difficulty in making up their minds as to their movements and programs, and as my plans depend partly on them, my movements are also rather vague. There is some talk of doing "Riders to the Sea" here before they go to London, and if they do so I shall have to stay and see how things go. They are going to do "The Shadow of the Glen" in London I believe, probably towards the end of March.[3]

I hope all your affairs go prosperously, I can think of no new or shining word to carry my gratitude to you for your aid; believe that it is profound, and that I remain always

very sincerely yours
J. M. Synge

P.S. Has Mathews read the Aran stuff and made up his mind about it?[4] I have photos, you know, that could be drawn from if he think illustrations a[re] needed.

MS, Gilvarry

[1] *The Shadow of the Glen* and *Riders to the Sea* appeared in Mathews's Vigo Series in May 1905; *The Tinker's Wedding* was again revised by JMS, and a two-act version published by Maunsel of Dublin in December 1907.

[2] *The Shadowy Waters* by Yeats was first produced, with Lady Gregory's *Twenty-Five* and *The Townland of Tamney* by Seumas MacManus, by the Irish National Theatre Society at the Molesworth Hall, 14 Jan 1904.

[3] The London Irish Literary Society had offered to sponsor a second visit by the Fay company to London on 26 Mar 1904.

[4] On 19 July 1904 Mathews wrote to Yeats, 'I think I did hint to Mr Dermot Freyer that I was a bit doubtful about issuing the Aran book this year . . . . I find

the Aran MS. very attractive but think it should come on later — the coming publishing season will probably be a bad one — and next year perhaps things may boom again.' (TCD)

To STEPHEN MacKENNA

Kingstown. Jan. 28 [1904]

Dear MacKenna

It is hardly possible to carry on a crystalised controversy between Dublin and Berlin, but, all the same, I have a couple of things to say to your letter[1]

You seem to feel that we should not deal with modern matters on the stage in Ireland, because Ireland is "blessedly unripe" for them. — Do you think that the country people of Norway are much less blessedly unripe than the Irish? If they are not should Ibsen never have been played in Norway, and therefore never have become an efficient dramatist? Do you think that because the people I have met with in the valleys of Würzburg and the Rhein, are quite as unripe as those of Wicklow or Kerry, that Sudermann and Hauptman should be driven from the boards of Berlin? The Dublin audiences who see Mde Rejane in Ibsen, Mrs P. Campbell in Sudermann, Olga Netherstole in Sapho etc,[2] are hardly blessedly unripe.

Heaven forbid that we should ever have a morbid sex-obseded drama in Ireland, not because we have any peculiarly, blessed sanctity which I utterly deny — see percentage of lunatics in Ireland and causes thereof — but because it is bad drama and is played out.

On the French stage the sex-element of life is given without the other ballancing elements; on the Irish stage the people you agree with want the other elements without sex. I restored the sex-element to its natural place, and the people were so surprised they saw the sex only.

I do not believe in the possibility of "a purely fantastic, unmodern, ideal, spring-dayish, Cuchulainoid National Theatre", because no drama — that is to hold its public — can grow out of anything but the fundamental realities of life which are neither modern or unmodern, and, as I see them, are rarely fantastic or spring-dayish. Single plays, of course, may and should be what you describe, but I do not think, that while life is what we know, any group of writers will produce work chiefly spring-dayish, without giving themselves up to a wilful, and insincere cult of joy, that would make their work useless, and demoralise their souls. I think squeamishness is a disease and that Ireland will gain if Irish writers deal manfully, directly, and decently with the entire reality of life.[3]

You ought to come over to London in March and see my plays, talk with self and Yeats, make yourself the beginning of a relation with the publishing branch of the coterie.[4] Many compliments to Madame, I fear there is not much chance of my reaching Berlin

Yours
J. M. Synge

I am much better, but still a bit shaky

MS, Lilly

[1] MacKenna's letter from Berlin (?early January 1904, TCD) commented, '. . . I do not know which of yez is in the right . . . . You should be free as artist, . . . whether you should be played I do not know: . . . I like the philistine idea of a purely fantastic unmodern . . . ideal, breezy — spring-dayish Cuchullainoid etc. national theatre . . . . I believe in the ripeness and unripeness of nations and class Ireland blessedly unripe . . . . Give us our own literary nationhood first, then let us rise to our frieze-clad Ibsens. (I know, of course, you hate the word Ibsen . . .) I would like to see your play in book form, not on boards . . . nor for myself, but for the people . . . . The stage might regenerate Ireland, used Cuchulainly.'

[2] Madame Réjane (Gabrielle-Charlotte Réju, 1857–1920), although best known on the Paris stage for her comic roles, had a striking success in New York in 1895 as Madame Sans-Gêne, and performed *Sapho* (adapted by Clyde Fitch from Daudet's novel) at the Theatre Royal, Dublin, in 1901 and in a French version of *A Doll's House* in June 1903. Stella Patrick Campbell (1865–1940) had already achieved prominence in Arthur Wing Pinero's *The Second Mrs Tanqueray* (1893) and *The Notorious Mrs Ebbsmith* (1894), and in Sudermann's *Magda* (1896), all three of which had been performed at Dublin's Theatre Royal. Olga Nethersole (1863–1951), famous for the passionate 'Nethersole kiss', made a career of performing the 'fallen woman' in problem dramas. In New York in 1900 she was arrested but legally absolved of alleged indecency as the heroine of *Sapho*, which she performed at the Gaiety Theatre, Dublin, during the week of 10 Oct 1903.

[3] A draft of this letter (TCD; published in the *Massachusetts Review*, Winter 1964, and elsewhere) varies considerably from the final text:

It is hardly possible to thresh out a critical question like the one — or rather perhaps the score — you raise, by slinging crystals at each other from Dublin to Berlin, but all the same I'm going to give you a volley.

You say we should not deal with modern matters on the stage in Ireland because Ireland is blessed[l]y unripe.' Bon! Do you think that the peasantry — the people — of Norway are less blessed, or greatly less blessed than the Irish? Do you think that if they are as innocent as the Irish, then Ibsen should not have been played in Norway, and, therefore, have never become an efficient dramatist? Do you think that because the people I have met in the valleys of Würzburg and the Rhein are as unripe as those of Kerry and Galway that Sudermann and Hauptmann should be driven from the boards of Berlin? The Dublin audiences who see Mde Rejane in Ibsen, Mrs. P. Campbell in Sudermann, Miss Olga Netherstink in Sapho etc. etc. are hardly blessedly unripe! They want to suck smut every evening and to rise up every morning and say, 'Behold we are the most virtuous nation in Europe. Thank God we are not as other men!'

Heaven forbid that we should have a morbid sex-obseded drama in Ireland, not because we have any peculiar sanctity which I utterly deny — blessed unripeness is sometimes akin to damned rotteness see percentage of lunatics in Ireland and causes thereof — but because it is bad as drama and is played out. On French stage you get sex without its ballancing elements: on Irish stage you the other elements without sex. I restored sex and the people were so surprised they saw the sex only.

I do not believe in the possibility of 'a purely fantastic, unmodern, ideal, breesy, springdayish, Cuchulainoid National Theatre.' We had the 'Shadowy Waters' on the stage last week, and it was the most DISTRESSING failure the mind can imagine, — a half empty room, with growling men and tittering females. Of course it is possible to write drama that fits your description and yet is fitter for the stage than the S. Waters, but no drama can grow out of anything other than the fundamental realities of life which are never fantastic, are neither modern, nor unmodern, and as I see them rarely spring-dayish, or breezy or Cuchulainoid!

The stage, even if it agreed to all your adjectives, would not regenerate — or for the matter of that un-regenerate — Ireland any more than the symphonies of Beethoven can regenerate Germany and Guillaume the twitterer — I mean the gneuter

P.S. 1 Feb

So far with controversial vehemence which is pen-deep only. I am interested in your view, and probably we would agree or nearly agree as to the plays that are proper for Ireland though — as often has happened — we reach the same point by different ways. When I deny Ireland's peculiar sanctity, I do so as compared with other potato-fed, thinly populated lands of same latitude, and I do not know that there is anything blessed in anaemia.

I have as you know perambulated a good deal of Ireland in my thirty and if I were tell, which Heaven forbid, all the sex-horrors I have seen I could a tale unfold that would wither up your blood. I think of course that single plays may and should be spring-dayish etc. But while life is what it is and men are what they are I do not think any group of writers will write such work chiefly unless they do so with a wilful insincerity of joy that would make their work useless, and destroy the power of their souls. I think squeamishness is a disease, and that Ireland will gain if Irish writers deal manfully, directly and *decently* with the entire reality of life. I think the Law-Maker and the Law-Breaker are both needful in society — as the lively and volcanic forces are needed to make earth's crust habitable — and I think the Law-Maker is tending to reduce Ireland or parts of Ireland to a dismal morbid hypocracy that is not a blessed unripeness. On the other hand I feel of course the infinitely sweet and healthy piety of a great deal of Irish life — I will use it gladly in my work and meanwhile it is perfectly safe from any fear of contamination from my evil words. Your position comes to this — You prefer the Dublin young men to spend their evenings listening to the obscene folly of the English Musical Comedies to seeing sincere and

4 Doubtless a reference to both Yeats and George Roberts (see p. 80).

To W. F. TRENCH[1]

31 Crosthwaite Park | Kingstown | Co Dublin
Monday [?15 February 1904]

My dear Sir

I received your letter and the patterns[2] a day or two ago, and I am greatly obliged for the kind help you have given us. The Leenane stuff comes very near the general effect of the darker shades the men wear on Inishmaan and will do excellently for some of the clothes. I am in hopes of matching it somewhere in Dublin and if that cannot be done we will get it from Leenane direct.

The real Aran stuff is, of course, much bluer, but I think it is the proportion of the white wool and the roughness of the texture that will tell on the stage by lamp-light, rather than the exact shade of the dark thread.[3]

I hoped to get pampooties from the islands, but ⟨tho⟩ I have not had any answers yet to my enquiries about them, and we shall probably have to to make them ourselves from the patterns I have.[4] It was very kind of you to take so much trouble about the caps. Those I remember on the island were certainly dull in colour but that may have been largely due to the effect of the turf-smoke and salt-water.

Thanking you again, very cordially, I remain, dear sir,

Your faithfuly

J. M. Synge

MS, TCD

[1] Wilbraham FitzJohn Trench (1873–1939), graduate of Trinity College, Dublin, where he was Professor of English Literature from 1913; a specialist in Shakespearian drama and Aristotle's *Poetics*, he was at this time teaching at Queen's College, Galway.

[2] This letter has not survived, but evidently included samples of cloth. Every effort was being made to be scrupulously faithful to the Aran Islands setting for the production of *Riders to the Sea*, which was to have its first performance later that month. Lady Gregory wrote in early February to Yeats, who was still lecturing in America,

> I am distracted trying to get Synge's 'properties' together for staging *Riders to the Sea*. I luckily took the flannel myself to the Gort dyer, and found he was going to use Diamond dyes instead of madder, and only 2 lbs. arrived. No real Aran caps can be got so far, or tweed. I am trying to stir Synge up to go to big shops and look for something near it, and get as little as possible for this time and the real stuff after, for *Riders to the Sea* will probably be a stock piece for a long time and ought to be well staged. However, I am promised a spinning wheel tomorrow.
>
>   (*Seventy Years* [Gerrards Cross, 1974], 414)

[3] 'The men wear three colours: the natural wool, indigo, and a grey flannel that is woven of alternate threads of indigo and natural wool' (*The Aran Islands*, in *Prose*, 59).

[4] In *The Aran Islands* JMS wrote:

> the sharp-edged fossils which abound in the limestone have cut my shoes to pieces. The family held a consultation on them last night, and in the end it was decided to make me a pair of pampooties . . . . They consist simply of a piece of raw cowskin, with the hair outside, laced over the toe and round the heel with two ends of fishing-line that work round and are tied above the instep. In the evening, when they are taken off, they are placed in a basin of water, as the rough hide cuts the foot and stocking if it is allowed to harden.   (*Prose*, 65)

On 25 Feb 1904 Lady Gregory reported to Yeats,

We, Synge and I, are still struggling with the things for his play. He has to deal with Aran Islanders, I with nuns, and I do think they might run a race backwards! However, yesterday, 'An ass and car went into the country' and brought back the spinning wheel in triumph, and it has been sent off by the nuns, but the red petticoats aren't ready yet, and the pampooties will have to be made in Dublin, a very good thing too, there is no object in bringing local smells into the theatre.   (*Seventy Years*, 414–15)

Martin McDonagh of Inishmaan finally replied on 26 Feb 1904:

Now about the pampooties. The price is half-crown a pair. But if you want a pair yourself I'll send them to you and welcome. But I wouldn't like to give them to anybody else without a half crown if they want them . . . . Sending you a little bit of flannel, but I have to say to you that it is very dear and very scarce, although I might be able to get some, if you want me to do so. The price of it is from 3/ to 3/6 per yard.

(TCD; translated in David H. Greene and Edward M. Stephens, *J. M. Synge 1871–1909* [New York, 1959], 106)

To D. J. O'DONOGHUE[1]

31 Crosthwaite Park | Kingstown
24.II.04

Dear O'Donaghue

Many thanks for your note. I will be very glad to do what you ask — though I fear it will be a little hard to get an extract from my Aran stuff with any any sort of completeness.[2] I will look you up in a day or two and talk it over with you, I suppose you are sometimes at home. This week I am rather on my head with rehearsals and preparations for 'Riders to the Sea'.[3] Perhaps we may meet at one of the performances I am likely to be there each evening.

A bientôt
J. M. Synge

MS, Lockwood

[1] David James O'Donoghue (1866–1917), journalist, editor, biographer of Carleton, Mangan, and Emmet, and from 1909 librarian of University College, Dublin. About 1896 he moved from London to Dublin to take over a publishing and bookselling business established by his brother. He was introduced to JMS in Paris by MacKenna, with whom O'Donoghue had shared rooms in Dublin in 1898, but they were never close friends and their relations were to cool considerably over *The Playboy*. In his biographical dictionary, *The Poets of Ireland* (1912), O'Donoghue described JMS as 'a man of quiet, friendly and charming disposition'.

[2] O'Donoghue was apparently planning a volume of writings to be published in connection with the Irish exhibition at the Louisiana Purchase Exposition, which opened in St. Louis, Missouri on 30 Apr 1904.

[3] *Riders to the Sea* received its first performance, by the Irish National Theatre Society, at the Molesworth Hall on 25 Feb 1904, alongside a revival of AE's *Deirdre*.

To FRANK FAY[1]

31 Crosthwaite Park | Kingstown
Friday [4 March 1904]

Dear Mr Fay

It was very good of you to come out to look for me last Sunday and I was very sorry indeed not to have been able to see you. I was in bed with an abcess on my face — at the root of an old tooth — which without being in any way serious made it impossible for me to talk, and distorted me so completely that you would not have known me. It came on after the show on Thursday evening — I'd had a tooth ache all that day and I suppose got a chill in some way. I regret endlessly to have had to miss the two other performances as there were many things, I wanted to consider with a view to London.[2] It cant be helped, and it is well I saw one. What do you think of Chanal?[3] I do not know at all how long it will be before I can go to town again in the evening. I have been up again today and yesterday, but I am very weak as I had high fever and the abcess is not quite gone. I will go in as soon as I can safely[4]

Yours very sincerely
J. M. Synge

MS, NLI

[1] Francis J. Fay (1870–1931), who worked as a clerk-stenographer with a firm of accountants, Craig, Gardner, became one of the leading actors and voice teacher for the company of actors established in 1902 by his brother Willie. William G. Fay (1872–1947), leading actor and stage manager for the company, was a former electrician who received his early training in repertory companies touring England and Ireland. The two brothers organized various dramatic societies in Dublin, these gradually evolving from 'comedy combinations' to more serious nationalist groups leading, finally, in the spring of 1902, to W. G. Fay's Irish National Dramatic Society (called the Irish National Dramatic Company by October 1902). Frank Fay's theatre criticism, which appeared in the *United Irishman* from 1899 to 1901, has been edited by James Kilroy, *Towards a National Theatre* (Dublin, 1970).

[2] Willie Fay had decided to include *Riders to the Sea* in the London bill, as well as *The Shadow of the Glen*. Padraic Colum reported to JMS on 29 Feb 1904 (TCD) that the show 'was very much improved on Saturday' and that the actress playing old Maurya, Helen Laird ('Honor Lavelle'; see p. 95), was 'a different woman when she came in the second time (after the vision)'.

[3] The drama critic Arthur Clery ('Chanel'), writing in the *Leader* for 5 Mar 1904, called the play 'hideous in its realism . . . the most ghastly production I have ever seen on a stage. It had all the horrors of a nightmare and reminded me of a visit to a dissecting room . . . . If he can learn to avoid the morbid, and to take a saner and less crabbed view of existence, I think he may be capable of writing a really valuable play . . . which, while it is healthy, will be effective.' JMS had evidently heard there would be a review of the play.

⁴ According to Mrs Synge's diary, JMS was not well enough to go into town until 11 Mar 1904, and then only briefly.

To GEORGE ROBERTS¹

31 Crosthwaite Park | Kingstown
March 16. [1904]

Dear Roberts

I am getting on all right but my temperature is a little uncertain so I am afraid to go in tonight for fear of another chill. I therefore enclose the words for Miss Walker,² she will know where they come in. Perhaps I may come in on Monday night, if not I will see you all in London. I suppose you will take over the spining wheel,³ it helps the scene so much.

In haste

Yours sincerely
J. M. Synge

P.S. Will you kindly send me 4 Samhains.⁴ I will pay for them when I see you next. —

MS, Berg

¹ George Roberts (1873–1953) founded the publishing firm Whaley & Co. in 1904, with James Starkey (see p. 95), then in 1905 Maunsel & Co with Joseph Hone (see p. 229) and Stephen Gwynn (see p. 131) as co-directors. He served as secretary and then member of the reading committee of the Irish National Theatre Society until he resigned in 1905 on the formation of the limited society. His first wife was the actress Mary Garvey (Maire ni Garbhaigh; see p. 91), who had a small part in *Riders to the Sea*. In his rather inaccurate memoirs, published in the *Irish Times*, 13 July–2 Aug 1955, Roberts described the painstaking care JMS took with this production.
² Mary Walker (d. 1958), later Mrs Eamon Price (she used her Irish name, Maire Nic Shiubhlaigh, when performing), was given the role of Nora Burke in *The Shadow of the Glen*. She and her brother Frank had been members of W. G. Fay's Irish National Dramatic Society; later two sisters, Eileen O'Doherty and Betty King, also joined the company. Mary Walker after some hesitation joined the seceders from the company in 1905, returning occasionally to perform in certain roles for which she had become noted. (Some considered her a better Nora Burke in *The Shadow of the Glen* than Molly Allgood [see p. 166].) Her reminiscences (with Edward Kenny), *The Splendid Years* (Dublin, 1955), not only give valuable information about the early years of the movement but the most detailed description of the difficulties of mastering the language of JMS's plays.
³ For *Riders to the Sea* (see p. 77, n. 2). It was used effectively in the opening scene by Cathleen the older daughter, played by Sara Allgood (see p. 95).
⁴ The October 1903 issue of the journal *Samhain*, edited by Yeats, in which *Riders to the Sea* was first published.

To FRANK FAY

4 Handel Street | [London]   W.C.
Sunday night | 10.iv.04

Dear Mr Fay

Many thanks for your letter. We have indeed had a great success with our show,[1] and a good deal of criticism has been most interesting although I still believe — as I once said to you — that our real critics must come from Dublin. It it only where an art is native, I think, that all its distinctions all its slight gradations, are fully understood. For instance most of our recent London critics have spoken well of the two plays we gave them that were perfectly obvious — I mean "Riders to the Sea," and the "Pot of Broth," but most of them failed to grasp "Seanchan,"[2] and the "Shadow of Glen," both of which demand an intellectual effort to make them comprehensable or at least a repeated hearing. However that may be we have so far *no critics* in Dublin so we have to make the best of London. I do not think Archer wrote the notice in the Manchester Guardian.[3] At least they say at the Irish Lit. Soc. that the Guardian sent a man down specially from Manchester to do our shows, and further the opening paragraph of the notice seemed to imply that the writer had not seen our company before. Who ever he may have been he seemed to understand the theatre, — he was the only critic I think who put his finger on the faults in the writing of "Broken Soil"![4] Have you seen Max Beerbom in Yesterday's Saturday review? [5] What he says of dramatists' technique is excellent, much more sensible, it seems to me, than Archer's sort of snub at our short plays in the "World." Still Max B. writes some amazing folly — as you will see — as where he says Irishmen cannot be vulgar. I wish he could see "Sold."[6] Archer seems to criticize — at least our prose plays — as dramas first, and literature afterwards.[7] The whole interest of our movement is that our little plays try to be literature first — i.e. to be personal, sincere, and beautiful — and drama afterwards. I daresay Archer admires Sudermann!

To come nearer home. Frankly I think our Irish audiences are a little to be excused for staying away — that is rather an Irish way of expressing it. With Sheanchan we drew good houses, but "Broken Soil" is not strong enough as the main-piece of an evening, Shadowy Waters is still less so, and Deidre is weak also. I am not blaming our choice of plays, we gave the best we had, but I think we should not take a gloomy view of our audiences because they did not let themselves be persuaded that weak plays were strong. When we have a bigger, and better repertoire — that is the matter of life and death — we will draw better audiences. I do not much believe in trying to entice in people by a sort of political atmosphere that has nothing to do with our real dramatic movement. By all means have 98 plays — I will do one if I can — but STRONG , good, dramas only will bring us people who are interested in the drama, and they are, after all, the people we must have —[8]

I think the verdict of the London Gaels that "In the Shadow of Glen" is perfectly unobjectionable will make the Dublin writers a little afraid of making themselves ridiculous by attacking us again on the moral question.

I dont know that I can give you any criticism on the acting that would be of value. You should try and get more people — though I suppose that is not easy. The soldier and the monk in Seanchan were dreadful, — the soldier especially.[9] You are perfectly right that it is practice the crowd needs most — i.e. of course, practise of playing in public. Camden Street work[10] is all very well but it will never take them beyond a certain pitch. Again all our women are too young; where else will you see such girls holding an audience — as they did after all — in serious drama? It was worst in the Shadow of the Glen, Miss W. is clever and charming in the part, but your brother is so strong he dominates the play — unconsciously and inevitably — and of course the woman should dominate. You were admirable I think in both your parts.[11]

I am very well but in agony and horror over my play with the blind people. It is exceedingly difficult to make it work out. I will be back in Ireland in 3 weeks about and hope to see you all then before I go off for my summer wandering I fear I have written incoherently I am tired, excuse it.

Very sincerely
J. M. Synge

P.S. Please remember me to everyone.

MS, NLI

[1] JMS's two plays were performed with Yeats's *The King's Threshold* at the matinée on 26 Mar 1904, at the Royalty Theatre, London. On 5 Apr 1904 Frank Fay wrote to JMS, who was still in London, 'Have we not had an extraordinary triumph . . . . As usual you have had to go out of your own country to be appreciated.' (TCD)
[2] i.e. *The King's Threshold.*
[3] William Archer (1856–1924), playwright, translator of Ibsen, and at this time dramatic critic of the *World*; he also occasionally wrote for the *Manchester Guardian* and would later serve in the same capacity on the *Tribune* and the *Nation*. One of the most influential writers on theatre in London, he became vice-president of the Society of Dramatic Critics.
[4] *Broken Soil* by Padraic Colum was performed with *The Pot of Broth* on the evening of 26 Mar. The *Manchester Guardian* critic on 28 Mar 1904 commiserated with Colum for having his 'second rate tragedy' follow just a few

hours after *Riders to the Sea*; 'there is no taste of the mouth about speeches . . . with a metaphor followed out into its furthest recesses . . . . Mr Colm writes altogether like one who has only half succeeded as yet in working the current theatrical convention out of his system.'

5 Henry Maximilian Beerbohm (1872–1956), author and caricaturist, half-brother of the actor Beerbohm Tree; in 1898 he succeeded G. B. Shaw as drama critic of the *Saturday Review*. Beerbohm wrote on 9 Apr 1904 that *The Shadow of the Glen* 'illustrates a very odd thing about the Irish people: their utter incapacity to be vulgar. What this farce would be like if it were translated by an Englishman, into English life, and were enacted by English players, I shudder to conceive.'

6 During the summer of 1903 Yeats's objections to *Sold*, a one-act play by James Cousins (see p. 120), led to a reorganization of the society and the initiation of a reading committee to recommend plays rather than having the entire group vote on their acceptance.

7 In the *World* for 29 Mar 1904, Archer wrote, 'A writer of genuine dramatic instinct is still but half way — if as much — towards being a real dramatist. As yet the Irish theatre has given us only dramatic sketches — no thought-out picture, with composition and depth in it . . . . *Riders to the Sea* . . . is . . . a tragic incident, not a drama. Its essence indeed is far more lyrical than dramatic. Mr Colm's *Broken Soil* tries to be drama, but is an eclogue.'

8 The word 'strong' is underlined three times. For JMS's response to Fay's request for 'a drama of '98', see *Plays* Book I, 215–17.

9 The soldier was performed by T. Keohler, the monk by Fred Ryan, both members of the Society since 1901. Thomas Goodwin Keohler (after 1914, Keller) (1874–1942), poet and theosophist, was to be one of the signatories of the 1904 letter of acceptance of Miss Horniman's offer of the Abbey Theatre (see p. 89). He became a member of the Theatre of Ireland company in 1906, and contributed his version of 'The Irish Theatre Movement' in three articles in the *Sunday Independent*, 6, 13, and 20 Jan 1929. Frederick J. Ryan (1870–1913), whose journalistic pseudonym was 'Irial', was secretary of the Irish National Theatre Society 1903–4, after his play *The Laying of the Foundations* entered the repertoire in 1902; when the Society moved to the Abbey Theatre, he became treasurer (1904–6). He was one of the founders of *Dana* (1905–6), and in later years went to Egypt where he was associate editor of the *Egyptian Standard*, and still later, in England, editor of the journal *Egypt*.

10 Camden Street Hall, 34 Lower Camden Street, Dublin, had been rented by the Society during the summer of 1902 and was still being used for rehearsals; according to Willie Fay, 'The hall was cold and so was the audience . . . . The roof leaked. The stage was so small that you couldn't swing a kitten, let alone a cat.' (*The Fays of the Abbey Theatre*, with Catharine Carswell [1935], 124–5)

11 Frank Fay played the leading roles in both *Broken Soil* and *The King's Threshold*; Willie Fay played the Tramp in *The Shadow of the Glen*, Bartley in *Riders to the Sea*, the Beggarman in *The Pot of Broth*, a minor role in *The King's Threshold*, and served as director and stage manager.

To LOUIS ESSON[1]

> 4 Handel Street | [London] W.C.
> Monday [25 April 1904]

Dear Mr Essen

I have just got your note and I am very sorry to say that I am leaving for Ireland tomorrow or next day[2] and my time is so much filled up I fear I will not be able to meet you. My address in Ireland is

> 31 Crosthwaite Park
> Kingstown
> Co Dublin

If you should come over drop me a line and — if I am at home — we can have our chat over there instead of here. If you are still in the British Isles in October next, you might find the opening of our I. Nat. Theatre company's season an interesting time to come over

With sincere regrets that I cannot meet you I remain

> yours sincerely
> J. M. Synge

MS, Walker

[1] Thomas Louis Buvelot Esson (1878–1943), Australian dramatist and critic, was in London with Leon Brodzky (see p. 173) from around March 1904. Apparently he did visit Dublin and at JMS's urging returned to Australia early in 1905 to create a national theatre; the result was the Pioneer Players, finally founded in 1922 in Melbourne. Esson recorded his memories of JMS in *Fellowship* (Melbourne), April 1921, 138–41: 'He was full of race and fine breeding, courteous, sensitive, sincere . . . a simple man; but there was something strange and alluring about him, an indescribable charm expressed in his voice and manner, and, above all, in his curious smile that was at the same time ironic and sympathetic.' The article gives a detailed description of observing JMS at a rehearsal of *The Well of the Saints*, and records a number of his critical comments.

[2] JMS did not leave London until Friday, 30 Apr 1904.

To RICHARD I. BEST[1]

> 31 Crosthwaite Park | Kingstown
> Tuesday [3 May 1904]

Dear Best

I felicitate you heartily on your post[2] — I heard only the other day that you had got it. I came home from London two days ago and if possible I would like to see you and Magee[3] some-time tomorrow or Friday, — partly for good-fellowship sake, partly because I am charged by the 'Academy' to do them Irish literary paragraphs, first instalment of which must reach them next week and I want to know what is to be said of "Eriu" and "Dana".[4] Did you see my review of Jubainville in Speaker?[5] It was in their number for April 2nd/04.

Yours ever

J. M. Synge

MS, NLI

[1] Richard Irvine Best (1872-1959), Irish scholar, bibliographer, and from 1924 to 1940 director of the National Library of Ireland; he was later Senior Professor of the School of Celtic Studies in the Dublin Institute for Advanced Studies and from 1948 to 1956 chairman of the Irish Manuscripts Commission. In Stephen MacKenna's earliest surviving letter to JMS (?mid-October 1897), he writes, 'Remind me when we meet to give you a note to a delightful Irishman in Paris, who loves the things of *Spirit* and is one of the most charming chaps that exist – a jewel of a man with great knowledge and reading and real *uncant-ified* culture' (TCD). Best and JMS met in January 1898, and when Best later installed JMS in his own former room at 90 rue d'Assas, he offered him useful advice not only on basic living but on his writing, and even helped him purchase his first typewriter (see p. 54); Best's rough notes on JMS are in the NLI.

[2] Best was elected third assistant director of the National Library at the meeting of the Trustees on 25 Mar 1904.

[3] William Kirkpatrick Magee ('John Eglinton'; 1868-1961), assistant librarian of the National Library, essayist and editor, with F. J. Ryan, of *Dana* (1904-5). He published five volumes of essays, editions of George Moore's letters, a memoir of AE, and a volume of poems, *Confidential, or Take It or Leave It* (1951), which includes a memoir of his early school friend Yeats.

[4] The *Academy and Literature* (London), under its new editor, W. Teign-mouth Shore, regularly published unsigned paragraphs on Irish matters; those during May and June 1904 were probably by JMS. *Dana*, 'A Magazine of Independent Thought', founded and edited by Magee and Frederick J. Ryan, ran for only twelve issues, from May 1904 to April 1905. *Eriu*, the journal of the School of Irish Learning, Dublin, was edited by Kuno Meyer (1858-1919) and John Strachan; its first issue also appeared in 1904 and included the first printing of the *Leabhar Oiris* (The Book of Chronicles), edited by Best, who served as Honorary Librarian to the School. Founded by Kuno Meyer in 1903, the School was incorporated in 1926 in the Royal Irish Academy, which continues to publish the journal.

[5] In his review of Henri d'Arbois de Jubainville's *The Irish Mythological Cycle and Celtic Mythology*, translated by Best (Dublin, 1903) (*Speaker*, 2 Apr 1904), JMS praised the 'care and taste' of the translation and the additional notes provided by Best (*Prose*, 364).

To LADY GREGORY

31 Crosthwaite Park | Kingstown
May 11./04

Dear Lady Gregory

Many thanks for your note and the cutting from Inquirer.[1] I was interested in what you told me of the 'Trilogy' I wish I could have seen it too.[2] The company has been taking a holiday but begins work again tonight I believe. We — the reading comittee — have provisionally passed a new play by one Boyle.[3] It is very weak in places but it has a ground-work of good dialogue — (with strange slips into news-paper phrases) — and a comic character that W. Fay is very anxious to play. They are sending it over I believe to W.B.Y. It will make a useful comedy I think.

I am hard at work overhauling my play and generally sharpening the dialogue, but the more I do the more there seems to be done. I hope you will pass through Dublin before the end of June, I shall be here most probably till then.

Yours sincerely

J. M. Synge

MS, Berg; *TB*, 49

[1] An article by H. Bryan Binns on *Riders to the Sea*, 'the central achievement of the Irish players at the Royalty Theatre', appeared in the *Inquirer*, 30 Apr 1904.

[2] On 22 Apr 1904 as part of the annual Shakespeare Festival at the Memorial Theatre, Stratford, F. W. Benson produced an abridged version of E. D. A. Morshead's translation of *The Oresteia* by Aeschylus.

[3] *The Building Fund* by William Boyle (1853–1923), a friend of Parnell and Redmond, and an authority on the works of James Clarence Mangan. Boyle was known in Ireland for his poems and short stories of the peasants, especially *A Kish of Brogues* (1899). *The Building Fund*, the first play submitted to the Society, was not produced until 25 Apr 1905. Two more of Boyle's plays, *The Eloquent Dempsy* and *The Mineral Workers*, were produced in 1906.

To RICHARD I. BEST

31 Crosthwaite Park | Kingstown

Friday [?17 June 1904]

Dear Best

I have not been much in town lately or I would have looked you and Magee up in the Library. I hope the matter of your appointment turned out all right. My brother has just come back from China,[1] and he is asking news of his fiddle, am I to tell him you are going to buy it, or no? Where and when are you best found anywhere? I am off to Kerry or some other wilderness in about a fortnight, and if you have moment free I could look you up meanwhile, if you are — as I suppose probabble — still overrun with your employments, let me know about fiddle, and we can meet some other time.

Tell Magee I am now working at the stuff for Dana,[2] but I fear it wont be brilliant

Yours ever

J. M. Synge

MS, NLI

[1] The Revd Samuel Synge and his wife, both medical missionaries, had returned on a two-year home leave, arriving in Kingstown on 7 June.

[2] Advance advertising listed JMS among the contributors to *Dana*, and on 8 Mar 1904 Magee had written (TCD) asking him for 'the article you spoke of — I think you said on Anatole France — as soon as possible'. Nothing by JMS appeared in the short-lived magazine, however, although various drafts of an article on Anatole France exist in his notebooks.

To STEPHEN MacKENNA

[31 Crosthwaite Park, Kingstown] Ireland

Sunday| [19] June/04

Dear MacKenna

I have kept putting off writing to you in the hope of lighting on a suitable moment of lucidity but it hasn't come, so you must have of my dregs. I'm sorry to hear you've been ailing. You should try and get yourself a filling of fresh air this summer. I should think there are many ways of sliding out into the country from where you are and even if Glen Cullens are not to be had, I suppose Saxon meadows smell as they should and you'd most likely find them able to brace you up body and soul.[1] Don't let yourself talk the bosh that you ain't a strong man no more, we get waves of good health and bad, but if we aren't organically krank, the bad waves pass off with a little persuading and leave us live and kicking. I spent last winter with my ten toes in the grave, and now I'm riding my 70 miles in the day, with a few mountain ranges thrown in, doing more and doing it more easily than ever before. Next month maybe I'll be down again. Breathe, eat, sleep smoke not too much, and you'll be fine.

I haven't seen the spring quite so intimately this year as last — I've been too busy at my play — but not the less I've seen many wonders. I miss my talks with you at Cintra[2] infinitely, but when I'm out pilgrimaging on the hills it's a kind of relief to know you aren't there any more shut up in your cellar. Last year *whenever* I came on miraculous bog-cottons and blue-bells and garlics which you did not see, I used to scratch my head and say "those d——d MacKennas." You will understand the emotion, I do not doubt; it is deedly sympathetic, I suppose, at base. Now I see you enthroned with a folio of Plotinus[3] looking out through the blue mists of

Thames, and it seems all right. I hope your quarters continue to delight you, I won't be over there, I fear, till spring next — if then. Have you seen Yeats again? He is over there still and as you have probably heard his play "Where There is Nothing", is to be done over there by the Stage Society at end of this month.[4] It isn't at all among his best work, yet it would be interest[ing] to see it. Did you see Muray's Hypolitus, and if you did what did you make of their method of chorusing?[5]

I have just got my new play off my hands, it was read to the company on Friday and goes into rehearsal at once,[6] it is a much bigger affair than the others and is in three acts. We hope to begin our new season in October in our new Theatre. Everything is settled now I believe *except patent* an important point, so we are still keeping whole affair *out of papers — no paragraph!* Miss Horniman (entre nous) is coming out herocaly and is laying out about £1000 (dit-on) on the premises which in their way will be unique in Dublin.[7] She — Miss H. — by the way has been casting my horoscope it's pretty bizarre as far as it goes — my hour isn't know[n] — so it is avowedly a little vague. It deals with my temperament and tendencies, I am interested, but of course, entirely unconvinced. If you were here I'd show it to you.[8]

Madame Esposito is translating "Riders to the Sea" into Russian and French, her Russian I cant judge, in French it loses a good deal as she has put it into standard healthy style, — but hasn't managed to give it any atmosphere or charm. She hopes to get it into a Russian review, and we are thinking of trying the Mercure de France, they like young movements.[9]

As soon as I get the rehearsals of my play fairly underway I'm off to the South and West, to forget theatres and all that is connected with them for two months or three. That, I think is essential for one's soul.

I concur cordially in the damnation of [*Dana* — Moore's article] appears a misbegotten abortion, a disgrace to [? Ireland and Paris], and [Eglinton] is a fearful instance of pedantic degeneration. He was too refined and too cultured to have any of our enthusiasms, or to take part in any of our movements, and now he has come to admire the drivel of George Moore, and to ⟨? to the wind!⟩! His own article, however, as you say is all right. After all it is better to rave after the sun and moon as Yeats does than to be as sane as [Magee].[10] I've promised him some stuff next month, and as I like and respect Magee I will do what I can, but I fear for "Dana" there is no hope.

Chesterton's portrait is superb, all his features are caught with an admirably subtle diffidence that defies praise.[11]

Yours
J. M. Synge

My compliments as always to Madame, I suppose you and she are revelling in music now "the season" is on. While I'm hearing the blackbirds and the wild geese crying in Ireland. Excuse raggy paper; can't find anything else.   J.M.S.

MS, TCD

1 In May 1904 the MacKennas had moved to London, taking rooms at 3 Clements Inn, the Strand, and MacKenna immediately wrote to JMS, rejoicing in their new surroundings while lamenting that they had been too busy to cycle into the countryside; he wrote again a month later, complaining of his health. (Both TCD) Glencullen is a famous Irish beauty spot eight miles from Rathfarnham on the way to Enniskerry.

2 The house in Dalkey where the MacKennas had lived for some time in 1903 before taking up a post in Berlin.

3 In his letter from Berlin in early March 1904 (TCD), MacKenna had asked for advice in persuading the newly established firm of Maunsel & Co. to publish his translation of Plotinus in instalments; a rough translation of the First Ennead was now complete.

4 *Where There is Nothing*, written by Yeats with the help of Lady Gregory and Douglas Hyde late in 1901 to prevent George Moore from absconding with the plot, received its first production by the Stage Society of London, directed by Harley Granville-Barker, at the Court Theatre on 27 June 1904.

5 The *Hippolytus* of Euripides, translated by Gilbert Murray, was produced by the New Century Theatre under the direction of Harley Granville-Barker, at the Lyric Theatre, London, the week of 30 May 1904. The *Academy* commented (4 June 1904), 'The choruses chanted by the Queen's maidens and the hunters grouped about the steps which led up to the Palace were impressive, but they became, however, a little monotonous towards the end of the story.'

6 Frank Fay read *The Well of the Saints* to the company on 17 June 1904 at the same time as Lady Gregory's *Kincora*; JMS's play went into rehearsal in July.

7 Annie Elizabeth Fredericka Horniman (1860-1937), a friend and colleague of Yeats in the Order of the Golden Dawn, had frequently acted as his amanuensis, especially on theatre business; she had been the anonymous backer in 1894 of his *The Land of Heart's Desire* at the Avenue Theatre, London, and in 1903 had designed and made the costumes for the first production of *The King's Threshold*. Now she had volunteered to build him a theatre in Dublin to fulfil his artistic aims. Her formal offer to Yeats, as president of the Irish National Theatre Society, of the use of the Abbey Theatre was accepted by the company, and on 6 July 1904 she returned the signed contract. At the same time she made arrangements for Joseph Holloway (see p. 117) to act as theatre architect and W. G. Fay to serve as stage adviser.

8 Miss Horniman's letter, dated 26 May 1904 from London, includes the following details:

Your mental capacities cannot help being good . . . and you should be able to learn languages pretty easily. There is also a certain vigour about your mind which may make you enjoy a healthy pugnacity . . . . Serious & perhaps gloomy ideas attract you & tragic stories please you & you will write them best . . . . You are not liable to insanity because . . . your mind is well-balanced. Strange unexpected events will turn up in your love affairs & spoil them . . . . Being of a very affectionate disposition . . . this is not fortunate.

I think that you are very unlikely to marry . . . & if you did she would be eccentric & not a good match, . . . nor a good temper . . . . In regard to popularity it is very obvious that the Church cannot possibly support you, . . . nor would the ordinary people appreciate you; yet a certain amount of success is certain . . . . But your imaginative faculty is of a disturbing nature to other people . . . as well as to yourself. Your sense of beauty . . . is strong and well-balanced, yet you can appreciate the bizarre . . . as well as that which is gentle & mysterious . . . . Your imagination is drawn towards changing vague images . . . which are full of rich beauty, and they are perhaps sombre too . . . . Comparing your planets with those in Mr Yeats nativity I find it clear that his influence has been excellent for both of you . . . and you will add to the prosperity of his theatrical schemes.   (TCD)

⁹ No translation by Mme Esposito (see p. 128) was published, and if one was done it has since disappeared. Nor is there any separate notice of JMS's work in the *Mercure de France*, although Henry-D. Davray published there a monthly survey of English literature and, in 1905 (LIV, 19–32), a lengthy article on the Irish literary movement.

¹⁰ Before giving this letter to E. M. Stephens, MacKenna heavily scribbled over some words, cutting others out with scissors, and explaining in a note, 'cut about for discretion, criticism of (or name for) Geo. Moore's art'. In late June 1904 MacKenna had written to JMS (TCD) of his disappointment with the first issue of *Dana*, commenting favourably only on Eglinton's own article and condemning George Moore's as 'not fit to wrap ham in'. Moore's article, 'Moods and Memories', was the first of a series of six impressions of Paris; Eglinton's, 'The Breaking of the Ice', was a lengthy review of a volume of personal reflections by the Revd P. A. Sheehan, *Under the Cedars and the Stars* (Dublin, 1903). The issue also included a brief review by Oliver St. John Gogarty of the anthology *New Songs*, edited by AE (Dublin and London, 1904).

¹¹ A photograph of G. K. Chesterton (1874–1936), the influential critic, essayist, and novelist whom JMS had met in London in 1903, appeared on the first page of the *Academy and Literature*, 14 May 1904; JMS also preserved a silhouette of Chesterton among his papers, perhaps sent by Marie MacKenna in the letter of late June 1904.

To FRANK FAY

[31 Crosthwaite Park, Kingstown]
Thursday night [? 1 July 1904]

Dear Mr Fay

I have just come home from our long day in the country¹ and found your letter waiting for me. Miss G.² mentioned the matter of the speech about priest to me directly but I had not time to go into matter fully with her and see what she meant. In your letter you quote your objector as saying *"these things are not true."* What put the simile into my head was a scene I saw not long ago in Galway where I saw a young man behaving most indecently to a girl on the roadside, while two priests sat near by on a seat looking out to sea and not pretending to see what was going on. The girl, of course, was perfectly well able to take care of herself and stoned the unfortunate man half a mile into Galway. The way the two priests sat stolidly looking out to sea, with this screaming row going on at their elbows tickled my fancy and seemed to me rather typical of many attitudes of the Irish church party. Further though it is true — I am sorry to say — that priests do beat their *parishioners*, the man in question — in my play — may have been a tinker, stranger, sailor, cattle-drover, — God knows what — types with which no priest would dream of interfering.[3] Tell Miss G — or whoever it may be — that what I write of Irish country life I know to be true and I most emphattically will not change a syllable of it because A. B. or C. may think they know better than I do. The other speech you refer to is not fresh in my mind, we can discuss it when we meet. You understand my position: I am *quite ready* to avoid hurting people's feelings needlessly, but I will *not* falsify what I believe to be true for any body. If one began that where would one end? I would rather drop play-writing altogether.

I told Miss G. today, on the spur of the moment, that the said man in the side ditch was a Protestant and that if the priest had touched him he would have got six-months with hard labor for common assault — perhaps as good an answer as any. She seems to have thought that I was sneering at the priest for not doing his obvious duty, an idea which of course never entered my head.

If there are passages in the Saint's rôle that give unnecessary trouble, I will do what I can to make them better if the reading comittee, — or if that is not possible — you yourself — will point them out to me

Excuse scrawl and believe me very sincerely yours

J. M. Synge

P.S. Dont imagine for a moment that I am in any way annoyed at your note on the contrary I am glad to know what is thought.

MS, NLI

[1] Synge had arranged to go to Lough Bray with Frank Fay on 1 July 1904.

[2] Mary Garvey (d. 1946), who performed as Maire ni Garbhaigh, was a member of the original Irish National Theatre Society; she resigned in 1905 when the theatre became professional, and later married George Roberts. A letter to her from Frank Fay, dated 14 July 1904 (NLI), notes: 'I spoke to my brother about not casting you for any part in *The Well of the Saints* and understood him to say he would not.'

[3] The passage referred to occurs in Act II of *The Well of the Saints*: 'TIMMY [*jeeringly*]. Looking on your face is it? And she after going by the way you'd see a priest going where there'd be a drunken man in the side ditch talking with a girl.' Joseph Holloway also objected to the simile, and Frank Fay replied on 14 Jan 1905, 'I spoke to Synge long ago about the passage about the priest — but he saw the incident and wont alter it and I am sorry I ever spoke about it . . . . Synge is not a "kindly" dramatist but I think he may yet be a great one

that will make the country talked of again. We mustn't try to clip his wings even if he splash us now and then.' (NLI) Evidently Synge later thought differently about the passage himself, and in the amendments he made in his own copy of the 1905 edition, he changed the simile to 'And she after going by with her head turned the way you'd see a sainted lady going where there'd be drunken people in the side ditch singing to themselves'.

To LADY GREGORY

> c/o Mrs Harris | Mountain Stage | Glenbeigh | Co Kerry[1]
> 10/VIII/04

Dear Lady Gregory

Many thanks for your letter which came yesterday; I would have written to you sooner but I thought I might as well wait for the news you promised me and thank you for it at the same time. I am delighted to hear that there is no difficulty about our patent; I should have thought the smallness of the Abbey house would have been guarantee enough that it would not draw away the travelling companies from the other theatres.[2] Probably the opposition was more against the granting of new patents in general, than against our actual house. I would have liked to see the encounter between W. Fay and O'Shaughnessy,[3] I have often heard of the latter's ferocity. I suppose by this time all is settled and W. B. Y. is pursuing pike again at Coole.

My journey went off all right, and though I had a terribly wet night in Tralee I was able to ride on here the next day. When I came up to the house I found to my horror a large green tent pitched in the haggard — and thought I had run my head into a G.L. settlement at last. However it turned out to be a band of sappers only,[4] who have since moved on.

Tomorrow is the great Puc. Fair at Killorglin[5] and I hope to spend the day there. The weather has been fairly fine so far, but I have had a turn of asthma and have not done much since I came. It is going away from me now. You must be glad to have Kincora safe off your hands at last. I hope the company will like it in its new form.[6]

The luncheon basket was most useful to me on my way and since I came here, and I must thank you again for it and all your kindness during my delightful visit to Coole. Please remember me to your party[7] and believe me

> Yours sincerely
> J. M. Synge

MS, Berg. *TB*, 55

---

[1] From 1 Aug to 1 Sept 1904 JMS stayed in Philly Harris's cottage in Kerry.

² The Abbey Theatre auditorium was 42 feet wide and 51 feet deep, with a seating capacity of 562; the stage was 40 feet wide, 16 feet 4 inches deep, with a proscenium opening of 21 feet and height of 14 feet. The owners of the professional theatres in Dublin had objected to the Society's application for a patent, but after a hearing on 4 Aug 1904 the application was granted in Lady Gregory's name.

³ Thomas Lopdell O'Shaughnessy (d. 1933), K.C., from 1905 Recorder of Dublin, was counsel for the rival theatres.

⁴ Instead of Gaelic Leaguers, he had encountered Royal Engineers.

⁵ The 'Puck Fair and Pattern' at Killorglin, Co. Kerry, dating back to 1613, lasts for three days in August — 'Gathering Day' on the 10th, 'Puck' Fair Day on the 11th, 'Scattering Day' on the 12th. On the evening of Gathering Day a large goat decked with ribbons is borne in triumph to the town square, where he presides for the next two days over the cattle, sheep, and horse fair; shops remain open all night.

⁶ JMS had spent two weeks at Coole assisting Lady Gregory with the revisions to her folk-history play, *Kincora*, first produced 25 Mar 1905.

⁷ Yeats wrote to Charles Ricketts on 26 July 1904 from Coole, 'Synge and AE the poet are staying here, and though they have come to their task from the opposite sides of the heavens they are both stirring the same pot — something of a witches' cauldron, I think' (*Letters*, ed. Wade, 436).

To LADY GREGORY

31 Crosthwaite Park | Kingstown
11/IX/04

Dear Lady Gregory

I was to have started to Aran tomorrow morning, but I hear that there is smallpox in Kilronan, so I am a little uncertain what I shall do.¹ My people want me not to go at all, and of course if it should spread, it would not be pleasant to be there in an epidemic; the people are so helpless and it is so impossible to help them.

I have seen about four rehearsals since I came up, which include two or three of the first act of Kincora. It works out, I think, as a thoroughly sound healthy act, but I cannot say so much for the cast. There are three very gawky strangers — one of them — who does Malachi I think — with a trick of intonation that is very irritating and will be very hard to stop. Wright is doing Felim and is also very bad. Roberts and Starky seem by comparison finished actors,² and F. Fay almost a miracle. Miss Walker is not promising as Gormleith. Among so many men in vigourous parts her voice and manner seem hopelessly languid and girlish. For the first time both the Fays take a gloomy view of her, and admit that she seems to have no feeling for the part. A few evenings ago Russell³ raised the question of the opening program and there was a somewhat violent discussion. W. Fay is very reasonable, but F.F. is as mad as a March hare. A.E.

and myself urged W. Fay — and I am sure you will agree — to rehearse
Kincora as hard as he could for some weeks, and then, if he found it
impossible to get a satisfactory show out of his cast, to reconsider
his opening program. The difficulty is that F.F. is dead against my
my play or Cuchulain[4] so one does not know what to suggest. He
says my work is only adressed to blasé town-dwelling theatre-goers,
that as long as we play that sort of work we are only doing what
Antoine does in Paris[5] and doing it worse, that he wants a National
Theatre that will draw the people etc. etc. etc. He's got Brian Boru
on the brain it seems. I do not know whether all this is his own
feeling only — in which case it is of no consequence — or whether
there is a Neo-patriotic-Catholic clique growing which might be
serious. Colum finds my play unsatisfactory because the Saint is
really a Protestant! Miss Laird has been frozen out because she is a
Protestant.[6] I expect once things get into full swing again it will be
all right, but the good people have been too long left to themselves
without anything exciting to do. W. Fay is in dispair at an epidemic
of love-making that has come over them at last with a vengence. It
makes the rehearsals much more amusing than they were, but it is
easy to see that the good people are much more taken up with each
other than with the plays. I think F.F. is one of the ones who have
not escaped — but *that is very much between ourselves*. I mean the
Co. especially the Fays must not know that I am telling tales out
of school.

   They have very little to show for the two months work they have
given my play. F.F. and Miss Esposito are the only ones who know
their parts at all beyond the first act. I think W.F. will be very good
though is not easy to judge him all through yet, as he is so much
taken up with the words. Miss Esposito is better than I expected,
Miss Algood much worse, Roberts is very middling,[7] and I dont
quite like F.F. though he is always adequate. So you see my prospects are not very golden either. F.F. sits in the corner during my
rehearsals muttering he'd like "to cut their ^(bloody) throats." Holloway[8] suggests that we should begin with old work as we are sure of
a new audience, it is not a bad idea, but I dont know what we could
take. I think it would be no harm if you would write to W. Fay in in
a couple of weeks and ask him how things are getting on; or it would
be better still if W.B.Y. could come up towards the end of the
month and have a look at things. Even if I do not go to Aran I will
go away somewhere for a month. W. Fay has asked me to stay for
a week more to help with the "Well of the Saints" rehearsals so I
will not get off till the end of the week. I am very glad I came up.

   I will be very pleased to have the "Shadow of the Glen" put
into Samhain, and I send you the MS. with this.[9] Should I consult

or notify Mathews about it? I have heard nothing more from him since.

I think that is all I have to say. You must not think the affairs of the Company are in too bad a state; things look worse when they are written down than they really are.

Yours sincerely
J. M. Synge

MS, Berg. *TB*, 62

[1] Instead JMS left on 17 Sept 1904 for a two-week visit to Sligo and North Mayo; he never visited Aran again.

[2] Udolphus ('Dossie') Wright (1887-1952) joined the company early in 1903 and remained with it as electrician, stage manager, and actor of small parts until his death; he performed Phelan in *Kincora*. James Sullivan Starkey ('Seumas O'Sullivan'; 1887-1952), poet, editor, essayist, and bibliophile, was a member of the early nationalist-oriented company and a signatory of the acceptance letter to Miss Horniman in 1904. He performed small parts in the plays of both Yeats and JMS; in *The Rose and the Bottle* (1946), he offers his own version of the founding of the National Theatre. Starkey was associated with George Roberts in the short-lived publishing business Whaley & Co., and was later joint editor with Seumas O'Connolly (see p. 162) of the Maunsel Tower Press booklets. In 1923 he founded the *Dublin Magazine*.

[3] George William Russell ('AE'; 1867-1939), poet, painter, economist, editor, mystic and philosopher, joined the Irish Literary Society in 1895, and became a banks organizer for Plunkett's Irish Agricultural Organization Society in 1897. He was editor of the *Irish Homestead* from 1905, later of the *Irish Statesman* (1923-30). Elected vice-president of the Irish National Theatre Society after the successful production of his only play, *Deirdre*, in 1902, he resigned his office in April 1904 over differences with Yeats, but continued to play an active role in the Society. He strongly advocated nationalism over artistic standards and was to sympathize with the 1905 seceders.

[4] *On Baile's Strand* by Yeats, first performed at the opening of the Abbey Theatre on 27 Dec 1904.

[5] André Antoine (1858-1943), founder of the Théâtre Libre of Paris (1887-95), the Théâtre Antoine (1896-1906), and later director of the Odéon (1906-16), whose innovations in acting and production provided an example of realism and ensemble playing followed by most of the 'free' theatres of Europe. Frank Fay had earlier recommended Antoine as a model to Yeats; another early admirer had been George Moore.

[6] Helen S. Laird (1874-1957), whose stage name was 'Honor Lavelle', was a member of the original company formed from Inghinidhe na hEireann (The Daughters of Erin, founded by Maud Gonne), but left when she joined the faculty of Alexandra College in 1904; she married Constantine P. Curran in 1913 and returned to the stage for the 1915-16 season of the Irish Theatre.

[7] Vera Esposito, whose stage name was 'Emma Vernon', was the daughter of the composer Michele Esposito; she first performed with the Society at the Molesworth Hall in *Riders to the Sea* and was one of the few members who remained when the company became professional. In 1905 she left to seek work in London, and after returning joined the rival Theatre of Ireland in 1906; she married Dr Maurice Dockrell. Sara Allgood (1883-1950), whose younger sister Molly became JMS's fiancée, was originally a pupil of Frank Fay; she joined the .

company in 1903 and rapidly became one of its leading actresses. She left the company in 1913, but returned to the Abbey in 1923 to perform in O'Casey's *Juno and the Paycock*. After many years of touring in England and Australia, she went to Hollywood in 1940, where she performed character parts in films until her death. Emma Vernon played Mary Doul, Sara Allgood Molly Byrne, and George Roberts Timmy the Smith, in the first production of *The Well of the Saints*.

⁸ The architect Joseph Holloway was a chronic playgoer.

⁹ Yeats published *In the Shadow of the Glen* in *Samhain* No. 4 (December 1904); simultaneously the American lawyer, and collector and patron of the arts, John Quinn (1870–1924), issued a copyright edition in New York.

To FRANK FAY

15 Maxwell Road [Rathgar]¹
Tuesday [?November 1904]

Dear Mr Fay

What about the French lessons?² I had dinner early and waited in for you all the evening on Saturday and you didn't turn up. Will you have one or two this week? Please let me know what time you'd like.

Yours
J.M.S.

MS, NLI

¹ In order to be closer to the theatre, JMS had moved into rooms in Rathgar, fifteen minutes' tram ride from the Abbey.

² Evidently Fay, who was especially interested in the technique of French actors, had asked JMS to coach him in French.

To JOHN MASEFIELD

15 Maxwell Rd | Rathgar | Dublin
17/XII/04

Dear Masefield

Many thanks for your letter and the Guardian. I will certainly have a shot at them with some articles and pars.¹ About reviewing I am less certain as it takes so much of one's time. I will ask you more about their conditions when you come over. I am delighted to hear that you are doing our Theatre and that we shall soon see you here.²

Very cordially yours
J. M. Synge

MS, Texas

¹ From October 1904 to March 1905 Masefield was responsible for the daily 'Miscellany' column of the *Manchester Guardian*. On 15 Dec 1904 he wrote to JMS (TCD), asking him if he was interested in doing any work and offering 5/- a Miscellany paragraph

² The official opening of the Abbey Theatre took place on 27 Dec 1904, when *On Baile's Strand*, *Kathleen ni Houlihan*, and *Spreading the News*, a new play by Lady Gregory, were among the plays performed; other items in the repertory were produced during the week to vary the bill. Masefield attended the opening and wrote two articles for the *Manchester Guardian*, on 2 Jan 1905 (unsigned) and 4 Jan (signed), in each praising both plays and players.

To GEORGE ROBERTS

15 Maxwell Road | Rathgar
23/XII/04

Dear Roberts

I have been ill for a week with influenza and I go down to Kingstown today for a few days to try and pick myself up. My address will be as formerly: —

31 Crosthwaite Park
etc.

I hope to get up for the shows next week. I suppose 'The Shadow' will be on Wednesday, Friday, and Saturday matinée?¹ Please send notices or programmes to that effect to the two addresses on back of this. They have both promised to come. Has Yeats heard anything of Bullen?²

Yours sincerely
J. M. Synge

[*overleaf*]

W. Henn Hinde Esq
12 Lower Merrion St.

———

George Yeates Esq
25 Lower Baggot Street

Also please enter enclosed list on your permanent address-book. Dont lose it, as I think the names are likely. You might look out addresses of Madden, Griffith, and MacNeill in Directory.³ Anytime *after present show* will of course do. You probably have directories nearer to your hand than I have.

MS, Berg

¹ *The Shadow of the Glen* was performed during the opening week of the new theatre.

² On 9 Nov 1904 the publisher A. H. Bullen (see p. 104) had written to Yeats (TCD) agreeing on his recommendation to publish *The Well of the Saints* in the series Plays for an Irish Theatre, and to pay JMS a royalty of 15 per cent of the published price; Bullen suggested that two or three illustrations from the designs Yeats was hoping to get from his brother Jack (see p. 112) also be included.

³ JMS was suggesting names of possible subscribers for the entire season of plays at the Abbey Theatre. Henn William Hinde, a civil engineer, was a family friend of the Synges (Robert Synge had been trained as an engineer before going to South America); the Dublin Post Office Directory lists his address in 1904 as 2 Lower Merrion Street. George Wyclif Yeates was JMS's dentist. Patrick J. Griffith had been JMS's first violin teacher in 1888 and remained a good friend. JMS's diary records frequent visits also to a MacNeill who may have been the musical-instrument maker in Capel Street referred to by Samuel Synge as 'John McNeile' (*LMD*, 142). Although I have found no reference to him in family records, the Madden referred to may be P. J. Madden who lived near Mrs Synge, in Clarinda Park, Kingstown.

PART FOUR

1905

*

In Search of Another Ireland

In Search of Another Ireland

Dublin and the West

*

THE first week of 1905 saw Synge at the new theatre, conducting rehearsals of *The Well of the Saints* which was scheduled for production February 4–11. Encouraged by John Masefield, he rescued two earlier articles, 'An Impression of Aran' and 'The Oppression of the Hills', which were published in the *Manchester Guardian* on 24 January and 15 February 1905. Meanwhile in Dublin he was once again the centre of a newspaper controversy, for Arthur Griffith, editor of the *United Irishman*, took the occasion to renew his attack on the theatre and, through Synge, on Yeats, by reviving his objections to *The Shadow of the Glen*. Ever ready for battle, Yeats plunged in with a lengthy argument – extending over several weeks – concerning Griffith's charges of 'Ephesian drama', and finally forcing publication of Synge's innocuous letter affirming his source in Aran. Privately, Synge expressed his indignation by sketching several scenarios on the theme of 'Deaf Mutes for Ireland' and once again tackling a much more extensive farce, 'National Drama', which he and Yeats seriously considered publishing in retaliation.

But by then thoughts of *The Playboy of the Western World* were beginning to stir, and although *The Well of the Saints* was hardly a success – George Moore later claimed it emptied the theatre, and even Frank Fay was hard put to defend it – the production brought Synge to the attention of several continental theatres. Instrumental in this was a young Frenchman, Henry Lebeau, who with the Breton writer Anatole LeBraz visited Ireland for three months in 1905, and who almost immediately acclaimed Synge's genius. Lebeau's article, published in the same month in Paris and Dublin, praised *The Well of the Saints* as

un oeuvre subtile et gracieuse, l'esquisse d'un drame plutôt peut-être qu'un drame proprement dit, mais le raffinement de l'observation, l'usage discret et adroit qui y est fait du symbolisme, et aussi la langue, une langue à la fois savante et populaire, adroite utilisation par la plume d'un artiste du dialecte anglais parlé par les paysans de l'Ouest de l'Irlande, en font tout l'opposé du banal et du vulgaire. (*Dana*, April 1905)

On the strength of Lebeau's article, sent him by George Moore, the German translator Dr Max Meyerfeld immediately wrote for permission to translate Synge's play. Meanwhile, a Dublin journalist visiting Prague praised Synge's work to the actor-translator Karel Mušek of the Bohemian National Theatre, who requested permission to translate *The Shadow of the Glen*.

On 15 February 1905 Synge moved back to Crosthwaite Park to assist his mother, who had been ill for some time; her diary reported increasing concern over her son's involvement with the theatre and his succession of visitors. He spent much of April sitting for John Butler Yeats, who had been commissioned by Hugh Lane to paint portraits of all the leaders of the literary revival; in addition to an oil painting, the elder Yeats produced at least three pencil sketches during 1905, and after Synge's death would recall with pleasure their long conversations in the studio on Stephen's Green.

Despite recurring attacks of feverish cold, Synge spent a week in Donegal in May, fishing with his brother Robert, returning to spend time in Annamoe with his cousin Edward, the artist, who had inherited a family property, Uplands, from one of Synge's favourite elderly relatives, 'Cousin Emily' Synge.

On 8 May 1905 Elkin Mathews finally published *The Shadow of the Glen* and *Riders to the Sea*, and later that month Synge was commissioned by the editor of the *Manchester Guardian* to write a series of articles on the west of Ireland, with Jack B. Yeats as illustrator. From 3 June to 3 July the two friends travelled north from Galway through Connemara and Mayo, those 'Congested Districts' which suffered from poverty, infertile lands, and too small holdings. Twelve articles appeared in the paper between 10 June and 26 July 1905.

George Roberts, managing director of the newly established Maunsel & Co., immediately sought permission to publish the articles as a book — a project which would not be realized until after Synge's death (and then only over Yeats's objections). Roberts did succeed, however, in persuading Synge to retrieve the manuscript of *The Aran Islands* from Mathews and to give the publishing rights in it to Maunsel.

Meanwhile, eager for more adventures, Synge again went west. He returned to Kerry for a week, from 7 August, before crossing to the Blasket Islands for a stay of two weeks — an experience he would later consider even more valuable than that of Aran. With many regrets he left the Great Blasket for Mountain Stage and the last two weeks of his stay in the west.

His re-entry into theatre business was sudden. With Miss Horniman's encouragement and the eager support of the Fay brothers, Yeats and Lady Gregory were planning to take control of the hitherto democratic and unbusinesslike company. At Yeats's request George Russell reluctantly agreed to draft a constitution establishing the National Theatre Society Ltd., and after a brief policy meeting at Coole in mid-September, Synge was dispatched to Dublin to work with Russell in persuading the players to resign from the original Society of amateurs and sign professional contracts. In late September Yeats reported to Lady Gregory, 'Synge is taking the reorganization very much in earnest and will I think make a good director. He has a plan for bringing a Gaelic company from the Blasket Islands, we will have to consider it presently. Synge would stage manage it himself.' (*TB*, 83) This particular plan did not come off, but his election with Yeats and Lady Gregory to the board of directors of the new limited company plunged Synge into a round of negotiations, decision-making, even the rewriting of fellow dramatists' plays, to such an extent that on 29 September Yeats suggested he become managing director for six months.

However, when the new season opened on 2 October, Synge was once again in bed with a fever, from which he did not fully recover until the beginning of November. He was also concerned about the swollen gland in his neck, which was becoming more noticeable. But when the company visited Oxford, Cambridge, and London where all three of his plays were performed, during the last week of November, he felt well enough to accompany them. Mrs Alfred North Whitehead was later to recall vividly his appearance in Cambridge:

There was one young man, shabbily clad, who said almost nothing and coughed dreadfully. After lunch someone took them the rounds of the college, but this young man stayed behind with Alfred and me. And then! Three hours, he talked brilliantly. We hadn't got his name. But after they were gone, we told each other, "No matter who he is, the man is extraordinary."
(Lucien Price, *The Dialogues of Alfred North Whitehead*
[Boston, 1954], 107)

Synge remained in London after the performances, once again under the wing of Yeats.

Back in Dublin for the first performance of Lady Gregory's *The White Cockade* on 9 December, he joined in Abbey business as the directors and the Fays attempted to replace those players who had left for nationalist reasons. Among the contracts issued was one to a young actress who had 'walked on' during the first production of *The Well of the Saints*. Her name was Molly Allgood and by early December, under the stage name of 'Maire O'Neill', she had taken on the role of Cathleen in *Riders to the Sea*.

To A. H. BULLEN[1]

15 Maxwell Road | *Rathgar* | Dublin
14/I/05
A. H. Bullen Esq

Dear Sir

 I have pleasure in returning corrected proofs of first half of the
Well of the Saints.[2] I am sorry I have had to make a good many
corrections in one scene of the first Act, as the MS. was used by our
company for rehearsing — since it has been in my hands, — and I
find that the prompter has written in a certain number of technical
stage directions which could not be left in the printed volume.
Mr Yeats promised to send me back this MS. to revise stage-directions
etc. before it went to press, but he seems to have forgotten all
about it at the last minute.

 I will send the rest of the proofs tomorrow or Monday they, as
far as I see have few errors.

Yours faithfully
J. M. Synge

MS, Berg

[1] Arthur Henry Bullen (1857–1920), Elizabethan scholar and friend of
John Butler Yeats, in 1897 published W. B. Yeats's *The Secret Rose* (under
the imprint Lawrence & Bullen), and in 1903–7 (under his own imprint) the
series, Plays for an Irish Theatre, which included four volumes by Yeats (*Where
There is Nothing, The Hour Glass and other Plays, The King's Threshold and On
Baile's Strand,* and *Deirdre*), as well as *The Well of the Saints.* From 1891 to
1900 he had been in partnership with H. W. Lawrence, from 1902 to 1907
with Frank Sidgwick. In 1904 he founded the Shakespeare Head Press at Stratford, which issued Yeats's eight-volume *Collected Works* (1908).
[2] *The Well of the Saints* was first published in February 1905 by the Abbey
Theatre itself, as volume I of the new Abbey Theatre Series; sheets for the
edition were printed by Bullen, who later issued the play in his own series,
adding an introduction by Yeats.

To D. J. O'DONOGHUE

15 Maxwell Road | Rathgar
25/I/05

Dear O'Donaghue

 I have been so over-whelmed with influenza and rehearsals lately ·
that I have been to see nobody — that is why I have never got round
to see you as I hoped —

I am doing some articles now for the Manchester Guardian,[1] and I want you to let me know if the stuff I gave you for the St Louis book[2] has ever been printed — as — if it has not — I am thinking of boiling it down for the Guardian. I know I was to retain copyright in any case but I suppose the Guardian would not like matter that is already in print —

Bullen is bringing out my new play in a few weeks, and this time I am getting satisfactory terms

tout à vous
J. M. Synge

MS, Healy

[1] 'An Impression of Aran' appeared in the *Manchester Guardian* on 24 Jan 1905 (*Prose*, 49).

[2] Presumably the 'extract from my Aran stuff' referred to at p. 78. I have found no further reference to a 'St Louis' publication

To ELKIN MATHEWS [1]

31 Crosthwaite Park | Kingstown[2]
[c. 29 January 1905]

Excuse delay in answering yours of the 20th. You are perfectly right about the 3rd play. You had another in two acts "The Tinkers Wedding," but the day I called on you last spring you gave me back the MS. as I wanted to make some corrections in it. Being in two acts, it is about as long as the other two plays together, so if they are long enough to fill your volume, I suppose you would hardly have room for "the Tinkers" with them. As far as I am concerned I would rather have the two plays you have brought out now together, and hold over the third as a character in the Tinkers Wedding is likely to displease of a good many of our Dublin friends ⟨and this reason with our new theatre to fill there is perhaps no⟩ and would perhaps hinder the sale of the book in Ireland —

Now as to the terms we spoke of last year. Would you think it possible to give me a per-centage — even a lower one, say 10% from the first — instead of the 12½% when the book had paid its expenses as I think you suggested? If you wish to hold to this latter arrangement how many volumes do you count necessary to pay off the expenses? i.e., after the sale of how many volumes would my royalties begin? Further ⟨for⟩ what terms of years ⟨do you⟩ shall we name *five* ⟨I think⟩ or six I suppose?

Please let me know at once if you

MS fragment (draft), TCD

¹ Charles Elkin Mathews (1851–1921), bookseller and publisher, formerly in partnership with John Lane, with whom he founded *The Yellow Book*; he published many of his authors, including Yeats, in the slim Vigo Cabinet Series.
² Although he was still living in Rathgar, JMS evidently wrote this draft while visiting his mother, who was ill, and perhaps after consulting his brother-in-law Harry Stephens (1856–1935), a solicitor.

To THE EDITOR, *UNITED IRISHMAN* ¹

The Abbey Theatre, | Abbey Street, | Dublin
[*c.* 1 February 1905]²

Sir,

I beg to enclose the story³ of an unfaithful wife which was told to me by an old man on the middle island of Aran in 1898, and which I have since used in a modified form in *The Shadow of the Glen*. It differs essentially from any version of the story of the Widow of Ephesus with which I am acquainted. As you will see, it was told to me in the first person, as not infrequently happens in folktales of this class.

Yours &tc.,
J. M. Synge

United Irishman, 11 February 1905

¹ Arthur Griffith (1872–1922), editor of the *United Irishman* (1899–1906) and *Sinn Fein* (1906–14); founder of the Sinn Fein Party and leader of the delegates who signed the Anglo–Irish Treaty of 6 Dec 1921, in 1922 he replaced de Valera as President of the new Republic. Although starting out as a supporter of the dramatic movement, Griffith, like Maud Gonne, objected on political grounds to JMS's play, which he dismissed on its first production as 'Ephesian drama'. The attack on Synge was renewed in January 1905, with a continuing debate between Griffith and Yeats.
² JMS apparently wrote this letter at Yeats's urging some time before 4 Feb 1905, for on that date Griffith wrote in the *United Irishman*, 'Mr Synge forwards us a tale he states he took down in Aran.' The letter finally appeared, at Yeats's repeated request, in the issue of 11 Feb.
³ Griffith did not print the enclosure, which was doubtless Pat Dirane's story as later published in *The Aran Islands*, Part I (*Prose*, 70).

To ELKIN MATHEWS

[15 Maxwell Road, Rathgar]
[?5 February 1905]

Dear Mr Mathews

I must again apologise for delay in answer[ing] your letter. I have new play ⟨doing it's⟩ going on first week in the Abbey Theatre¹ all this week and I have been very much taken up. I now send revised texts of The Shadow of Glen and Riders to the Sea.

As to the term you offer I would rather the per-centage coming from the outset, but as I understand the trade price sometimes fluctuates I think it would be more satisfactory to have the royalty on the published price. If 10% is too high I will consider any other that you care to offer.

The term of years I mentioned I suppose will suit you?[2] As to the preface by Mr Yeats or Lady Gregory I would rather not have [one. Mr Yeats has] spoken favorabl[y] of my work in Samhain and also in a short preface he has done for the new play in three acts which Mr Bullen is bringing out, so I fear if I get any more introductions people will cry out that we are log-rolling! I hear that

MS fragment (draft), TCD

[1] *The Well of the Saints* received its first production on 4 Feb 1905.
[2] The agreement finally signed on 22 Mar 1905 (TCD) was for seven years at 10 per cent.

To JOHN MASEFIELD

15 Maxwell Road | Rathgar | Dublin
8/II/05

Dear Masefield

Many thanks for your letters etc. I am very sorry you could not get over again to our present show. The new play has been attacked directly or indirectly in nearly all the papers, and our audiences have become very thin indeed. However the company is playing very excellently and the few who do come seem to be enthusiastic so it is exciting all the same.

I enclose another article.[1] It is cut down from a longer one that I have had on my hands for years, and I am not sure that I have not ruined it in the cutting down. If it appears unsatisfactory to you please fire it back to me without showing it to the Ed.[2] and I will send something better when the plays are over.

I will certainly let you know of my movements if there is any chance of my going to England but my finances are in a parlous state and I may not get over at all this year. I hear great accounts of your play[3] from Yeats

Tout à vous
J. M. Synge

N.B. After this week my address will be

·31 Crosthwaite Park
Kingstown
Co Dublin

MS, Columbia

¹ Probably 'The Oppression of the Hills', published in the *Manchester Guardian* on 15 Feb 1905 (*Prose*, 209).

² C. P. Scott; see p. 110.

³ Probably *The Sweeps of Ninety-Eight*, written in 1905.

To SARAH PURSER¹

15 Maxwell Road | Rathgar
15.II.05

Dear Miss Purser

I am very much obliged for your note, but very unfortunately I cannot, I fear, get to see you this evening. I move back to Kingstown with bag and baggage late this afternoon, and as my mother has been ill and I am going out there to take charge of the house, I cannot either put off my going or come back to town for the evening as I might otherwise do. I may come back to Rathgar in about six weeks, but in any case I am often up and down from Kingstown and if you will allow me I will come and see you as soon as you come home from London. Is Wednesday your evening at home or shall I go on chance? My Kingstown address is 31 Crosthwaite Park Kingstown I have not had an evening free since I saw you at the Theatre but now the play is over I am at liberty again and delighted to be so!

Yours sincerely
J. M. Synge

MS, NLI

¹ Sarah Henrietta Purser (1848–1943), artist, founder in 1903 of a stained-glass workshop, An Túr Gloine (The Tower of Glass), which provided the windows for the Abbey Theatre; later she worked with Hugh Lane for the establishment of a gallery of modern art in Dublin and in 1914 became a trustee of the National Gallery of Ireland. Renowned as a witty conversationalist, she held 'at homes' in Mespil House from 1911, on the second Tuesday afternoon of every month, which became a Dublin institution. At this time she was living at 11 Harcourt Terrace, a much smaller residence.

To KAREL MUŠEK[1]

31 Crosthwaite Park | Kingstown | Co Dublin
March 10th [1905]

Herrn Karel Musek

Dear Sir

I must apologise for long delay in answering your kind letter and thanking you for the cuttings and the translations which you were good enough to make for me. I have been ill with influenza the last few weeks or I should have written to you long ago. I am sending you a copy of 'Riders to the Sea' — for the moment I have no copies of the 'Well of the Saints' left, but I will get you one if you have not got it. I shall be very much pleased if you decide to translate either of these plays for the National Bohemian Theatre. Please let me know what you think about the matter when you have made up your mind.

I hope you will be able to come to Ireland next summer as you say in your letter. If you do please let me know before hand as I might be of use to you even if I am out of Dublin myself

With many thanks and best compliments

Yours sincerely
J. M. Synge

Many thanks for the programme and 'Posters' which interest us greatly.   J.M.S

MS, Berg

[1] Karel Mušek (1867–1924), actor and régisseur of the Bohemian National Theatre, Prague, had first heard of the Irish National Theatre when the barrister and journalist R. J. Kelly (see p. 159) visited Prague and sent him a copy of *The Shadow of the Glen*. He eventually translated *The Shadow of the Glen*, *Riders to the Sea*, *The Playboy of the Western World*, and *The Aran Islands*, and in a foreword to the published translation of *The Playboy* (Stará Riše, 1921), described his meetings with JMS in 1906. He also translated plays by Shaw, Maugham, and Galsworthy.

To FRANK FAY

Kingstown
Thursday [? March 1905]

Dear Fay

I forgot to remind you about the Manchester Guardian article that you promised to lend Lebeau.[1] Can you let me have it to send him. I think he will do a very full and serious article[2] about our work so it is worth our while to help him. Of course he will let you have it again.

Yours cordially
J. M. Synge

MS, Pepper

¹ Henry or Henri Lebeau, a young French travel writer and university teacher who visited Ireland from February to May 1905 with the Breton writer and critic Anatole LeBraz (1859–1926), and became a close correspondent of JMS for the remainder of his life. The *Manchester Guardian* article was probably one of the two by Masefield (see above, p. 97).

² 'The Well of the Saints' was published over Lebeau's name in the *Revue de l'art dramatique*, 15 Apr 1905, and reprinted in the April issue of *Dana*, where it was signed 'A Lover of the West'.

To C. P. SCOTT[1]

31 Crosthwaite Park | Kingstown | Co Dublin
18.V.05

Dear Mr Scott

I am much obliged for your letter of the fifteenth, and I will very gladly undertake the work you propose, and In a day or two, I will write more fully ⟨and lay⟩ to suggest a certain tour — which I think would cover the ground most fully — and to ask you a few questions on points of detail as to my letters. Till then please excuse this hurried line and believe me

very truly yours
J. M. Synge

MS draft, TCD

¹ Charles Prestwick Scott (1846–1932), editor of the *Manchester Guardian* from 1872 to 1929 and Liberal MP for Lancashire 1895–1906, had written asking JMS if he would be interested in doing a series of articles on the Congested Districts of the west of Ireland. He continued to suggest topics for series of articles throughout JMS's life.

To MAX MEYERFELD[1]

31 Crosthwaite Park | Kingstown | Co. Dublin
26.V.05

Dear Sir

A small edition of "The Well of the Saints" was issued at the time of the performance for sale in the theatre, so I have pleasure in sending you a copy. I should be very glad to have it translated into German but — as you will see — it will not be easy to render adequately a great part of the dialogue which depends for its effect on the peculiar colour-quality of the dialect I have used. I imagine in the German 'Volkslieder' one would get a language that would be pretty nearly what is needed, but when you have read the play you will see for yourself. If you will kindly let me know when you decide whether it appears' suitable for translation, I will have pleasure in sending you my conditions, if you wish to undertake the work. I know German pretty well — I spent some 13 months in Germany some years ago — and I would be glad to help you in your version in any way I could. The article you saw in 'Dana' was originally written for the "Revue de l'art dramatique" of Paris and appeared there in the No of April 15.

Yours faithfully
J. M. Synge

MS, NLI

---

[1] Dr Max Meyerfeld (1875–1952) of Berlin, theatre critic for the *Neuen Zürcher Zeitung* and translator of Robert Burns, John Galsworthy, George Moore, and Oscar Wilde, had been given the April 1905 issue of *Dana* by George Moore. His interest in JMS roused by Lebeau's article (see p. 110), he wrote on 22 May 1905 (TCD) asking to read *The Well of the Saints* in the hope of translating it into German. Some of JMS's letters to Meyerfeld were published in the *Yale Review*, July 1924.

To STEPHEN MacKENNA

31 Crosthwaite Park | Kingstown
30.V.05

Dear MacKenna

A line only to wish you God speed, and felicitations for your new post[1] if it is working out felicitously. I envy you Paris. I send with this post another booklet containing the Shadow of the Glen[2] which made all the row. Did you get the Dana I sent you, if you did not you'll find the article for which I sent it to you in "La revue de l'art dramatique et musicale" for Avril 15 where your unworthy servant as the representative of Irelande overclouds in bulk all over barbarous tribes. I cannot write as I am packing to go off to the west to do articles on the Irish Distress by special commission of Manchester Guardian, an interesting job, but for me a nervous one, it is so much out of my line, and in certain ways I like not lifting the rags from my mother country for to tickle the sentiments of Manchester. However terms are advantageous and the need of keeping some rags upon myself in this piantic[3] country has also to be minded —

My compliments to Madame. When occasion is ripe let me know what way the chestnuts are smelling in the Luxembourg. To think of you in the Rue du Luxembourg — you luxurious dog — and me chewing blighted spuds upon the quaking bosom of a Connaught bog.

Yours
J. M. Synge

Copy of MS, Skelton

¹ After spending the winter of 1904-5 in Russia, MacKenna returned to London in March, but was soon posted to Paris where, except for brief assignments, he remained until the spring of 1907.
² The Vigo Cabinet edition, published on 8 May 1905.
³ Irish for 'difficult'.

To LADY GREGORY

31 Crosthwaite Park | Kingstown
30.V.05

Dear Lady Gregory
    I send you a copy of Mathews volume in case you care to have it although you have the pieces already in Samhain. I wont be in Dublin, I fear, for next "show"¹ as I am going to the west immediately to do articles for the Manchester Guardian on the Irish Distress with Jack Yeats,² as illustrator, in my company. A German worthy is in treaty with me about translating the "Well of the Saints" into German but I fear the dialect will be too much for him. I have written to W.B.Y. to enquire what I should demand as to terms etc.

Very sincerely yours
J. M. Synge

MS, Carpenter. *TB*, 67

¹ Padraic Colum's *The Land* received its first production with a revival of Yeats's *The Hour Glass* on 9 June 1905.
² Jack Butler Yeats (1871-1957), artist brother of W. B. Yeats, and also a dramatist, lived in Devon but frequently visited and exhibited in Ireland; JMS had been to one of his exhibitions in London. Jack Yeats described their tour of the west in the New York *Evening Sun*, 20 July 1909, and made various sketches of JMS on the road; later he advised him on Christy Mahon's costume for *The Playboy of the Western World*, and illustrated *The Aran Islands* (1907).

To MAX MEYERFELD

Carna Hotel | Carna | Co. Galway | Ireland[1]
June 14th 1905

Max Meyerfeld Esq

Dear Sir

I very much regret delay in sending you the conditions we spoke of. I wished to consult with one or two people[2] and I have not yet heard from them as I am away doing a series of articles for the Manchester Guardian.

The chief point about the translation is, that I do not want to give away the rights of translation unless you are sure of finding a publisher for the work. If you find a publisher I am ready to agree to any arrangement at the usual conditions.

I trust you will excuse me for the long delay and let me hear from you again. I remain

Yours very truly
J. M. Synge

P.S. Your card[3] only reached me today but I suppose this will be sent after you if you have left London. Please address to me as before 31 Crosthwaite Park Kingstown etc

MS, NLI

---

[1] JMS and Jack Yeats began their lengthy tour of the Congested Districts on 3 June 1905, staying no more than two nights at each place.

[2] Yeats had written on 1 June 1905 (TCD) advising JMS not to grant rights to a translator until a publisher had been found, but offering to seek further advice from Arthur Symons.

[3] Meyerfeld had written from London on 27 May 1905 (TCD).

To MRS KATHLEEN SYNGE

Deehan's Royal Hotel, | Belmullet, | Co. Mayo.
[*c.* 16] June, 1905

My dearest Mother,

We have just arrived here and found your parcel with pyjamas, and cigarettes, and also got the six pounds all right, and your letter. We left Gorumna on Monday and sailed across to Carna, where we stayed till yesterday morning. We started for here at 11 a.m. with a two hours' drive to the Clifden line, then we had to train all the way back to *Athlone* and wait there 5 hours to get the connection for Ballina, so that in the end we reached Ballina at 3 o'clock this morning, then drove here the 40 miles on the long car, in a downpour most of the way, and got here at 10.30. I am all right and have had no Asthma since I left Gorumna on Monday; it is a mysterious complaint. In Gorumna I could have thrown a stone from my bed into the sea, yet I was pretty bad; and in Carna I was among bogs and I was quite free of it — and the two places are only 8 miles from each other. I hope you got over move[1] successfully. I must post this now.

Please direct, or ask A.[2] to direct, everything here for the present.

Y[our affectionate son]

J. M. Synge

LMD, 128

[1] Mrs Synge had moved to Greenanmore House, near Rathdrum, Co. Wicklow, on 15 June 1905; she did not return to Kingstown until 6 Sept.

[2] Annie Isabella Stephens (1863-1944), JMS's sister, who lived next door at 29 Crosthwaite Park.

To MRS KATHLEEN SYNGE

Deehan's Royal Hotel, | Belmullet,
Saturday [24 June 1905]

My dearest Mother,

We are leaving here tomorrow or next day for the centre of Mayo and then going home. I will want some more money probably, but I cannot get it yet as I dont know where I'll be.

It is extravagantly hot at present, and not very easy here to rake up fresh matters for an article every second day.[1] It is a great thing that we have had such fine weather. I dont know how we should have managed if it had been wet. My typewriter broke down yesterday, but I managed to patch it up again, and I hope it may last till we get home.

I am getting on very well, but I have so much writing I have no time for letters.

Y[our affectionate son]

J. M. Synge

LMD, 129

[1] Twelve articles appeared at intervals of three to four days in the *Manchester Guardian* between 10 June and 26 July 1905; JMS and Jack Yeats were in the west from 3 June to 3 July.

To MAX MEYERFELD

31 Crosthwaite Park | KINGSTOWN | Co. Dublin
10.VII.05

Dear Sir,

I Am sorry there has [been] another delay in answering your letter of July 3.rd. I have just come back from the west of Ireland, and I have been much occupied the last few days.

I am glad to hear that you think it will be possible to get the play performed in one of your theatres. I am afraid I can hardly promise to make a version into ordinary English of the whole play[1] — just at present at least, it would not be possible — but I can do a few pages at first, and then any particular passages that you find difficult. I do not think you will find the general language hard to follow when you have done a few pages, as the same idioms are often repeated, and the purely local words are not very numerous. However I perfectly understand that it will be a difficult language to translate, and, if you give me time, I will do anything I can to help you.

As to the conditions I am informed that the following are the most usual and satisfactory, but I am of course ready to consider any modification you may suggest. The agreement I propose would be that I should make over the translating rights to you for a term of years — say for five years — with the condition that you have the book published within a given time, six months I suppose would be a reasonable period, or it can be longer if you wish. Then I should have a royalty representing say half profits. The acting rights could be arranged for some what on the same lines, but it is perhaps as well to wait till I hear if these conditons are likely to suit you, or what others you may suggest, before going more fully into the matter.

If you decide to undertake the work it would perhaps save time if you would let me know a few passages or pages in the play that you would like a version of, so that I could do them for you and send them at once.

Yours faithfully
[*signed*] J. M. Synge

TS, NLI

[1] Meyerfeld had asked (3 July 1905, TCD) for 'an English transcript' of *The Well of the Saints*.

To STEPHEN MACKENNA

31 Crosthwaite Park [Kingstown]
July 13th / 05

Dear MacKenna

This unhappy island has sunstroke, which doesn't suit it, and I've got cold. To be quite myself this morning — I'm alone in the house — I sniffed through Massinger and Heywood and Heine, and Rabelais and Rafftery, and Chaucer — here you breathe — and Milton and Marlow and Maeterlinck, and Merimée, and Lever,[1] and the ten commandments and the minor prophets and the map of Ireland, yet the divil a good did they do me till I went to my upper chamber and dived into a press of papers where I came on stray letters written in Cintra and Clamart and in Boissonade,[2] and in Clements Inn and Berlin, and in the fashionable roadway of the Luxembourg, by one, Stephen MacKenna. That's nearly all I have to say, and I'm so bloddy hot I think I'll stop. It's 23° Cent. on my table and whatever that may be in Paris it's the mischief here. What are you at? I've sent you a Dana, and a book, and a letter and the Lord knows what, and not a word out of you!

I've just come home from the Guardian business. Jack Yeats and myself had a great time and I sent off 3 articles a week for four weeks running. Would you believe that? But he, being a wiser man than I, made a better bargain, and though I had much the heavier job the dirty skunks paid him more than they paid me, and that's a thorn in my dignity! I got £25.4.0 which is more than I've ever had yet and still I'm swearing and damning. However we had a wonderful journey, and as we had a purse to pull on we pushed into out-of-the-way corners in Mayo and Galway that were more strange and marvellous than anything I've dreamed of. Unluckily my commission was to write on the "Distress" so I couldn't do any thing like what I would have wished to do as an interpretation of the whole life. Besides of course we had not time in a month's trip to get to the bottom of things anywhere. As soon as I recover from this cold affair I'm off again to spend my £25.4.0 on the same ground. There are sides of all that western life the groggy-patriot-publican-general shop-man who is married to the priest's half sister and is second cousin once-removed of the dispensary doctor, that are horrible and awful. This is the type that is running the present United Irish League anti-grazier campaign[3] while they're swindling the people themselves in a dozen ways and then buying out their holdings and packing off whole families to America. The subject is too big to go into here, but at best its beastly. All that side of the matter of course I left untouched in my stuff. I sometimes wish to God I hadn't a soul and then I could give myself up to putting those lads on the stage. God, wouldn't they hop! In a way it is all heartrending, in one place the people are starving but wonderfully attractive and charming and in another place where things are going well one has a rampant double-chinned vulgarity I haven't seen the like of.

My compliments to Madame and you

J. M. Synge

MS, TCD

[1] Charles James Lever (1806–72), prolific novelist and medical practitioner both in Irish country villages and fashionable European resorts, was sometime editor of the *Dublin University Magazine*. His best-known works such as *The Confessions of Harry Lorrequer* (1839), *Charles O'Malley* (1841), and *The Martins of Cro'Martin* (1856) combine a fine comic sense and ear for colourful dialogue with a sensitive awareness of the implications of contemporary events on Ireland.

[2] MacKenna had lived at 6 rue Boissonade, Paris XIVe (a short distance from JMS's room at 90 rue d'Assas), from the autumn of 1899 until moving to Clamart a year later.

[3] The United Irish League was founded in Co. Mayo in 1898 by William O'Brien of the Nationalist party, who sought a settlement to the land question through an alliance between the Protestants of the north and the Catholic middle class of the south. The League advocated the division of grazing estates into peasant holdings.

To JOSEPH HOLLOWAY[1]

31 Crosthwaite Park | Kingstown
July 20th / 05

Dear Mr Holloway

Many thanks for your kind note and the address of the man we spoke of.[2] I should think he is sure to write to me before he prints or plays his translation but I am glad to have his address. It will be very interesting if he puts it on the stage.

I am off again in a few days to the west or south of Ireland for the rest of the summer. I was lucky to come in for Sarah[3] during the couple of weeks I was at home.

Yours sincerely
J. M. Synge

MS, NLI

[1] Joseph Holloway (1861–1944), architect for the Abbey Theatre, was a drama critic and staunch member of the Irish Literary Society. His 'Impressions of a Dublin Playgoer' provide, in 221 almost indecipherable volumes (NLI), a virtually day-by-day account of theatre in Dublin over a fifty-year period, and

offer a picture of the puritanical, nationalist views of the Abbey Theatre's opponents.

² Evidently Karel Mušek, who had written to Holloway's friend R. J. Kelly on 8 July 1905 (NLI) concerning his plans to translate *The Shadow of the Glen*.

³ Sarah Bernhardt (1845–1923), the French actress specializing in tragic and strong dramatic roles and noted for her 'divine' voice, had performed with Mrs Patrick Campbell in *Pelléas et Mélisande* by Maeterlinck at the Gaiety Theatre, Dublin, twice only, on 17 July 1905.

To MAX MEYERFELD

31 Crosthwaite Park | Kingstown | Co. Dublin
July 26th [1905]

Dear Sir

I have been laid up with influenza for the last ten days or I should have written to you sooner.

I now send you a version — as you will see a rough and bald one — of the first scene and some notes on first act that I hope may be of use to you. I will send you a version of the chief scene of Act II in a few days, and then if you will please let me know of any particular scenes that you are likely to have trouble with, I will do them for you as soon as I can.[1]

I am likely to go away again into the country next week but this address will always find me.

Very truly yours
J. M. Synge

MS, NLI

[1] JMS's transcription and notes on *The Well of the Saints* are published in *Plays* Book I, 269–71 and 274–5.

To MAX MEYERFELD

31 Crosthwaite Park | Kingstown | Dublin | Ireland
July 31st [1905]

Dear Sir

The little edition of the play is nearly all gone so I could not find a spare copy of the printed text — a more expensive edition is coming out shortly with a preface by W. B. Yeats. — I have however gone over one of my old manuscripts and written in explanations where they seemed necessary, and I am sending you this version today. One scene — the 2nd of Act II — I have rewritten for you in full, and put into its place in the MS.[1] If there is still any passage (or passages) that you are in doubt about please do not hesitate to point them out to me.

Yours very truly

J. M. Synge

MS, NLI

---

[1] See *Plays* Book I, 272-4. Meyerfeld had written on 27 July 1905, 'I do not find the greatest difficulty in the use of strange and obsolete words, but in the construction of the sentences' (TCD).

To LADY GREGORY

c/o Mr William Long | Ballyferriter | Dingle | Co Kerry

4.VIII.05[1]

Dear Lady Gregory

Many thanks for your kind invitation which came unfortunately just as I was setting out for here, and as I had engaged my room and ordered a car to meet me I could not change my plans. I am in the centre of the most Gealic part of Munster — 10 miles beyond Dingle close to Smerwick Harbour — and I am making great strides with the Munster dialect. I have realised that I must recussitate my Irish this year or lose it altogether, so I am hard at work. I am staying in a sort of little inn for the present but I may move on any day if I can find a cottage anywhere round the neighbourhood. I like this neighbourhood in many ways greatly and the people are very ready to talk Irish and be friendly which is a help. So many of the Mayo people are hard to get at, for one reason or another, that I did not have much talk up there.

I saw Fay the day before I came away and he told me all about the present state of affairs in the company.[2] I wonder how it is going to end. I think it would probably be best to put off any very very sweeping changes for another year, but that of course will depend on the way things turn out.

If there are any developments I am always eager to hear news of them one seems so out of the world in places like this. I do not know how long I shall be here but letters or anything sent to Kingstown will always come on to me as I keep my people posted with my various addresses. There is are very wild Islands — the Blasket Islands — not far from here and I would like to get on them for a while if it is possible but so far the weather has been so rough I have not even been able to row out to them.

I hope your play[3] is coming on, mine has made no proggress since as after all I was not able to do anything in July as I was down with a sort of influenza.

Thanking you again for your invitation which I am very sorry to have missed I remain

Yours very sincerely
J. M. Synge

MS, Berg. *TB*, 71

[1] A misdating for 8 Aug 1905; JMS and Frank Fay went to Kilternan on the 5th. From 7 Aug until moving to the Blasket Islands on the 13th, JMS lodged, for 3/6 a day, in a cottage in a village just south of Smerwick Harbour on the tip of the Dingle peninsula; his description of the experience in *The Shanachie* (Summer 1907), 61-70, offers no information concerning his host, nor do his notebooks or Mrs Synge's diaries.

[2] When Miss Horniman offered (12 June 1905, NLI) to guarantee up to £500 in salaries to allow the Irish National Theatre Society professional status, the nationalist core of the company interpreted this as a further erosion of the original ideals of the movement. The principal objectors, who later seceded and established a rival company, were Padraic Colum, Thomas Keohler, Frank Walker (see p. 161) and his sister Mary (Maire Nic Shiubhlaigh), James Starkey, Mary Garvey, George Roberts, James Cousins, and H. F. Norman. James Henry Sproull Cousins (1873-1956) was a poet and dramatist whose early play *Sold*, when objected to by Yeats, caused one of the initial disagreements in the Society. He describes the early years of the movement, before he and his wife became ardent Theosophists and went to India, in *We Two Together* (with Margaret E. Cousins; Madras, 1950). Henry Felix Norman (1868-1947), an early friend of AE and member of the Theosophical Lodge in Dublin, edited the *Irish Homestead* from 1899 to 1905 when he and AE changed places, Norman becoming an organizer of rural banks in the Irish Agricultural Organization Society.

[3] *The White Cockade.*

To LADY GREGORY

Ballyferriter [Dingle, Co. Kerry]
Friday 11th [August 1905]

Dear Lady Gregory

The plays[1] have just come. I am delighted to see that yours is finished, but I have not had time to read it yet, and will not for a day or two as I spend the day with John Eglington — who is staying 20 miles from here — tomorrow and the next day I move on bag and baggage to the Great Blasket Island!

It is probably even more primitive than Aran and I am wild with joy at the prospect If all goes well I may stay there for some time. I will read the plays carefully and let you know what I have to say about them as soon as I can, and also I will tell you of my new abode. I am to go out in a curragh on Sunday when the people are going back from Mass on the mainland, and I am to lodge with the King.

le meas mor[2]

J. M. Synge

MS, Berg. *TB*, 73

₁ *The White Cockade*, and perhaps a play by Stephen Gwynn.
₂ Irish for 'with great regard'.

To MAX MEYERFELD

Ballyferriter | Dingle | Co Kerry
12/VIII/05

Dear Sir

I got your letter a day or two ago and I have pleasure in answering your questions

p 8. l. 20 *playing shows* = playing little plays, or performing in circuses such as are seen in country fairs

p 9. l. 18 *it wonder enough we are ourselves* = we are such fine-looking wonderful blind people that we are wonder enough for this place, and we dont wish you to do anything here that people would think of instead of us.

p 11. l. 18 *naggin* is a small measure of quantity, half a pint, I think.

p 11. l 21 *hid in the thatch* = she means hidden up under straw of roof inside house.

p 12. l 15 *sup of water* = a little water

p 20. last line. "skinny" girls = thin, lanky

p 22. l. 13 *stripping rushes for lights.* = the people used to make "rush lights" by taking the outside skin off rushes, and then soaking them the rushes in grease.

p 24. l 14 come now *till* we watch = come now so that we can watch, or come now and let us watch.

p. 24 l. 20 *on the way* = you should be thinking *how* sin has brought blindness etc.

p. 24 last line, "the words of woman and smiths" this phrase is almost a quotation from an old hymn of Saint Patrick. In Irish folklore smiths were thought to be magicians, and more or less in league with the powers of darkness. Perhaps the phrase cannot be translated (?)

p 25. l. 16 *the water would do rightly* = *the water would have the same effect — would do very well.*

p 28. l 12 "gamey eyes" — tricky, merry eyes.

p 29. l 6. a bad one = an ugly man.

p 31. l. 17. I'll speak hard to the two of you = say dreadful things to Molly and Mary Doul.

p 32. l 16. a wisp on any *gray mare* = a tangle of dirty hair on any *gray horse* = he is thinking of the dirty gray mountain ponies of Ireland and their knotted shaggy manes. mare = female horse.

Doul, "ou" as in "out". Byrne like "burn". Simon long English "Ī". Bállinatone, "Grianan", Annagolan = annagóulan the 'ou' as in 'out'. Laragh the gh is now usually mute otherwise it is a guttural. Glenássil. —

I am moving out to a very wild island off south west coast the Blasket Island, tomorrow for a couple of weeks, but letters to Kingstown will follow me. I will be very glad to explain any more phrases that turn up in following acts.

With best wishes

Yours faithfully
J. M. Synge

MS, NLI

To LADY GREGORY

c/o The King | Shawn Keane
The Great Blasket Island | Dunquin | Dingle | Co Kerry
Sunday 20.VIII.05

Dear Lady Gregory

Excuse this scribble I am writing out on a mountain top as I have difficulties in finding a place in the house. I have been here for a week today, and in some ways I find it the most interesting place I have ever been in. I sleep in a little cot in the corner of the King's room and in the morning — on state occasions — the princess comes in when we awake and gives us each a dram of whisky and lights our pipes and then leaves us to talk. When I get up and go in to the kitchen the little queen brings me a bowl of water to wash my face and the princess holds me a towel. In the evenings there are often 20 or 30 people in the house dancing and getting on. The old king himself[1] is the only person who speaks to me in English, so I am thrown back on my Irish entirely, and I have great trouble with it sometimes. I have to read and eat and write in the kitchen which is usually full of people so I have not been able to read your play as carefully as I would have liked. I went through it the other day out on the cliffs and liked it very much. So I am sending you back the MS. with many thanks for letting me see it — in case you may want it. The idea of the whole thing I think is admirable,[2] and I liked most of the scenes. Once or twice I felt doubtful if there was quite current enough in a scene, but I cannot be sure that it was not the fault of the gannets and choughs that were distracting my attention. The language seemed a bit too figurative once or twice — in Sarsfield's part especially I think — but a few strokes of blue pencil would put that all-right, if you think it worth while to make any more revision. I would like to see it again when I get back to Ireland, I feel strangely far away from stage-land, and I dont feel that my judgment now is of any value. I will read the other play when I can and send it back to you. The weather is so broken I cannot often read comfortably outside and I am continualy disturbed in the house. The posts here are very uncertain, there may be no more here before I leave, so my address is still Kingstown. I would like to stay here a good while but when the schoolmaster comes back I may have to go at the end of the week, or I may knock up, as the conditions in bad weather are trying. We were weather bound yesterday but a curragh may set off tonight so I am getting this ready. This place itself is magnificent, I can see now from Valentia to Loop Head, all the Kerry mountains and the Atlantic outside.

Yours very sincerely
J. M. Synge

MS, Berg. *TB*, 76

[1] The King (about whose name JMS drew a box in the address above) has been identified by Robin Flower as Pádraig o'Catháin (Shawn Keane); see Greene and Stephens, *J. M. Synge*, 188–9, and *MUJ*, 175–6.

[2] In her notes to the published version of the play, Lady Gregory recalled, 'When my *White Cockade* was first produced [9 Dec 1905] I was pleased to hear that J. M. Synge had said my method had made the writing of historical drama again possible.'

To MAX MEYERFELD

The Great Blasket Island | Dingle | Co Kerry
August 21st 05

My dear Sir

I received your card and your second letter[1] last night. I am sorry for delay in answering your questions but there is only one post here in the week (— if the weather is bad there is none at all —) so things are slow in reaching me. I will try and get a curragh to take this letter ashore tomorrow as no post goes till Saturday next.

Now for your questions! —

p. 37   l. 13 whacking your thorns = hacking, chopping, or cutting your sticks (of hawthorn).

p. 39   l. 15 rake ashes from = rake out ashes *from under* the forge.

p. 41   l 8 slipping each way = slipping every way, in every direction.

p. 45   l.7 sneezing = he has been sweating and snuffling and sneezing with a cold in his head (spoken in derision

p. 51   l 20 Cahir (kăhĭr) — city of Iveragh. The nominative is on page 54 here it is a genetive, pronounced ēe-v'ráu and ēe-vráu-ig the 'au' as in caught. The town is Caherciveen in Kerry

p. 51   l 21 Reeks = *Mountains*, the Macgillicuddy's *Reeks* in Kerry, near Cork border, are well [known] mountains in Ireland

53,   l. 19. a man looking on bad days etc. = a man who has been for a long time looking at the bad weather and ugliness, which Martin now finds in the world. looking on = looking at, in this dialect

59   l 19 raise your voice = speak out loudly, cry out.

60.   l 9 *Hell's long curse.* can hardly be translated literally It means a great curse, or the great curse of Hell. Any strong peasant curse would do.

65   l 2 wicket = misprint for wicked.

70   l 12 a bit of comfort = any consolation. He means that if he had anything to comfort or console him for all their misery, as she has in her hope of beauty, he would be nearly as well off as before the cure.

70   l 20 griseldy = grisly.

71   l. 5 There's talking, There's = *voilà*. He means That is grand talk (ironically) for a clever woman! Great talk indeed!

71   last l. great talking = great talking or chatting with each other

73   l 15 sloughs = bogs.

73   l 18 yeomen = guards

p. 80   l 20 The image of the Lord thrown upon men, = the image of God reflected by men, he is thinking of text, 'God created man in his own image'

p 81   l 23 'creels' = tall basket or hampers for fish or turf.

p 87   l 18 and be looking out on the holy men, = he will be looking himself at the holy men of God. (He is merely wheedling or flattering the saint, to hide his intention)

p 88   l 21 the little splash = gurgling sound of the water in vessel.

p. 91 1 10 a slough of wet = a wet quagmire or bog. Do you
   remember the 'Slough of Despond' in Pilgrim's Progress?
   of Bunyan The word is used in same sense in Ireland now.

I am very much pleased that you have liked the little play as you
have worked at it. I agree with you that the way I have treated their
going blind again is open to criticism, but if I had taken the motive,
that their blindness was a punishment, I would have got out of the
spirit of the play, or have fallen into needless complications or
commonplaces so I passed lightly over the matter as it was not really
essential to what is most important in the play. I do not know how
long I shall be out on this island, if I am back in Kingstown before
you publish the translation I would be glad to see a proof. Please
excuse the scrawl I have written, I am working in a tiny cottage
kitchen with half a dozen people talking Gaelic round me.

Thanking you for all the trouble you are talking with my work I
remain

Yours faithfully
J. M. Synge

P.S. I suppose of course you received the letter I sent you 10 days
ago

MS, NLI

1 Meyerfeld's request of 4 Aug 1905 (TCD) for a reply to his letters elicited
an explanatory postcard from Annie Stephens on 17 Aug, explaining that her
brother was 'travelling in the South of Ireland & I have no address at present to
which I can forward letters. I expect to hear from him in a few days.' (NLI)

2 Meyerfeld's letter of 9 Aug 1905 asks, 'There is only one thing which
seems to me open to attack: Why don't you give any reason for their going blind
again? In fact, we have too much pity for these poor beggars — why should they
lose their sight again without having done any mischief?' (TCD)

To W. B. YEATS[1]

[The Great Blasket Island, Dingle, Co. Kerry]
[*c.* 21 August 1905]

everyday literary plays which this one[2] is just like what one meets
everywhere. It is, of course, in many ways a very capable piece of
work — both in dialogue and putting together, although there are
points I do not like — but I think it is too near the conventional
historical play and has too much conventional pathos to be the sort
of thing we want. On the other [hand], we seem to be short of
plays, and it is hard to say on what pretext we should vote against
this stuff however little we may like it.

I got Boyle[3] from F. Fay last night and have read two acts of him.

He sets one's teeth on edge continually, and yet I think it is certainly worth revising and playing. It hovers over being a good picture of the patriot publican, and yet it is never quite right and it is very often quite wrong. Your brother and I saw something of these kind of people when we were away for the *Manchester Guardian*. They are colossal in their vulgarity, but their vulgarity is as different from cockney vulgarity as the Mayo dialect is from the Cockney. Boyle does not seem able to distinguish between the two and sticks in English Music Hall vulgarity of the worst kind. I rather agree with Fay[4] that you would be more likely to get Boyle to put it to rights than Colum. Boyle would be sure to resent in his heart having Colum appointed to direct him, besides Colum seems never to know his own [mind] and if Boyle was sulky Colum would give in at once. I think it is probable that I leave this Island at the end of the week, though I am likely to stay on in the neighbourhood another month. Please thank Lady G for her letters . . . .

J. M. Synge

TS copy (fragment), NLI. *TB*, 77

[1] William Butler Yeats (1865-1939), poet, dramatist, essayist, and prime mover of Ireland's literary renaissance. He first met JMS in Paris on 21 Dec 1896, shortly after he had met Lady Gregory, but he did not involve JMS in theatre plans until somewhat later (see *TB, passim*). Yeats spent each summer at Coole during the first decade of the twentieth century.

[2] Probably the play sent by Lady Gregory with hers; see p. 121.

[3] William Boyle had submitted his second play, *The Eloquent Dempsy*, to the company.

[4] Yeats had sent JMS a copy (TCD) of Willie Fay's objections to Yeats's plan of having Colum revise Boyle's play, on the grounds of Colum's incompetence and insufficient knowledge of the country people: the play was finally revised by Yeats and JMS.

To MAX MEYERFELD

Ballyferriter | Dingle | Co. Kerry
September 1st/05

My dear Sir

Many thanks for your letter of August 26th which I have just received. Now as to your two questions: 'Bride' is simply an Irish Christian name, a shortened form of Bridget (Brigid in Irish), and it has nothing to do with the English 'bride.' At the end of Act. II you are right in supposing that Martin wishes to deceive God, his theology — folk-theology — is always vague and he fears that even in Hell God might plague him in some new way if he knew what an unholy joy Martin had found for himself.

As you ask me to tell you something of my life I will try and do so as briefly as I can. I was born in 1871 near Dublin — my father was a barrister and landlord —. I went to various local schools and had private tutors till 1887 when I entered Trinity College Dublin, taking my degree (B A) in 1892. Meanwhile I had given a great deal of my time to music — I took the scholarship of Harmony and Counterpoint in the Royal Irish Academy of Music about the same time — and in 1893 I went to Germany, (partly for a holiday), but I stayed there studying music for nearly a year. I saw that the Germans were so much more innately gifted with the musical faculties than I was that I decided to give up music and take to literature instead. I went back to Germany for a few months to work at the language only, and then on the first day of 1895 I went to Paris for six months. The next year I went to Italy and learned Italian, and then I spent six or seven winters in Paris going back to Ireland for half the year. In 1898 I went to the Aran Islands to learn Gaelic and lived with the peasants. Ever since then I have spent part of my year among the Irish speaking peasantry in various localities as I am now doing once more. I have the MS of a book giving an account of my life on the Aran Islands which Mr Elkin Mathews has promised to publish shortly. During the last 10 years I have written a certain number of short articles and reviews for various papers, but my first real success was with the two little plays — which I suppose you have seen or heard of — 'Riders to the Sea' and "The Shadow of the Glen", which were played in Dublin by our Society and also in London March 1904 where they were very well received. Since then I have given up Paris and give all my time to writing for the little Theatre we have in Dublin. I hope to have another play ready before very long, and I shall be glad to let you see it if you wish.

I am not fond of photographs and I have not been taken for ten years, there, is however a sketch of me by Mr J. B. Yeats — the father of the poet — in the last number of "Samhain"[1] and if you like I will send you a copy when I go back to town in a few weeks.

I shall be interested to hear the decision of the Manager of the 'Deutsches Theater' when he gives it to you, but as I leave here tomorrow for another part of Kerry — the *Iveragh* neighbourhood — it would perhaps be best if you would kindly direct to my address in Kingstown.

I am trying to pass a long wet day in a little country inn so you must excuse me if I have written of myself at too great length and believe me with best compliments

Sincerely yours

J. M. Synge

MS, NLI

¹ *Samhain*, December 1904, included a portrait of JMS by John Butler Yeats, opposite p. 34.

To MME NATHALIE ESPOSITO¹

> Mountain Stage | Glenbeigh | Co Kerry
> Friday [8 September 1905]

Dear Madame Esposito

Your line and invitation for Tuesday reached me last night; as you see I am still on my travels so I must ask you to let me put it off for a week or two till I get back to town. The weather is as bad as it can be now, and as I am writing the water is splashing down through the thatch all round me. If it goes on like this I will not stay out here much longer, as I cannot write or do anything in this sort of place.

In August I was out for a fortnight on the Great Blasket Island off the Kerry coast, and I had a wonderful time there. I slept in a corner of the king's room — there is a king of the island — and his two daughters attended on me — one of them — who was married a few months ago and still lives in her father's house — a curiously charming person. The girls had no English so I had to get on with them as best I could in Irish. Every evening twenty or thirty men and girls used to come up into our house to dance and amuse themselves in the kitchen so that we had great festivities. The worst of that sort of place is that I feel so miserably lonely for weeks after I leave it. Here I am in another peasant cottage but the people are more civilised and they haven't got the peculiar attractiveness of the islanders.

I heard from F Fay the other day that rehearsals are going on again, and I am beginning to feel that I ought to be back at work again myself, but it is a great thing to get clear away and forget all about the Abbey affairs for a month or two in the year. I will feel very 'out of it' when I begin to write again, at present as you must, notise I cannot even write a letter!

> Very cordially yours
> J. M. Synge

MS, Esposito

¹ Madame Esposito, née Nathalie Petrovna Klebnikoff, wife of the composer Michele Esposito and mother of Vera ('Emma Vernon'), had been a strong supporter of the theatre movement from its beginnings; Joseph Holloway (diary, NLI) recalls her serving as wardrobe mistress during rehearsals in December 1904.

To FRANK FAY

c/o Mrs Harris | Mountain Stage | Glenbeigh | Co Kerry
Friday. 8th/Sept [1905]

Dear Fay

I am sorry I have been so long in "answering" your letter, I have had several moves, and in these places it is not easy to get a quiet place to write. I sent you Boyle's play some time ago and I hope it reached you safely. I also wrote Yeats my opinion of it in brief. I have not much more to say of it and I suppose by this time it has · gone through the committee for good or bad. I think it has a good deal of vitality but it is not possible in its present state, though a little revision would make it possible. I have had no news of what took place at the general meeting

There is the most terrible rain going on here now and the thatch is dripping and spashing about my ears, in spite of tin buckets stuck about the floor to catch the drops —

A letter and any news would now be an infinite blessing to

Yours cordialement
J. M. Synge

MS, NLI

To MAX MEYERFELD

Glenbeigh | Kerry
September 12th/05

Dear Sir

I got your very welcome letter a day or two ago, and I am of course delighted with the good news you give me.[1] I need hardly add that I am extremely grateful to you for the kindness of your letter, and indeed for all that you have done. I only hope now, for your sake as well as my own, that it [will] turn out a success on your German Stage. The title you have chosen is, I think, admirable, and you were of course perfectly right to change Bride's name as you have done.[2]

My Christian names are John Millington, my family were originally called Millington, and Queen Elisabeth is said to have changed their name to "Synge" they sang so finely. Synge is, of course, pronounced "sing". Since then they have been in Ireland for nearly three centuries, so that there is now a good deal of Celtic, or more exactly, Gaelic blood in the family.

I hope to get back to Kingstown in 10 or twelve days and as soon as I arrive I will let you know so that you may send me the proofs if it is not too late. As you say there would be no use in sending them out here to Kerry it would take too long.

Now I can only congratulate you in turn for your success in the difficult task of translating my dialect, and thank you once more very warmly for all the trouble you have taken.

With best compliments and regards

Very sincerely yours

J. M. Synge

P.S. My new play[3] is an ironic comedy about a man who kills his father I will send it to you when it is finished as I would only give you a false idea of it if I told you the plot.   J.M.S.

MS, NLI

[1] Meyerfeld wrote on 5 Sept 1905 (TCD) that his translation of *The Well of the Saints* would be produced at the Deutsches Theater in Berlin and would be published 'in a very short time'. S. Fischer Verlag brought it out on 13 Jan 1906, the day after the play opened.

[2] Meyerfeld originally suggested 'Der Wunderquell' (The World of Wonders); the play was produced and published as *Der Heilige Brunnen*. Bride's name was altered to Nora.

[3] *The Playboy of the Western World.*

To W. B. YEATS

c/o Mrs Harris | Mountain Stage | Glenbeigh | Co Kerry
Tuesday [12 September 1905]

Dear Yeats

I have just got your letter, and a very doleful one from F. Fay. I will certainly go up for the meeting as we are evidently in for a tussle[1] — I enclose a line to Lady Gregory telling her that I will go to Coole as suggested and then we can talk things over thoroughly before we go to Dublin. I cannot bring or send you the Tinker MS. I am sorry to say, as I have not got it with me, and I am afraid to set my pious relations to hunt for it among my papers for fear they would set fire to the whole. I can give it to you in Dublin if that will be time enough. I have heard from my German translator to say that "The Well of the Saints" has been accepted by the director of the 'Deutsches Theater' — the first Theatre, he says, of Germany — for production during the coming season. His translation is to be published very soon in Berlin.

So till Saturday

Yours very sincerely

J. M. Synge

P.S. My garments and fine linen are rather dishevelled after 6 weeks in Kerry hovels. I suppose Lady Gregory wont mind!

MS, Berg. *TB*, 80

---

[1] A special general meeting of the Society was called for 22 Sept 1905 to discuss reorganization of the company to protect Miss Horniman's guarantee. At Yeats's request George Russell had drawn up rules for a limited company, but Russell's preference for a limited form of democracy — including a reading committee for selection of plays and a permanent business committee resident in Dublin — caused not only Yeats but the Fays many misgivings.

To LADY GREGORY[1]

> c/o Mrs Harris | Mountain Stage | Glenbeigh | Co. Kerry
> Tuesday [12 September 1905]

Dear Lady Gregory

Yeats tells me that you kindly invite me to Coole for a consultation on our way to the meeting. I will be very glad to go, and, if nothing unforeseen occurs, I will get to Gort at 7.20 P.M. on Saturday. I will leave here before post comes on Saturday and there is no post on Friday so if you have any change of plans to tell me of it must get here by Thursday morning or by wire. I hope you got Gwynne's play[2] all right with my thanks.

A bientôt

> Yours very sincerely
> J. M. Synge

MS, Berg. *TB*, 81

---

[1] Enclosed with the preceding letter.

[2] Stephen Lucius Gwynn (1864–1950), novelist, biographer, poet, travel writer, was MP for Galway City from 1906 to 1919. As secretary of the Irish Literary Society, London, he had been responsible for the company's first visit to London in April 1903, and on his return to Ireland in 1904 he became actively involved in the Irish National Theatre Society. According to Joseph Holloway, Gwynn was among those authors whose plays were rejected by the Society; none, in any event, was produced by the company. He was co-director with Joseph Hone and George Roberts of Maunsel & Co., founded in 1905.

To FRANK FAY

Glenbeigh | Kerry
Tuesday [12 September 1905]

Dear Fay

Many thanks for your letter. I am going to Coole on Saturday and then on to Dublin for the meeting. I have just heard from my German translator that the 'Well of the Saints' has been accepted by the director of the 'Deutches Theater' — the first Theatre of Germany — for production during the coming season. Dont be afeard we'll carry the day still, and be damned to them all.

Yours
J. M. Synge

MS, NLI

To MAX MEYERFELD

c/o Lady Gregory | COOLE PARK, | GORT, | CO. GALWAY.[1]
Monday [18 September 1905]

Dear Dr Meyerfeld

Very many thanks for the MS. which I have just received. I have only had time to look at a few pages yet, but I have read enough to feel the style and method of your translation and I am entirely delighted with it. I will go through it all carefully and send it back to you as soon as possible.

In haste

Yours sincerely
J. M. Synge

MS, NLI

[1] Written on Coole Park stationery, from Lady Gregory's home.

To MAX MEYERFELD

31 Crosthwaite Park | Kingstown | Co. Dublin
September 23rd/05

Dear Dr Meyerfeld

I must ask you to pardon me for the long delay in sending back your M.S. I have just come home and till now I have not had a moment to myself. As I said I am delighted with your translation and very grateful to you for it. There are only a few remarks I have to make as to possible changes of a couple of passages, I make them merely as suggestions for your consideration, and then you can do as you think best —

Act I Mary Doul's first speech. Would it be better (clearer) to say "Am Loch in der Mauer vorbir." I mean does Loch give the sense of 'gap', as definitely an opening in the wall?

p. 22. l. 5 "schwarzen Farbe." Martin means merely the soot and dirt of the forge. To use *Farbe* so definitely when he is just restored seems a little dangerous, and as he recognizes Patch by the colour of his hair and his nick-name, it would perhaps be better to use some phrase such as, "the soot on his face", or the dirt of his face, or head.

p. 24. l. 14 I would be inclined to strike out "*wahrhaftig,*" it seems to weaken the speech.

p. 25. l. 19 "grosszuziehen" 'rear' as used by Irish peasants includes the idea of 'bringing forth,' as well as 'bringing up' and as is shown in Mary's next speech the first idea is really what is in their minds. Could you get a popular word with the two meanings? If not it would perhaps be best to make Martin say that she was never even fit to *have* a child.

p. 26, l. 14 I suppose you use 'Verstand' intentionally instead of Gehirn?

Act II. p. 5. l. 8. Could you insert at the beginning of Timmy['s] speech "*Dunkler Tag?* Es ist nicht wahr u.s.w." I made this addition when the play was performed to emphasize the situation.

p. 11 l. 9. 'nichtsnutzig' has hardly the sense of coaxing, i.e. flattering, wheedling or the like.

p. 12. l. 10. Would it go better without 'wirklich'?

Act. III.

p. 3. l. 17. The literal translation of 'Dying oath', seems a little long and cumbrous for a moment of such excitement. Would it not be better to substitute some terse expression of the same value?

p. 6. l. 20 *Kitty Bawn* means *white Kitty*.

p. 8. l. 9. "Hier in der östlichen Welt." He does not mean here in the east of Ireland, but away in the 'eastern world,' a sort of wonderland very often spoken of in Irish folk-tales.

l. 16 in aller Mund sein, gives a good sense but it is not quite accurate. She means that they will have a good time talking and quarreling with each other as they were doing at beginning of Act I.

p. 10. l. 10. Here again does Loch give the right sense of *opening* in the wall?

p. 16. l. 9. Perhaps Torfkörbe would be better (?)

Well, those are the only points I have to mention and as you see they are none of them important. Sometimes in the translation there is an inevitable loss of terseness, which does not signify in a reading version, but I dare say when the play goes into rehearsal a few words or speeches will have to be cut out here and there. Indeed in our own performances here I made a very few cuts and changes, which I will point out to you when the time comes. Our Theatre Society is going to London in November I believe, and will play the "Well of the Saints," there then, and perhaps also in Oxford.

I am sending you by this post a copy of Samhain which has a drawing of myself, not a very good one I think, still it is better than a photo. I will also send you a copy of the edition of the 'Well of the Saints' with W. B. Yeats' introduction when it comes out, as it might interest you.

With best compliments and cordial thanks

I remain yours sincerely
J. M. Synge

MS, NLI

To LADY GREGORY

31 Crosthwaite Park | Kingstown
Thursday [28 September 1905]

Dear Lady Gregory

I believe Yeats has kept you posted in the way things have been working out since we came up. Everything seems to be going on well but one does not quite know what the company will do at the next meeting. It will be a pity if there is a split bad enough to stop the London visit. I suppose you will come up next week, I think you will be wanted at the meeting, even if things go fairly smoothly.[1] I am trying not very successfully to pick up the threads of my play. It is hard to begin again after such a long holiday. I tried to find out from the Espositos what is thought of OBrien Butler's music, but I did not hear anything very definite. They evidently do not consider him a person of any importance, but I do not think Signor Esposito has ever heard his music.[2]

Yours sincerely
J. M. Synge

MS, Berg. *TB*, 82

[1] At the meeting on 22 Sept 1905 the nationalists were overruled and agreed to the appointment of a committee, George Russell, JMS, and F. J. Ryan, to draw up Articles of Association for the new society, distinguishing it from the original Irish National Theatre Society. On 24 Oct the new Limited Society was registered with Yeats, Lady Gregory, and JMS as the board of directors, W. G. Fay as stage manager, and F. J. Fay as secretary.

² The Irish composer O'Brien Butler (*c.* 1870–1915), whose real name was Whitwell, composed an opera *The Sea Swan* (1903), a sonata for violin and piano on Irish themes, and songs, including the music to Thomas MacDonagh's 'Marching Song for the Irish Volunteers'. Michele Esposito (1855–1929), Italian pianist, composer, and teacher, had been professor of pianoforte at the Royal Irish Academy of Music since 1882 and conductor of the Dublin Orchestral Society since its establishment in 1899; in 1905 he received an honorary Doctor of Music degree from Trinity College. The Abbey directors may have been considering Butler for the post of performer/composer which was eventually filled by Arthur Darley (see p. 170).

To GEORGE ROBERTS

31 Crosthwaite Park
Nov 7th/05

Dear Roberts

I was sorry not to be able to see you on Saturday, but it was my tenth day in bed and I was not able to talk. I am much better now, still letter-writing is rather an effort so I will be very brief — If you are going to publish a full edition, at the ordinary price, of the Aran book, and if you agree to give me 15% on published price from outset, I am willing to let the royalties on the expensive edition be arranged by Mr Gwynne later on in any way that is fair as you suggest —

In that case if you will write to Mr Elkin Mathews for me I would be much obliged as I am hardly able to write to him now and you are in a hurry.¹ Put it to him as nicely as you can explaining how the idea arose, and telling him that I am not well enough to write myself.

How would "Three Islands of the West" do for a title? or "Three Islands of Galway". We shall have to talk over title before we finally decide.

If I do not get stronger quickly I am afraid I wont be able to do the article for you at all for the annual.²

Three or four hours work would put it all right so let me know when it would have to be ready and I will do what I can

Yours sincerely
J. M. Synge

MS (?dictated), Kansas

¹ *The Aran Islands*, published jointly by Maunsel & Co. and Elkin Mathews, did not appear until 1907.

² The newly founded Maunsel & Co. were planning a quarterly journal of Irish writing, *The Shanachie*, under the editorship of Joseph Hone. Each year's issues of this 'Irish Miscellany', to which JMS became a regular contributor, were to be bound as a volume, but there were only six issues (Summer 1906 to Winter 1907). 'The Vagrants of Wicklow', JMS's first contribution (*Prose*, 202), appeared in the second issue, Autumn 1906, 93–8.

To ELKIN MATHEWS

31 Crosthwaite Park | Kingstown | Co Dublin
Nov. 11./05

Dear Mr Mathews

I have been very unwell for some time or I would have written to you sooner about our project for my book on Aran. It has been suggested that the new publishing house in Dublin — Maunsel & Co — should bring it out, and I have thought it best to agree for several reasons. One or two of my plays have made me very unpopular with a section of our Irish Catholic public and I feel it will be a great advantage to me to have this book printed and published in Dublin on Irish paper — small matters that are nevertheless thought a good deal of over here. Then I can get terms here very much more satisfactory than those that you were good enough to offer me. It is nearly two years now since you first spoke of publishing the book, so I dare say you do not feel very sure of its fate, and I am sure you will be just as glad that we should take the risk over here.[1] I have asked Mr Roberts of Maunsel and Co. to write to you about what copies you would like etc. I hope the little plays are going pretty well.

Yours faithfully
J. M. Synge

MS, Lockwood

[1] JMS wrote three drafts of this letter before sending this final version. Earlier drafts (TCD) offered a further reason, 'We are all anxious to make this house a success', and emphasized even more the delay in publication.

To MAX MEYERFELD

31 Crosthwaite Park | Kingstown
Nov. 13/05

Dear Dr. Meyerfeld

Very many thanks for the copy of your translation[1] It looks very nice and reads well. I am very sorry for delay in sending you the list of the 'cuts' I have made. I would have sent them long ago but I have been ill for the last month and unable to do anything. I will send them if possible this week. Our company is to play "The Well of the Saints", at Oxford and Cambridge next week — with some of our other plays — and then in London the week after. It may interest you to know that 'The Shadow of the Glen' has been translated into·

Czech, and is to be played at the National Bohemian Theatre at Prague before long — on the seventh of February I believe.

My new play is not yet finished, this illness I have had has kept all my work back.

I will write again in a day or two with the cuts, but I did not like to let another day pass without thanking you for the translation

Yours sincerely
J. M. Synge

MS, NLI

1 JMS returned this copy of the translation to Meyerfeld; it was not published until the spring of 1906.

To LADY GREGORY

31 Crosthwaite Park | Kingstown
Wednesday [15 November 1905]

Dear Lady Gregory

I hope you got over all right. I have just got an invitation from a Mrs or Miss Gotch at Oxford asking me to put up there, but I am writing to say that you have already arranged for me somewhere else. Is not that so? I hope to go over on Monday — if all goes well. I cannot go sooner as I have got a book to review for the Guardian[1] and I am trying to correct Aran MS. for the press. I wrote to Mathews saying that I had decided to give it to Maunsel but I have had no reply from him yet.

I hope everything is going well, I am getting along fairly.

Very sincerely yours
J. M. Synge

MS, Berg. *TB*, 84

1 JMS's review of A. H. Leahy's *Heroic Romances of Ireland*, vol. I, was not published in the *Manchester Guardian* until 28 Dec 1905 (*Prose*, 371).

To MAX MEYERFELD

31 Crosthwaite Park | Kingstown | Dublin
Nov. 19th/05

Dear Dr. Meyerfeld

I enclose a list of the cuts and stage alterations which we have made in the Well of the Saints.[1] Some of the cuts are very unimportant and I merely made them because I thought the speeches *spoke* more lightly without the words I cut out. In your translation it is hard to say whether the same cuts are advisable or others. I seemed to feel that in the German the first scene of Act II was a little inclined to drag but really these are points on which you and the stage manager who directs the rehearsals will be able to judge much better than I can. Till one gets into the actual rehearsal it is I think better to do as little cutting as possible, then if a speech drags on the stage it must of course be amended. I have not been well enough yet to go into the Abbey Theatre to compare my notes of the cuts with the "prompt book," if I find any more changes in it I will let you know of them as soon as I can. I am going to London and Oxford if I am well enough to see the plays there, but I shall be back here in ten days or a fortnight.

With best compliments
Very truly yours
J. M. Synge

N.B. The cutting of lines 8 to 13. p. 27 I did not think necessary but the stage manager thought they retarded the climax.

MS, NLI

---

[1] The enclosure is now missing.

To W. B. YEATS

31 Crosthwaite Park | Kingstown
Sunday [19 November 1905]

Dear Yeats

Thanks for invitation for tomorrow evening, I will turn up if I get across all right. My neck[1] is much better, but I have been so unwell in my stomach the last few days that I began to fear I would have to drop the trip altogether. However I have decided to start tomorrow for London and if I am not well enough for the Oxford and Cambridge round, I will go out and stay with a cousin in Surrey till you all come back to London.[2] I do not know whether I am wise to go, but I will see if I am better or worse for the day's travelling tomorrow and make my plans accordingly.

Yours sincerely
J. M. Synge

MS, Berg. *TB*, 85

---

[1] An enlarged gland had again appeared in his neck, undetected symptom of Hodgkin's Disease.

[2] Before going to London for the week of 27 Nov, the company were to give two performances in Oxford on 23 Nov, and two in Cambridge on 24 Nov; JMS finally joined them in Cambridge, after staying with his cousin Edward M. Synge, the etcher, at his house at Byfleet, Surrey.

To GEORGE ROBERTS

> 31 Crosthwaite Park | Kingstown
> Thursday [December 1905]

Dear Roberts

Lebeau is doing a rather full article about our work[1] and he wishes to see Yeats' preface to the Well of the Saints. If you have a couple of the lose prefaces still lying about could you let me have one or two of them to send him. I would be greatly obliged.

When do you want to go to press with the Aran book? I am not having the operation[2] at present after all — I am so much better, — so I can get up the MS for you whenever you like. I suppose *five years* would suit you as the term for which you would wish the copy-right?

> Yours faithfully
> J. M. Synge

MS, Kansas

[1] No further article by Henri Lebeau seems to have appeared.
[2] For removal of the enlarged gland in his neck.

To SUSAN MARY YEATS[1]

> 31 Crosthwaite Park | Kingstown
> Thursday [December 1905?]

Dear Miss Yeats

Many thanks for your note and invitation which Fay handed over to me last night. I will very gladly go out tomorrow evening with the players, so please believe me with best thanks and wishes till then

> Yours sincerely
> J. M. Synge

MS, TCD

[1] Susan Mary (Lilly) Yeats (1866–1949), sister to W. B. Yeats, was in charge of the embroidery in Dun Emer Industries and hostess of Gurteen Dhas, Dundrum, the house she shared with her father and sister Lolly; the Abbey Theatre players were frequent visitors.

To W. B. YEATS

31 Crosthwaite Park | Kingstown
Dec. 31st/05

Dear Yeats

I got your letter a day or two ago. I have not been able to get into the Theatre yet, as the weather has been very bad and my cold is still hanging about, though nearly gone. It has not got into my chest which is the great thing. I am to meet Ryan[1] there on Wednesday to see how things are going on, and I will then take over the key. Your proposal about the fifty pounds is I think a good plan, but I doubt that it would be worth while putting the £100 into Deposit till we see how our expenses go when we are touring.[2]

Fay has been out here with your letter about Miss Walker.[3] It is annoying but I think it would be worse than useless to take proceedings. We could only proceed against her, I suppose, for damages for breach of contract, but she has left us a fortnight — from the 28th to the 9th to fill her place, and in any case she can leave us at a month's notice so that we are not in a strong position. The only loss we could sustain would be on our January show the profits of which judged by our last show — the accounts would of course have to be produced — would be nil, and we would be hooted out of court! All the same great capital would be made out of it by the enemy[4] so that we would be considerably more unpopular than ever. On our side meanwhile we have absolutely nothing to gain. If Miss Walker comes back for the month against her will, she will be utterly useless and demoralizing to the rest of our people, while we pay her, her wages for making mischief.

I suppose you feel more than I do that she should be made an example of, but we would be so obviously punishing ourselves more than we could punish her, that we would lose more prestige than we could gain. That at least is how I feel about it, and I am inclined to think that this is a sort of case in which the *three of us* should be of one mind *before* a definite line of action is taken up. Fay is not excited about the matter, but he has some theory that proceedings are out of the question, because she has not actually taken up her contract. That, however, does not sound very convincing. For the rest he is in the best of spirits, and is evidently pleased with the new people he has seen.

He is bargaining with MacDonal[5] and it is better to let him make as good a bargain as he can, for there is no fear of losing the man altogether. If we begin giving 25/d weekly to those that ask it we'll have Miss Esposito asking it before long.

We must be careful not to let our next show clash with the General Election.[6] That would mean another empty week.

Yours sincerely
J. M. Synge

MS, Berg. *TB*, 85

[1] F. J. Ryan continued to serve as liaison between the discontented nationalists and the new Limited Society.

[2] An agreement with the seceders concerning division of finances, costumes, and properties had been drawn up; Miss Horniman had placed all responsibility for the future business transactions of the limited company in the hands of the three directors, and Lady Gregory had been active in the negotiations with Ryan and Keohler.

[3] Mary Walker (Maire Nic Shiubhlaigh) had been undecided about turning professional; see p. 149.

[4] i.e. the seceders.

[5] Francis Quinton ('Mac') McDonnell (1883–1951), whose stage name was 'Arthur Sinclair', joined the company late in 1904 and had rapidly become one of the leading actors. In 1915 he led a mass resignation over St. John Ervine's management of the theatre, and in 1926 became Molly Allgood's second husband, touring with her and Sara Allgood in his own company until they separated.

[6] It took place on 12 Jan 1906.

PART FIVE

1906

*

The Creation of *The Playboy* and a Love Returned

The Creation of *The Playboy*
and a Love Returned

*

ON 9 December 1905 Henri Lebeau wrote from England, 'No doubt you brought away the young girl with the walk of a queen' (TCD). We do not have Synge's reply, but by early 1906 he was sufficiently impressed by Maire O'Neill's performance in *Riders to the Sea* to arrange for her to replace her older sister Sara as Nora Burke in *The Shadow of the Glen*. He conducted their rehearsals himself and, through the speeches of the Tramp, courted her — and won. When he accompanied the players to Wexford on 26 February, his relationship with Molly was apparent to all, and by the time the company made its first extensive tour of England, from 26 May to 9 July, Miss Horniman's tart letters had forced a reluctant Lady Gregory and Yeats to face an embarrassing realignment within the ranks.

Perhaps in part to keep this new relationship from his mother and to enjoy in privacy a love which, though stormy, was returned at last, in February Synge again took rooms in Rathgar. But he was also heavily committed to the theatre, where he increasingly acted as buffer between Yeats's hasty temper and the players, especially those who were uncertain whether to throw in their fortunes with the new limited company or to side with the more comfortable nationalist aims of the seceders. As the only director residing permanently in Dublin, Synge was expected also to handle many of the administrative matters, such as the appointment and training of a new business manager and the year's programming, and to interpret Miss Horniman's demands to an overworked, harassed Willie Fay. Involvement with theatre business reached one of its peaks during the English tour when his services varied between that of advance publicity man and company manager. When he returned on 9 July he moved into the new house his mother had taken in Glenageary, Kingstown, in order again to be near her daughter and son-in-law. While Mrs Synge was in County Wicklow for the summer, he took his meals with the Stephens family, spending as much time as possible walking with Molly in the country.

Synge could now consider himself a playwright of international stature. His plays were receiving critical acclaim in England. In Berlin

Max Meyerfeld's translation of *The Well of the Saints* was produced in January by Max Reinhardt's Deutsches Theater (though not directed by Reinhardt); although the production was not a success, the play was favourably received as a literary work. However, Meyerfeld judged *The Tinker's Wedding* too parochial for a German audience, and returned the manuscript without translating it. More successful was the production in Prague on 7 February of *The Shadow of the Glen*; when the translator Karel Mušek arrived in Dublin on 24 July he brought with him news that the play was to be performed by the Bohemian National Theatre during their regular winter season.

Meanwhile, the writing of *The Playboy of the Western World* continued to be troublesome. Bothered by interruptions at the theatre and quarrels with Molly, Synge took his typewriter and bicycle to County Kerry on 25 August, but spent most of his time there out among the hills and heather writing to his 'Changeling' back in Dublin. His notes — and many of the rhapsodic descriptions sent to Molly — became the basis of a series of articles published the following year in *The Shanachie*, and many of his observations eventually worked their way into his play; but when he returned to Dublin on 12 September, unwell and further distressed by misunderstandings with Molly, *The Playboy* seemed no further ahead.

Recurring bouts of asthma and other bronchial and stomach upsets continued to plague him throughout the autumn, and his work was interrupted not only by demands at the theatre but by family and social responsibilities. His brother Samuel returned to China on 25 October, leaving his mother even more dependent on Synge's company; visiting friends — Jack Yeats and the American poet Agnes Tobin — demanded attention; dealing with Willie Fay's courtship and elopement required time-consuming diplomacy. On 13 October he braved his mother's displeasure by taking his nephew and Florence Ross to the theatre's opening season 'Conversazione', but still delayed confiding in her about his love affair.

He published little this year: two book reviews for the *Manchester Guardian* ('A Translation of Irish Romance' on 6 March and 'The Fair Hills of Ireland' on 16 November), and 'The Vagrants of Wicklow' in the second issue of *The Shanachie* in November. However, proofs of *The Aran Islands* trickled in throughout November and December, and while the anguish of completing *The Playboy* intensified, his love for Molly spurred him to return to poetry.

Finally, after a particularly severe lung infection which kept him housebound for two weeks — forcing Molly to visit Glendalough House for the first time — he packed up his papers once more and went to England. There, he stayed for a fortnight with

Edward Synge in Surrey and made two forays into London. From the safety of his cousin's house he at last wrote to his mother about Molly; and when he returned to Dublin on 14 December, *The Playboy* was almost completed.

To MAX MEYERFELD

31 Crosthwaite Park | Kingstown | Dublin
3/I/06

Dear Dr. Meyerfeld

Has anything been settled about the date of the production of the Well of the Saints? It was very successful at Oxford and Cambridge so I hope it may go well in Berlin where it will also get an intellectual audience also.

Several Germans[1] have asked me to let them translate my little one-act plays, or at least to start negot[iat]ions with them with that object in view. What shall I say to them? You spoke last summer of a possibility of doing them yourself — in which case of course I would give them to no one else. If on the other hand you do not feel inclined to undertake them I would open negot[iat]ions with the others. I do not want to hurry your decision unduly in any way but I would like to hear what you feel about it when convenient. I am hard at work on my new play now — it was delayed by my illness — and I hope also to bring out a little two-act comedy — The Tinker's Wedding — very shortly, which I wrote some time ago but quite forgot to mention to you. We have never played it here as they say it is too immoral for Dublin! There is however some talk of having it done in London before long — though nothing is decided as yet. I am inclined to think it would do rather well in German, in any case if it is published I will have pleasure in sending you a copy. My book on the Aran Islands goes to the press in a few days and is to be published in the spring.

With best wishes for the season
believe me very sincerely yours
J. M. Synge

MS, NLI

[1] Anna Wilke of Königsberg had written several times (TCD) requesting permission to translate and produce one of his plays, other than *The Well of the Saints*, in Germany.

To LADY GREGORY

31 Crosthwaite Park
Friday 5th [January 1906]

Dear Lady Gregory

Thanks for your letter. I have not written till today as there has been nothing definite to say. Yeats and I have been corresponding

rather vehemently all the week but he sent me a humourous and
pleasant telegram last night which I take to mean that he has come
over to our view about the proceedings. Meanwhile I met old Mr
Yeats last night and heard the other side of the story — Miss Walker
is staying with them,[1] so that one can now see pretty well what
happened.

Miss W. was not very eager to come to us — because she is afraid
of the Fays, and their theory is that we are all absolutely in the
Fay's hands! — however she started negotiations with W.B.Y., as I
suppose you know, and all went well till Friday night Dec. 22nd.
That evening I dined at the Nassau with W.B.Y Kettle[2] and Fay.
After dinner W.B.Y. and Fay went to the Abbey T. to meet Miss
Walker and get her to sign her contract, as she had agreed to do,
while I discoursed [with] Kettle. When they came back I thought
there was storm in the air, and after Kettle went, it turned out that
Miss W. has refused to sign on the spot but promised definitely to
sign and send it in before morning. W.B Y. added that this new
vacillation had made him loose his temper with her, for the first
time, and he was rather excited about the whole thing. He thought
she was not going to sign at all and he began planning a vehement
letter that he would write her the next morning when he found the
contract had not arrived. I tried to put oil on the waters but it was
no use. That night I got cold so that I was not in again. I heard barely
that Miss W. had signed and then nothing more till Fay turned up on
the 31st with her resignation. On the 23rd — the Saturday after
her signed contract had come — it seems W.B Y. wrote to her defining her duties as costume woman etc. and apparently the irritation
he felt with her went into the tone of his letter.

Here I only know what Mr. Y. told me last night. He says that
Miss W. told him what was in the letter, word for word, and that it
was very scolding and annoying in tone. When Miss W. got it she
said to herself, "the Fays have turned Mr Yeats against me too. They
are all against me now. I wont have anything to do with them."

I have written all this to let you know how things are, with a view
to future movements towards getting her back. You want her back.
W.B Y. will want her back when it comes to doing verse plays without
her. I want her back. Fay, *for the moment* does *not* want her,
because he is very naturally sick of the whole crew, but he will come
round — can be brought round. For the time being however we'll
all have TO LET THE HARE SIT. Please dont say anything about what
I have written here to W.B.Y. He has given in gracefully and I dont
want it to look as if I was fussing on about the matter.

It is rather serious the way people are misrepresenting all our
doings in Dublin. Mr Yeats had everything by the wrong end and was

quite hostile, but when I explained everything to him, he quite came over and urged me again and again to write out a plain statement of what we had done and send it round to everyone — he added "to Russell for instance." — ! ! !

I don't see that we can do anything but quietly live things down and explain ourselves in a friendly way to anyone we can. There is a whole folk-myth — of the evil spirit type — built up round the Fays. It is funny but extremely inconvenient.

I hope your dance went off well.[3]

Yours sincerely
J. M. Synge

P.S. One moral from the story is that W.B.Y. must not be the person to deal *directly* with the actors, as he is rather too impetuous. In this case it couldn't be helped as she wrote to him, and you were away. If you had been here of course we would have had her all right.

MS, Berg. *TB*, 91

[1] W. B. Yeats's father, John Butler Yeats (1839–1922), was a painter, essayist, and raconteur. The actress Mary Walker was working as an embroidress in the Yeats sisters' Dun Emer Industries at Dundrum.

[2] Thomas Michael Kettle (1880–1916), political essayist and editor of the short-lived *Nationist*, who joined the seceders later this year; from 1906 to 1910 he was MP for East Tyrone, from 1910 the first Professor of Economics at University College, Dublin. When *The Playboy* was published, his was one of the first reviews to praise the play and the playwright's vision (*National Democrat*, April 1907).

[3] As usual, Lady Gregory was acting as hostess over the Christmas season to a large party at Coole.

To JOHN GUINAN[1]

[The Abbey Theatre, Dublin]
[Early January 1906]

Your play has several good qualities, a sort of strength or grit in the dialogue, humour and a sense of character. The central idea, however, is rather thin. The opening dialogue wanders a little, & it is a bad plan to introduce a character, Mrs. Seery, merely for the sake of exposition & then to drop her out of the play. Mat's scene (p. 7 end to 9 beginning) is quite useless & does not help the story in any way. The difficulty of your play as you have worked it is to keep up the interest — to increase the interest — while Timmy is out in the cowhouse, & you have hardly managed to do so. To drop the interest about the second third of a one-act play is quite fatal to its success. Once or twice you use expressions like 'I was never any great shakes in a shindy', which at least in *their associations* are not peasant dialect, & spoil the sort of distinction one can get always by keeping really close to the actual speech of the country people. On the whole, however, your dialect — is it not Kerry dialect — is very good. If you write any more plays we would be glad to see them.

MS (Holloway) fragment, NLI

---

[1] John Guinan (1874–1945), playwright, short-story writer, and civil servant, worked in the same office with George Fitzmaurice, with whom he collaborated on at least one play (*The Wonderful Wedding*). Four of Guinan's plays were eventually produced at the Abbey Theatre: *The Cuckoo's Nest* (1913), *The Plough Lifters* (1916), *Black Oliver* (1927), and *The Rune of Healing* (1931). JMS's criticism of Guinan's *Rustic Rivals* (perhaps an early version of *The Plough Lifters*) was given by W. G. Fay to Joseph Holloway, who quoted it in his diary for 10 Jan 1906 (NLI).

To LADY GREGORY

[31 Crosthwaite Park] Kingstown. Jan. 11. 06

Dear Lady Gregory.

Many thanks for your letters, and the copies that which I was very glad to see. Your letters to Coulum were, I think, exactly what was wanted.[1] I saw his letter last night, and another to Fay in much the same strain. He is hopeless I fear. Fay asked him to come round and talk things over with him (Fay) but Colum says he cannot come "as he has already given too much time to the problem." As he refuses to see Fay, I feel a little disinclined to ask him to meet me, as perhaps he would refuse also. However I will try it presently [as] it seems advisable. I have not consulted the lawyers yet, as everything is still so vague, I will do so of course when there is some clearer issue, if we cannot arrange our *preliminary* matters, as I feel would be best, without them. I have not heard what Yeats thinks of the arrangement I proposed to you, so it is too soon to do anything yet. I do not at all understand about the patent.[2] My memory of what was given in the papers was just what you send me today, but Fay and Miss Hornaman, I think, have since quoted words that are not in it "That Dame Gregory is licensed to carry on a well-conducted theatre ect., etc." and I also understood that they had taken legal opinion on the point that we are independent of the I.N.T.S. for Irish plays and that it was decided in our favour. Certainly the authorities seem to have interpreted it that way, as they have refused to give special licenses for certain 'Lets' on the grounds that our patent covered the performances given, which, however, had nothing to do with the I.N.T.S. That is a point we shall have to have legal advice on before long. I always believed that the Vice P. became members independently of their office and would remain so whether elected V.P. or not. I think that must surely be so, but if elections are made by a bare majority things will become very difficult after next annual meeting so it is important to do what we can now. I think it will be better to wait tall we are all together at next show before attempting anything very definite, but till then of course it is well to get as many points clear in our minds as possible, and to have the various points on which we want advice clearly arranged. If the 'others' have as strong a possition as your copy of the patent seems to show[3] it wotn do to make them finally and firmly our enemies by rash legal proceedings such as asking for an injunction to stop their show.

I felt very much agrieved at the phrase you quot from old Mr. Y's letter.[4] I explained everything to him so fully, it is painful to see him harping back to that ridiculous cry.

Yours sincerely
J. M. Synge

P.S. I think Fay must have correspondence with the lawyer re patent. I will look it up. The second par. of W.BY's letter to Miss Walker[5] was not in copy I saw. I think it was quite right in tone.

'Well of the Saints' is to be played first time *tomorrow* in Berlin.

TS (MS emendations), Berg. *TB*, 108

1 On 9 Jan 1906 Lady Gregory had sent JMS copies of her two letters to Padraic Colum, the first in reply to his appeal for a reuniting of the company as 'a people's theatre', the second after she received news that the seceders had put his play *The Land* into rehearsal (TCD; see *TB*, 102–6). To JMS she expressed concern that the seceders at the next general meeting could vote them out and put in their own vice-presidents in order to take control of the original society.

2 The Warrant for Letters Patent (22 Dec 1904) licensing Lady Gregory (in place of Miss Horniman, who was not an Irish resident) stipulated that 'no play shall be performed until it has been recommended by the Reading Committee [of the original Irish National Theatre Society]' (quoted in full in Peter Kavanagh, *The Story of the Abbey Theatre* [New York, 1950], 213–22). The only reference to officers occurs in the *Rules of the Irish National Theatre Society* (30 Dec 1903; amended 6 Apr 1904): 'The President, Vice-Presidents, and Secretary shall *ex-officio* be members of the Society' (NLI).

3 'The patent shall only empower the patentee to exhibit plays in the Irish or English language written by Irish writers on Irish subjects, or such dramatic works of foreign authors as would tend to interest the public in the higher works of dramatic art; all foregoing to be selected by the Irish National Theatre Society under the provisions of Part 6 of its rules now existing' (TCD).

4 The phrase Lady Gregory quoted (6 Jan 1906, TCD) from a letter of J. B. Yeats (Berg) is 'the mad poet is in the hands of vulgar intriguers.'

⁵ W. B. Yeats's letter of appointment to Mary Walker (TCD), including a final paragraph apologizing for his hasty temper.

To WHITNEY, MOORE AND COMPANY¹

[The Abbey Theatre, Dublin]
[*c.* 13 January 1906]

Letter to W & Mo.

Gentlemen

Mr W. B. Yeats and Lady Gregory are out of Dublin at present for a week but they both join me in asking if you would kindly give information on the following points in connection with the working of the National Theatre Society.

1st. You are doubtless aware that the National Theatre Company Limited has been formed by certain members of the Irish National Theatre Society in the hope of carrying on the work in a more efficient way. A considerable number however of the other members of the I.N.T.S. however has decided for various reasons [not] to take part in the new company. We are now informed that these members are rehearsing one of the plays of the repertoire and intend to play in public as the Irish National Theatre Society This rehearsing and — performance if it takes place — break the Rule [on page] seven of the Rules of I.N.T.S. which reads as follows —² as Mr. Fay , the stage manager, was given no notice of the rehearsals and not consulted. Now we wish to know if we decide that these performances will tend to do us harm in any way [*illegible*] what steps could be taken to restrain them. Would the breaking of rule seven enable us to get an injunction against them for instance if we thought the matter sufficiently serious?

2nd. We understand that the patent gives Lady Gregory power to carry on a well-conducted theatre in the Abbey Theatre, quite independently of the I.N.T.S. except in regard to foreign masterpieces — which it is stated I believe, must be chosen by the reading committee of the I.N.T.S. In the newspaper version of the patent however a clause is given as follows — After speaking of the I.N.T.S. it says the patent shall cease if the Nati[onal] T[heatre] is dissolved. Could you tell [us] if that clause is in the patent, and if so whether the dissolution of the Irish National Theatre Society would endanger our patent.

3. We are most anxious to leave the members of the I.N.T.S. who have not joined the new company perfectly free to go on acting as they seem to desire so long as they do not compromise us or endanger

our patent. If I am right in the reading of the patent with regard to foreign masterpieces do you think it would be possible to draw up some agreement with the old company which would guarantee our rights for the foreign [plays] and the patent, and leave us — who are in New Company free to resign out of the old and continue our work independently. Do you think the following would put us in a safe position. If the Irish N.T.S. would sign agreement to appoint a nominal sub-reading committee which would be empowered to give us or any of Miss Horniman's tenants the necessary authorisation to play any foreign masterpiece we decided to produce. Then if seven of the members would further agree to keep the old I.N.T.S. in legal muster during the serving of our present patent. Then all of us who are in the New company would resign out of the old and leave the members free to carry on their work their own way. A simpler way would of course be for the old members to form a new Society and leave old one to us with the patent, but it is feared they do not wish to adopt this course.[3]

I shall be greatly obliged if you can let me have your opinion on these points. I believe Mr. Yeats will be back in Dublin shortly and then we wish to come to some understanding as the present state of things is unsatisfactory in many ways and confusing for the public.

Yours faithfully,
J. M. Synge

MS (draft), TCD

[1] Whitney, Moore and Company (later Whitney, Moore and Keller) of Dublin were the solicitors for the Abbey Theatre until about 1930.

[2] Clause V(k) of the *Rules* (not copied into this draft) reads: 'Any acting member taking part in any performance other than those given by the Society, shall give notice of such engagement to the Secretary, who shall submit same to the Committee, who shall decide whether or not such performance is prejudicial to the interests of the Society. If, against the decision of the Committee, any such acting member should take part in performances other than those given by the society, the Committee shall have power to suspend any such person from membership until the matter has been brought before a Special General Meeting of Members, whose decision shall be final.' (NLI) The rule was invoked to expel P. J. Kelly in 1904 and would be invoked again in 1908 against the Fays.

[2] The seceders were adamant in their refusal, on political grounds, to give up the name of the Irish National Theatre Society. However, Miss Horniman brought about an agreement, drafted by the end of January 1906, by sending a formal letter to Yeats transferring her gift of the free use of the theatre to the new limited society.

To MACMILLAN AND COMPANY, NEW YORK

[31 Crosthwaite Park, Kingstown]
[*c*. 15 January 1906]

Dear Sir,

I am greatly obliged for your letter of Dec. 22nd which I have just received.[1] Mr. Fisher Unwin to whom you addressed it, sent it by some mistake to [a] cousin of mine so it was considerably delayed

I should be very glad indeed if you bring out my plays or some of them in America I do not gather which but so far I have made no arrangements with Mr. F. Unwin about their publication. He only wrote to me in fact suggesting such a thing a few days ago.[2] I do not know which of my plays you have seen and whether you saw them in Samhain or in the book form.

This is how I stand. Mr. Elkin Mathews has published two of them in one Vol. 'The Shadow of the Glen,' and 'Riders to the Sea' [*illegible*] and Mr. A. H. Bullen has published another, 'The Well of the Saints,' (it may interest [you] to know that this play was [produced] in Germany in [translation]) and by reason of many delays I have not yet finally agreed on all points in our agreement so I do [not] know whether the American rights are in my hands or his.

Meanwhile, I am bringing out another The Tinker's Wedding before long in Dublin and I am at work on another play[3] which I hope to finish in a month or two but with regard to which I have so far made no arrangements with regard to publication. I am inclined to think that the Well of the Saints would be one of the best of them all to try in book form in America so I will find out at once how I stand and let you know. I will also send you if you wish a MS. of The Tinker's Wedding, as soon as it is ready — I have a few trifling alterations to make in it. If you should be inclined to bring it out I would delay publication here so that your edition might be out in time to get me stage copyright in America. 'The Well of the Saints' and The Shadow have already been printed in New York for copyright purposes only.

MS fragment (draft), TCD

---

[1] No letter from Macmillan of around this date exists among JMS's papers. In August 1907 E. Byrne Hackett of Baker and Taylor, encouraged by John Quinn, proposed an edition of the collected plays, but this also came to nothing.
[2] A letter from T. Fisher Unwin dated 3 Jan 1906 (TCD), which may have enclosed the enquiry from America not received by JMS until 14 Jan, expressed interest in any of his manuscripts; I have not found his reply.
[3] *The Playboy of the Western World.*

To MAX MEYERFELD

31 Crosthwaite Park | Kingstown
Jan. 18th [1906]

Dear Dr. Meyerfeld

I am much obliged for your letter, the translation and the News-paper cuttings.[1] I am sorry the play had so little success, I suppose with notices of that kind it has no chance of getting into the other theatres. Will they play it again at the D. Theater? I found here that it grew on people as they knew it better, and many who did not like it when they first saw it at our Theatre, were enthusiastic about it when they saw it again. In any case I can only thank you once more for all the trouble you have taken, and hope for better luck. I have a few changes to make in the Tinker's Wedding then — if you have still any wish to see it[2] — I will be glad to send you a copy of the MS. to see what you think of it. I suppose after Friday's reception of my work you are not likely to translate the one-act plays.

Will the translation of the 'Well of the Saints' be reviewed in your literary papers as *a book*? If it gets any *interesting* reviews I should be greatly obliged if you would let me know of them.

Believe me always
faithfully yours
J. M. Synge

MS, NLI

[1] The translation and cuttings were not preserved; Meyerfeld recalled later that *Der Heilige Brunnen* (*The Well of the Saints*) 'had no success at all. After some six or seven performances — in a bill with Oscar Wilde's "Florentine Tragedy" — it was withdrawn' (*Yale Review*, July 1924, 690).

[2] On 8 Jan 1906 Meyerfeld had written, 'I am very anxious to read the Tinker's Wedding. A comedy, especially if it is "immoral", will always interest the German public.' (TCD)

To LADY GREGORY

[31 Crosthwaite Park, Kingstown]
[26 January 1906]

Dear Lady Gregory

I have a bit of a cold so I will not be in tonight. The German cuttings[1] are hard to make anything out of their style seems so outrageous in translation. I send two fragments as I promised though

I doubt they are much use. If added — or if the first of them is added
to the Era notice it might make a pare.[2]

Yours sincerely

J. M. Synge

[*Enclosure*]

One paper tells the story then goes on: —

Because this is rather long drawn and told in three acts this has been
taken as beginngers work. As if where the still thread of unending
mournfullness spins itself round our hearts, and where brilliant
world-humour is spread over human scenes you must work in the
green-room art of your craftsmen (Handwerker artisans) who measure
out their acts with their watches in their hands.

"Weights and measures must cease where what is immeasurable
and imponderable in poetical origality begins" says Gottschall[3]
from whom you have still something to learn.

Leave this Irishman as he is; if he goes on as he has begun you may
live to hear more of him. He unrolls for us here a piece of the World-
soul, and exhibits with daring strokes a side of human life which lies
close on the borders between tragedy and humour. Yet he holds us
and makes us thrill if a heart still beats beneath our jackets.

'Der Roland von Berlin' critises points in construction such as the
position of strongest point in play — the quarrel and jeering crowd —
in the first act. Then they say

"What gives me a sympathy with this new name is that he does not
go off into sentimentality, that he does not weep and sigh and
coquette with high tragedy. Behind this legend I see a laughing
face; a little moved he looks into it, a little only, then he raises his
eye-brows in irony and laughs again.

Herr Synge may not be a dramatist may not be a great poet but he
has one thing that I like in him, a thing that for many good Germans
is a book with seven seals, that is, Humour.[4]

N.B. I'd like to quote about the 'Humour' but I dont want to tell
Dublin I'm maybe no dramatist. That wouldn't do —

MS, Berg. *TB*, 112

[1] On 20 Jan 1906 Meyerfeld sent him more reviews of the Berlin production;
they seem not to have been preserved.

[2] *The Era* (London), recognized organ of the theatrical profession, published
a report of the cast and production of *Der Heilige Brunnen* on 20 Jan 1906. No
further 'paragraph' (a news item, unlike a paid advertisement) appears to have
been published.

[3] Rudolf von Gottschall (1823–1909), German editor, critic, and author.

[4] JMS has drawn two large question marks across this sentence.

To MAX MEYERFELD

THE NATIONAL THEATRE SOCIETY, LIMITED,
ABBEY THEATRE, DUBLIN.[1]
Jan. 27. 06

Dear Dr Meyerfeld

Many thanks for your letter[2] and the additional cuttings and pictures. I am glad to see that some of them are pretty favourable. Perhaps the book may have a chance after all. I will send you a MS. of the Tinker's Wedding as soon as I can, in a week or two I hope. If it is not giving you too much trouble I wonder if you could send me a couple of programmes of the first show of the "Heiliger Brunen." The Secretary of our Theatre and one or two of our friends are keeping all documents in connection with our work and they would like a programme of the 'Well' at the 'Deutsches Theater' to put with them. It is hardly fair to trouble you about such a trifle, but if you can manage to let us have them I will be greatly obliged.

Very sincerely yours
J. M. Synge

MS, NLI

  [1] Printed letterhead, also listing: 'Directors: W.B. Yeats, J.M. Synge, Lady Gregory. | Stage Manager: W.G. Fay. | Secretary: F.J. Fay.'
  [2] Apparently that of 20 Jan 1906 (TCD); see preceding letter.

To KAREL MUŠEK

31 Crosthwaite Park | Kingstown | Co Dublin | Ireland
February 5th/06

M. Musek!
Dear Sir,

I see by a leaflet sent me some time ago by Mr. Kelly[1] that you are playing my "Shadow of the Glen" in Prague this month. I would be much obliged if you would kindly send me a couple of programmes of your performance, and if I can get German notices in the papers I would like to see a few of them. I have just received copies of the larger edition of the "Well of the Saints" and I will have great pleasure in sending you a copy, if this letter reaches you alright as I am not quite sure that I have your correct address! I need not say that I will be greatly interested to see how my little play succeeds in Bohemia.[2]
Your movement there must, in many ways be like ours in Ireland.

With best compliments
I remain dear Sir,
Yours faithfully
J. M. Synge

MS copy (Mušek), TCD

¹ Richard J. Kelly (1886–1931), barrister and author, J.P. for County Galway, editor and managing director of the *Tuam Herald*, had introduced Mušek to the plays of the Irish dramatic movement while on a visit to Prague (from which city he later received a silver medal for distinguished services). He and JMS do not appear to have met, although they corresponded.

² Mušek replied on 12 Feb 1906, sending copies of reviews of the production of *Ve Stínu Doliny* arranged by the 'Circle of Bohemian Writers' at the Inchover Theatre, Smíchov (a suburb of Prague). 'Your play,' he writes, 'although a little foreign to our people has met with a very good success and will be repeated . . . . For the arrangement on the stage I must thank Mr Kelly, who has kindly sent me some cards with real Irish interiors and types of the people.' He asks permission to translate *The Well of the Saints* or *Riders to the Sea* 'for our National Theatre, for the next winter season' (TCD).

To MAX MEYERFELD

31 Crosthwaite Park | Kingstown
Feb 8th/06

Dear Dr Meyerfeld

I am much obliged for your letter and the Bank-note for ten pounds. I do not know whether a formal receipt is necessary, I enclose one to make sure. I hope to send you a MS. of the 'Tinker's Wedding' very soon

In haste

very truly yours
J. M. Synge

MS, NLI

To LADY GREGORY

57 Rathgar Road | Dublin¹
Feb 16th [1906]

Dear Lady Gregory

Many thanks for MS. of 'Le Medecin.'² I think he is entirely admirable, and is certain to go well. This is just a line to acknowledge the MS. as I suppose I shall see you in a day or two.

My play has made practically no way since as I have been down for ten days with bronchitis and not able to work. My lung is not touched however and I have come off well considering.

I got into the Theatre yesterday and arranged for the advertising. I hope I shall be all right by next week.

Very sincerely yours
J. M. Synge

P.S. By the way I got £10. the other day royalties of five shows of the Well of the Saints in Jan. This morning I had Bohemian cuttings on Shadow of Glen. It seems to [have] done very well.

MS, Berg. *TB*, 113

1 On 6 Feb 1906 JMS moved into rooms in Rathgar.
2 *The Doctor in Spite of Himself*, Lady Gregory's Kiltartan adaptation of Molière's *Le Médecin malgré lui*, which JMS later, according to Joseph Holloway's diary (NLI), praised for its energy.

To LADY GREGORY

57 Rathgar Road
March 1st [1906]

Dear Lady Gregory
    I saw Russell last night. He says Colm, Miss Laird, Starkey, Miss Walker, Roberts, and Ryan, have promised to resign if terms are come to that are satisfactory. There are two difficulties. Roberts will not resign, he thinks, or let his friends resign unless he gets an agreement about the books to *himself personally*, he says that this agreement is the one asset on which his claim to partnership is based.[1] I do not think the point is important enough to make it worth our while to upset negotiations about it. We had best give him an agreement as long as he behaves himself. I entirely agreed with you that Russell had to know about Miss Horniman's move,[2] and told him last night in confidence. He thinks that as they particularly want propaganist plays the move would simply be looked on as an underhand way of refusing them the theatre altogether, and that any hint of such a thing would upset our negotiations once and for all. It is most provoking. I have written Yeats a long letter[3] which he can show to Miss Horniman saying that, I, for my part, refuse to negotiate with the opposition if they are kept in the dark about this point, and that if they are told they will refuse to make terms. If you agree with me you had better write to him to that effect also to strengthen his hand in dealing with her.

Very sincerely yours
J. M. Synge

P.S. Russell and cie will vote us a safe majority before going off if Miss Garvey and F. Walker[4] stay on. He has not seen Koehler yet.

MS, Berg. *TB*, 117

1 On 22 May 1905 Miss Horniman had given Roberts permission (Houghton Library, Harvard) to call the series of plays published by Maunsel & Co. 'The Abbey Theatre Series', with the right to sell the books in the theatre.

² Miss Horniman was demanding the right to see the list of all plays proposed for production in the theatre, including rentals, and refusing to let the theatre for the production of those she considered propaganda.

³ This letter has not been discovered.

⁴ Frank Walker (Prionnsias MacSiubhlaigh) had, like his sister, been a member of Fay's early dramatic society, recruited from the nationalist groups, and chose not to stáy on with the new company; Mary Garvey returned occasionally.

To W. B. YEATS

57 Rathgar Road
March 7th [1906]

Dear Yeats

Every thing will go smothly, if we give Roberts the right to sell books during our shows, and agree that the new society¹ shall be treated exactly as other tenants if they want the theatre. Miss Horniman wrote practically saying she would agree to anything we thought necessary. I have told Russell that she will let to them as to anyone else and that satisfies him. *Now you and Lady Gregory had better draw up a list of* the new Members that are to go in to give us a majority and quorum. Russell and I will draw up an agenda paper of the matters that are to go before the meeting, and he will show it to his friends individually and get their agreement to it. Then at the meeting he advises — I think wisely — that there should be no speech-making what ever. The resolutions can be put one after the other and carried straight off. When can you come over? We cannot play till Easter Week in Dublin (April 16) but I think it would be unwise to let the matter hang on, now that things are agreed on. Heaven knows what new difficulty might turn up in the next five weeks. You might come over to see how Baile's Strand is going, and then we could fix off everything. It would probably be best for you to come the day before meeting so that Russell may not have time to fight with you.

Yours
J. M. Synge

Of course I will send you and Lady G. a copy of agenda paper when it is drawn up.

MS, Berg. *TB*, 118

¹ The seceders eventually took the name The Theatre of Ireland.

To LADY GREGORY

57 Rathgar Road
March 10 [1906]

Dear Lady Gregory

Thanks for your letters. I believe the U.I. attack[1] must be got up by one of the 'Irreconcilables' who wants to have a row and stop our negociations. I agree with you that it is best to take no notise of it. I wrote to Yeats as soon as I saw it advising him not to answer, and I have just heard from him to say that he agrees and will not. So all is safe for the for the moment. I think it is doubly important however to hurry on our arrangements, so I will try and arrange with Russell to-night about drawing up the agenda paper for the meeting. Yeats says he can come over any time after end of next week so I think it is best to face the inconvenience and get it over. The U.I. may say something we shall have to answer and then no one knows what will be the end of it.

Every thing is going well at the Abbey. I have just performed the delicate operation of getting Sara Algood out of Nora Burke's part — where she was impossible — and getting Molly Algood[2] in. Molly A's voice is too young for the part but she feels it, and has some expression.

Russell does not know who is at bottom of U.I. business   He says he will try and find out.

Yours sincerely
J. M. Synge

MS, Berg. *TB*, 119

[1] A leading article in the *United Irishman*, 10 Mar 1906, criticized 'the attempt to convert the Abbey Theatre into "a Theatre of Commerce" ' and quoted a letter (possibly by Seumas O'Connolly) attacking Yeats for abandoning the 'fundamental principle of the original society . . . the development of a national drama'. O'Connolly (Seamus O'Conghaile), honorary secretary of the Theatre of Ireland, was co-editor with James Starkey of the first two issues of the Tower Press Booklets (1906–8).

[2] Molly Allgood ('Maire O'Neill') took over the heroine's role in *The Shadow of the Glen* from her sister, who had inherited it when Mary Walker left the company.

To MAX MEYERFELD

31 Crosthwaite Park | Kingstown[1]
March 10th/06

Dear Dr Meyerfeld

I am much obliged for your letter — there is no hurry about the money you can send it whenever it is convenient. There is a rumour here that the German Company which plays in London are going to do the 'Well of The Saints' there next year[2] and one of Wilde's plays — I suppose The Florentine Tragedy — have you heard anything of it? I suppose they make the same business arrangements as German companies playing in Germany.

I am sorry for delay in sending you 'The Tinker's Wedding,' I have had to revise it a little, and I have had influenza which has kept me back in all my work. I hope to send you the MS. to look at next week if possible. Remember it is a little play written before the 'Well of the Saints' but never played here because it is thought too immoral and anticlerical, my new play in 3 acts will not be finished for some time yet. We hope to play it here in the early autumn.

'The Shadow of the Glen' was played in Prag[ue] in February and seems to have succeeded very well. Please excuse the unavoidable delay in sending MS. and believe me very truly yours

J. M. Synge

MS, NLI

[1] Although he was still living in Rathgar, JMS visited his mother regularly and continued to use her address interchangeably with the Dublin one.

[2] The German Theatre company offered a regular four months' season of classic and modern plays in the Great Queen's Street Theatre, London, from November 1902 to 1907, after a season in St. George's Hall in 1901. On 9–10 Mar 1906 they produced Schiller's *Maria Stuart*, but there is no record of their having ever produced *The Well of the Saints*.

To LADY GREGORY

57 Rathgar Road
March 19 [1906]

Dear Lady Gregory

I got your letter this morning. We were very much taken aback when we heard from Miss Horniman that you were in London, as we had just sent cheques to Coole, and had no money for Dundalk.[1] Fortunately Fay has a few pounds of his own in the bank so we got through on them and some of Horniman's petty cash. It might have been an awkward predicament.

There has been some muddling I dare say you have heard about the circulars. F. Fay does not carry out my directions and does things inspired by his crazy conscience without telling me so that I never know where I am. He is doing so much in a number of ways for his pay that one cannot use any authority and his temper has been somewhat dangerous. Miss Horniman is getting on my nerves too, but the printing is all going out this week and then please God there'll be a respite.

We got a tremendous House in Dundalk — the largest we have ever played to in Ireland — but our resception was not very good. The Pot of Broth, failed absolutely and there was no applause at all when the curtain came down although it was an excellent performance, I never saw Fay better.[2] Demsey just got through with a certain amount of applause here and there and I think an interested house. Kathleen went off best, and Miss Allgood was wonderful, especially in her singing part at the end.[3] A number of people were very enthusiastic about her and the play, but there was hardly any applause at the end, and one did not feel any real enthusiasm (apart from one or two political outbursts) — in the house. The audience was quite different from any we have played to yet, very intelligent, ready to be pleased, but very critical, and, of course, not perfectly cultured — Dr. Bunbury[4] was a favourite! The men who got us down were admirable people businesslike, intelligent, and in a sense really critical. If we can draw there again on the strength of the Saturday show I think we may win Dundalk; they want us down again in May — in the race week, and we should probably go. The Building Fund and Spreading the News, and Riders to the Sea, might get them. I went down on the company's funds I hope with your approval. Fay is evidently anxious that I should do so, as — apart from any help that I can give him — he wants us to feel the difficulties of playing our plays to these country audiences, and also he is afraid I think that if none of us were there we might throw the blame on some careless[ness] of his when there was a failure. I will tell you more about it when you come over.

I am to meet Russell tomorrow night to draw up the agenda; I suppose as it has gone on so long the date you suggested the 7th of April would be as good as another. Last week Russell missed me and I missed him so we did not get it done. However as there has been no further row in the U.I. there is not so much hurry as I feared there might be.[5]

Yours sincerely
J. M. Synge

If you are *not* coming over this [week] before Saturday please let me know in time so that we may send a cheque for signature. Yeats assured me before he left that he had signed a number to keep us going, but when I got the book there was not a signed one!!

MS, Berg. *TB*, 120

[1] The company played for the first time in Dundalk, Co. Louth, on 17 Mar 1906.

² W. G. Fay played the trickster-tramp in *The Pot of Broth*, the one-act farce by Yeats and Lady Gregory.

³ Sara Allgood played the old woman representing the spirit of Ireland in *Kathleen ni Houlihan* by Yeats and Lady Gregory.

⁴ A character in *The Eloquent Dempsy*, played by F. J. Fay; the author of the play, William Boyle, came from Dundalk.

⁵ The meeting with the dissidents appears finally to have been held about 10 Apr 1906.

To MAX MEYERFELD

31 Crosthwaite Park | Kingstown
April [? 7th 1906]

Dear Dr. Meyerfeld

I am extremely sorry for delay in sending you the 'Tinker's Wedding,' I have been revising it ever since, and only got the clean copy last night. So I send it to you now with very many apologies. I may work at it a little more still as in some ways I am not wholly satisfied with it, but it will not differ much from what I am sending you; please let me know when convenient if you think it would have any chance in Germany.

Now I want to ask you about another man. A German gentleman who knows Mr. Yeats is getting up a bill of Irish plays — one-act ones I think — and he wishes to include my 'Riders to the Sea' or "Shadow of the Glen," but I have told him that I would not give him leave to translate them without consulting you, as you had spoken of translating them yourself. What do you feel about it? If the bill is made up and played I would not, of course, like my work to be omitted¹   Please write me frankly your opinion and meanwhile excuse me for my delay and believe me

Sincerely yours
J. M. Synge

Please let me have the MSS. of the T. Wedding back when you have read it as I have to make arrangements for publication etc.

MS, NLI

¹ Evidently Yeats's arrangements with the unknown German did not work out.

To MOLLY ALLGOOD[1]

57 Rathgar Road
Saturday [*c.* 7 April 1906]

Dear Molly

I am going out tomorrow, so, if it is fine, meet me at ten minutes past ten at *Harcourt Street*.

Dont be late

Yours
J. M. Synge

MS (photo), NLI. *LM*, 1

[1] Molly Allgood (1887-1952) joined the company in 1905, playing 'walk-on' parts as 'Maire O'Neill'; as early as December 1905 she was given the role of Cathleen in *Riders to the Sea* by Willie Fay (TCD). Holloway's diary for 27 Jan 1906 reports, 'Maire O'Neill's Cathleen was ever and always attuned to the scene — the pathetic stops in the voice, and subdued demeanour of resigned sadness were present in her interpretation' (NLI). Lady Gregory also wrote approvingly to Yeats of her performance in *The White Cockade* (December 1905, Berg). Not only did she play Nora Burke in *The Shadow of the Glen*, she soon rivalled her sister Sara as leading lady of the company, eventually performing Pegeen Mike in *The Playboy* and JMS's Deirdre. She remained with the company after JMS's death until her first marriage, in 1911, to G. H. Mair. After a second marriage, to Francis McDonnell, she toured America and worked, mainly in London, on the stage and in film and radio.

To LADY GREGORY

ABBEY THEATRE, | ABBEY STREET, | DUBLIN
[7 May 1906]

Dear Lady Gregory

Wareing[1] is very anxious that we should have our properties costumes etc as perfect as possible. But our spinning [wheel] has practically given out so I think we [should] have another spinning wheel if you could perhaps find one down there. It could be paid for out of company's funds. I would like [it if] Miss Allgood should learn to spin so that there may be no fake about the show.[2]

I am just scribbling this to catch the post we hope to see Yeats tomorrow

Yours sincerely
J. M. Synge

MS, Berg. *TB*, 122

[1] Alfred Wareing (1876-1942), business manager for Herbert Beerbohm Tree, undertook the management, his wife assisting him, of the company's first

extensive British tour, from 26 May to 9 July 1906. Wareing was later founder of the Glasgow Repertory Theatre (1909), director of the Theatre Royal, Huddersfield (1918–31), and librarian of the Shakespeare Memorial Library (1931–3).

2 Lady Gregory did find a spinning wheel at Coole, but Molly does not appear to have learned to spin.

To MAX MEYERFELD

ABBEY THEATRE, | ABBEY STREET, | DUBLIN May 14 1906

Dear Dr. Meyerfeld

I received the M.S. of the Tinkers and your kind letter. I am glad to hear your opinion about my 'peasant' plays, though naturally I do not share it.[1]

I am afraid there is no chance of my being in London this season. Our company however plays in Cardiff on the 28th of this month and week following then a week in each of following towns Glasgow, Aberdeen Newcastle on Tyne, Edinburgh and Hull ending the 7th July. If you could arrange to see any of our shows it might interest you. My two one-act plays are to be given in each town. I shall be going round myself also but probabl[y] a little before the company.

Yours sincerely

J. M. Synge

MS, NLI

1 Meyerfeld had written on 13 Apr 1906,
I need hardly tell you that there is no chance whatever for this comedy in Germany. It is too undramatic and too Irish — in fact, no one in this country would understand it . . . . I should like to ask you why you stick to Ireland. Ireland is not the world, and it seems very doubtful to me whether you will ever be able to conquer the world by dealing exclusively with Irish peasants . . . you must give up this speciality if you want to preserve your name and fame. (TCD)

To MAX MEYERFELD

Cardiff
May 28th [1906]

Dear Dr. Meyerfeld

Many thanks for your kind letter.[1] I am extremely sorry that I cannot get to London to see you. Could you not come to Newcastle-on-Tyne, on the 18th of June, or to Edinburgh on the 24th and see our company and our plays and myself. I should be extremely glad to make your acquaintance personally. I hope my new play may be finished during the summer but of course this tour delays me.

Very sincerely yours
J. M. Synge

MS, NLI

---

¹ Meyerfeld had written from London, 23 May 1906, again urging JMS to let him translate *The Playboy* when it was finished, adding, 'please keep in mind that you are not only writing for the Irish National Theatre, but the German stage also expects very much of you' (TCD).

To KAREL MUŠEK

Kings Theatre | Glasgow
June 2nd/06

Dear Mr Musek

I beleive in the hurry of getting off on our tour I have forgotten to answer your kind letter.¹ I am much obliged for all the trouble you are taking with my work, and I hope "The Well of the Saints" may be found suitable for your National Theatre. I sent you a booklet the other day with an account of the plays we are doing on our present tour.² We play here in Glasgow next week, then a week in Aberdeen and three more in NewCastle-on-Tyne, Edinburgh and Hull, ending our tour on the 7th of July when we go back to Dublin. If you can come to Dublin then we shall all be delighted to see you. Mr Yeats and Lady Gregory would like to make your acquaintance also so please let us know in time when you are coming over, and we will do all we can to show you what is most interesting in this country. Perhaps you could come down to the west of Ireland for a while with us, it is much more interesting than Dublin. *Please write to me* at the 'Abbey Theatre, Abbey Street *Dublin.*

With best wishes hoping soon to see you very cordially yours

J. M. Synge

P.S. Please let me know *as soon as you can* what time you are likely to come to Ireland.

I was much interested to see your translation of Shaw.³ Many thanks for it.

MS, Berg

---

¹ Mušek had written on 21 May 1906 reporting that the manager of the National Theatre in Prague (perhaps G. Schmoranz, see p. 181) felt *Riders to the Sea*, which Mušek had translated, was 'highly characteristic, but for our people

a little too sad. Especially as we have played two years ago the Hollandish Drama "Hope", which is also taken from fisherfolk's life. However, I am translating the first act of "The Well of the Saints" . . . . My opinion of it is that it will suit our people; only it needs some abbreviations in the 2nd and 3rd acts.' (TCD)

2 *Irish Plays by Mr W. B. Yeats, Mr J. M. Synge, Mr Wm. Boyle and Lady Gregory Toured under the Direction of Alfred Wareing. Summer, 1906,* a 12-page illustrated brochure (reprinted in *TB,* 316).

3 With his letter of 21 May, Mušek enclosed his translation of *The Devil's Disciple,* which has since disappeared.

To LADY GREGORY

Glasgow
Saturday [9 June 1906]

Dear Lady Gregory

Thanks for your letter. We wrote 3 weeks ago for particulars about the hall at Longford[1] and their answer came yesterday evening. There are some difficulties Fay thinks about the size of our stuff but I have not had an opportunity of talking it out with him, yet, and I will hardly get him to day as he will be on his head with the two shows. We are distinctly a success in Glasgow we had £38 in the house on Wednesday and Thursday, and £41 last night

Things however are not going very smoothly. Mrs Wareing as I suppose you heard went off to London and they got down a Mr Bell[2] to replace her, a profundly self-satisfied and vulgar commercial man, that none of us can abide. He got Miss H[orniman] more or less into his hands, and at last she sailed round to Fay one evening just before the show to suggest that Bell should 'make up' the company. Fay broke out forthwith, and she describes her exit as that of "a strange cat driven out of a kitchen with a broom-stick"! She complains pathetically to me that everyone knows in Glasgow that she is paying for our show, and that she feels in rather a foolish position when she has to confess that she has no authority over it!! We will have to be very careful indeed about our next steps. I am not writing much to Yeats while he is with Miss Horniman he is so careless about his letters.

Fay is as uncertain as ever. One day he says we must go back for five more years work in Ireland before we try big tours [again], the next day I can see that he is hoping against hope that Minshull[3] will offer us a date here next winter. It is natural enough I suppose that he should go up and down as our prospects change. If we are to tour much we will have to get a business man who is one of ourselves, and who arranges with us, otherwise we'll soon be known as Miss Horniman's company. I think we shall be able to add Glasgow and

Edinburgh to our list of safe towns. There is very great interest taken in our work here now, for instance they have sold 52 copies of 'Riders to the Sea' in the last two days.

Fay says he cannot get up new pupils for the Hour Glass and rehearse it for the Longford Show. I think we had better give them Kathleen.

My address next week will be, 'Her Majesty's Theatre', Aberdeen. I have got out of the advance work and let Wareing go on ahead this time. It is all very well to go round with him if he wishes, but I objected strongly to doing the hack advance work alone fagging round with the little books to reporters and booksellers. I told Miss Horniman I thought it was a mistake from a business point of view to set one of the authors and directors to such work so I got off. I am far more use in the town while the plays are running.

Sincerely yours
J. M. Synge

Darley[4] has a cold and is rather alarmed about himself I hope he wont break down.

MS, NLI. *TB*, 127

[1] The company played in the Temperance Hall, Longford, on 12 and 13 July 1906.

[2] John Jay Bell (1871–1934), Scottish dramatist whose plays in the Scots vernacular were produced by Wareing's Glasgow Repertory Theatre, 1910–23.

[3] George T. Minshull, general manager of the Royal Lyceum Theatre, Glasgow.

[4] Arthur Darley (1873–1929), who had studied at the Royal Irish Academy of Music with JMS, joined the company as performer, between plays, of traditional Irish music. Although he did not perform regularly with them after this tour, he was occasionally heard as soloist in Dublin and London, and composed incidental music for some of the plays, including *The Gaol Gate*, Yeats's *Deirdre* and the revised *Shadowy Waters* (all 1906), and W.S. Blunt's *Fand* (1907).

To W. B. YEATS

c/o Mrs Wood | 2 Reed Street | Hull
July 2nd [1906]

Dear Yeats

The posters have been printed and are to go to the Bill Poster from Healy's[1] today. Our stuff will not go into the Hall so we have to take our new 'fit-up' and stuff. Shawn's[2] brother I believe is working at it, and Fay says he will be able to have everything ready in time. Can Miss Darragh get a girl in Longford to come on as second keener in

Riders to the Sea" so that we may leave Miss E. O'Demsey behind. I think it would be much better not to take her with us. Will Miss Darragh look after the front of the House? — I mean keep her eye on ticket sellers check takers etc. —[3]

I do not quite know how the company are acting, everything is done accurately but I sometimes fancy they are getting a little mechanical from so much playing of the same pieces to poor audiences. — In Dublin the continual change of programme keeps them up to the mark. — However a number of people in Edinburgh — Mrs Traquiere — if that is how you spell her — Paterson, and others[4] were so entirely carried away by our shows that there is no doubt our people are doing well if not always at their best. W. G. Fay by the way is not good, just now as he is too much occupied with his love affair.[5]

The Hour Glass is to be rehearsed here this week, and the Longford programmes are in hand. We cannot I suppose put in the children's names as we do not know who they will be. Frank F. thought Annie Algood[6] was to speak the children part. Poor Frank is in terrible dispair wondering what he will do with himself when the tour is over!!!

Yours
J.M.S.

MS, Yeats. *TB*, 129

[1] Hely's Limited, stationers of Dame Street, Dublin.

[2] Seaghan Barlow (1880–1972), stage carpenter and scene painter at the Abbey from its opening; his reminiscences were published in *Ireland's Abbey Theatre: A History*, ed. Lennox Robinson (1951), 69–76.

[3] Letitia Marion Dallas (stage name 'Florence Darragh'; d. 1917), an Anglo-Irish actress who became a member of the first repertory company at the Gaiety Theatre, Manchester, and later founded the Liverpool Repertory Company. James Agate described her performances as 'storehouses of treasure rather than living-rooms for a soul' (*Manchester Guardian*, 14 Sept 1909). She had apparently offered through her friend Miss Horniman to organize the touring in the Irish country towns. Eileen O'Dempsey, younger sister of Brigit (Anna Bridget) O'Dempsey, a member of the company, had been hired for the tour against the better judgement of the directors.

[4] Phoebe Anna Traquair (1852–1936), née Moss, daughter of a Dublin physician, studied at the Dublin School of Art before marrying Dr Ramsay Traquair, Keeper of the Natural History Library in Edinburgh, in 1873; she was best known as a muralist and illustrator, Yeats comparing her best work to that of Charles Ricketts. For James Paterson RSA (1854–1932), see p. 277.

[5] With Brigit O'Dempsey; see p. 172.

[6] Johanna (Annie) Allgood, younger sister of Sara and Molly, occasionally performed small parts for the company.

To LADY GREGORY

Hull
Wednesday [4 July 1906]

Dear Lady Gregory

I saw your letter to Fay last night, and he has talked his letter to Miss H. over with me.[1] I fear, however, his apology will have little effect — though it is well of course for him to write it — as she seems to have taken a regular craze against him. She has raked up every bit of unwiseness and carelessness that he has been guilty of in the last two years, and is so excited about it that I do not see any possibility of things going back to what they were before. I had no idea in Glasgow that the matter was so serious — neither Fay nor she seemed to make much of it — but as soon as I went to see her in Edinburgh the whole thing came out. She tells me in a letter I got yesterday that she has written to you fully as to the 'deadness or rather absense' of the acting at present, but I think there is no real falling off. We made as good an impression in Edinburgh — *with the right people* — as we have ever done anywhere. I have asked Fay to show you Mrs. Traquair's letter[2] and some others that will show you that things are not going badly. On the other hand there is no doubt that Fay is almost wicketly careless about everything. I am afraid that Miss O'Demsy will not improve him[3] — this of course is very much between ourselves — with Miss Harrison[4] and Russell he was always dealing with worthy ideas that gave him a sort of dignity, but now between the two O'Demseys I dont feel so sure about him. It is extraordinary how those two girls have lowered the tone of the almost the whole company. Bridget O.D. by the way has greatly improved in her acting but she is one of the most silly and vulgar girls I have ever met. The Bohemian man is coming to Ireland about the twentieth of July. Am I to tell him that you invite [him] to Coole or would it be better to wait till we see him?

Yours
J. M. Synge

MS, Berg. *TB*, 130

[1] Miss Horniman sent a series of letters to Yeats and Lady Gregory (NLI) expressing her increasing dissatisfaction with the behaviour of the company in general and Fay and Synge in particular; she was increasingly distressed also by Willie Fay's 'unbusinesslike' attitude towards accounts.

[2] Mrs Traquair had written to a friend in Edinburgh praising Sara Allgood's Maurya in *Riders to the Sea*: 'She was outside, station, time or circumstance an eternal thing. All the plays were delightful.' (Berg)

[3] Brigit O'Dempsey's romance with Willie Fay was a further source of irri-

tation to Miss Horniman; the girl's father, a Wexford lawyer, disapproved of the match.

4 Possibly the artist Sarah Cecilia Harrison (*c*. 1864–1941).

To W. B. YEATS

Hull
Saturday [7 July 1906]

Dear Yeats

I am glad to gather from your letter that you are going to Longford so that the care of the company will be for a while off my shoulders.

Fay wrote to Miss Horniman at Lady Gregory's wish. He showed me his letter in the theatre. I did not think it very good but I let him send it as I did not really know what he was to say. I did not tell him much of what Miss H. said to me as I thought she did not wish it. The way she speaks about the company's work in her letter to the directors is MOST ABSURD.[1] She is simply repeating what Wareing and *Co* have been saying and his quarrel with us really is that we are not stagy. Our our kind of people as I said are as enthusiastic about our work in Edinburgh as they have ever been. Paterson, the artist, gave the three girls bouquets in Edinburgh this day week. Miss O'Demsy has taken to starting conversations out of our window with bystanders during our journeys, but it is nothing very serious. I was going to speak to Fay about it today but after all the irritation about Miss H. I think it is better to let things stand. Fay and Miss O'D. will flirt till they are married dont make more of the matter than it deserves unless you want to please the mischief makers and make a permanent split with with Fay.

The Australian is most enthusiastic[2] and says we have a *splendid* company

J. M. Synge

MS, Berg. *TB*, 132

1 Miss Horniman sent a three-page typed letter of complaints to all three directors on 4 July 1906 (Yeats), offering 'Home Rule' and a £600 annual subsidy, adding that she would give further financial assistance when required but only for performances at the Abbey, and advising them not to consider touring again until 'the whole company are competent and the management adequate'.

2 Leon Herbert Spencer Brodzky (later Brodney; 1883–1973), journalist and playwright, founder in 1904 of the Australian Theatre Society, Melbourne. He published 'The Lesson of the Irish Theatre' in *The British–Australasian* (9 Aug 1906) and 'Towards an Australian Drama' in *The Lone Hand* (1 June 1908), based on his interviews with Yeats and JMS and three performances he attended in Hull.

To KAREL MUŠEK

Glendalough House | Glenageary | Kingstown | Co. Dublin[1]
July 12 [1906]

Dear Mr. Musek,

I am delighted to have got your letter[2] and to hear that you are coming over at last. I am just back from our tour so next week will suit me admirably. I will be delighted to call on you say at 12 o'clock on Tuesday wherever you are staying if you will let me know by telegraph or post card. If you are going to a hotel the Nassau Hotel Nassau Street is a small, moderate hotel where we have often stayed,[3] which might suit you. It is temperance however, i.e. there is nothing in the way of drinks. I am sorry I cannot invite you to stay with me but my people and the servants are all away in the country.[4] Please let me know where I am to call on you and believe me very truly yours

a bientôt
J. M. Synge

MS copy (Mušek), TCD

[1] JMS had moved with his mother to Glendalough House, which was near the new home of his sister Annie (Mrs Harry Stephens) in Silchester Road, Glenageary.
[2] Of 12 June 1906 (TCD), enclosing a programme announcing performances of *Ve Stínu Doliny*, 16–24 June 1906.
[3] Both Yeats and Lady Gregory regularly stayed at this hotel.
[4] Mrs Synge was in Co. Wicklow from 3 July to 6 Sept 1906 with her son Samuel and his family.

To LADY GREGORY

Glendalough House | Glenageary | Kingstown
July 12th [1906]

Dear Lady Gregory

I have just heard from Musek, the Bohemian, that he is to be here on Tuesday next

I saw Yeats yesterday and had a long talk over affairs. The only thing to be done is obviously to find out exactly what money we are to have and then arrange our expenses accordingly for the next four years.[1] I feel very bitter indeed against Miss Horniman, for the way she sided with this gang of busybodies and todies against us. I do not feel at all anxious to pin my career to her money. I feel inclined to fight it out here for ourselves and if we fail I'll go and live the rest of my natural life with the king of the Blasket Islands

Yours sincerely
J. M. Synge

MS, Berg. *TB*, 133

¹ Miss Horniman's patent for the theatre was granted only until 1910.

To LADY GREGORY

Glendalough House | Glenageary | Kingstown
July 13th [1906]

Dear Lady Gregory

Thanks for your card and invitation which crossed my letter of yesterday. I am afraid as I have promised to meet the Bohemian here on Tuesday I cannot go down tomorrow. After all there is nothing very urgent to settle as I do not see that we can make great changes at present. I am sorry of course not to be able to join the council of war at once, but in his way, Musek may be useful to us so I think I had better not run away just in front of him. How long does Fay stay with you?

Yours sincerely
J. M. Synge

MS, Berg. *TB*, 134

To LADY GREGORY

Glendalough House | Glenageary | Kingstown
July 14th [1906]

Dear Lady Gregory,

I find that I have mistaken our friend the Bohemian and that he is not coming till Tuesday the 24, so if I am needed for your consultations I could go down on Monday afternoon, and get back in time to take care of Musek. Perhaps Yeats would like to talk the matter out before he settles to his work.

If you think it would be well for me to go down at once — and if it still suits your arrangements — please let me have a line or wire on Monday morning and I will go by afternoon train. I am very sorry to have bothered you with so many contradictory letters. I hope Longford has been a success

Yours sincerely
J. M. Synge

MS, Berg. *TB*, 135

To MOLLY ALLGOOD

Glendalough House | Glenageary | Kingstown
(Monday) [16 July 1906]

Dear Molly

I saw Frank Fay today and heard from him that you had come back to Dublin instead of going to Sligo, and that you had gone now to Balbriggan[1] for a week. I have been wondering what had become of you it seems strange that you would not send me a line to tell me where you were. If I had known you were in Dublin I might have seen you on Saturday. I go down to Lady Gregory's tomorrow morning for a week and then come back here to meet the Bohemian who is to arrive on the 24th. I hope I shall see you then before I set off again. I hope you are enjoying yourselves, I have been dull enough these days here.

I was at the Espositos last night they are full of the Trinity Show.[2] This address will always find me.　　　　　　　　Yours ever

J. M. Synge

P.S. I wonder if this will find you?[3]

MS, TCD. *LM*, 1

[1]　A small coastal resort 22 miles north of Dublin.
[2]　During the week of 25 June 1906 Vera Esposito received favourable reviews as Lydia Languish in the Trinity College Amateur Dramatic Club production of *The Rivals*, at the Queen's Royal Theatre, Dublin.
[3]　Molly has written 'Idiotic' across the top of the letter.

To MOLLY ALLGOOD

Glendalough House | Glenageary | Kingstown
July 19th [1906]

Dear Molly

I have come back as I had nothing more to do at Gort when we had once arranged everything. I enclose a fragment of a letter I began to you last Thursday. I got your card this morning forwarded to Lady Gregory's before I left. I asked you not to send me post cards to avoid gossip please dont do so next time. Did you get my other letter. I heard accidentaly of your walking arm in arm with Wright at Longford. Is that true? Please let me know when you are coming back to Dublin. The Bohemian comes next Tuesday I believe.　　　　　　　　Yours ever

J. M. Synge

[*Enclosure*]

July 12th

Dear Changling

I suppose you are getting into Longford by now, I've been feeling very lonesome all the morning thinking of you posting away over Ireland without me. I had a lot to say to you yesterday before you went off but I couldn't get an opportunity. It doesn't much matter however as you know all I had to say. The Bohemian man Musek, is his name is coming here on Tuesday, and then I suppose I'll go to Lady Gregory's for a while but after that I dont know yet where I'll turn to. I am writing this on the chance of getting your adress but I wouldn't be surprised if you've forgotten mine. I've just written five letters so I'll write no more to you now

MS (photo), NLI; encl. MS, AS. *LM*, 2

To MOLLY ALLGOOD

Glendalough House | Glenageary | Kingstown
Thursday night [19 July 1906]

Dear Changling

Why dont you write to me? We have not seen each other for ten days and I've had nothing from you but a few wretched lines on a post card. It makes me imagine all sorts of things when you are so queer and silent. I have a lot of things to tell you about my talks with Lady Gregory and Yeats but I will let that wait. Also ⟨about⟩ the story about Wright which came out at a moment and in a way that was peculiarly painful and humiliating to me. Why — However I did not start this letter to scold you as I'm better again though I have been more distressed about it than I can say.

I think I am going to stay about Dublin for the present and finish my play so I may see a good deal of you this next while, when you come back and the Bohemian goes. When my play is finished I'll go off myself for a while; I think to the Blasquet Islands.

I came up with Fay yesterday and he, I think, went to Enniscorthy in the evening. He got influenza or something at Gort and was ill for two days. We have arranged the affairs of the company satisfactorily on a new basis and everything is going to be much more regular and orderly than it has been so far. That is our only chance.

Friday morning

I have got your letter at last — and I am much better. I think about you a lot indeed I'm nearly always thinking about you in one way or another, but my thoughts aren't always pleasant ones as Cardiff[1] and other incidents come up in spite of me. I'm glad to hear that you are lonesome its very good for you. I wonder in the end if you will stay out there a week or a fortnight. I thought I heard some of them saying that Lady Gregory was sending Sally the money she had lost.[2] *Dont say* anything about it, of course, unless it comes. I am longing to have a good walk with you again, but of course you should stay on the fortnight if you are able. I shall probably be very busy next week with the Bohemian. Is Wright at Balbriggan too as he met you at the station?

I am sending you one of my photos, not one of the good ones, as one has gone to an Australian paper, and I am giving the other to my nephew[3] to photograph again. I'll give you a better one when I get it. You dont seem to have got the letter I sent to your Dublin address on Tuesday, but it doesn't matter as there was not anything in it. I am afraid the letter I wrote you yesterday wont have made you happier, so I am sending this off early to cheer you up. You see I began it last night as I had begun to relent.

I dont know whether I shall stay here to work at my play, or get lodgings somewhere. It is not very convenient here as I have to walk a quarter of a mile to my sister's for every meal, and one gets tired of it. Now good bye to you and be good and lonesome and write to me again at once if you want another letter as much as I do.

Your old Tramp alias Dan Burke!

MS, TCD. *LM*, 3

[1] Apparently the scene of one of their first major quarrels, while on tour.
[2] Molly's sister Sara, who was with her in Balbriggan, was known for her carelessness about money.
[3] Probably Frank Stephens.

To MOLLY ALLGOOD

Glendalough House | Glenageary | Kingstown
Friday night [20 July 1906]

My dear little Changling

I am writing this to you in my bed at one o'clock as I am not able to sleep and I wont have time to write to you tomorrow as I am going to Wicklow to see my old mother. I got your second letter this evening. It seems to have been a different occasion of walking with Dossy Wright that I heard of — some time when he had B[rigit] O. D[empsey] on one arm and you on the other — so I was more hurt

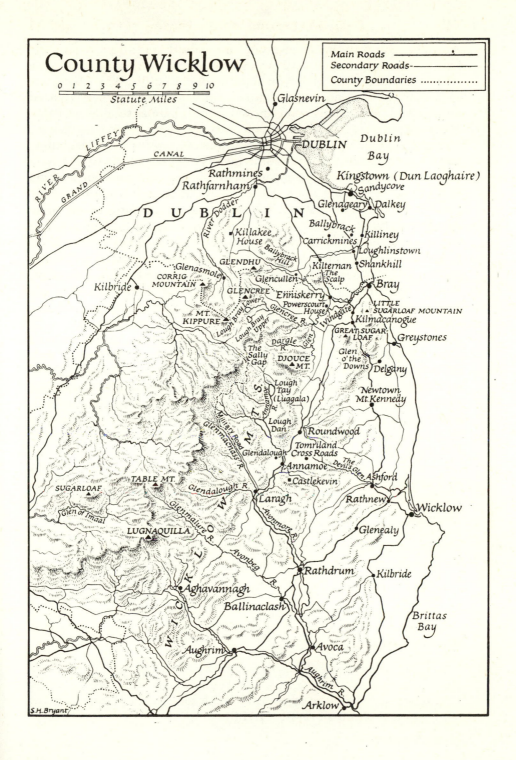

County Wicklow

Main Roads ——————
Secondary Roads ———————
County Boundaries ················

0 1 2 3 4 5 6 7 8 9 10
Statute Miles

S.H.Bryant

than ever. As for your excuse you are as well able to keep on your feet as any one I know, and even if you weren't a sprained ankle is a trifle compared with what you have made me suffer. Why I have felt the whole thing so much is of course, that it seems as if you have been doing all the little things you know I cannot bare as soon as ever you get away out of my sight. Dont you want me to have full trust in you, changling? Dont you know that a suspicious love is more degrading than ennobling? and yet everytime just as I am beginning to trust you fully − I always trust you in one sense − you do some foolish thing that upsets everything again. However let us drop the matter for the present We are fond enough of each other, I am sure, to get these things right by degrees. I had a long ride today up by the lower end of Glen Cullen and Kilternan (where we once walked from Carrickmines). It was a very beautiful day here with a wonderful lustre in the sky and a clear blue sea. I read your little letter up there in the hills and I felt over-joyed that I have got you. I have had a lot of trouble and lonesomeness in my life, changling, and for God's sake dont dissappoint me now. Perhaps you think I am too strict, but it is really only a little outer dignity and loyalty that I ask you for beyond what I have got already. These little loyalties are not unimportant as they are a part of the courtesy and therefore of the comeliness of love, and unless love is kept courteous and comely it looses its 'humaness' and cannot be trusted to last through life. Polished wood wont rot, and it is the same with polished love. Surfaces are not important in themselves but if the surface goes the heart rots −

This is d——ly philosofical but it's a roundabout way of saying you must see Dossy hanged before you take his arm again. Dont imagine that I'm trying to copy your handwriting, but I've a cramp in my back and my hip's asleep on me from writing sideways with my paper on my pillow. By the way dont think that I signed myself 'yours *etc.*', mine was 'yours *ever*', a very different story!

The cocks are crowing themselves hoarse under my window so I'd best ring down the curtain and have a sleep

Believe me
my worthy changling
Yours fervently
J.M.S.

Is that any better?

P.S. Saturday morning. I am to meet Musek the Bohemian on Tuesday at 12 o'clock so I dont know yet when we'll be able to meet. I need not say it will be as soon as I can manage it. I hope you got my letter and photo all right.   J.M.S.

MS, AS. *LM*, 6

To LADY GREGORY

Glendalough House | Glenageary | Kingstown
July 24 [1906]

Dear Lady Gregory

I have been with Karel Musek all day today and I like him. He will go down to you on Friday by the nine fifteen train. He asked if he should write to you but I told [him] I thought he need not mind as I would let you know. He brought me a very aimiable letter from his director[1] telling me he was going to do the Shadow of the Glen in their National Theatre next winter.

I have recommended Musek, 'Kathleen' and 'Spreading the News'. You should read him the latter when he is with [you]. I have promised that you will show him the inside of a real cottage in the West as they want to reproduce one exactly for our plays. They have £12,000 a year *and* all scenery and light from the government so they can afford to do things well. I have had a lot of interesting talk with him about the working of their pay system etc, and learned some things that may be useful to us by and by.

I had a good journey up the other day with Fay and I have [been] toying with my play ever since but have not made much way. When I pass on Musek I will begin in earnest. Please remind Yeats not to disparage acting qualities of the 'Well' as they talk of doing it too!

Yours sincerely
J. M. Synge

MS, Berg. *TB*, 135

[1] G. Schmoranz, director of the Theatre Royal, the National Bohemian Theatre in Prague; his letter in French is dated 15 July 1906 (TCD).

To MOLLY ALLGOOD

Glendalough House | Glenageary | Kingstown
Tuesday [24 July 1906]

Dear Molly

Will you and Sally come to the Abbey about 4.30 on Thursday to meet Karel Musek the Bohemian. I am going to ask F. Fay and Darley to come in too. He wants to hear the keen and see some of our Aran dresses etc.

He brought me a most flattering letter from his director calling me chèr maître — (dear Master) and telling me he is going to put on the 'Shadow' next winter in their regular repertoire at the *National Theatre* — which will mean royalties! Musek himself is going to do

Micheal Dara. They have £12,000 from the government to play with and all scenery and light, so they can afford to do things well!

Could you and Sally bring in means of making tea and cakes *at my expense* on Thursday? If its a bother dont mind and we'll let him starve, if it isn't perhaps you might tell Mrs Martin[1] we're coming, so that she may have clean cups!

I hope you weren't *too* tired after your walk, and that you got home safe. We had a great day!

Yours ever
J. M. Synge

MS, Texas. *LM*, 7

---

[1] Mrs Catherine Martin acted as Abbey Theatre caretaker from its opening. Her reminiscences were published in *Ireland's Abbey Theatre*, 67–9.

To MOLLY ALLGOOD

Glendalough House | Glenageary | Kingstown
July 27th [1906]

Dear Molly

Saturday and Sunday are bad days for the country now so I think we wont go out till Monday or Tuesday. I'll write you a line again to fix the time. Please let me know what I owe for the tea, it was very nice. I liked your dress very much, but I'm not quite sure of the hat. It is very smart and becomes you, but I'm inclined to think it is just a shade too fly-away. I'll make up my mind when I see it again. I wish you'd write me a line to keep me going till we meet. I'm trying to work but I'm unsettled and I'm not making way with anything. If I dont make way next week I'll go off to the west maybe and rest myself. I must go sooner or later so it would be as well to get it over.

Did you get my last letter to Balbriggan?

Your old Tramp

MS, TCD. *LM*, 8

To MOLLY ALLGOOD

Glendalough House | Glenageary
Saturday [28 July 1906]

Dear Molly

I meant that Sunday and Saturdays were bad for our outings because of the crowds in trains and in the glens. However I am longing so to have a walk with you that we will go in spite of them tomorrow *Sunday*. Come down from Westland Row to Bray by the train that goes from W. Row at a *quarter to 12* (taking a return ticket to Bray) and I'll join you in the train at Sandy Cove or Glenageary. That is if it is fine of course. I hope you will get this in time, I suppose you will. I dont think my letter to Balbriggan was very business like, yesterday evening I nearly died of 'lonesomess' so I am as badly off as you are.

Yours ever and always
The Tramp

P.S. I am not sure whether you will get this letter so I will not wait for you in Bray, so dont miss your train. I enclose 3/0 two for the tea and one for your train   J.M.S.

MS, TCD. *LM*, 9

To LADY GREGORY

Glendalough House | Glenageary | Kingstown
July 29th [1906]

Dear Lady Gregory

I got a note from Colum last night saying that they want the costumes at once and that they have a list of what belongs to them.[1] Could you send me a list − typed if possible − of what I am to give or not to give so that I may not be entirely at their mercy. They will not mean to take anything that is not theirs but very possibly they do not remember or do not know the various things you paid for from time to time. If you could send me a list I could go through the things with Miss Sara Algood who would know which was which and then the sooner they have them the better. I have been so busy with Musek and my play that I have forgotten to get hold of Mrs Collar[2] − if it is possible − but I will try tomorrow or next day. I hope Musek arrived all right.

Yours sincerely
J. M. Synge

MS, Berg. *TB*, 136

---

[1] Padraic Colum as secretary of the newly-established Theatre of Ireland had applied in an undated letter to JMS (TCD) for the 'peasant costumes due to us for some months past'.

[2] Apparently a mistake for Mrs Carlyle; see p. 185.

To MOLLY ALLGOOD

[Glendalough House, Glenageary]
Tuesday [31 July 1906]

Dear Molly

I have only a moment to write a business line.

Will you and Sally please meet me tomorrow at the Abbey between 3 o'clock and half-past to go through the clothes. I have asked
Colum to come at 4 o'clock, but it would be best if you would come
earlier so that we could sort the things out first. I have got a list from
Lady Gregory of the things she paid for so it will not be difficult.

I believe Musek comes back on Wednesday; I suppose in the
evening. I am afraid I'll be with him on Thursday, but when he goes
we'll have a long day in the country.

Yours lonesomely
J.M.S.

If you cant come tomorrow please send me a card tonight to say so,
if possible   J.M.S.

MS, TCD. *LM*, 9

To MOLLY ALLGOOD

Glendalough House [Glenageary]
Friday [3 August 1906]

My dear Changling

I was with Musek all day today and I am to see him again *tomorrow*
(*Saturday*) so I cant go to walk with you. However my cousin[1]
is not coming down till Monday so I can go on *Sunday* if *it is fine*.
Will you come down by the *quarter to* ELEVEN from Westland Row?
I will join you like last time at Glenageary or Sandycove, and if you
are not in the train I will take it for granted that you are not coming.
It is better to get off an hour earlier as I must be home a little earlier
in the evening. You can send me a line if you feel disposed to say
if you are coming, and anything nice that you can think of. I'm
fagged out with my efforts to amuse Musek all day, he goes away
tomorrow evening. I like him very much but it is hard to talk to him
continualy as his English is so uncertain.

Your old Tramp
J.M.S.

MS, TCD. *LM*, 10

[1] Probably his childhood companion Florence A. Ross (1870–1949), daughter
of Mrs Synge's sister and a member of the household from 1891 until she joined

her brother in Tonga in 1895. For some years she lived with relatives in New Zealand and the Argentine before returning to England to work as an illustrator, and finally settling in Ireland as a professional artist. She was one of the few members of his family who encouraged JMS's work in the theatre and shared his nationalist sympathies.

To LADY GREGORY

> Glendalough House | Glenageary | Kingstown
> Sunday [5 August 1906]

Dear Lady Gregory

I packed Musek off last night; he was very much pleased with his visit to you.

I have just got the address of the Mrs Collar, who has to do with the Congress.[1] What shall I say to her. All our peasants costumes — are gone — except the few of yours — and I dont feel quite sure that everything would be ready to give a satisfactory show at the end of the month. I saw the programme of the Congress the other day in the paper and everything is being done rather elaborately so if we do it we must do it well. I shall be away and you and Yeats will be away also so it would mean leaving everything to Fay and I rather think he might bungle things and do more harm than good. On the other hand it would be a fine advertisement. I wonder could Yeats come up for the one night to receive them and see that everything is right? Please think it over again and let me know.

I am pleased with the way my play is going but I find it is quite impossible to rush through with it now. So I rather think I shall take it and the typewriter to some place in Kerry where I could work. By doing so I would get some sort of holiday and still avoid dropping the play again — which is a rather dangerous process. If I do this I will be beyond posts so you and Yeats would have to stir up the Fays about the Congress matter if it is to come off. I do not think it is worth putting off my holiday for it, as if I do not get a good summer I generally pay for it in the winter in extra bouts of influenza and all its miseries.

Walker and Miss Laird came for the clothes and were very civil but at the same time painfully thorough!

> Yours sincerely
> J. M. Synge

MS, Berg. *TB*, 137

1 No one named Collar is listed in the newspaper reports of the Institute of Journalists which was holding its annual conference in Dublin during the week beginning 31 Aug 1906, but Mrs James Carlyle, wife of the vice-president of the Institute, is mentioned as a member of the reception committee.

To MOLLY ALLGOOD

Glendalough House [Glenageary]
Tuesday night [7August 1906]

Dear Changling

I have just got your little note. I waited about in my sister's garden till it was near the post hour, sitting on a dark seat by myself under a chesnut-tree and feeling very lonesome. My sister was going about with her husband watering their flowers, and the nephews were doing other things and I wanted my changling to keep me company and to cheer me up. Then I came home here and presently the post came. Changling do you think I can live on 'little purple grapes'?[1] If you want to write such little notes I must have them by the *half dozen* at least. What are those few lines for a very starving man? I wanted to hear how you got home, and how you supped, and how everybody's temper is, and what you did yesterday, and what you read or didn't read, and God knows what, and yet you're too lazy to tell me! What there was, was very tasty so I wont scold you this time, but the next time I want a good fat letter with talk in it, that I can chew the cud with at my ease. I haven't taken any steps yet about going away, so I dont know when it'll come off. I have been hammering away at my play till I am dizzy but it is too hot and I am not doing much good. My brother[2] is to be here tomorrow morning I believe, I am rather amused at the prospect of our talk, I dont mind him a bit.

Wednesday

My brother has been here but it was something else he wanted to talk about that hadn't any thing to do with you. I will write and tell him some day I think. I did not get a good opportunity or I would have told him today. You know I am longing to see you but I do not know if we could manage it tomorrow. My cousin has put off her coming home till tonight so I may have to attend her tomorrow it is a nuisance I'm half afraid we wont meet till Sunday, or shall we take Saturday instead?

If you will write me more I'll write you more; at present you dont deserve it. You'll hear from me again very soon in any case about our walk. I'm sorry to write so scrappily but I mean a great deal more than I find the right moment to say.

Yours always
The Tramp

P.S. Write to me again tomorrow please. *Dont forget.*

MS, TCD. *LM*, 10

¹ Molly's term for the *fraughans*, small blue berries that grow among the heather.

² Probably Samuel Synge, whose wife was returning to Ireland with their infant son, born in England on 12 July 1906.

To MOLLY ALLGOOD

Glendalough House | Glenageary
Friday. 10th [August 1906]

My dear Changling

I have been looking out all day for a letter from you but none has come. The last post hasnt passed yet so one may come still. I have missed you this week somehow more than ever before but I have kept valliantly to my work and I have got through a great deal. It is wonderful how the play begins to grow in one's mind when one gives one's whole time to it, after a few days of misery the ideas begin suddenly to come of themselves and then all is plain sailing. Why didn't you write to me yesterday? I meant to write you a nice letter this evening that would please you, but my head is too tired. I wish to Heaven this play was finished. Now it's nine o'clock so I'll stop for a moment to see if a letter is coming, if it comes at all it will be here soon———————————————————————————————

No letter, I'm curiously disappointed I made sure you would acknowledge the book I sent you yesterday, but may be it has not reached you.

Will you come down by *the quarter to eleven* train *from Westland Row on Sunday* and let us have a good walk. I will join you as before. Come unless it is it is really wet as I suppose it will be our last chance before I go away Send me a line if you can

Yours ever
The Tramp

I dont know why you will not write to me, it is very strange

MS, TCD. *LM*, 12

To LADY GREGORY

Glendalough House. Glenageary. Kingstown
August 12th 1906

Dear Lady Gregory

Thanks for your letters. I have had no visit or letter from Mr Henderson. I wonder if he is not inclined to try us. It is a pity to begin the season's work under the old regime. Did Magee refuse our offer I heard nothing more of him.[1]

I wrote to Mrs Collar and got her reply which I enclose last night. Shall we let the matter drop, or suggest organising a show ourselves for any of the journalists who would like to come. As I said last week in that case some one of us would have to be there I think to receive them.

They open rehearsals tomorrow I believe so I will go in and try and arrange something about the Galway tour. Do you want one night only, in Athlone and Mullingar and two in Galway? And what part of September would suit you best?

I expect to go off next week so Fay will have to look after things a good deal. I will have lists of the peasant costumes that remain sent to you at once so that you may know what is wanting.

I went to the Oireachtas on Thursday to see their plays. The propagandist play done by the Ballaghadereen company was clever with some excellent dialogue, and the peasants who acted it were quite admirabl with far more of the real peasant about them than our people have ever had. I felt really enthusiastic about the whole show although the definitely 'propagandist' fragments were of course very crude. The play was call[ed], I think an t-Aruige mor (the big change) (I think I have spelled it wrong) it would probably read badly.[2]

The Land on the other hand was most dismal, so bad that I came away after the first act. The people didn't know their words, and Frank Walker and two or three others were absolutely inaudible. Miss Garvey might have been talking comskatcan for all that one could catch, and was more sentimental and stagy than ever. I never saw such a show — I wonder what Colum thought of it.[3]

I enclose a leaflet they were distributing.

Yours sincerely
J. M. Synge

I shall be very glad, thanks, to go down and read you my play if it is finished in time, but there is still a great deal to do. I have had a very steady weeks work since last Sunday and have made good way, but my head is getting very tired, working in hot weather takes a lot out of me.

MS, Berg. *TB*, 140

[1] W. A. Henderson (1863-1927), secretary of the National Literary Society of Dublin from 1898 and a close friend of Joseph Holloway, was an aspiring journalist, chiefly remembered for his many scrapbooks, including 'The Playboy and What He did' and '1904-1907 The Irish National Theatre Movement' (NLI).

The directors had asked Henderson to take on the new position of business manager, having apparently first considered offering it to W. K. Magee.

² The Oireachtas, a festival of Irish art, music, and drama, was sponsored each year by the Gaelic League. Among the festival productions JMS attended with his cousin, Florence Ross, in the Rotunda Hall on 9 Aug 1906 was *An tAthrughadh Mór*, a comedy by Felix Partridge about the speaking of Irish, presented by members of Craobh Bhealach a'Doirin, the Western Players.

³ *An Talamh*, an Irish translation of Padraic Colum's *The Land*, was presented at the festival by the newly established Theatre of Ireland.

To MOLLY ALLGOOD

Glendalough House [Glenageary]
Wednesday [15 August 1906]

Dear Changling

I was very glad to get your note yesterday, but I have not had time to write to you and even now I am in a hurry.

I understand that I am to go to tea with you tomorrow (Thursday) at 4 o'clock. If anything has turned up to keep you busy at that time send me a line — POSTED EARLY — or a wire, please, to put me off. I am not going away this week so I hope we may have another walk next Sunday. We might go up Big Sugar Loaf perhaps.

I had F.J.F[ay] out here last night and we had a pleasant talk.

Excuse this hasty *business line* as we are to meet tomorrow.

Your old
Tramp

I was in the Scalp¹ this afternoon and stood *lonesomely* under a tree in a big shower I hope tomorrow'll be fine so that I may admire your roof!

MS, Texas. *LM*, 12

¹ A narrow gap in the rocks through which the main Dublin–Enniskerry road passes, about two miles north of Enniskerry.

To SAMUEL SYNGE¹

Glendalough House, [Glenageary]
Thursday [16 August 1906]

Dear Sam,

I am, of course, no expert in publication matters of this kind, but the estimate you have been given seems to be reasonable enough, if perhaps a bit on the high side. I should think anyone who wanted the

booklet[2] would be quite ready to give a shilling for it. I presume
they mean to bind the *whole* 500 for the sum they quote, not the
first two hundred only. The real cost of printing is the 'setting up,'
so perhaps it would be worth your while to ask them at what figure
they would print you an extra five hundred before the type is
broken up. You might find it so cheap that it would be worth
trying; according to their letter the binding of your edition will
be £5, then if you deduct the 'setting-up' cost again, the cost of
printing off five hundred cannot be much. I suppose the trade price
will be about /10d., then their commission comes off, so your share
of price will be about /8¾d.; I would say to them that you presume
they undertake Distribution. I do not think you can expect them to
do much advertising for their 500 pence. I think the corrections and
alterations refer to changes you might make when reading the proof.
I suppose books are sold in the offices of Shipping Companies,
Cook's, etc. I do not know. Let me know if I can tell you anything
more. The great danger of publishing at one's own expense is that as
the publishers have nothing to lose and little to gain they take no
trouble in pushing and Distributing the work.

Yours affectionately,

J. M. Synge

LMD, 268

¹ The Revd Samuel Synge (1869–1951) had been very close to JMS, his
younger brother, in childhood. In 1896 he became a medical missionary in
China, where he married a fellow medical missionary, Mary Harmar (1864–1939);
with their baby daughter Edith (b. 1904) they were in Ireland on leave from June
1904 until October 1906, when they returned to China until 1914. In 1932
Samuel Synge published *Letters to my Daughter: Memories of John Millington
Synge*, based on letters written between 1914 and 1928.
   ² *A Few Hints on the Care of Children at Sea*, a 30-page booklet, was published by J. Bale, Sons & Danielsson in London in October 1906, just before
Samuel Synge returned with his family to China.

To MOLLY ALLGOOD

Glendalough House [Glenageary]
Friday night [17 August 1906]

Dearest Changling

   I'm very dejected tonight again I dont know why except that I'm
dead tired and that I was annoyed and bored to death at dinner by
a foolish lady who was praising the English and abusing the French.
I dont fit well in to that family party[1] somehow, they are rich and
I am poor, and they are religious and I'm as you know, and so on

with everything. I used to feel very desolate at times but now I dont so much mind as I've a changling of my own to think about and write to. I dont like hanging about their house as a poor relation — although I am a paying guest — as I know that they — or most of them — in their hearts dispise a man of letters. Success in life is what they aim for, and they understand no success that does not bring a nice house, and servants, and good dinners. You're not like that are you? I wish we could keep each other company all these evenings. It is miserable that we must both be lonesome and so much apart. I hope you'll read steadily when I'm away. I hate to preach at you or schoolmaster you, — I like you so perfectly as you are — but you must know, that it will make life richer for both of us if you know literature and the arts, the things that are of most interest to me and my few personal friends, that you'll know one of these days.

It is quite an autumn evening here tonight cold and blustery. I like autumn but I always get a pang of regret when I feel that the summer is over. I have just been having a little walk by myself in the dark and I have a greater yearning than I can describe to you, to have you with me, to make much of me, and cheer me up.

Your old Tramp

P.S. Remember you are to come down by the quarter to eleven on Sunday. Dont miss it, if you are coming at all. I hope it may be fine enough for us.   J.M.S.

MS, TCD. *LM*, 13

[1] i.e. the family of his sister Annie, Mrs Stephens.

To MOLLY ALLGOOD

[Glendalough House, Glenageary]
Monday night [20 August 1906]

Dearest Changling

I've written the letter to Kerry and I feel lonesome at the thought of it. I hate the thought of leaving you for so long especially as you will have this tour[1] with no one to look after your comfort. Please go home to your people as soon as you can after I am gone and make it up with Sally.[2] She is your natural companion in the company and it will be very unpleasant on tour if you are not on good terms. For the sake of *my* ease of mind do make it up if you can.

I am writing this letter to put with some books I'm sending you tomorrow. I meant really to tell you only how nice you were in the Green Room today. Will it make you vain if I tell you I felt proud of my little changling she looked so pretty and quiet and nice. I think mountain air and little purple *grapes* — not papers mind — must be the natural food of changlings they seem to agree with you so well! Or — to carry out the contrasts of my play — would you rather have the pig's leg, you spoke of with such fond enthusiasm last night?

I hope you'll like the books, please treat them kindly. Do you think I'm a fool to spend my time writing to you — six hours after I leave you — when I ought to be reading? If I'm a fool now its folly to be wise.

Your old Tramp.

Can you read all this?

MS, TCD. *LM*, 14

---

1 The Galway tour the company was to make in September.
2 After a quarrel with her sister Sally, apparently over the relationship with JMS of which neither family approved, Molly had moved from her mother's home at 37 Mary Street to stay with her eldest sister, Peggy (Margaret, Mrs Tom Callender; 1879-1959), at Park Chambers, 13 Stephens Green North.

To LADY GREGORY

Glendalough House | Glenageary | Kingstown
[22 August 1906]

Dear Lady Gregory

Many thanks for your kind invitation, but I had already written to the cottage where I go in Kerry and I think I had best go there as I want to be among peasants for a while, and it is a good mountainy place for this hot weather.

I am to see Henderson tonight and I will let you know what I think of him. I do not think I'll get off till Friday or Saturday. I'm taking my play and typewriter with me so that I will be able to work it up while I am away. How is your new play[1] getting on?

Yours sincerely
J. M. Synge

MS, Berg. *TB*, 146

---

1 *The Gaol Gate.*

To MOLLY ALLGOOD

c/o Mrs. Harris | Mountain Stage | Glenbeigh | Co Kerry
[27 August 1906]

Dearest Changling

I enclose a lot of scribbles to you that I did out on the rocks today and yesterday. Tell me if you can read them and if you care for more. They are a bit scrappy I fear. It isn't an easy place some how to get time to write I am nearly always out or talking to someone, and when I come in and sit myself down I dont seem to be in the right mood. I have been in moods since I came here, however, that were very right indeed. I wish I could have written to you then. You would have been very pleased I think with what I had to say.

I had a very good journey down on Saturday and I felt in great spirits, I was so pleased to have you to think about. I had a honeymoon couple oposite me in the train. The good lady's wedding ring was too tight for her and her finger was puffed up double its size, above the ring which of course they could not stir. Unless they look out she'll lose her finger.

I had a great welcome from them all here and although I'm very lonely at times I'm glad to be here. It is very heavy and close today, and I've got a bit of a headache so dont mind the thinness of this letter. I'll send you a fine one one of these days. Be good, and write me a long letter. I daresay I'll be back in three weeks.

Your old Tramp.

[*Enclosures*]

Dearest Changling

I'm out sitting on the cliffs over the sea, on Sunday morning in a gale of wind with rainbows, and clouds & showers and sun flying over me. It's just 11 o'cl. the time of our train at Sandycove! What a pity you aren't here with me, you'd enjoy it all so much. An old man I know came into the kitchen last night and shook me by the hand: "A 100,000 welcomes to you", he said, "and where is the Missis?" "Oh" I said "You'll have to wait till next year to see her"!

There is an old tramper staying in the house who is eighty years old and remembers the famine and the Crimean War. He is one of the best story-tellers in the county and he told us some last night in Irish. He says he used to be good at it but he has lost his teeth now and he isn't able "to give them out like a *ballad*." This morning when I went into the kitchen he was sound asleep on the wooden settle in his bare feet with nothing over him but his coat.

This perfectly fresh wild beauty of the sea and sky is a delight to me, but it makes me sick when I think that you are left behind, and of all the more or less vulgar or beastly talk of Mac,[1] and his friends that you are more or less forced to listen to. Read your Arthur,[2] that will keep your mind full of wild beautiful things like the beauty of the world. When I had to live in London I always kept some book like 'Arthur' on my hands and found it a great plan for keeping myself up when I was in ugly surroundings.

Monday

I'm out again on my perch over the sea. This morning there is a dead hot calm, with heavy clouds, and I can hear the sea birds clapping their wings in the cliffs under me. The air is full [of] the smell of honey from the heather, and there is a seal sneezing and blowing in the sea just under me. It is all wonderful & if I only had my changling with me! I am thinking of you a great deal and I have bad fits of loneliness. Never mind every day now is bringing us nearer, and there's a great time coming!

MS, TCD. *LM*, 15

1 Francis McDonnell.
2 Probably *Le Morte Darthur*, translated by Sir Thomas Malory whom JMS refers to in his notebooks (see *Prose*, 348).

To MOLLY ALLGOOD

c/o Mrs Harris | Mountain Stage | Glenbeigh | Co Kerry
Tuesday [28 August 1906]

Dearest Changling

All your letters have come this morning, you know they couldn't come any sooner as there are only the three posts in the week. I am delighted to hear from you. I am very lonesome too, and not very well. I dont know which of them to answer first. Yes, dont let us squabble any more, it is a wretched degrading sort of business. I am very glad to hear that your people are coming round. Sally shook me very cordially by the hand when I told her I was going away to Kerry for a month. I think she sees that she has been making rather a fool of herself, and I'm sure she'll be all right now. We are all fools at times so we cannot blame her, and you know I've a great respect for her in many ways.

I am very glad you saw the flats,[1] but you do not say a word as to how you like the place now you have seen it. Dont talk about it by the way or you'll have the Fays down there and then we could not go. It is too soon yet I think to take one, I would rather see them for myself first, and in any case I could not pay four or five months rent for nothing, and in the end perhaps see some thing else that would suit us better Even if they are not to be had when we want them people are sure to be moving in and out continually so we would be sure to get a nice one in the end. Are Peggy and Tom [Callender] going to settle there? The most charming relations if they are *too* near are in the way at times. However we'll have a good look at them when I go home and then we'll see what to do.

Dont be alarmed about turning into a saint I dont think there's much danger! I had no opportunity to speak to Fay about your teeth so I'll write about it when I am writing to him next. I daresay I shall only stay here for three weeks after all, in which case I ll be back in a little more than a fortnight, so cheer up!

I haven't touched my play since I came down. It is too hot somehow to sit over it in the house, and my head is acheing a good deal so I think I'll be the better for a bit of a rest. You'll get this I suppose on Wednesday morning and I ought [to] have an answer on Thursday. There is no post here tomorrow, or Friday. The letter you wrote yesterday was in time so you'll easily be able to catch the post.

This [is] a dull sort of letter I'm afraid but I'm writing it in a hurry to have it finished before my dinner as I will be going out afterwards and I can post it then. I'm thinking of you a great deal, and I hoped for a photo this morning I think you had better send me the two and I can keep the two of them at least till I go home.

Write as often as you can, it does me good

Your old Tramp.

This is a beautiful day and the country is wonderful I wish you were here to enjoy it with me. I can only half enjoy it now by myself. Never mind we'll have great walks presently.

MS, TCD. *LM*, 16

---

[1] New flats were being built in the old part of Dublin near St. Patrick's Cathedral, called the Coombe, where restoration was taking place.

To MOLLY ALLGOOD

[Mountain Stage, Co. Kerry]
[28 August 1906]

Dearest. I'm am lying in one of the most beautiful spots in the whole world, with my head in among the heather that is fragrant with honey. I have masses of mountains all round me and a wonderfully blue sea and sky. Down in the valleys a number of little people are working at their oats and hay, the women looking so comfortable in their little red petticoats and bare legs. Wouldn't we be happy, changling, if we could live like that?

I posted a letter to you ½ an hour ago — not as nice a one as you deserve — and now I am at it again! Although I am lonely and depressed these days I am glad I have come out here to see all the glories of the world. I am out on a ride now over a high mountain gap — the Windy Gap — and I am resting in the heather on my way up. I'm off again —— ——

I have come out through the Gap & I am resting again. I have Carntual[1] on my left — the highest mountain in Ireland — full of ragged peaks with white cloud twisted through them like a piece of lace. Just under me there is a great basin, six miles across, full of woods and rich bogs and a blue river and lake. Outside it there is a circle [of] grey mountains ——

I'm resting again, now down among the woods. The richness and colour and sweetness of every thing is beyond words, at least beyond any hasty ones I can write now. It almost seems as if you were riding with me today I am thinking of you so much. Dear Changling! You do not know what I would give to have you with me here —— It is good for anyone to be out in such beauty as this is and it stirs me up to try and make my Irish plays as beautiful as Ireland — I wonder if you could act a *beautiful* part? If it was in your compass — as we say of singers — I think you could. We must try you.

Tuesday night

This isn't much of a letter but perhaps you will like to have it, so I'll post it tomorrow on my way to the fair[2] — I start early. I hope you aren't dissappointed that I have not decided on the Comb it is too soon. You were good not to go out wandering on Sunday. Good night, changling, I'll soon be back again.   Your old Tramp.

MS, TCD. *LM*, 18

1 Carrantuohill.
2 See p. 197.

To LADY GREGORY

                    c/o Mrs. Harris | Mountain Stage | Glenbeigh | Co Kerry
                                                             30.VIII.06

Dear Lady Gregory

I saw Henderson last week, and we went through his duties. He seems very willing and I think he may do very well, if he does not take fright at us. He still thinks it was a terrible thing for Yeats to suggest that Irish people should sell their souls, and for you to put his sacred majesty James II into a barrel![1] I think he will be very energetic in working up an audience, an important part of our work that we have rather neglected. By the way the annual meeting of our Company must be held I suppose before the year is up. I wonder if Yeats remembers it, I suppose he had better fix a date and then get Ryan or F.J.F[ay] to give whatever notice is necessary. It would be as well to have it before we pay off Ryan, as otherwise we shall all be sitting about looking with curiosity and awe at the ballance sheet. Henderson will be free towards the end of September. We suggested that he should go down with the Co. on the Galway tour, to see how things are worked to talk over the beating up of our first-show audience with you and Yeats. It would be as well probably to have him with the company as W.G.[Fay] will be in 'advance' so they will be like a flock of sheep without a shepard. I have been here for nearly a week, but I have a touch of asthma and am not acclimatized yet.

Yours sincerely
J. M. Synge

MS, Berg. *TB*, 146

[1] A reference to Yeats's *The Countess Cathleen* and Lady Gregory's *The White Cockade*.

To MOLLY ALLGOOD

[Mountain Stage, Co. Kerry]
Thursday [30 August 1906]

Dearest

The post man has just walked in over the hill with your two letters — by the way the Post Offices have just sent out notices that if people persist in putting stamps on *the backs* of *their letters* they will decline to deliver them, that wouldn't do!

I'm afraid I'm spoiling you by writing to you every day — I wont keep it up after this week, so be prepared! I didn't write any thing to you yesterday (though I posted Tuesday's notes) as I was out at Killorglin fair[1] in the morning and then up into a mountain pass — on my feet in the evening. The fair was very amusing as usual and I met a great many country people that I knew. I saw three lustre jugs in a little crockery shop, and I'm going to buy them — or at least two of them — for *our* use! They are worth 2/6 I believe in Dublin, and it is well for us to have something that we can *pawn*!

I wonder what *Madame Giraffe*[2] would say to me if she thinks Fay too poor. That's the Giraffe's doing you may be sure. I am glad Miss Yeats was friendly to you, she likes you, she told me so six months ago. She is extremely nice I think, if you — I wont finish that it was to be about your millionaire. N.B. Dont take my spelling for gospel sometimes I make my words French by mistake. I wonder what will become of me if you all go to America and leave me behind. Do you take that into your consideration? That would mean 6 months instead of three weeks remember!

Last night I was out on my little hill over the sea about nine o'clock in the moonlight. It was extraordinarily peacefull and grand and I was wondering how you were getting on in the Abbey (it was rehearsal time) listening to the blather of Mac and Co. My walk yesterday afternoon too was wonderful, I was high up on a mountain path looking down a thousand feet of sloping heather into the sea. Then there was Dingle bay perfectly calm and blue, and in the background another line of mountains ending with the Blasquet Islands about 15 miles away. I was up there till sunset and the colour was strangely beautiful. After all while the fine weather last it is better to spend my time in places like that than to be fumbling over my play. So far I haven't looked at it, and I am not sure that I will, there is too much movement in this cottage somehow to get my mind to work. I am getting good from this change I think though I get a sort of Hay-fever at night that worries me. What is worse since last year my bed has got full of fleas — saving your presence or absence — and they bite me nearly into a fever, I killed three or four last night and I saw a lot more that got off!

Do you know Joy,[3] Colm's friend? He was to be at Killorglin these days and I wrote to him there, but have not heard so I suppose he has gone. He is one of a family of 17 and his mother died two or three months ago, as another was coming! His father is a publican in Killorglin, but is paralized or something and never appears! It is an extraordinary story — told me by a little Killorglin girl of ten who is staying here — you had better *not* repeat it. Now will that suit you for today's letter? I dont know, by the way, whether you will get this tomorrow or not as I am going to post it in Cahersiveen M. Doul's Cahir-Iveraghig[4] — and I may not catch the post. I cannot go down to the Glenbeigh post every day.

Your old Stager.

MS, TCD. *LM*, 19

1 The famous 'Puck Fair', held each August in Kerry.
2 This may refer to Miss Horniman.
3 Maurice Joy (1884–1944), a poet and occasional essayist, editor of *The*

Irish Rebellion of 1916 and its Martyrs (New York, 1916); he was one of Horace Plunkett's secretaries for several years.

⁴ Cahirciveen, Co. Kerry; Martin Doul in *The Well of the Saints* calls it Cahir Iveraghig (city of Iveragh), pronounced Kăhĭr ēēvráu-ig, the 'au' as in 'caught'.

To MOLLY ALLGOOD

c/o Mrs Harris [Mountain Stage, Co. Kerry]
September 1st [1906]

Dear Changling

Your note — a short one — has just come. I sent you a long letter on Thursday — posted in Caherciveen which does not seem to have reached you when you wrote yours. Tell me if you got it all right. I'm sure I'm writing to you about double as much as you write me, amn't I? I have just heard that the MacKennas are in Dublin for a week and want to see me. I shall be very sorry if I miss them. I have written to Fay on the teeth question and I hope he will devise something. What would you say if I was to turn up in Dublin this day week? It is possible I may go up then as I am not very well, and I find I cannot possibly work at my play here. I woke up the othernight feeling that you were in difficulty or danger or something and I didn't like it, so I was glad to hear this morning that you are all right. Of course you wont go with Power[1] unless your sisters go. I am dissappointed at getting such a scrap of a line from you this morning, and now I cannot hear again till Tuesday. Well if you dont write to me! you know our bargain. Joking apart I've three more letters to write so this must do for you today.

Your old T.

P.S. I've got my other letters written so I may come at you again. I think it's a shame for you to send me such a scrap with a whole side of the paper untouched! I bathed yesterday in the sea for the first time for about 25 years, and found it delightful. I have bathed and learned to swim in Wicklow rivers but the blue fresh sea some how is far more exciting. I was afraid to stay in more than a minute or so as I have a sort of asthma and I didn't want [to] make it worse. These moonlight nights here are most wonderful. Last night when I was coming back from the cliffs about 9 o'clock I came on the little girls belonging to this house and two or three others, and I got them to dance and sing Irish songs to me in the moonlight for nearly an hour. They were in bare feet of course, and while they were dansing a little divil of a brother of their's kept throwing in dried furze-thorns under their feet, so that every now and then one

of them would go lame with a squal. I am glad you like Catriona.[2]
Wont the arthur books keep you going for a while still? Have you
read any of the second volume? Have you read Shakspeare? Remember in three little weeks there'll be another new moon, and then with
the help of God, we'll have great walking and talking at the fall of
night. Do write me some decent letters before Tuesday's post.

                                                                J.M.S.

MS, TCD. *LM*, 21

[1] Ambrose Power, who was organizing a dance party (see p. 219), acted with
the company from late 1904 until 1907 when he resigned over a quarrel with
W. G. Fay. He returned to the company from 1908 to 1911, playing small parts.
  [2] The novel by Robert Louis Stevenson, published in 1893 as a sequel to
Kidnapped.

To MOLLY ALLGOOD

                                   c/o Mrs Harris | etc. [Co. Kerry]
                                   Tuesday [4 September 1906]
Dearest Changling
  No letter has come from you. I can hardly believe that you have
not written, so it is perhaps the postman's fault, he may be drunk
after the races yesterday or God knows what. As soon as I get my
dinner I'm going down to the post town to make the divil's own row.
I have invented seven new curses — for my private prayers of course
only — during the last hour and a half. Tell me when your sister goes
to the Hospital, and when you go back to your people.[1] Am I to go
on writing to P[ark] Chambers after you go back it, seems rather
absurd?
  I'm a good deal better and I dont think I'll go home at present,
not at least till my three weeks are up. I am only here ten days now
but it seems an age. I have not even opened my play yet, after all
it is far more important for me to be out in the fresh air now, getting
a stock of health to carry me through next winter, than to be finished
with the play a few weeks sooner or later. I am in such a rage now
with this postman or whatever it is that I cannot write. Fortunately
I have some scribbles to send you that are more likely to please you.
                                                                Your T.
What about the photos?
If you have written to me since please write by return and tell me
when and where you posted it. If you have *not* written, if it is *your*
fault ——!!![2]

[*Enclosure*]

Sept. 3. 1906

D.C. I couldn't write yesterday or today — at least couldn't post to you — so I've come down now under the cliffs — right on the edge of the sea — to watch the sunset and tell you my news. I've been at races today near here, at Rossbeigh with Philly Harris, the man of the House, and some of his family. They — the races — were run on a flat strand when the tide was out. It was a brilliant day and the jockeys and crowd looked very gay against the blue of the sea, but some how all the movement and festivity made me miss *someone* even more than I do when I'm out alone in the hills so I got rather dejected. I think I'm getting lonesomer every day, I wonder if you are? I suppose we'll survive two or three weeks more?

It is wonderful out here tonight. I told you I'm on the edge of a long bay with mountains on both sides. The sun sets over the sea now right at the mouth of it, and throws the most marvelleous lights and shadows on the hills that I am facing. The bracken on them is turning red the last few days, which puts a sort of warm bloom on them in the late evening light. Between them and me, of course, there are 8 or 10 miles of fresh purple sea with sea gulls and cormorants and one seal that is watching me. You remember how we enjoyed the smoky backyard kind of sun we had at Whitly Bay[3] so you can fancy how you'd like this radiant place if you were here! I could write sheets to you about the wonders I see day by day, but it is as well to wait till you see them for yourself some day.

Tuesday (morning)

I'm out on the road above the cliffs that I was under last night, waiting for the post — with letters from you I hope — and watching the people picking carregeen moss.[4] Dozens of men & women are out in the sea up to their waists — in old clothes, poking about for it under the water. They only find it at the lowest spring tide so the sea is far out and as smooth as a lake It is a day with thin grey clouds wonderfully clear and silent & beautiful but I can just here the voices of the people talking and laughing in the sea under me. My poor changling to be shut up in Dublin when I am in such a divine place!

Found your letter all right after an hour's hunt in Drunken Postman's pocket. Thanks. Tell me all about Dosey mind.[5]

MS, TCD. *LM*, 22

---

1 Molly chose, however, to stay on with the Callenders; see p. 202.
2 Across the top of this letter Molly has written the word 'reconcile'.

³ Probably Whitley Bay, a seaside resort ten miles north of Newcastle on Tyne, which the company visited during the 1906 tour.

⁴ Carragheen moss, a variety of seaweed exported for commercial use as a gelatine and also used for medicinal purposes.

⁵ These sentences apparently added after writing the covering letter above.

To MOLLY ALLGOOD

c/o Mrs Harris [Mountain Stage, Co. Kerry]
Thursday [6 September 1906]

Dear Changling

I have just got your little note. That is strange news about B. O'Demsey.¹ I wonder how it will end, I have no news of it from the others.

Now about yourself. We talked over your staying on at St[ephens] Green by yourself as you know. You agreed not to stay there as I did not like it for you. Now at the LAST moment you tell me that you are going back of your definite word, and going to do what I asked you not. What does it all mean? Do you think —— I had better not write what I think. I am too distressed. You seem determined that I am never to TRUST you. I do not so much mind your staying on as the way you seem utterly to disregard your word. If there is any reason for you to change your plans why do you not give it to me. I am very unwell and *now* very wretched. I am going home in a few days.

Yours J.

Surely you might have had the courtesy to consult me at least about your plans!

P.S. You can write here again as I do not leave till next week.

Later

P.S. Dearest. Perhaps you understood that our bargain was that you should not stay on in the Green *unless* your mother agreed. If so, though, that is *not* my recollection of what passed, it makes things a little different, if your mother really agrees.

Why are you staying on? I dislike EXTREMELY² the idea of your being there as a sort of caretaker. In any case it is outrageous that you should make these plans without letting me know. I cannot understand why you treat me so badly.   J.M.S.

Please write by return The thought that I cannot trust you is anguish to me. You have finally ruined my holiday.

MS, TCD. *LM*, 24

¹ The latest rumour in the stormy courtship of Willie Fay was that Brigit O'Dempsey had resigned from the company and returned home.
² Underlined five times.

To MOLLY ALLGOOD

[Mountain Stage, Co. Kerry]
Saturday [8 September 1906]

Dearest

The post has passed the first post since I left Dublin with no letter from you. I expect to go home on Tuesday evening or Wednesday morning next so please <u>WRITE</u>¹ here again. I am very unwell — nothing at all serious but an ailment brought on by the damp, and unsuitable food, that causes me intense pain at times, I nearly fainted yesterday I was so bad — however I always get all right at once when I get back to civilization. I suppose you have taken what I said badly, it is vain trying to write of these things. We can talk it over next week together. I was very unwell while I was writing, and, as you must have seen, it was a shock to me to think that you made nothing of what we had talked of so much. Believe me, dearest, as always

your old T.

Is it not cruel of you to leave me without a letter? I have had no news of the Directors or the affair of B. O'D.

Yours
J.M.S.

Write me a nice letter *by return*. I will call for it at the post town on Monday.

MS, TCD. *LM*, 25

¹ Underlined four times.

To MOLLY ALLGOOD

Glendalough House | Glenageary | Kingstown
Wednesday [12 September 1906]

Dear Changling

I got home this morning, and I hope I'll soon be all right again. Very many thanks for the tie which is admirable. I cannot write you a letter today, this is merely to announce my arrival. If I feel well enough I shall probably be in at the Abbey tomorrow. (Thursday) Shall I see you then I wonder. Wont it be fun to see ourselves again?

I have not heard whether the Galway tour is on next week or off. You are all great hands at *not* 'Spreading the News'![1]

Yours
J.M.S.

MS, AS. *LM*, 26

1 The title of one of Lady Gregory's most popular plays.

To MAX MEYERFELD

Glendalough House | Glenageary | Kingstown | Co. Dublin
September 14 [1906]

Dear Dr. Meyerfeld

Many thanks for the £2.8.0[1] which I have just received.

I hope to have my new play ready in a few weeks time, and I will send you a copy as soon as possible. I have been working at it most of the summer — except for a few weeks which I spent in Kerry — but as you know play writing is slow work. I think it will be a much better *acting* play than the "Well of the Saints" and I hope you will think it suitable for translation.

I will write to you again more fully when I am able to send you a copy

With many thanks very sincerely yours

J. M. Synge

P.S. Please note change of address which is permanent.

MS, NLI

1 On 8 Sept 1906 (TCD) Meyerfeld had sent him the royalties for the February performances in Berlin of *The Well of the Saints* and again requested to see the new play.

To MOLLY ALLGOOD

[Glendalough House, Glenageary]
18th. IX. 06

Little treasure of my soul

I am delighted with your picture, it is very pretty and distinguished though it does not of course quite give your expression — photographs seldom do that.

I was very pleased with you the other evening, you were very self-possessed and charming, and got through very well, I think, considering your inexperience. Isn't Miss Tobin nice?[1] I have to go to Waterford with her tomorrow for the day — she wants to see the place as some of her people come from there — and she does not like going alone, so she asked me to go with her. Today I have to work at my play — I am getting very unhappy about it as it wont come out right. I am beginning to fear there is some inherent defect in the story as I am treating it. I am at my wits end with it. Tonight I may go to see Mrs Tanqueray at the Gaiety[2] I am not sure, Thursday please God I'll see you, I am famishing, it is heartrending as you say.[3] I nearly went in to call on you on Sunday I got so lonesome. Never mind next Sunday we'll have a *long long day* in the Mountains. Could you come by the quarter to *ten* train the days are so short now? I have a very old friend[4] to see this week — she is over from England for a few days only — and I may wire to you on Thursday to have tea and cakes for her at the Abbey. She is a writer on art.

I am much better again now, nearly well in fact. You have no idea how much I have suffered. Good bye, my treasure, till Thursday I suppose

J.M.S.

I am sick and tired of this sort of thing. I think in a week or two we had better make ourselves 'official' and then defy gossip. I may drop in and see your mother some day *unbeknownsted*!

MS, TCD. *LM*, 26

---

[1] The American poet Agnes Tobin (see p. 309) had given a dinner for the company who undertook a copyright performance of one of her plays; on 17 Sept 1906 she wrote to JMS, 'I shall never forget how beautiful that dear girl looked at dinner with her wreath — it was something to burn candles before' (TCD).

[2] Olga Nethersole's company was performing *The Second Mrs Tanqueray* by Arthur Wing Pinero at the Gaiety Theatre.

[3] Molly was away with the company, performing in Galway, 18–19 Sept.

[4] Probably Hope Rea (b. 1860), whom JMS had met in Florence and whom he visited regularly on his trips to London. Author of *Tuscan Artists, Their Thought and Work* (1898, 1904) and of individual studies of Donatello, Rembrandt, Rubens, and Titian, she was interested in theosophy and later published several folk miracle plays.

To MOLLY ALLGOOD

[Glendalough House, Glenageary]
[18 September 1906]

Dearest

I have just got your note. I hope my letter has reached you by this time and made you all right. I was thinking of going to town yesterday that is chiefly why I did not write to you, the rest was laziness. Your photo only came last night at 9.30 and I wrote to thank you this morning so I dont think I was very bad was I? Dont think for a moment that I take offence at imaginary triffles, or that I would leave your letter unanswered for a reason of that kind. You may be sure when I have anything I dont approve of I'll let you know fast enough.

I'm very sorry indeed that I have made you uneasy, you must have seen by my note this morning how far you were from knowing the real state of things when you said that I didn't seem to want to see you or hear from you. Since I was away I seem to value you more profoundly than ever, you need never doubt me, my little heart, if you treat me well. I put up your photo last night on a stand next my bed so that it was the first thing I saw this morning. Good bye

J.M.S.

MS, TCD. *LM*, 28

To MOLLY ALLGOOD

[Glendalough House, Glenageary]
Friday [21 September 1906]

Dear Changling

I have no paper[1] and I am in no humour for writing so this is merely to carry out my half-promise and to bid you good day. I am still under the cloud you put over me in the Park, I hope it may wear off before tonight.

Dont forget Sunday by the quarter to eleven from West[land] R[ow]. I hope to Heaven we may have a good day.

J.M.S.

Evening — The cloud is lifting again. Am I too hard on you, treasure, for your little sins? If I am forgive me.

MS, AS. *LM*, 28

[1] The letter is written on the back of a page from one of the final drafts ('G', 18 Sept 1906) of Act I of *The Playboy*.

To MOLLY ALLGOOD

[Glendalough House, Glenageary]
Saturday. 7.A.M. [22 September 1906]
In my little Bed

My Own

I dont suppose I shall get a word with you tonight, and I will not be well enough I fear to walk tomorrow, so I want to write you a line to thank you for your notes. Dearest, yesterday morning I sat down to write you a letter that would have made your hair stand on end, but fortunately when I got the pen in my hand I wrote to Germany instead. I was greatly troubled all day — far more so than you imagine — by our quarrel on Thursday. And my first impulse was to give you a terrible scolding but I am going to drop my dignity and appeal to you instead. Dont you know, changling, that I am an excitable, over-strung fool, — as all writers are, and *have to be*, — and dont you love me enough to be a little considerate, and kindly with me even if you do not think that I am always reasonable in what I want you to do? Surely you wouldn't like to worry me into consumption or God knows what? And with the continual, deadly strain of my writing I haven't much health over to shake off the effect of these hideous little squabbles that harass me indescribably, because my own darling, I love you indescribably. When you know how my whole heart has gone out to you, why do you speak to me as you did on Thursday, or break your word to me as you did a few days before? We may have a beautiful life together, but, if we are not careful, we may put ourselves into a very hell on earth. Do let us be careful,

J.M.S.

MS, AS. *LM*, 29

To MOLLY ALLGOOD

[Glendalough House, Glenageary]
Monday night [?24 September 1906]

My dearest Changling

I believe I promised to write to you today, and I am a man of my word so here goes!

I have just been out having a little turn on my cycle in the twilight, which was very clear and quiet so I am in a peaceful mood. What shall I say about our squabble last night? It haunted me and distressed me more than I expected. I could not go to sleep thinking of it last night, and it was back into my head before I could get my eyes open this morning. You gave me an utterly hard hostile look, when I tried to put things right that is not pleasant to think of. Some people seem to be able to have disputes and forget them but I am not like that so we must not do that sort of thing again. Please write me a good letter tomorrow, when you get this, that will put me to rights again.

As to the matter we fought over it was small in itself, but such things mean a great deal. We can talk it over better than we can write of it, I am always afraid to say much in a letter, letters are so easily misunderstood by a little over emphasizing some thing that is really put lightly.

When am I to go to tea with you? On Wednesday afternoon I suppose you will be rehearsing I could go on Thursday instead if you are free then. Let me know in time.

I was sorry to leave you so soon today but as you refused to have tea with me there was nothing for it. I was rewarded for my industry in coming home to work by getting some of the best speeches down that I have got hold of since I began work this time. Dont forget to write to me *at once*

Your old Tramp

MS, TCD. *LM*, 29

To MOLLY ALLGOOD

[Glendalough House, Glenageary]
Thursday [?27 September 1906]

Dearest

I am getting on well again today, and I have just got your note, thanks. You ought to have some smelling salts to hold under F.J. [Fay]'s nose when he goes to sleep!

You made me a wee bit uneasy last night, dear Heart, by some of your talk, and the moods you told me of. I thought you had come round altogether to like the sort of life you'll have with me best — the life I mean that we have out on the hills, and by the sea on Bray head and in the art we both live for — but if you begin again hankering after commonplace pleasures and riches and that sort of thing we shall both be made wretched. I do not mean of course that we want to be poor or that we shouldn't amuse ourselves, but I fear there is something a little different in your head now. Write me a nice letter, my own heart, and cheer me up again, I dont really believe that it's anything more than a passing whim, but I'd like you to tell me so again. I have often told you that I am sure with a little care we may have a beautiful life together, but that a little carelessness — especially with you as you are so young and so quick and an actress — might easily ruin our happiness for ever. Forgive this preaching, my life, I dare say it is very absurde.

Your old Tramp forever.[1]

MS, TCD. *LM*, 30

[1] At the bottom of this letter Molly has written 'peculiar' twice.

To LADY GREGORY

Glendalough House [Glenageary]
Saturday [29 September 1906]

Dear Lady Gregory

I saw Henderson at the Abbey last night. He is anxious that we should offer subscription tickets at one guinea for *ten consequetive Saturday* nights, ie, for half our season. He thinks he could get at least a hundred sold, and thus get us some money in hand and gain us the nucleus of a regular audience. What do you think? If we do it we must get the matter in hand at once, and also make out a provisional programme for the whole series, as we should have to announce what we are going to do. I asked Fay to send you a rough programme today of what he would suggest. We should have to make our announcement as interesting as we could and include, I think, either Oedipus or the Antigone.[1] I think the experiment would be worth trying. It is almost as easy to get people to take such tickets as to come to *one* of our shows, but if they take the tickets they will come to ten, and thus save our energies. It might leave our audience the other days a little worse than ever, but we would have the pit as before, and after all the stalls have been practically empty lately.

Henderson suggests the Saturday before we open — the 13th I think it is, for our At Home. Will that suit you? Henderson is a nervous quiet creature and Fay I think is likely to sit on him if we dont take care. I cannot be in there very much just now as my play takes all my time.

It will be impossible to get any good of Fay till his private affairs are arranged. He showed me your letter[2] — or Yeats I forget which last night, and I of course agree, but I have always understood that misstating age in an affair of the kind was a sort of everyday thing that had not dangerous consequences and did not in any way affect

the legality of the marriage. It was Koehler I think who put it into
Fay's head. Fay's view now is that Scotch law is the same as the
English or Irish on these points, so that Scotland was no advantage,
but he is quite muddled and everyone he consults tells him something different. You know that Miss O'D. was with relatives of the
Allgoods in Glasgow, but her talk of love matters shocked them —
perhaps needlessly — and they would not keep her. This I heard
privately from Miss S. Allgood last night and I do not know whether
Fay knows himself why she was turned out, *so please keep it private*.
I wonder if Father O'Donavan³ could help them in London, one
is a little slow to bring more people than necessary into the matter,
but Fay certainly wants advice from someone who really knows.
I got him to go to a priest here, who was first very encouraging,
but is now making difficulties. I do not know why he has changed,
it may be that Fay himself was too hopeful about him at first, and is
now too depressed.

Yours sincerely
J. M. Synge

MS, Berg. *TB*, 147

¹ The directors approached various people, including Robert Gregory, 'John
Eglinton', Gilbert Murray, and Oliver St. John Gogarty for suitable translations
of classical plays, without success.
² Willie Fay and Lady Gregory had been corresponding throughout September about his marriage plans; at this time Brigit O'Dempsey was staying with the
William Boyles in London.
³ Probably Jeremiah O'Donovan (1871–1942), the novelist 'Gerald O'Donovan', a radical priest who served as administrator of the Loughrea parish from
1897 to 1904; he invited the Irish National Theatre Society to perform for his
Cathedral Fund there in 1903. From late 1904 he appears to have been based
in London where he was friendly with George Moore; he left the priesthood
shortly after.

To MOLLY ALLGOOD

[Glendalough House, Glenageary]
Saturday Morning 12.30 [29 September 1906]

Dearest
    When I got home last night I saw to my horror a letter lying on the
table which I made sure was from Jack Y[eats].¹ When I opened it
however it was only from my cousin, about Monday,² so, so far,
I am free for tomorrow. Please come by the *quarter to eleven tomorrow Sunday*. I am tired this week and I think that will be early
enough for both of us as we are working so hard!

You must not mind if I seem a little distant at the Theatre, every one is watching us, and even when we are publicly engaged I do not care to let outsiders see anything. Isn't that the best way? Remember what a public nuisance Fay and Co. became! Last spring we had to do our talking in the Theatre as we did not see each other elsewhere but now, thank God, we can have our talk on green hills, that are better than all the green rooms in the world. Please dont be hurt, I am only defending myself because you said I wasn't nice last night! Twenty two hours and a half, the Devil mend them, till we meet again.

Your old
J.M.S.

You had better look in your letter box tomorrow morning in case I should be stopped still. I hope I wont.

MS, TCD. *LM*, 33

1 Jack Yeats was in Dublin preparing for an exhibition of his sketches, from 1 to 20 Oct 1906, in Leinster Hall; during October he and JMS went walking and also spent an evening attending a melodrama at the Queen's Theatre.

2 JMS had arranged to go into town on the Monday with Florence Ross, perhaps to the opening of Jack Yeats's exhibition.

To W. B. YEATS

Glendalough House | Glenageary | Co Dublin
Oct 4th [1906]

Dear Yeats

I have got your two letters. My idea about the seats was to have productions always full price, revival Saturdays always six penny seats, but perhaps it is too complicated, so let us work as you suggest beginning on Mondays.

The Deirdre matter[1] is a puzzle. My play, though in its last agony, is not finished and I cannot promise it for any definite day. It is more than likely that when I read it to you and Fay — when you come up for the At Home — there will be little things to alter that have escaped me. And with my stuff it takes time to get even half a page of new dialogue fully into key with what goes before it. The play, I think, will be one of the longest we have done, and in places extremely difficult. If we said the nineteenth (19th) I could only have some six or seven full rehearsals, which would not I am quite sure be enough. We could not rehearse it in the evening till the Mineral Workers[2] are done with, then Fay goes to Scotland to get married, and however speedy he is we cannot hope to get much work out of him that week so there would be only a fortnight (6 rehearsals) over. In the Playboy he has a very big part and I do not see that the thing can be managed. I am very sorry, but what is to be done? Would you like to put on Kincora or the Well-of-the-Saints, in November? I do not think it would be a good plan as we should have new productions every month to begin with. It seems a pity to put on Miss Darragh in Advent and in the Christmas season when business is sure to be bad. However I do not know that Advent makes much difference. When we were drawing up the list Henderson sent you I asked Fay if he could have the playboy by the 17th and he thought he could not. Could we make up a bill with Lady Gregory's Canavans³ for November? If F. Fay could play my playboy there might be some chance of being ready as he learns quickly but I fear some of it would be altogether out of his range. The devil of it is that our programme ought to go to press tomorrow. Would it be possible for you to wire instructions tomorrow morning. If we do not get the printing in hand at once it will be late for the 'At Home' and we will miss getting the thing talked about and lose subscribers. (I'll be at Abbey *tomorrow — Friday — night* can you write so *that I get it by evening post* THERE). Kathleen was omitted from list (with Demsey) by oversight, so was the Jackdaw⁴ from the Kings Threshold week. Of course if we play every Saturday as a subscriber Saturday we will go through the programme a little faster. You saw that in our list we omitted *one* of each of the two *New production Saturdays*.

Please tell Lady Gregory that I got her letter and saw Fay last night. Scotland seems to be all right so that matter will be arranged easily enough.

An idea strikes me. Suppose you begin rehearsing Deirdre IN THE DAYTIME on the 27th of November, — after first night of Playboy — I suppose whole cast is made of paid company — you could have *eleven* or 12 rehearsals and play it the 10th. Wouldn't that do? My difficulty is that I can only have full rehearsals — with my big cast *three nights* in the week and of course W. G. Fay's memory. Then what about the Canavans, are they paid company or whole crowd? Give us some decision. You and Lady Gregory will be able to hit on something.

Yours

J. M. Synge

MS, Berg. *TB*, 153

¹ Yeats had written on 3 Oct 1906 (TCD) that his new play *Deirdre* required the attendance at rehearsals of Lady Gregory, who had helped him with the scenario, Robert Gregory, who was designing it, and Florence Darragh, who was

appearing as a guest performer, and consequently the production should be early in December rather than when JMS had suggested. It was finally produced on 24 Nov 1906.

2 *The Mineral Workers*, a new play by William Boyle, included in the cast non-permanent members of the company who could only rehearse in the evenings.

3 *The Canavans*, a three-act historical comedy by Lady Gregory, received its first production on 8 Dec 1906 along with a revised version of Yeats's *The Shadowy Waters*, also starring Florence Darragh.

4 *The Jackdaw*, a comedy by Lady Gregory, which was not produced until 23 Feb 1907; instead she wrote her one-act tragedy *The Gaol Gate* for production with *The Mineral Workers* on 20 Oct 1906.

To MOLLY ALLGOOD

[Glendalough House, Glenageary]
Thursday night | 7.30 [? 4 October 1906]

Dearest

Just a line of greeting. I have been slaving off and on all day and now I am going down to the pier. Fancy, two days more and then *Sunday*! How I look forward to it! I hope rain or Jack Yeats wont stop us. Could you come by the quarter to ten next time do you think? I want to take you to Enniskerry on the long car[1] and then to Glen Cree, it is a lovely place and I'd like you to see it before the autumn is over.

I am going to make Christy Mahon come in dressed as a jockey from the mule race in the third act, wont Fay look funny!

This is a miserable scrap but excuse it I'm wearied out. Till the Day of Judgement and after it.

Your old T.

MS, Texas, *LM*, 32

1 An uncovered four-wheeled horse-drawn car in which the passengers sat in two rows back to back, making regular journeys from Bray station to Enniskerry village by way of the Dargle Glen and Powerscourt Demesne.

To MOLLY ALLGOOD

[Glendalough House, Glenageary]
Saturday *Midday* [6 October 1906]

Treasure

I am sending you a line to remind you of tomorrow, I am so afraid you might forget!! Do not come of course if it is a wet day, but if it is raining *at a quarter to ten* and clears up before a *quarter to eleven*

come then. I have had so much letter-writing to do this morning —
for the Theatre — I have not had time to touch my play. I am going
to the Tree show,[1] I think, this afternoon. I dont want to go a bit
but I think I ought to pay my respects to Wareing. I may want his
help some time.

The weather glass is rising so perhaps it will be fine tomorrow
Please Goodness it will. I hope we will not make any mistake, sometimes it rains in Dublin and is fine here or the other way round. Look
in your box again tomorrow morning, and be very happy. So till
tomorrow good bye

Your old Tramp

MS, Texas. *LM*, 35

<hr>

[1] Herbert Beerbohm Tree (1853–1917), English actor-manager, was known
for his lavish Shakespearian productions; when not performing in Her Majesty's
Theatre in London, his companies toured under the management of Alfred
Wareing, with Dublin's Royalty Theatre one of their regular stops. During the
first week of October 1906 the repertoire included *Nero* by Stephen Phillips,
Colonel Newcome by Michael Morton, and *Antony and Cleopatra*, as well as
revivals.

To MOLLY ALLGOOD

[Glendalough House, Glenageary]
Monday night 12.30 [8 October 1906]

Dear Heart

I have been in bed for half an hour and I've suddenly taken a
notion that I must write you a line before I go to sleep My little
treasure if you knew how I longed to have a little chat with you all
the evening but it wasn't possible. I wonder if you felt I was neglecting you? It couldn't be helped. Perhaps you'll think I'm an ass to
write to [you] so soon when I've nothing to say except that you're
my only changling and I'm always thinking about you, and yearning
to be with you even when I seem to be taking no notice of you at
all.

Be good and faithful to your old Tramp and we'll have great times
yet. I dont know why I am writing all this A thousand blessings on
you

J.M.S.

MS, AS. *LM*, 34

To MOLLY ALLGOOD

> Glendalough House [Glenageary]
> Wednesday [10 October 1906]

Dearest

Would you like to walk with your old Tramp *tomorrow*? *Thursday*. I will go up by the train that gets in about 20 minutes to three, and I'll go to the bridge between *Capel St.* and *Parliament St.* at *three o'clock (tomorrow — Thursday)* If you're there we'll take an outing either to Lucan, or by the Palmerston tram to the Dodder and so to the glens.[1] If you are *not* there, I'll take it you cant come and I'll go and see Jack Yeats If they have a rehearsal of the Gaol-Gate or anything tomorrow afternoon, so that you cant come, dont trouble about it, and we'll have our walk some other time. If it is wet — regularly wet — I wont be there. You wont get this till tomorrow morning so there wont be time for you to answer. It will not matter if you aren't there, but as I do not know whether you can come I will not wait after five past three, and if by any chance I am not there then dont wait for me. It is not a pleasant place. I've a lot of nice things to say to you but they'll do tomorrow. Ever your old

> J.M.S.

MS, TCD. *LM*, 34

[1] Among the Dublin Mountains beyond Rathfarnham on the outskirts of Dublin are Glendhu (the Pine Forest), Glenasmole (Glen of the Thrushes), and Glencullen.

To MOLLY ALLGOOD

> [Glendalough House, Glenageary]
> Thursday [11 October 1906]

Dearest

What a Day! No chance for our walk. I shall be at the Abbey tomorrow afternoon and perhaps evening, so we'll meet then.

I have had a very nice letter from my brother he seems quite pleased.[1] I wish you could see him before he goes away. He is to be here I believe tomorrow morning and will stay about a week, then to China for seven years.

How are you feeling? Wasn't it strange how I felt your depression and got up in the middle of the night to write you a letter of consolation. It wont be my fault if we aren't happy changling, and I'm sure it wont be yours so please God we're safe.

Ever, my own dearest, your old Tramp.

MS, TCD. *LM*, 35

---

¹ Perhaps concerning the publication in October 1906 of his booklet, *A Few Hints on the Care of Children at Sea*; see p. 190.

To MOLLY ALLGOOD

[Glendalough House, Glenageary]
[?13 October 1906]

. . . Please come [do]wn to Bray tomorrow if fine, by the quarter to *ten* from W. Row.

I was awake nearly all night — you know why — and I am not good for much today. Is that the way you are going to comfort me and help me in my work?

Yours ever
J.M.S.

[I had hoped for] a l[etter from you]˙today but [the postman] passed —

I have no other paper

MS fragment, TCD. *LM*, xx

To MOLLY ALLGOOD

[Glendalough House, Glenageary]
Monday [15 October 1906]

Dear Polly

I enclose the immortal ballad — It will do to sing by and by if I get too stiff to stand on my head.

I find there is more work than I thought to be done on the second Act of my play so I'll have to make another desperate go at it this week, last week somehow I didn't get much done

I hope you aren't tired after yesterday. I had a great sleep last night and feel ready for a fine week's work. This afternoon I was through the edge of Bray on my cycle along a bit of the road we were on last night. It was hard to believe it was the same place. You've made me want to act by telling me I couldn't be understood.

Fiddle de-dee! Dor*t* you remember how clear I was when I was teaching you Nora B[urke]? Perhaps I'll see [you] tonight, perhaps I wont be in till Wednesday.

Goodbye dearest your
J.M.S.

[*Enclosure*]

The NEW ORIGANAL BALLAD of MISS POLLY POP-GUN . . .

Young Polly Popgun and her man went out one autumn day,
When hips and haws and blackberries their millions did display.
Then he and she did quarrel sore upon a mountain lane
And first she swore and then she bit and then to ease her pain
A black and bloody smudge she laid upon her lovers cheek
Who stood upon the pathway there in patience mild and meek,
And then in passion and in pride she snivelled loud and long
Till all her griefs he squeezed away upon his bosom strong.

MS (encl. TS), TCD. *LM*, 36

To MOLLY ALLGOOD

[Glendalough House, Glenageary]
Tuesday [16 October 1906]

Dearest
    Your note has just come. I've been hard at work all day — except of course for my outing, when I came in for a big shower in Glen Cullen and got soaked to the skin. I have not had a word with my brother yet, the days seem to slip by and I never see him alone. I am very bothered with my play again now, the Second Act has got out of joint in some way, and now its all in a mess. Dont be uneasy changling, everything is going on all right I think, I will go and see your mother soon, I dont much like the job so I keep putting it off. Besides of course I'm very hard at work again now, as if possible I want to read my play to the Directors next week. Wont it be a blessing if I can finish it then? I felt very lonesome today up in the country without you. I half thought of going in to town to take you for a walk but I thought it better to stick to my work. I dont know when I shall be in. When I go in the afternoon I nearly always get to the Abbey before *three*, so dont wait for me in that stuffy hole. I may be in tomorrow possibly, but it is not likely. If my letters keep you late in the morning, I'll have to knock them off again!!! I am sorry you are getting back into

your bad ways. You want someone to look after you eh? This letter wont do you much good I'm afraid but I'm very tired. Good bye Pop Gun.[1]

MS, TCD. *LM*, 37

[1] The letter is unsigned and across the top Molly has scribbled in pencil: you may stop your letters if you like, I dont care if I never heard from you or saw you again so there! & please dont let thoughts of me come into you your head when you are writing your play. It would be dreadful if your speeches were upset   I dont care a 'rap' for the theatre or anyone in it the pantomime season is coming on & I can easily get a shop; in fact I shall go out this afternoon & apply for one.

M. Allgood

To MOLLY ALLGOOD

[Glendalough House, Glenageary]
Thursday [18 October 1906]

Dearest

I'm looking forward to a luxurious shave by and by. I didn't thank you for the admirable article because my speeches of gratitude to you dont 'come off'.

By the way I think we made more of the Fay incident last night than it deserved. He really said very little. If he says anything more I have my answer ready — only please keep good time and please be civil to him — civil I mean as you would be to the manager of any other business you were in. You'll never get a perfect manager till you go to Heaven, and W.G. is a good fellow at bottom — you have often said so —

I have done a good morning's work, and ended my second act again, I think nearly right this time. How is your tooth-ache? my brother is off in town again today so I have not been able to ask him. He is extremely busy, of course, these few days bidding good-bye to all his friends. This is a lovely clear day I wish we were going out, we could have done so only for this OEdipus dinner with Magee.[1] I've an idea for next Sunday that we might meet at Carrick-mines and walk round through the mountains to Rathfarnham, I must measure it on the map to see how far it would be? We mustn't tire you too much as you have the long week's playing before you! I saw in the Mail a lot of adds of rooms for 5/0 a week, in fairly good localities, I'll *soon* be after them. I hope you are in good spirits. Keep cheerful its the best way

ever your old Tramp.

P.S. You cant write sentimental letters I find in the morning! I'm sending you a little book I promised you long ago. Please take great care of it and let me have it when you have read it.

MS, TCD. *LM*, 38

---

[1] Although a translation of *Oedipus* by W. K. Magee ('John Eglinton') was one of the possibilities for the winter programme, the production did not materialize.

To MOLLY ALLGOOD

Glendalough House [Glenageary]
Friday night [19 October 1906]

My own Treasure

I have just got home and found your little note! What a pity it was that I had to spoil our pleasant evening by letting you go home by yourself! I could not get rid of Stewart,[1] but I went after you as soon as I could, with him. I saw you in the distance and hurried after you. Just as we were overtaking you, you turned into a chemist's I said "There's Miss A, going home alone," and made a run to catch you, but you shut the door in my face!! I had told him I was going by the 10.45 train so I couldn't wait for you.

Darling when I think of your little smiles today I am carried away with delight. It was worth being lonely for years and years because it has made me value a priceless love like yours more than other men could do. Isn't it glorious that we have found each other I will be very careful not to let my little Changeling be lonesome any more, and not to hurt her little feelings. My own darling please be careful too. Of course you wont go to [Ambrose] Power's danse, the thought would be ANGUISH to me!! It's foolish but that [is] how I'm made. I know you are not likely to want to go, but I've just put this in as I heard Sally asking Power to take the two of you, and perhaps you might have let her persuade you without thinking how much it would hurt me. I dont know what would become of me if we quarreled now, I feel as if we knew each other too well to quarrel any more. You hardly know, my own changling, how entirely you've got hold of your old Tramp by the heart. I am sometimes frightened when I think what it would be to lose you. We wont talk of such things. Come down *by the quarter to eleven on Sunday* if fine, unless you hear to the contrary. Ten thousand blessings on you

Your Tramp

MS, TCD. *LM*, 39

¹ Joseph Holloway's diary (NLI) lists a 'Stuart' among those attending the dress rehearsal at the Abbey on 19 Oct 1906; this may be C. T. Stewart, nephew of the sculptor John Hughes, who also lived in Kingstown.

To MOLLY ALLGOOD

[Glendalough House, Glenageary]
Saturday [20 October 1906]

Dearest.

I was taken with a very lonesome turn last night, on my way home. It is painful being so near you and hardly seeing you at all. This state of affairs cant last much longer, only I dont want to start making fusses till my play is off my hands. I had no notion that you had such a beautiful voice, at least, it seemed beautiful to me. I liked your whole show of Mary except one gesture that seemed forced. You see Darley is quite friendly.¹ I knew he was, when in his ordinary humour.

By the way I was unspeakably pained and offended by your note, and P.O that I got on Thursday night. What have I done that you should write to me as if I was a dunning Jew? It was well your second letter came or I'd have been raging all day yesterday.

I'm not at all well, inside, I'm sorry to say — it is the worry of my play that is knocking me up I think — but I hope I'll be all right tomorrow. Please come down as usual by the *quarter to eleven train*, I'll be able to get as far as the train in any case and go to Bray with you and back. That is of course if it is *not* a *wet day*. It is looking doubtful this morning, but the glass is high and it may clear off again. I hope to go in this evening if I am not too unwell, but I shall be much occupied with a not very pleasant job. I've had a long morning at my play, by degrees the unfinished pages are getting fewer and fewer — Thanks be to God —

Good bye my own little treasure, till tomorrow with the help of God — (tonight doesn't count)

Your old T.

P.S. If my ailments get *much* worse I'll write tonight to put you off, but I dont think that will be necessary.   J.M.S.
Did you get the book?
P.S. Little Heart. Some times I haven't any words deep enough and tender enough to tell you all I feel for you. I am ashamed of my arid little letters when I have posted them, and of my foolish tempers, sometimes, when I bid you good-bye. But dont doubt your old Tramp. Anything that is profound, you surely know, cannot be expressed easily, and our feelings, little heart, are profound indeed!

MS, TCD. *LM*, 31

[1] Molly was rehearsing one of the leading roles in Lady Gregory's *The Gaol Gate*, in which she sang a *caoine* composed by Arthur Darley.

To MOLLY ALLGOOD

[Glendalough House, Glenageary]
Sunday [21 October 1906]

Little Heart

Another wet day for us! It was as well maybe as I'm not very flourishing and a long walk wouldn't have been the best thing for me. I wasn't well enough to go in last night and I am not sure that I'll get in tomorrow, by Tuesday however I ought to be all right, as there is not much the matter with me.

Little Heart, this morning I was brimming over with tender things to say to you, but I didn't write them, and now I've forgotten most of them. I was going to tell you how proud I was to be a man of letters so that I could write my little changling things other men wouldn't know how to get into words. That's a good idea, I think, worth putting into a sonnet if I get the mood. Then I was going to talk about other profound things that I've forgotten altogether. These two idle days I've had time to think and you've never been out of my mind; I've felt very happy to have a little changling of my own to think of, even though I've been lonesome, and longing to have you here to pet me and keep up my spirits.

I've a new idea. Do you think you could write a little comedy to play in yourself; say about your life in the convent school? I could give you a scenario, would not it be fun, and then you'd be able to patronise Miss Darragh, and Mrs Bill Fay and the lot of them. I'm sure you've as much humour as Lady Gregory, and humour is the only thing her little farces have. Or could you write a comedy about the women at Kilmacanogue (that's how it's spelled) or about some incident of your early career? The one thing needful is to get hold of some little centre of life that you know thoroughly, and that is not quite familiar to every one. I'm sure your old grandmother would be a lovely character in a play. Think about it, little heart, and, when you're acting, notice how the scenes etc. are worked out, one into the other. This is all a wild idea, but it would be fun to try; no one would know but ourselves and of course I'd help and advise you. You could write out your MSS on the typewriter, so all is complet!

I wonder how the show went last night[1] I suppose I shall hear from you tomorrow. By the way what afternoons are you free this week? Our best way would be to meet at Carrickmines and have a walk to Kilternan and round about, and then I could send you back

by Harcourt Street again, and wander home here. I believe my
brother goes on Thursday. I have not had a word with him yet on
'Ourselves', we are both so busy I never see him except at meals.
He is in town nearly every day bidding people goodbye and so on.
I dont know whether I shall be able to post this tonight. It is very
wet and I dont want to give myself a chill. I hope I shall hear from
you tomorrow morning, and that it will be a nice letter.

Ever, my little Heart, your old

Tramp

MS, TCD. *LM*, 40

¹ Too ill to attend the opening of the season, when *The Gaol Gate*, *The
Mineral Workers*, and *Spreading the News* were performed, JMS had sent a
telegram to the theatre the night before.

To MOLLY ALLGOOD

Kingstown 22 October 1906 10.35 A.M.

Allgood Care Callender Park Chambers Stephens Green North
Dublin.
Congratulations   Much better   Synge

Telegram, TCD. *LM*, 41

To MOLLY ALLGOOD

[Glendalough House, Glenageary]
Monday morning [22 October 1906]

Little Sweetheart

I cannot tell you how delighted I was to get your letter this
morning. I am much better — nearly all right again — but I will not
go in tonight unless I feel quite fit.

I am in a great hurry with this as I want to catch the early post.
You'll be expecting something. I am delighted to hear of the success
of everything. When I read of the compliments you got I had tears
of pleasure in my eyes to the wonder of my family. Yes you have
a lovely voice, I think, it will be worth anything on the roads

Now I must run. I posted my letter to you in Dalkey myself on
Saturday, I went round there in the afternoon and was the worse for it.
Goddbye, dearest till very soon, I hope. Write if I dont go in tonight

Your old Tramper

MS, TCD. *LM*, 41

To MOLLY ALLGOOD

[Glendalough House, Glenageary] My Bed
12.30 [23 October 1906]

Little (or big) Heart!

Did you think I neglected you tonight? My poor little heart I couldn't hepl it, I had a lot of business to talk with WBY etc.[1] When he and I went across to the tea-room he launched out into *your* praises, in quite a pointed way as if complimenting me also. He says you are curiously charming in Boyle and he cannot make out how you do it as there is so little in the part.[2] He said a lot more nice things about your cleverness and imagination that I wont tell you. I think our troubles are nearly over with the help of God! Come down in good time tomorrow (Wednesday) I shall be there from 7.20 I think. We might manage a walk perhaps on Friday. I feel as if my little illness and our last letters have made us nearer than ever.

Good bye J.M.S.

MS, TCD. *LM*, 42

[1] In addition to discussing theatre programming with Yeats, JMS was in discussion with George Roberts concerning the copyrighting of Maunsel's Abbey Theatre Series in the U.S.

[2] Molly played the small role of the daughter Kitty in *The Mineral Workers*.

To MOLLY ALLGOOD

[Glendalough House, Glenageary]
Thursday (afternoon) [25 October 1906]

Dearest Pop.

Come down tomorrow (Friday) if you can by the *quarter to* two from Westland Row, taking 3rd return to Bray. I will join you at Glenageary and we can have four hours together. You can go back to Dublin by the train I went up by last night, that will be time enough I suppose. Get your dinner of course before you come.

I showed my brother your photo today he beamed at it most cordially and said with conviction "Thats a *very nice* face."

Also I heard people in the Tea-rooms last night saying how good the 'younger girl' was in the G.Gate".

Now are you buttered up enough for one day?

I've a crow to pluck with you all the same, Miss P.P.!

In a hurry

ever yours
Tramp

P.S. Of course tomorrow depends on a fine day. Dont come if wet there would be no use.

MS, TCD. *LM*, 42

To MOLLY ALLGOOD

[Glendalough House, Glenageary]
Friday [26 October 1906]

Dearest

Rain again! I wish you'd pray that it may be fine on Sunday, I dont know what'll become of us if it's wet!

My brother went off last night. It was very sad seeing him going off on the boat for seven years — he is one of the best fellows in [the] world, I think, though he is so religious we have not much in common. My old mother bore up wonderfully well, though she cried a good deal of course after he was gone. She kept saying now and then, "It seems so hard that I must live without him". The whole thing gives me a 'grief-lump', in my throat!

I found your little note waiting for me when I came back from the boat, and it pleased me very greatly. It made me feel the way I felt long ago in Wexford when you were so nice and good, before we got into the Cardiff complications and all the little troubles we have had since. If you like to thank God in my name for having given you to me you can, I feel nearly ready to do it myself today I am so happy and pleased with you. I'll be up tomorrow evening, — this evening I must stay with my mother, — and then please Heaven we'll get our walk on Sunday. Good bye my little heart

J.M.S.

Do you realise how free you'll be when Deirdre's on? I hope there'll be a moon then!

MS, TCD. *LM*, 43

To MOLLY ALLGOOD

[Glendalough House, Glenageary]
[31 October 1906]

Darling

I was very delighted to get your note this morning. I expected it last night, and was dissapointed. I dont know whether I shall be in tonight or not. I wrote to Yeats asking him to fix a directors' meeting for various matters and he has not answered me, so I am not very eager to go in till he does so.

I had a dreadful turn of dispair over the Playboy last night — it seemed hopeless — but I have come through the difficulty, more or less, that was in my way. I am feeling very much 'done up' with it all and I fear I cant leave it for a walk this week. It is too bad, but I must get done with the thing or it will kill me. I am sorry to hear that you are having gloomy dreams, you must be done up too. I am too worn out to write much of anything to you now, but if you had seen my misery when the post passed last night without a letter from my little Changling you would forgive me. I dont know what will become of me if I dont get the Playboy off my hands soon, I nearly wrote in to them last night to ask them to put on the 'Well of the Saints' instead of it in December so that I might have a few months more to work at it but I dont like the thought of having it hanging over me all this winter when I ought to be so Happy! Parts of it are the best work, I think, that I have ever done, but parts of it, are not structurally strong or good, I have been all this time trying to get over weak situations by strong writing, but now I find it wont do, and I am at my wit's end. It's well I have the thought of you to comfort me! or I dont know what I should do. Write to me very often your letters are my only comfort.

Ever my little Heart your J.M.S.

MS, TCD. *LM*, 44

To MOLLY ALLGOOD

[Glendalough House, Glenageary]
Nov 1st [1906]

My little Life

Yes, you have comforted me a good bit. I like being lectured and I'll try and keep up my spirits and work ahead. I have heard from Yeats and I am to be in tomorrow afternoon, and probably evening so I shall get my eyes on you again. This is a wretched day, it is well we had not arranged for a walk. I half hope I have got over the weakness in my Second Act that has been worrying me so much, but it is too soon to say with certainty. Any little change seems a great improvement at first, but after a while you find out that it is the novelty only that is taking you, and that in reality the 2nd state is worse than the first. I hope the next play I write I'll have you at my elbow to advise me and cheer me up. I have no one out here to talk over my troubles with and I get frightfully depressed.

What a lot of things you got the Fays![1] I will give him a copy of the 'Well' too to make up for the smallness of my subscription. I wonder shall we get a word together tomorrow, I shall probably be dining with W.B.Y. *and her Ladyship*

We'll have Sunday again soon in any case with the help of God. That is something to look forward to!

Yours forever
J.M.S.

MS, TCD. *LM*, 45

---

[1] W. G. Fay and Brigit O'Dempsey were married in Glasgow on 29 Oct 1906, returning to Dublin on 1 Nov.

To MOLLY ALLGOOD

[Glendalough House, Glenageary]
Saturday [3 November 1906]

Dearest

I've had a great morning's work my play is getting on. Two or three more weeks ought to finish it. I am going in tonight but I write this in case by any chance I should not get a word with you. Please come down tomorrow — if it is not a wet day — by the usual train at a *quarter to eleven*. The weather is looking very uncertain but we must hope for the best. It cant always rain!

I am very glad that you liked 'Auccassin and Nicolete,'[1] it is a very beautiful little thing, I think, filled with the very essence of literature and romance. Keep it of course as long as you want it. Then I will poke out something else for you.

Did I send you the "Ordeal of Richard Feveril", by Meredith before I went to Kerry? I was looking for it the other day to send it to you but I couldn't find it.

Pray for tomorrow.

Ever your
J.M.S.

MS, TCD. *LM*, 45

---

[1] JMS may have been introduced to this thirteenth-century legend of Provence by Petit de Julleville's lectures at the Sorbonne in 1895; it is also discussed by Walter Pater in *The Renaissance* and the English translations by F. W. Bourdillon and Andrew Lang were well known.

To MOLLY ALLGOOD

[Glendalough House, Glenageary]
[?5 November 1906]

Dearest

I am in great form today for my work. So much so that I am not going in to town to see this old play of [?MacManus][1] I hope you got home all right. I had the best sleep I have had for weeks and I feel in great spirits. The P.Boy is very nearly done I think this week should get me through with it! Wont that be great? I shall be in tomorrow or next day most likely, in any case, I'll let you know of my movements of course, we must try and fit in a walk this week, I suppose there will be a rehearsal on Wednesday evening?

This letter will be *thick* enough I hope![2]

Ever your Tramp

MS, TCD. *LM*, 51

[1] During the first week of November 1906 the Gaelic League's Samhain celebration took place in the Abbey Theatre; on 5 Nov *Orange and Green* by Seumas MacManus was produced with *The Sword of Dermot* by James Cousins and *An tAthrughadh Mór* by Felix Partridge.

[2] It is written on a postcard.

To LADY GREGORY

Glendalough House | Kingstown
(Monday) [5 November 1906]

Dear Lady Gregory

I am afraid I cannot take you the Playboy tomorrow. The Manchester Guardian seems to be in a hurry for my notice of Gwynne's book[1] so that will take me some time this week. I have only very little now to do to the Playboy to get him *provisionally* finished, so I hope to be able to read him out on Thursday or Friday if that will suit you and Yeats.

Yours sincerely
J. M. Synge

MS, Berg. *TB*, 158

[1] His review of *The Fair Hills of Ireland* by Stephen Gwynn, which appeared in the *Manchester Guardian*, 16 Nov 1906, commented on the 'pleasantness' of the book, 'which is likely to bring many minds into a more intelligent sympathy with Ireland, where, for good and for bad, the past is so living and the present so desirous to live' (*Prose*, 387).

To MOLLY ALLGOOD

[Glendalough House, Glenageary]
[5 November 1906]

Little Heart

I am just off to the post with the Aran book proofs[1] so I have only time to write you a hurried line in spite of all your injunctions! I feel in great form after yesterday and I have had a good morning's work. I hope you aren't the worse. There was a very bad thunder storm in Kingstown — much worse than what we got — about five o'clock — the flashes we saw I suppose in the Rocky Valley.[2] We got off very well. Let me hear from you soon.

My mother asked me again if I was alone, and I said I had 'a friend' with me. I must tell her soon. Do you really want more books. I will send you as many as you like but I dont want to plague you with books that you have no time to read. Remember to get Cuchulain of Muirthemne from the library and read 'The Sons of Usnach'[3] in it. It is charming. Now ten thousand blessings on you I'll write more the next time

Your old Tramp

MS, TCD. *LM*, 46

[1] Proofs for *The Aran Islands* were arriving from Maunsel & Co. in batches.
[2] By Great Sugar Loaf in the Wicklow Mountains near the tiny village of Kilmacanoge.
[3] Translated by Lady Gregory; the source of JMS's next play, *Deirdre of the Sorrows*.

To MOLLY ALLGOOD

[Glendalough House, Glenageary]
Tuesday [6 November 1906]

Dearest

This is a mere line. I was too occupied with my play to go in last night, but hope to be in tomorrow or next day, and in any case on Friday to meet Henderson. I am working now at very high tension and if I can keep it up perhaps I shall have finished in a fortnight. Wont that be great? I do not know whether I shall be able to walk on Thursday or not. I am rather afraid of taking my thoughts off my work even for one evening. Hadn't we a *splendid* day on Sunday?

Ever yours

J.M.S.

MS, AS. *LM*, 47

To JOSEPH HONE[1]

[Glendalough House, Glenageary]
Nov 6th [1906]

Dear Hone

I return proof[2] I was out when it came last night so could not see to it then.

Please give enclosed line to Roberts

Yours sincerely
J. M. Synge

MS, TCD

[1] Joseph Maunsel Hone (1882–1959), one of the founders of Maunsel & Co., was editor of *The Shanachie*, to which JMS contributed articles for five of its six numbers, starting with 'The Vagrants of Wicklow' for Autumn 1906 (no. 2). Later Hone became a prolific translator of works from the Italian and French, wrote biographies of, among others, Berkeley, Thomas Davis, George Moore, Henry Tonks, and W. B. Yeats, and edited the letters of John Butler Yeats. He was elected president of the Irish Academy of Letters in 1957.

[2] Possibly of 'The Vagrants of Wicklow'; or another batch of *The Aran Islands.*

To MOLLY ALLGOOD

[Glendalough House, Glenageary]
Tuesday night [6 November 1906]

Dearest

I am so very sorry to hear of the pain in your back. Is it quite gone? I blame myself very much for taking you such a long way when you weren't very well. Do let me know tomorrow how you are. I feel uneasy about you. I did not let myself believe all the talk you made the other night but it did trouble me a bit so I am glad you have disowned it. I am dreadfully busy these days I have a book to review for the Manchester Guardian, and a lot of proofs to correct for my Aran book, and of course the P.B. To make matters worse a spring has just broken in my type-writer so I dont know what I shall do. I may have to go to town with it tomorrow morning and I may look in at the Abbey but I dont know. I want to read the P.B. to the Directors and Fay on Thursday or Friday so I dont know about a walk, in any case we cannot go unless you are *quite* well. Let me know. I am too tired now to write any thing of interest. Did you go to the conversazione at the National Literary?[1] I had a bit of a ride this afternoon and I was wishing you were there to enjoy it the air was so beautifully clear. I wonder what I shall think of Miss D[arragh]. You will be very unwise if you let her *see* that you dont like her. She is playing her game, and you had better play yours. I mean that you should be affable, and reserved at the same time, so that she will not know whether you like her or not. That is the wisest plan, though it is not easy perhaps for little changlings! Now take care of yourself and let me know how you are. Excuse this matter of fact note I am writing against time and I am very tired.

Yours forever
J. M. Tramp

I've found the little spring of my T.Writer so I may be able to patch it up myself for the present. *Remember to write* tomorrow

MS, TCD. *LM*, 47

---

[1] The National Literary Society of Ireland, founded in 1892 by Yeats and others, met regularly during the winter months and frequently the papers given there provided a forum for debate on the Abbey Theatre and its playwrights.

To W. B. YEATS

Glendalough House | Kingstown
Nov. 7th [1906]

Dear Yeats

Thanks for card. I'll come in tomorrow afternoon. Two of the matters we have to arrange were postponed, I think, from last meeting in order that we might have Ryan's advice. Would it be well to get him down tomorrow either after his work or in the evening? He was to advise us as to Miss Horniman and the minutes the form of the notice we are to send Bank about Henderson and the I.N.T.S. money.

I hope everything is going on well. I would have been in during the week but I could not leave the Play-Boy. I am nearly in distraction with him, and consequently am very unwell.

Yours
J.M.S.

I'll bring in OEdipus tomorrow.
P.S. We'll have to come to some arrangement with Ryan, I think, as to his overseeing of the accounts for the present.

MS, Berg. *TB*, 159

To MOLLY ALLGOOD

[Glendalough House, Glenageary]
Nov. 8/06

Dear Heart

I am greatly relieved to hear that you are better, I got very anxious last night when no letter came. Of course I will keep myself free for Sunday so that we may walk if it is fine. We had better take the quarter to eleven train as you have a show on Saturday night. If your back is not well of course we wont be able to go very far, you had better ask Peggy if she thinks you are well enough for a long walk. The Playboy is very nearly ready, I am writing to Lady Gregory by this post to ask her to fix a time for me to read it to them. Then there will be the job of making a clean copy. My M.S. at present could not be read by anyone but myself, it is all written over and corrected and pulled to bits. I will send you the Cuchulain please take great care of it, as it is a presentation copy from Lady Gregory. Have you finished Aucassin and Nicolete?

What wretched weather it is! My mother is in bed with a very bad cold, I hope I wont get it. I sent off my review to Manchester yesterday, and got more proofs to correct. I am kept busy! I hope you are taking care of yourself and not sitting too much in the Green Room with the window shut. Remember if your health gives way we wont be able to have our long walks. It is only very strong women who can walk as you have been doing, so you must keep very strong, changeling.

What are you changing about now? You seem greatly impressed with your changable attributes! Forever

J. M. Tramp.

P.S. This reads very scrapily I fear, but it means well, when my morning's work is over I am always too tired to write to you as well as I would like. Forgive my tired brains![1]

MS, AS. *LM*, 48

[1] At the top of this letter Molly has tried three times to spell 'Prague'.

To LADY GREGORY

Glendalough House | Kingstown
Nov. 8th [1906]

Dear Lady Gregory,

May I read the Play Boy to you and Yeats and Fay some time tomorrow, Saturday or Monday according as it suits you all. A little verbal correction is still necessary and one or two structural points may need — I fancy do need — revision, but I would like to have your opinions on it before I go any further.

Yours sincerely
J. M. Synge

MS, Berg. *TB*, 159

To SARAH PURSER

Glendalough House | Glenageary | Kingstown
Nov. 10 [1906]

Dear Miss Purser

Many thanks for your kind invitation, which was forwarded to me last night. Something seems always to get in the way when you send me a *first* invitation so I hope you will forgive me if I ask you to let me come some other evening instead. A brother of mine went off to China last week for seven years and my mother has rather collapsed in consequence so I do not like to leave her alone all this evening — when I shall be at the plays — and all tomorrow night as well. I am so sorry but I do not think I can help it, though I have been looking forward to your 'stained-glass scenario'[1] — that you promised me — ever since our 'At Home'.

I hope I shall see you tonight at the plays. I dreamed last night that Tolstoi was there escorted by two Japanese. It will be interesting if they turn up!

With many thanks

yours sincerely
J. M. Synge

MS, NLI

[1] Presumably plans for a window from her workshop, An Túr Gloine.

To MOLLY ALLGOOD

[Glendalough House, Glenageary]
Saturday [10 November 1906]

Dear Molly

I got your letter all right last night, and the letter and paper that you forwarded me. The letter was an invitation out to dinner on Sunday evening, but of course I have refused it. Your letter wasn't a bit nice, I wish you wouldn't write like that it makes me feel queer.

You were in a mighty hurry to take it for granted that I was going to have a reading of the P.B. on Sunday and to spoil our walk!

I dreamed about you last night — a very nice dream I think — but I have got it mixed up. I dreamed also that Tolstoi — the great Russian writer came to our plays with two Japanese to see 'Riders-to-the-Sea', and that there was a very bad house. I could not write a nice, letter this morning to save my life — it shows how little right I have to scold you for yours — I slept very badly, and I am tired and dull. You dont want me to invent sweet speeches when I'm not a bit sweet do you? We'll be able to see more of each other now, I hope, as the P.B. is nearly done, that will be a blessing. Come tomorrow, if fine, by the *quarter to eleven* please, I wish to God I could say something nice to you, but your letter and some of the things you have hinted (or seemed to hint) have frozen a little layer of ice round my old heart which as you know very well is a mass of love for my little changeling.

Your old T.

P.S. Dont imagine I'm huffed or anything, little heart, I'm only weary.

MS, AS. *LM*, 49

To MOLLY ALLGOOD

[Glendalough House, Glenageary]
Saturday afternoon [10 November 1906]

Little Heart

I wrote you a crusty sort of note this morning when I was tired and in a bad humour. I have taken a holiday from my work today and now — at 5 o'cl. — after a cycle ride through Kilternan, and the Scalp and Enniskerry, I'm in the best of humours and I could write you nice things till you were tired of them. What a pair of asses we are! We are so fond of each other and we get on so beautifully when we like, and still we keep pulling each other's hair, and saying stupid things till we both get miserable. It is such a pity that we cant have sense because we both know quite well I think, that we are all in all to each other, and will be so always. We must see more of each [other] if we can manage it now, and I think that will make things smoother. This little tiffette — by the way — was your fault wasn't it? It was a very slight affair in any case, and you were very good last night. I believe it is that wretched Playboy who has been making all the mischief, it is unnatural that we should be so near each other, and still not be able to see each other oftener.[1] We'll change all that with the help of God. I suppose you will get this tomorrow morning on your way to meet me. That we may have a fine day! now goodbye my own little treasure and forgive my growls.

Ever your Tramp.

A quarter to eleven on Sunday remember from W Row.

MS, TCD. *LM*, 50

---

[1] During this week the company were rehearsing during the day while the theatre was let to other local companies.

To MOLLY ALLGOOD

[Glendalough House, Glenageary]
Tuesday [13 November 1906]

Dearest

I was delighted to hear yesterday that you are well again. I did not think I could hear from you so early in the day, but I waited about all the same, cleaning my bicycle and fiddling about. Then just as I had given up hope and was going out a postman rode up to the gate on a bicycle and handed me your letter. I hadn't time to answer you yesterday as I have been working at my M.S. for the reading tonight. Unfortunately I have a cold and am very hoarse and unwell so I wont be able to do myself justice, I fear. My cycle blew up yesterday so I went down by the sea instead of riding and sat down in the cold wind like an idiot. I feel very depressed and anxious about tonight, a great deal depends on this play I think. I got a very gushing letter from George Moore last night praising my 'Vagrants of Wicklow' up to the skies.[1] Did you see what Martin Harvey said about 'Riders' in his speech in to day's paper?[2] I do hope my Play-boy will come off.

I am so glad we are not going to quarrell any more, of course as we have such *strong wills* once we decide not to quarrell we wont quarrell! Isn't that so? I awoke very early this morning and thought a lot and happily about you and our arrangements before I got up. I should think in another ten days I shall have done all I can do to the Play-Boy and then we'll come to business. I have a lot of proofs to correct today and I am so anxious about tonight I have not much peace of mind to write nicely to you. If I get a very bad cold out of this how shall I post your letters? Dont be alarmed if you a[re] a day or two without news. I'll try and let you know tomorrow how the play goes.

This is a poor sort of note I'm afraid but it is not wanting of feeling, little treasure, that makes it so. It is only my weariness and fears about tonight. Goodbye dear heart, and be good to your

old Tramper

MS, TCD. *LM*, 51

[1] George Moore (1852-1933), the novelist and sometime dramatist whose early participation in the Irish dramatic movement resulted in the ill-fated *Diarmuid and Grania* (written in collaboration with W. B. Yeats in 1901) and the entertainingly malicious trilogy, *Hail and Farewell!* (1911-14). He wrote to JMS c/o Maunsel & Co. on 11 Nov 1906 (TCD).

[2] Sir John Martin Harvey (1863-1944), actor-manager in the tradition of Sir Henry Irving, from whom he received his early training, was noted as much for his roles in romantic melodramas as for his Shakespearian performances; he frequently toured Ireland and North America and was seriously tempted to perform in *The Playboy*. His speech on 12 Nov 1906 to the Ladies' Auxiliary of the Lifeboat Saturday Fund referred to 'Mr Synge's masterly little play, entitled "Riders to the Sea," . . . as one of the strongest object lessons in the perilous nature of the life of those who "go down to the sea in ships" '.

To MOLLY ALLGOOD

[Glendalough House, Glenageary]
Friday [16 November 1906]

Dear Heart

I've had a bad turn enough, but I'm much better though I'm in bed still. I may get up for a while this evening but I am not sure yet. Dont be uneasy about me, dear heart, it is only a bout of influenza, made sharper by my trip to town Tuesday when it was coming on and the excitement of the "reading". I would give the world and all to see you, but I'm afraid we cant well manage it. I couldn't of course have you up here and downstairs we'd have to face the whole crowd, — my cousin is staying here now[1] — and my sister and elder brothers and nephews are all in and out. We would have no peace or satisfaction I'm afraid, and so alas! you had better wait. I hope I shall be in town again by Monday or Tuesday, but if I am not I will arrange for you to come down some way or other, so that I may have a look at my little changeling again. Dear Heart write to me every day, I lie here listening for the post man's knock. I think of you a great deal and changeling I love you infinitely. I cannot write any more now. It tires me and I have a line to write to Lady G.

Ever my dear Heart
Your old Tramp

MS, TCD. *LM*, 52

[1] Florence Ross had come to Glendalough House on 15 Nov 1906.

To MOLLY ALLGOOD

[Glendalough House, Glenageary]
[18 November 1906]

Dearest.

It is cruel — cruel — cruel — to leave me without a line from you
when I am so ill and miserable. Did you not get my letter asking you
to write to me every day? I am very unwell, we got the doctor out
from Dublin to see me last night.[1] He hopes I will soon be all right.
I am to go in to him on Wednesday or Thursday. Are you offended
by my last note or what has happened? I was so weak when I was
writing I could hardly hold the pen. I am to stay in bed all day today
what a change from the Sundays we have had!

You have no notion, darling of my heart, how much and how
tenderly I think of you. You must not be uneasy about me. I am
mending now, and in a few weeks, I hope, I'll be as well as ever.
It is all that accursed Playboy. There is no chance now of putting
him on in December. Why dont you write. I wish I had asked you
to come down today in spite of everything. When I put you off
coming, I felt so weak I didn't feel capable of making the explanations a visit would have entailed

Yours forever
J. M. Tramp

MS, TCD. *LM*, 53

[1] Dr Alfred R. Parsons (1864–1952) of 27 Lower Fitzwilliam Street came at
about 10.30 p.m. on the 17th; according to Mrs Synge's diary, he thought 'the
bronchial tubes caused bleeding', but there is no other description of JMS's
illness. Parsons, visiting physician to the Royal City of Dublin Hospital, was
known for his careful diagnoses and open-minded approach to new remedies.

To MOLLY ALLGOOD

[Glendalough House, Glenageary]
Tuesday (afternoon) [20 November 1906]

Dearest

Thanks for your two letters. I enclose a scrawl I wrote yesterday
morning when the post passed and left me. Even when your note
came at 2. yesterday I was a little dissappointed that you had written
so few lines when you had all Sunday on your hands. I got all the
earlier ones last week, and was delighted to get them. I am up now
again, and have been downstairs for a while. If you come — I leave
it to yourself, you know I will be overjoyed to see you — you might
come by the quarter to two from W.R. to Glenageary, and go home

If you come to Glenageary station ask for Adelaide
Road. Turn to right down it towards the sea,
our house is a good bit down on the right, the last
house before a big bare field. 'Glendalough House'
is on the pillars of the gate, but very faint.
You could also come by tram and walk up Adelaide
Road, when our house would be the first big house on
your left, but the trams are very slow and cold.

I am a little better to-day, I think
but it is very tedious. If I am
well enough I go in to the doctor
on Thursday or Friday afternoon.
Perhaps you could meet me at W. Row
and walk as far as the sea cons with
me. I will let you know if I can what time I am
going. My dear old love how hard it is to be parted
for so long. I promise I'll take more care from this to the
day of judgement and let my plays take of Themselves.
By the way if you come give a nice little double knock! I wonder

To Molly Allgood, 20 November 1906

by the quarter past three in time for your rehearsal. If you come to Glenageary station ask for Adelaide Road. Turn to right down it towards the sea. Our house is a good bit down on the right, the last house before a big bare field. 'Glendalough House' is on the pillars of the gate, but very faint. You could also come by tram and walk *up* Adelaide Road, when our house would be the first big house on your left, but the trams are very slow and cold. [*Map*]

I am a little better today I think but it is very tedious. If I am well enough I go in to the doctor on Thursday or Friday afternoon. Perhaps you could meet me at W. Row and walk as far as the Doctors with me. I will let you know if I can what time I am going. My dear old love how hard it is to be parted for so long. I promise I'll take more care from this to the day of Judgement and let my plays take [care] of themselves. By the way if you come give a nice little double knock!¹ I wonder if I shall get out soon. I am afraid of this cold weather and I am weak still I am afraid to write too much for fear of making my head ache.

Good bye dearest

J. M. Tramp

[*Enclosure*]

Monday morning [19 November 1906]

Dearest.

Why dont you write? This morning I made fully sure of a long loving letter When the post knock came I hammered on the floor with my stick for the servant and told her to get me my letter, but she said there was none for me. I turned over then in my bed and said to myself that now I had better try and die quickly as my little changeling had turned against me or something terrible had happened. These dissappointments I need not say are very bad for me. Why do you torture me? Little soul I did not know till these days how utterly I am wrapped up in you. Yesterday I thought in spite of all that you would come and see me. I suppose my letter stopped you. I am very weak still Even writing these few lines makes my heart thump. What times are you free this week? I cannot live without you much longer Why — why — why did I make myself ill like this just as life had become a delight and a blessing to me for first time in my life. — I wont post this till I see if a letter comes from you at two o'clock. If none comes I'll faint with agony. I give my letters to you to my mother to send to the post, and she knew, I think, that I was expecting you yesterday but we do not speak of you yet. I'm too shaky.

MSS, TCD. *LM*, 54

¹ Young ladies were trained to 'double knock' to distinguish themselves from tradesmen and postmen.

To MOLLY ALLGOOD

Glendalough House [Glenageary]
Thursday [22 November 1906]

Dearest

I am afraid you must be ill again as you have not turned up I hope you are not bad. Tomorrow I am going in to the doctor so do not come then. Saturday also is a bad day and the Fays are likely to come out on Sunday. I will let you know what we can do. I shall be uneasy now till I hear that you are not ill. I feel very much upset watching out for you these two afternoons and trying to keep the coast clear so that I might see you quietly in our dining room. It would almost be better to send me a wire to say you cannot come than to leave me in such suspense. However I'm not the worse, I think. I've been out for a little today, but I felt very weak on my legs. I showed my mother your photo the other night and told her you were a great friend of mine That is as far as I can go till I am stronger I am thoroughly sick of this state of affairs we must end it, and make ourselves public. Be sure to let me know how you are.

Good bye dear heart,

Your Tramp.

MS, TCD. *LM*, 56

To MOLLY ALLGOOD

[Glendalough House, Glenageary]
Friday [23 November 1906]

Dear Heart

I am not quite sure that you are going to meet me today so I had better send you a line. I felt quite cheered up by your little visit yesterday, and I think I am a lot better today. It was too bad that I had to let you trot off so soon, but it couldn't be helped. A whole pack of them were waiting to have tea in the room where we were, and besides by the time my cousin's¹ visit was over too I was dead fagged out. I hope you will meet me this afternoon. It is curious what a little thing checks the flow of the emotions. Last evening because there was a sort of vague difficulty or uncertainty about our positions in this house we were as stiff as strangers. I felt beforehand that it would be like that, so I was not dissappointed, and I am *delighted* that you came. I do things gradually by nature and we have made a great step in the right direction. It is much better to let my mother get used to the idea by degrees than to spring it on her too suddenly. I wish you could have seen your solemnity as you walked into the room yesterday with your long coat and glasses, you looked like a *Professor of Political Economy* at the very least. Your little visit has made this room more interesting than it was yesterday, and I have the pleasantest remembrance of every little thing you said. I hope to Heaven the doctor will not find much the matter with me today.

How did you get home? As soon as you were gone I began imagining that you would get into the wrong train and be carried off to Bray and then have no money to take you home. I saw you as plainly as possible standing in your long coat on the platform in Bray explaining your case to the station master and porters! It looked very funny. Dear heart I wish I had you here every day what a difference it would make

Tenderly your
J. M. Tramp

I had a letter from Miss Tobin this morning she heard from Sally that I was ill.

MS, TCD. *LM*, 56

¹ Edward Synge the etcher was in Kingstown staying with JMS's brother Robert; he invited JMS to Surrey to recuperate.

To MOLLY ALLGOOD

[Glendalough House, Glenageary]
Friday Night [23 November 1906]

Little Heart

This is my second letter to you today, I'm afraid I'm spoiling you! Well I had to wait *two* long hours before I saw the doctor so that it was a quarter past five when I got away. I am grateful to you for coming to meet me I liked you (in spite of your hat) more than I am going to say. But to get to the point. The doctor says I've got on very well, but I've a very slight irritation on one lung still, so it is well for me to be carefull, and he advises me to put off Playboy and go to England for a fortnight. So, dear heart, I think I'll go for your sake as much as for my own. You would not like me to knock up regularly would you? The other day when I felt so very ill I kept wondering over and over what my poor little changeling would do if I died and she was left to fight along by herself. I dont like to think of it. You would get along well I dare say, but it is lonesome to think about. However I'm all right again and you'll have me back to you in two weeks ready for walks and mountains, and all our tramping as before. Please tell me as soon as you can what times you are free next week, I must have one little outing with you *before* I go.

I hope you weren't hurt by my sayings about your hat! Remember I'm so proud of my little changeling that I wont let anyone spoil her, not even you!! But forgive me, it wasn't nice of me to go on so much about it when you had taken all the trouble to come down and meet me. I'm afraid I cant see you on Sunday. I am a bit feverish still and I must be very quiet for a couple of days My cousin is coming out here that day. I hope I shall see you on Monday or the day after. Write me a long letter

Ever yours
J. M. Tramp

MS, TCD. *LM*, 57

To MOLLY ALLGOOD

[Glendalough House, Glenageary]
Saturday Morning [24 November 1906]

My dearest

I am much better today, I think, but I feel very sad, somehow, at the thought that I am not to see you till Monday or Tuesday. I am much more 'lonesome' now than when I was really ill. My little life how fond I am of you! I wonder if you are tired of all the times I tell you that. When you begin to be tired of it tell me. Dont you think I am right to go to England and get strong again? Mind you write a full real letter today or tomorrow or both, at least send me a line today if you have not time for a long letter. You will have plenty of time for that tomorrow. I wonder what you will do all day. I shall be thinking of you. When I go to England I'll write to my mother and tell her all. I am afraid I might say something too violent if we talked it over at first as I loose my temper so easily.

Forever and ever, my heart's light,

Your old T.

MS, TCD. *LM*, 58

To MOLLY ALLGOOD

[Glendalough House, Glenageary]
Saturday [24 November 1906]

My Heart's Joy

Thanks for your note — a very nice one — which I got this morning. My mother is too shy to say much about you, but I think she is pleased. She said you seemed very bright and she hoped I had asked you to come down again on Sunday and cheer me up. I said I hadn't but I would write. Today she has reminded me several times not to forget my note to you. So come down tomorrow (Sunday) by the *quarter to three*, like yesterday[1] and we'll have another little chat   If I can think of a suitable excuse I'll write to F. Fay and put him off coming tomorrow. I'm not quite up to entertaining him in any case.

The doctor says I am going on well, getting better slowly. I am not sad except at moments when I get depressed by being ill so long, and not able to see you. Now this must go to the post so that you may have it before you go to bed. Thousands of blessings

from your old Tramp

MS, TCD. *LM*, 59

[1] A mistake for 'Thursday'; see p. 240.

To LADY GREGORY

Glendalough House | Glenageary | Kingstown
Nov 25 [1906]

Dear Lady Gregory

I have had rather a worse attack than I expected when I wrote my last note, but I am much better now, and out as usual. One of my lungs however has been a little touched so I shall have to be careful for a while. Would it be possible to put off the Playboy for a couple of weeks? I am afraid if I went to work at him again now, and then rehearsed all December I would be very likely to knock up badly before I was done with him. My doctor says I may do it, if it is *necessary*, but he advises me to take a couple of weeks rest if it can be managed. A cousin of mine who etches is over here now and he wants me to go and stay with him for a fortnight in a sort of country house he has in Surrey, so if you think the Playboy can be put off I will go across on Thursday or Friday and get back in time to see the Shadowy Waters and get the Playboy under way for January. What do you think? If I go I would like to read the third act of Playboy to you before I go, and then make final changes while I am away as I shall have a quiet time. I hope to see Deirdre on Tuesday or Wednesday if all goes well.

Yours sincerely

J. M. Synge

MS, Berg. *TB*, 160

To MOLLY ALLGOOD

[Glendalough House, Glenageary]

Tuesday [27 November 1906]

Dearest

I forget whether I promised to write to you today or you to me. I was none the worse for our nice little walk yesterday, and I hope to be in at the Abbey tomorrow night. I am to go to the Nassau to finish reading the Playboy in the afternoon and I suppose they'll keep me to dine. Then on Thursday I think I shall [have] to take my cousin round to see old Yeats[1] and on Friday I'm off, so it was well we had our time yesterday. Let me know however, what time you are free the next two days in case, by any chance I should be able to arrange to see you again. I am sending you a couple of books tomorrow — two very well known novels that everyone reads, and that will amuse you I think. You had better keep the other books till I come back. You may like to dip into them again. I have been thinking about you a great deal, and very *happily* since yesterday — as I always do for the matter of that. I have just taken a notion — *dont tell any one* — that it would be grand if we could get the place you are in now when the Callenders go. I wonder if it would be possible. Something you said about the mountains made my mouth water. Goodbye my little heart till tomorrow night. I hope you have written.

Your old T.

MS, Texas. *LM*, 59

[1] J. B. Yeats had a studio at 7 Stephens Green North.

To MOLLY ALLGOOD

[Glendalough House, Glenageary]
Thursday [29 November 1906]

Dear Heart

I only slept for an hour and a half last night — I was even worse than in Cardiff — and I feel very much done up today. I wrote you a letter at four o'clock in the morning and another at ten, but I am not going to send you either of them at least not today. They are sad, not cross, ones, but I think my poor little changling was sad enough herself last night, so I do not want to sadden her more. I need not tell you how much I have suffered. You must see yourself how strange it all looked to me but I am telling myself that you are not experienced in the ways of the world and that I must not blame you for what you do in haste only. Why did you try and hide it, that is the worst of all? I am almost frightened sometimes when I think how wildly I love you. My life is in your hands, now, as well as my honour. You will very soon send me into my grave if you do not begin to act like a woman who loves — instead of the way you are doing. This was meant to be a cheerful letter, but I'm afraid it can hardly be called that. I am not well. The Playboy is rather a weight on me too, he is not turning out well. I am getting depressed again now so I had better come to an end. My address will be from to-morrow

Wintersells Farm
Byfleet
Surrey. England.

Please write to me very often and very nicely. Oh my little Heart *why* do you torture me?

Your old Tramp.

I send you some of the verses as I promised. Remember they are not particularly good examples of my verse although my heart is in them.
Write.

[*Enclosure*]
NB To be read last, but followed by p. 4 over again!
Dear Heart

It is four o'clock in the morning but I cannot sleep my mind is so full of misery. To think that the one evening in five weeks that I was able to go into the theatre you should go and leave me for hours, listening to every footfall with a sort of lump in my throat. And for such a reason! And the very day you wrote me a letter so filled with promises. I wish to God I had never been born. I did not allow myself to think anything while I was waiting in the theatre. I had begun to trust you so completely. You must know as well as I do the low scurilous thoughts medical students and their like have when they dangle after actresses! And to think that after all our walks among the quiet mountains, you should face that! [*deletion*] I wish I had died last week when I was so ill. It would have saved me the anguish I am feeling now. Do not think that I want to pain you. It is only because I love you so profoundly, that I feel as I do. You have my life and honour in your hands now, as well as your own, and oh my treasure for God's sake dont ruin our lives by the want of a little thought and a little will. I feel broken down and infinitely wretched. I wish I was not going away I would like to see you again my heart's light! before I go but that is hardly possible.

[10 a.m.]

Such dreary thoughts to haunt me. Do not think I am making too much of what has happened. Taking it as it [is] at the lightest it is much more than a trifle. If you had told me in the Green-room that you were going it would have been quite different.

I do not know whether I am right in sending you the letter I wrote last night in bed. Perhaps it is as well that you should know something of what I have suffered. Dear Heart wont you be better when we are married?

I wonder if I shall hear from you at two o'clock.

My address in England will be

       Wintersells Farm
       Byfleet
       Surrey. England.

[p. 4]

Later. I've had a good walk and I feel more cheerful again. Little Heart it frightens me sometimes when I think how wildly I love you. Oh do be a little more careful or you will kill me quite certainly. I do not think I ask you anything that it is not reasonable to ask and yet — !

I send you three[1] of the old verses you may like to have them for old times sake though you must not take them as specimens of my verse writing. They were really improvisations. Two others I have about you are better, but you could not read them they are so much pulled about. If you will write me a really nice letter every day when I am away perhaps I shall be able to do something with The Playboy still. I suppose I shall hear from you today.

       Yours ever
       Tramp.

[*Enclosures*]

I knew all solitude, it seemed,
   That any man might know,
— Dead year passed year — and then I dreamed
   I could find comfort so.

But now if you and I apart
   Must pass two days or three,
⟨Then I in my own lonesome heart
   Seem lost eternally.⟩

(*or*)   *Then in the desert of my heart*
      I perish utterly.[2]

We came behind the rain from Murphy's inn
And saw the splendour of the night begin,
Behind bare sycamores, that in the west
Clung to the sky like lace about the breast
     Of Women richly dressed.

We heard the thrushes by the shore and sea,
And saw the *golden* stars nativity,
   in the furze we met
Then ⟨seemed as best within⟩ a lonely cloud
Of strange delight, where birds were singing loud,
The rest was silence, with the smell
⟨Of furze and grass, and buds that swell⟩
       in its
Of golden ⟨In⟩ honey⟨'s⟩ golden well.

And then I asked why with your lips to mine
Had all these glories added eight or nine
New volumes to their glory? Were stars made new
Because your little lips were round and true?
         land
I asked what change you'd wrought in ⟨earth⟩ and sea
This more than Earthly Paradise to wake for me?
With what new gold you'd cased the moon,
With what new anthems raised the river's tune?
And why did every sound with rapture break
While my two lips were on your honied cheek?[3]

MS, TCD; encls. (poems) TS, AS. *LM*, 60

  [1] Only two poems were enclosed. Both are in typescript with manuscript alterations in ink (indicated by italics); passages in ⟨ ⟩ struck out.

  [2] Molly has written above the second version of the couplet 'I like this the best'; an even later version is printed in *Poems*, 41.

  [3] This version is quoted in *Poems*, 113.

To MOLLY ALLGOOD

Glendalou[gh House, Glenageary]
[30 November 1906]

Dearest

Forgive me, I am just off　my car is coming. I love [you] more [than I can] say so be happy till I come back to you　it will be very soon　write at once

With a thousand blessings

Your old
Tramp

MS, TCD. *LM*, 64

To MOLLY ALLGOOD

CITY OF DUBLIN STEAM PACKET COMPANY
ROYAL MAIL STEAMER "MUNSTER"
[30 November 1906]

My dearest Soul

I am off in the Mail and as it is going to be very rough I am writing this before every one gets sick. I was so sorry to hear this morning that you are unwell. Do take care of yourself, above all dont smoke much, it upsets your nerves and heart always if you are unwell. Forgive me for seeming hard on you. I will explain what I felt some other time. Now I only want to tell you how completly I am yours. Do let us be wise and open. Can you wonder that I felt upset and queer when you went off so secretly the only night in five weeks — and after such a bad illness — that I got in to see you.

Little Heart I am going to write to my mother now when I get over. Wouldn't it be lovely if I could get you down to stay with us at Christmas for a week. What walks we would have, and what talks over the fire! I feel very sad going away from my little changeling even for two weeks. I hope the next journey I set out on will be a very different one!!

How I wish I could put my arms round you now and make every [thing] right again. But — there was a roll I am going to catch it! Forgive me again dear heart and remember if you have suffered so have I, intensely and terribly.

Let me have a long loving letter every day　then I will come back well and happy and we will be always together How I wish I was coming back instead of going away

Yours tenderly and forever
J. M. Tramp

I shall be very anxious till I hear how you are!

MS, TCD. *LM*, 64

To LADY GREGORY

Wintersells | Byfleet | Surrey
Dec 1st [1906]

Dear Lady Gregory
Just a line to tell you I am over all right, and to give you my address in case anything should turn up.
I hope the Matinee[1] was a success. I am anxious to hear how the week ended. I think the change of place and ideas will help me to finish the Playboy. I have been looking at etchings and pictures all the morning and I feel revived. Too much Dublin I fear would ruin anyone.

Yours sincerely
J. M. Synge

MS, Berg. *TB*, 162

[1] As an experiment, the directors were introducing Saturday matinées at the Abbey.

To MOLLY ALLGOOD

Wintersells | Byfleet | Surrey | England
Dec 1st [1906]

Dearest Heart,
I have been thinking about you a great deal on my journey. I hope you are feeling all right again. I got over very well but I was rather fagged when I got here at eight o'clock in the evening. It is a nice old house and very nicely furnished in a quiet artistic way. I have been looking through a number of my cousins pictures this morning and admired them greatly. I wish he would give me some. I wonder how your Matinée will go off today, I do not feel that it will be much of a success. I suppose you will let me hear how it goes. I do not quite know if I shall be able to get a letter to you every day here as we are some way to the post. I will try. I suppose you will get this on

Sunday morning. I hope you will take a quiet day and rest yourself reading your books. Dont take too many cigarettes mind. I am writing under difficulties today as my cousin is fussing about at my table, and 'checking the flow of my emotions'. But never mind I am overflowing with them all the same, dear heart. Your little letter yesterday made me very sad whenever I read it. But between ourselves I dont quite see that I am the one to be blamed. If you had been very ill, and if you came up to see me before you went away for two weeks, what would you think if I went off to spend the evening with say a ballet-girl, and left you walking up and down the green [room] wondering what had become of me? would you have been quite pleased with me when I came back, ⟨and gone home quite happily.⟩ However, I do not want to scold my little changling anymore. When you are unhappy I feel like a hangman. I am depressed today I seem so far away from you. But still I think for your own sake as much as my own I was right to come over and pick myself up. Dear heart let this be our last misunderstanding, tell me always all you are thinking and doing, as I tell you what I do. Is that much to ask you? And for God's sake keep clear of the men who dangle after actresses. I know too well how medicals and their like think and speak of the women they run after in Theatres, and it wrings my heart when I think what that man may be saying and thinking of my little changling, who is so sweet and so innocent and whom I love so utterly. [*deletion*] Get yourself well and strong, my own little heart, before I go home, and we will have a happy Christmas — happier than anyone else will have in Ireland or out of it. Do write to [me] often. I feel so lonely here. I think it will help my work however to have a change of ideas. I have been thinking a lot about our future, I think you may turn out a very fine actress — if you can only preserve your sincerity — and if the Abbey breaks up at any time I cannot of course ask you to give up your art. We shall have to live in London part of the year, and I think as my wife you will have more chance than you would have by yourself, — I know so many writers etc. in London — of getting parts in the intellectual plays at the Court[1] or elsewhere. Then when we had a little money we'd go off to our own mountains and worship the moon and stars! Wouldn't that be a nice life? Keep your health sound, and keep your *distinction* of mind and all will be well. I cannot tell you how I love you good bye for 13 days

Your Tramp

MS, TCD. *LM*, 65

[1] The Court Theatre in Sloane Square, London, under the management of J. E. Vedrenne and Harley Granville-Barker, produced from 18 Oct 1905 till

20 June 1907 plays by Bernard Shaw, John Galsworthy, Granville-Barker, Ibsen, and other modern playwrights.

To MOLLY ALLGOOD

Wintersells | Byfleet | Surrey
Dec 2nd/06

Little Heart

I was delighted to get your note this morning and to hear that you are getting on well. I could not post a letter here today — there was no post out after ten o'clock — so you will have no news of me tomorrow (Monday). I wonder how you have passed your day, and if you care at all for the books. I have been dodging about in and out most of the day, and for a while sitting in my cousin's studio at the end of the garden while he was working at his etchings. He is very kind, and I cant help pitying him living here by himself with no one to talk to except his dog. It reminds me of my life before I had a changling to look to, and make much of — when she is good! It is strange what a difference you have made in my life, I used to be infinitely lonely, though I was so used to it in a way. How did you like the last verses about my lonesomeness? I sometimes wish that you had had some experience of lonesomeness before we met, it makes one value real fellowship more deeply. Try and write me a long letter the next time with talk in it so that I can talk back to you, as there is no news here to tell you. My cousin — Edward Synge is his name — has a great many books and I have been dipping into a number of them. It is about six now, and I am alone in his library with his dog, and he is down in his studio. I dont go down between four and dinner (at 7) so I have time to dream and write and think about my changeling. It is a beautiful old room full of cupboards and alcoves with bookshelves, and a lot of valuable etchings that he has bought or been given. I like these sort of times, when one can simply sit and think about all one has done or left undone, and all one is going to do. I wish we could make ourselves a beautiful home like this. It is a help, I think, to one's mind to have everything about one quiet and uncommon and beautiful. My next play must be quite different from the P.Boy I want to do something quiet and stately and restrained and I want you to act in it. I think I will work more easily when I have you at my elbow to advise me, and when we are in our own little abode. I think we ought to [be] able to make it nice. I have books that are not common and pictures that are not common and I'll have a little wife who is altogether unheard-of (!) I mean unlike anyone that has ever been — so we shall

be well away from all good commonplace people. I wonder if you'll
think this a very rambling letter. If you do you can write me another
as rambling as you like. Isn't that fair. I got the last batch of proofs
for the "Aran Islands" this morning so it ought to be out now before
very long. I am beginning to feel very ambitious again. That is a good
sign I think. My cousin here is just beginning to get real success now
with his work and he is more than ten years older than I am,[1] so
if I dont kick the bucket I ought to be able to do good work and
plenty of it still. You must help me and keep me up to it. How do
you like Deirdre now that you have seen it so often? I wonder
shall I have a letter from you tomorrow morning.

Monday [3 December 1906]

My Treasure

I got your second charming letter this morning, and it filled me
with joy. I will write and tell Lady Gregory as soon as she goes home
for Xmas about the 15th of this month. That will be the best way
I think. I wrote the enclosed[2] yesterday, and I am in a great hurry
now to go off to the post so I cannot put much into this line. I am
always thinking about you and wishing I was home again. I am not
very well as I have got a sort of asthma at night that disturbs me a
good deal. Take care of yourself Dear Heart and be quite well when
I go back. I am to lunch with Miss Tobin — did I tell you? — some
day this week. You need not be jealous! No one will run away
with me.

I am so sorry you will have no letter today. It could not be helped
as the posts are bad here on Sunday.

With endless love

Your old Tramp
J.M.S.[3]

MSS, TCD. *LM*, 67, 68

[1] Actually his cousin was only five years older.
[2] i.e. the letter of 2 Dec 1906 printed above.
[3] Molly has written 'frivolous' at the bottom of the letter.

To MOLLY ALLGOOD

Wintersells | Byfleet | Surrey
Dec 4 [1906]

Dear Heart

Another letter this morning. I am so glad to see that you are
cheerful again! I have not written to my mother since Saturday,

but I will tell her in my next letter. I dont know whether it would be any use to write to your mother, I should think it would do as well to go and see her when I go over. I am not very well yet as I have a sort of asthma at night that gives me a nasty cough. I haven't been able to do anything to the Playboy yet, next week I hope to work at him.

I often read over your little letters and they seem to do me good. I think of you a great deal and I get very lonely sometimes. Two other cousins were down here yesterday — sisters of the man I am staying with — one of them is a hospital nurse, the other a writer, who does school histories and that sort of thing.[1] They are very pleasant and kindly both of them. I have not heard yet from Miss T. what day I am to lunch with her. It is half-a-crown for a return to London so I cannot go up very often, although I am so close. I am glad you had such a good matinée. I am beginning to count the days till I see my little changling again. This is Tuesday, and on Friday half the time will be over. Is not that a comfort? I hope we shall have a fine Sunday, two days after I go back so that we may have a long day together. Dear heart we must be careful now another quarrel would kill us.

I am certainly stronger today, so I hope in ten days more I shall be all right. Good bye and be good I fear I am late for the post though I have been writing in a hurry. There is not much in my letter but I suppose you are glad to hear

Your old Tramp.

MS, TCD. *LM*, 69

[1] Edward Synge had four sisters, one of whom, Margaret Bertha (1861–1939), published, among other children's stories, anthologies, and histories, *Cook's Voyages* (1892), *A Child of the Mews* (1896), biographies of Gladstone (1898) and General Gordon (1900), *The Story of the World for the Children of the British Empire* (1903), and *A Short History of Social Life in England* (1906).

To MOLLY ALLGOOD

Wintersells | Byfleet | Surrey
Dec. 5 *Wednesday* [1906]

Little Heart

No letter from you today! The last I got was written on Sunday, and this is Wednesday. I have felt uneasy all day, wondering if you were ill, or if anything had gone wrong. I hope I shall hear tomorrow morning, it is evening now.

I am afraid some of my last letters may have seemed cold in comparison, with the full and loving ones of yours that I was answering, but you are too wise I think to mind even if they seemed so. It is sometimes hard here to get a good time for writing and in a strange place one's mind is a little distracted with the new people one meets

I dont know how I have lived so long without you, for you are a part now of every thought and feeling that I have. It is evening now and E.S. is down in his studio so that I am alone again in the library I told you about. I have opened the end window − it is a long narrow room with a window at each end − so that I can see the stars we used to walk about under, a long time ago! All that we feel for each other is so much connected with this divine world, that our particular affection, in a real sense, must be divine also. What is there in life, dear heart, to come near our walks down that winding road from Enniskerry when the stars themselves seemed like little candles, set round our great love that is more priceless than they are. The stillness of this dim room puts me into a sort of dream. Would to God that you were here that I might put my arms round you and feel that the reality and mystery of our love is stronger even than dreams. (I wonder am I writing nonsense? It sounds uncommonly like it)

Talking of dreams. I dreamt last night that I introduced you to my brother, and that he began at once retrimming your hat! The last thing he would notise. I dreamt also that Mac. and O'Rourk[1] fluffed so badly at the Abbey that the curtain had to be dropped on them! What a step from the sublime to the ridiculous!

Thursday [6 December 1906]

Dearest

Your rambling letter came this morning. Why didn't you write to me on Monday when you'd nothing else to do? How do you manage to write backwards I've tried to do it and I cant. Between ourselves it is very ugly. I dont mind the blots the 'J' is certainly an improvement.

Why do you think Miss D[arragh] 'knows'? I wrote to you last night a letter which you'll find with this.[2] I'm writing now in the garden in a sort of old Green House (that has only the roof and end left standing) so that I may get the air. It does not help letter-writing to have your paper blowing up every minute. Your letter was pretty 'rambling', but I know it is not easy to write good letters always when one writes often, and I want to hear from you very often indeed. I am going to write to my mother tonight. About yours is more difficult. I felt it hard somehow to write on such an important matter to a person I dont know. As soon as I speak to her

I will *feel* how to put things, but my mind becomes a blank when I think of writing to her now, and I am afraid my letter would be stiff or awkward. What do you think? I am not very well. The asthma has left me with a heavy cough, so that I am not much the better yet for the change. However I am picking up now I think, and I hope to look into the Playboy tonight or tomorrow. Tomorrow week I go home!!!

Your old Tramp.[3]

MSS, (5 Dec) AS; (6 Dec) TCD. *LM*, 70, 71

[1] Joseph A. O'Rourke (1882-1937) joined the company during the summer of 1906 and remained until 1916, joining Arthur Sinclair's Irish Players.
[2] i.e. the letter of 5 Dec 1906, printed above.
[3] Molly scrawled 'presume' twice at the top of Thursday's instalment.

To KAREL MUŠEK

Byfleet | Surrey | England
Dec. 6/06

Dear Mr Musek
I am much obliged for the post cards[1] you sent me a long time ago and the kind invitation to visit you in Prague; Please excuse me for not writing to you sooner but I have been so busy with my new play I have had little time for my correspondence. A few week[s] ago I got a very severe attack of influenza and I have come over here for a couple of weeks for change of air. We hope to do my new play at the end of January but it is a little uncertain as I have not quite finished it yet. We are doing very well at the Abbey this season. We play every Saturday night and usually the house is quite full. We also play a new bill for a week every month and do fairly well though, the Saturdays are our great success. Last week we played Mr Yeats' new play 'Deirdre', with an Irish actress Miss Darragh who has been very successful in London in the chief part. Next week we put on a new play of Lady Gregory's[2] which I have not seen yet even in rehearsal
My book on the Aran Islands will soon be out now I think.
Please give my compliments to Madame Musek and believe me
very truly yours
J. M. Synge
P.S. Please address as usual
Glendalough House, Glenageary, Kingstown, Dublin.

MS, TCD

¹ On 12 Sept 1906 Mušek sent a card (TCD) with a photograph of JMS at Carrickmines (reproduced in Bourgeois, opp. p. 14). JMS was apparently spurred to write by a letter he received on 29 Nov 1906 from Mušek's friend Richard Kelly (TCD) enquiring about *The Aran Islands.*
² *The Canavans* (see p. 213).

To MOLLY ALLGOOD

[Byfleet, Surrey]
Friday Night [7 December 1906]

Dearest

Your note written on Tuesday evening came this morning — why it took so long on the way is best known to itself — and was very welcome. It was a nice note. I wonder what put it into your changeling's head that I want you to be 'serious'. The lighter your little heart is the better — the only thing I dont like is a certain cheap, commonplace, merriment which is at times strongly felt among 'the company', but which you are naturally, thank God, quite free of. A kind of restraint in one's merriment — a restraint I mean not in the degree of it, so much as in the quality — gives style and distinction without taking any joyousness away. In a way I do perhaps want you to be serious, that is I want you to take serious things seriously, and to look where you are going so that you may not be a mere weather-cock twisting about after every breeze that blows on you. This isn't a lecture mind, but you mustn't get it into your head that I am a morose tyrant. Surely we are merry enough when we are out having our walks and taking our little teas at Kilmacanogue (i.e. Kilmaconic) aren't we?

I have posted the letter to my mother today!¹ So that is done. I will write to yours also if you like. I spoke about it in my last letter, and I'll wait to hear what you say in answer.

I went up to London today and lunched with Miss Tobin, she was very nice and kind. There is not of course the remotest sign of flirtation about us but I like her greatly, and value her friendship. She has taken a great liking to you and Sally. She says she would hardly know me I have changed so much since the summer, and I look so thin now and generally unwell. That is not very encouraging, is it? Your last letter was the right kind of thing as it is possible to answer what you say. You say that I'll think you sentimental because of what you write about the verses. It is hard to define sentimentality, but you may be quite easy in your mind, you are not sentimental, and never will be in the sickly sense of the word. A full vigourous affection does not get sentimental, it is only sickly, inactive half-

and-half people who are really attacked. A true affection naturally occupies itself with the little things as well as the big things that concern it, but it does not grow any less healthy for that reason.

I am glad you were at Don Giovanni. We must hear a lot of good music together. There are so few ways of enjoying the arts in Dublin, I feel I have been foolish to neglect music so much. Is this letter too philosophical for you? If it is, tell me, and I'll write to you next time about 'Jones', E. Synge's dog, and the 'Encumbrance' as we call the housekeeper's Baby!

Saturday Morning [8 December 1906]
Your note of Thursday has come this morning. It cut me like a knife. It brings tears into my throat when I see you trying to pick a quarrel with me again so soon after what has passed, and when I am so far away from you, and so utterly unwell. I have never said, or thought for an instant that you were either *'silly'* or 'sentimental'. I have written as best I could in any time that I could find, and fagged off to post with my letters to you in all weathers. If you do not care to have them I am sorry I took so much trouble.

Your old Tramp

P.S. Later.
You must know that you are never out of my mind, and that I love you as the very breath of my soul. It is perhaps because I am a writer that I am not able to write about this profound passion and love that I am filled with, except at times when I feel I can express it worthily.

When I get a loving letter from you I am full of joy for the whole day. But when you write as you have just written I feel utterly broken down.

Tramp

Dear Heart why do you write so snappily when you know how much it hurts me. If you only could know how I lie awake at night counting the hours till I get back to you you would know how unjust you are. This is Saturday I get back on Friday.

MS, TCD. *LM*, 71

1 Mrs Synge's diary for 8 Dec 1906 notes only, 'I got a long letter from Johnnie telling me' (TCD).

To MOLLY ALLGOOD

[Byfleet, Surrey]
Monday [10 December 1906]

Dear Old Changeling

Many thanks for your letter this morning. I wrote you a long one on Wednesday or Thursday that you dont seem to have got. Also a 'grumpy' one on Saturday that I suppose you got yesterday. I am better I think on the whole and I go back on Friday so do not post to me after 6.o'c. on Wednesday. Write as much as you can before that I live on your letters. I have not heard yet what my mother thinks. Why am I to put off telling Lady G.? I thought you wished it. Dear Heart I am looking forward to fine walks during your holidays. Unfortunately the P.Boy is hanging over me still I haven't been well enough to do much to him since I came over. There is a sort of open Green House in the garden — did I tell you before? — where I sometimes sit and work at him. I often dream of you now, pleasant little dreams but nothing remarkable. It shows how much I am thinking about you. I got the Irish Society all right. You come out very well but I am jealous of the public getting *my photo*, that was promised to me for my exclusive use. A woman was murdered in the village half a mile away from here last night. They are making a motor-race course all round this house and there are a lot of cut-throats about. Now, dearest, I'm afraid I must take a turn at the PlayBoy so I'll have to leave you with this shabby note. It is a shame but I cant help it I've been busy all the morning with last proofs etc of the Aran Book.
With a thousand blessings

Your old Tramper.

I am glad you liked David Copperfield. It is a good book. I dont think I have any more Dickens but we'll get you some. I wonder how you'll get on with Vanity Fair.

P.S. Now for a galloping Post Scrip. I've been through Act I. It is good I think and only needs a little more revision. I wish I could say the same for Act III!

Write me *one* more nice *loving letter at least* before I go home so that I may have happy meditations on my long solitary journey on Friday. Your last ones dont make me as happy as those you wrote first. Perhaps it is my fault as I may have been too business like on my side of the correspondence.

It is a glorious day here but very cold. I am nearly frozen in my Green House, but still it is pleasanter than indoors. I wonder if you got my last letter but one. I thought it would please you, and still (if you have got it), you do not say a word about it. I wonder how the Canavans are going. You might send me a paper or two if you can *afford it*!

Your old T.

MSS, (letter) TCD; (PS) AS. *LM*, 73

To MOLLY ALLGOOD

[Byfleet, Surrey]
Monday Evening [10 December 1906]

Dearest Heart.

This is my second letter to you today. When I am writing quickly in the morning to catch the post I do not seem to be able to say anything that is worth saying. It seems a very long time since our last walk which was only a fortnight ago, but I have never known days go so slowly as these have gone. Why do you say you had to stop writing or you would say something that you did not want to say?

I feel low and uneasy — I do [not] know why — since your letter on Saturday. My own heart, do let us make our love a deep and certain thing with no room in it for uneasiness or misgiving. You know how lonely I have been, and how I have taken you into the very essence of my life. I do still believe that our love will be a joy and blessing to us, Dear Heart [*deletion*] — I cannot write this evening I keep wondering what you were going to say and why you do not want me to tell Lady G. when you have asked me so often to do so —

Why are you so changeable when you know how much it hurts and harms me?

I dare say that this is all my own folly and depression, and that all the time you are the best little changeling in the world, but people who have had influenza are very easily depressed so I have a good excuse if I am foolish. Wont it be a blessing when we are together again? That is our only cure I think. I tremble sometimes when I think how much power I have given you over my life, and how recklessly you often use it. "I had better stop or I shall say something I dont want to say"!! That is a quotation

There are only four more days now till I start back again. That is a blessing! Remember to write me a BEAUTIFUL letter to cheer up my cold lonely journey.

J.M.S.

Post early on *Wednesday*.

Tuesday morning | Dec 10th/06[1]

My Thousand Treasures

I opened your letter this morning with terror — I knew I deserved a scolding and I was afraid I was going to "catch it"! You let me off very well and I am in wild good spirits now. Dear Heart in four Days — damn them — I will be in the Seventh Heaven again, with my little changling, my little jewel, my love and life, in my arms! Is not that something to live for. Dearest if you could see how I get up thinking of my little changeling, and go to bed thinking about my little changeling, about her little baby nose, and her little eyes, and her little voice, and her little bull-dog chin, and all her little soul and body that is mine forever!

Dear Heart, Dear Heart, Dear Heart if you knew how much you are to me! How I see you waiting for me at the door of the scenery room, and sitting on my knee among the quiet woods, and putting a new life into the stars and streams and trees and Heaven and Earth and all that therein is for me! I had better stop I think or I might blaspheme God in my love for you.

I send some lines I scratched off last night if they make you smile remember they are a first draft only. I send also a foolish letter I wrote last night.[2] Now for the Play Boy — God confound him!

Goodbye my own dearest Heart.

Your Tramp.

Many thanks for all your news. It interests me greatly. I fear you are right about Yeats' plays. Good bye again, my single darling love, my treasure of life.

MSS, (10 Dec) TCD; ([11] Dec) (photo) NLI. *LM*, 75, 76

[1] JMS misdated this letter; it should be 11 Dec 1906.
[2] Presumably the letter of 'Monday Evening' printed above. The poem is missing; perhaps it was 'I brought you where the stars and moon of night', quoted in Elizabeth Coxhead, *Daughters of Erin* (1965), 187, and *LM*, 76.

To MOLLY ALLGOOD

Byfleet | Surrey
Thursday [13 December 1906]

My Dearest,

This is a line merely to thank you for papers and your note. I was in London yesterday — lunching first, with Miss Tobin, then with her to a show of my cousin's pictures, then to dine with *him* at an Irishman's called Stopford,[1] talking till one o'clock at night, sleeping there and back here today about two o'clock when I got your note. I am off for Ireland tomorrow morning. I am terribly afraid I may be a good deal taken up with the Directors on Saturday and perhaps on Sunday — you know they are both leaving Dublin very soon. However in any case we shall have good times next week. I am inclined to shout with delight at the thought of going back to you.

Your old T.

Turn over

P.S. I heard from my mother. She says she thought 'the friend' I have been walking with was a man, but that my showing her the photo and the letters that came so often when I was ill made her think there was some thing. Then she says it would be a good thing if it would make me happier, and to wind up she points out how poor we shall be with our £100 a year. Quite a nice letter for a first go off. So that is satisfactory

Good bye till Saturday, afternoon or evening or both. I would like to go in early on Saturday but there would be no use as I shall be tired after the journey

Your T.

MS, TCD. *LM*, 77

¹ Edward Adderley Stopford (1843–1919), brother of the historian and nationalist Mrs Alice Stopford Green (1847–1929), was a tea merchant and wood carver who lived in Weybridge, Surrey; later he moved to Frankfort Avenue, Rathgar, Dublin, and worked with Horace Plunkett in the Irish Agricultural Organization Society.

To LADY GREGORY and W. B. YEATS

Byfleet, Surrey
Dec. 13th/06

Dear Lady Gregory

I am sorry I have not been able to answer your letter and papers sooner. I am going home tomorrow, but I think it is best to write you some of the things I have to say as it will help to keep matters clear. — This is, of course, to Yeats as well as to you, — I take his statement marked Dec. 2nd.¹

I think we should be mistaken in taking the continental Municapal Theatre as the pattern of what we wish to attain as our 'final object' even in a fairly remote future. A dramatic movement is either (a) a creation of a new dramatic Literature where the interest is in the novelty and power of the new work rather than in the quality of the execution, or (b) a highly organised executive undertaking where the interest lies in the more and more perfect interpretation of works that are already received as classics. A movement of this kind is chiefly useful in a country where there has been a successful *creative movement*. So far our movement has been entirely creative, – the only movement of the kind I think now existing – and it is for this reason that it has attracted so much attention. To turn this movement now – for what are to some extent extrinsic reasons – into an executive movement for the production of a great number of foreign plays of many types would be, I cannot but think, a disastrous policy. None of us are suited for such an undertaking, – it will be done in good time by a dramatic Hugh Lane[2] when Ireland is ripe for it. I think Yeats view that it would be a good thing for Irish audiences – *our* audiences – or young writers is mistaken. Goethe at the end of his life said that he and Schiller had failed to found a German drama a[t] Weimar because they had confused the public mind by giving one day Shakespere, one day Calderon, one day Sophocles and so on. Whether he is right or not we can see that none of the 'Municip. Theatres' that are all over Europe are creating or helping to create a new stage-literature. We are right to do work like the 'Doctor' and Oedipus because they illuminate our work but for that reason only. Our supply of native plays is very small and we should go on I think for a long time with a very small company so that the mature work may go a long way towards keeping it occupied.[3]

As you (Lady Gregory) say Miss Horniman's money – as far as I am aware – is quite insufficient for anything in the nature of a Municipal Theatre. The Bohemian Theatre has £12,000 a year and all scenery. The interest on the £25,000 would be I suppose £800 or £900, so that for us all large schemes would mean a short life, and then a collapse as it has happened in so many English movements. If we are to have a grant from some Irish State fund, we are more likely to get one that will be of real use if we keep our movement local –

I do not see a possibility of any workable arrangement in which Miss Horniman would have control of some of the departments.[4] ——

That is my feeling on the general question raised by Yeats' statement. Now for the practical matters. W. Fay must be freed, that I think is urgently necessary if he is to keep up the quality of his acting. An Assistant Stagemanager as we agreed will do this if we can find the right man.

For the verse plays, – Yeats plays, – I am ready to agree to almost any experiment that he thinks desirable in order to ensure good performances. Mrs Emery[5] — as you suggest — might be of great use. At the same time I think he is possibly mistaken in looking on the English stage for the people that are needed. Looking back from here with the sort of perspective that distance gives I greatly dislike the impression that 'Deirdre' or rather Miss Darragh has left on me. Emotion — if it cannot be given with some trace of distinction or nobility — is best left to the imagination of the audience. Did not Cleopatra, and Lady MacBeth, and Miranda make more impression when they were played by small boys than when they are done by Mrs P. Campbell — I wonder how one of "Dunn's Kids" would do in Dectora?![6] I would rather go on trying our own people for ten years, than bring in this ready made style that is so likely to destroy the sort of distinction everyone recognises in our own company. Still that is only my personal feeling and, as I said, I think it essential that Yeats should be able to try anything that seems at all likely to help on his work, which requires so much skill. —

To wind up. I am convinced that it will be our wisest policy to work on steadily on our own lines for the term of the Patent. After that we may get a grant from our Home Rule Government, or we may all have to go to the Work House — where I have no doubt W. G. F. would be exceedingly popular.[7]

I hope to see you both on Saturday probably at the Matinee and to talk over further details before you both leave. I have done very little to the PlayBoy as I got an attack when I arrived here of a sort of bronchial asthma which threw me back greatly. I am much better now and ready for work again.

Yours sincerely

J. M. Synge

MS, Berg. *TB*, 177

[1] Yeats's lengthy memorandum suggested the expansion of the theatre after 'the Continental pattern', training actors through the presentation of foreign masterpieces, and incorporating professional actors and actresses (such as Miss Darragh) on an *ad hoc* basis; he intimated that Miss Horniman would contribute £25,000 towards such a venture. Lady Gregory disagreed with various points, but emphasized the need for further training, especially in verse drama, and agreed that an overworked Willie Fay required assistance both in management and stage production. (See *TB*, 168.)

[2] Hugh Percy Lane (1875–1915), knighted in 1909, Lady Gregory's favourite nephew; an art collector and critic, he was governor of Dublin's National Gallery from 1904, its director from 1914 until he was drowned on the *Lusitania*. In 1908 JMS reviewed for the *Manchester Guardian* (*Prose*, 390) Lane's impressive collection of paintings by the French Impressionists which he intended to give to Ireland. When the Dublin Corporation in 1913 rescinded its promise to build the gallery Lane requested, he bequeathed the collection to the National

Gallery in London, where, despite a long legal battle waged by Lady Gregory, the pictures remained until a Loan Scheme was arranged in 1959.

 ³ JMS preserved his first draft of this reply among his papers, and is there even more explicit about his fears for the company: 'A larger and more expensive company with more expensive people in it, . . . would force us to play a great deal of foreign matter and destroy the distinctive note of our movement' (TCD).

⁴ Here the original draft is even more specific, obviously indicating the tenor of previous discussions: 'I object to giving Miss Horniman any control over the company whatever. If she is given power it ceases to be an Irish movement worked by Irish people to carry out their ideas, so that if any such arrangement becomes necessary I shall withdraw, — my plays of course might remain if they were wanted. I object to Miss Horniman's control not because she is English, but because I have no confidence in her ideals.' (TCD)

⁵ Florence Farr Emery (1860–1917), a close friend of Yeats and like Miss Horniman his colleague in the Order of the Golden Dawn, was a frequent performer of Yeats's poetry. She was one of the earliest actresses of Ibsen in England, and had provided both Shaw and Yeats with their first professional productions at the Avenue Theatre in 1894, under the sponsorship of Miss Horniman.

⁶ J. H. Dunne performed minor roles at the Abbey from December 1904 until January 1906, and again between March 1908 and September 1910; he was evidently never a member of the full-time company. Dectora was a character in Yeats's *The Shadowy Waters*, originally played by Maire Nic Shiubhlaigh.

⁷ Willie Fay took one of the comic roles in *The Poorhouse* by Lady Gregory and Douglas Hyde, later revised by Lady Gregory as *The Workhouse Ward*.

To MOLLY ALLGOOD

Glendalough [House, Glenageary]
Monday [17 December 1906]

Dearest

I feel as if I could hardly wait till tomorrow I am so eager to see you again.

I have had a little ride round by Bray, it was a most wonderful evening, and I never felt so happy between the memory of yesterday and the hope of tomorrow. What a joy to live in a place where the twilights are so glorious, and where I have such a little friend to share them with me. We'll make the old romances come to life again.

I hope you weren't tired after our beautiful outing.

Meet me tomorrow *Tuesday Wet* or *Fine* at Westland Row Station at 2 O'Clock. I'll be there unless I wire; if you cant come please wire to me before 12. Please dont be late it is such a wretched place to wait.

Ever and Ever
your old Tramp

I've thought of a very nice present for you!!!!!

MS, AS. *LM*, 78

To MOLLY ALLGOOD

Glendalough House [Glenageary]
Wednesday | Dec. 19/06

Sweetest Heart.

Do you remember that I told you once — in Liverpool I think — that the love of a man of 35 was a very, or at least a rather different thing from that of a man of 25? I was making a mistake. Last night I felt all the flood of fullness, and freshness and tenderness that I thought I had half left behind me. I can say now very truthfully that I have never loved anyone but you and I am putting my whole life now into this love.

I have no cold today after all and I have had a good morning's work at the Playboy, I am going out now for a turn on my bicycle and then I am going to work again. I am sorry I did not arrange to see you some time today. It is hard to be a whole day without you when you are so near, and your whole time is free.

My mother enquiried quite pleasantly about our walk and where we had been, she is coming round to the idea very quickly I think, but still it is better not to hurry things.

Meet me tomorrow at the same time and place 2 oclock, Westland Row and dont be late as we could so easily miss each other in that big station.

I hope you are not tired. Good bye dearest Heart

Your old Tramp

MS, TCD. *LM*, 78

To MOLLY ALLGOOD

Glendalough House [Glenageary]
Friday Night [21 December 1906]

Sweetest Heart

I am very sorry to say that I think I should stick at the Playboy all day tomorrow so that we shall not meet till Sunday. It is a nuisance, but I know you feel as much as I do how important it is that I should finish my job. My typewriter broke down this morning a little before twelve so I had to go into town and get a new spring put into it after lunch. Then I bought you a dear little watch, — dear in every sense — saw old Yeats, and came home too late to get through much work.

I heard from Musek last night, the letter was waiting for me when I got home. He sent me post-card photos of the Bohemian Nora and Dan Burke. The Shadow is to go goes on there in March.[1]

Dear Heart come down by *the quarter to ten* from Westland Row on Sunday — second class — to Bray as usual. We will have a great day. Of course do not come if it is wet. Write me a nice letter when you get this so that I shall have it tomorrow night to cheer me up after my days work. Hadn't we a lovely time yesterday. I think you'll like the little watch.

Forever your old Tramp

You had better put out your little head when you come to Glenageary there are so many seconds it would be hard to find you.

MS, TCD. *LM*, 79

1 *The Shadow of the Glen* was not finally produced at the National Theatre in Prague until 22 Aug 1907; Mušek himself played the Tramp and received from Frank Fay the 'scene plot' for the cottage interior.

To W. B. YEATS

Glendalough House | Kingstown | Dublin
Dec, 24 . . . 06

Dear Yeats

Lady Gregory has sent me Miss Horniman's letter,[1] wwth her very generous offer, and asks me to write what I think of it to you at once. I think the arrangement would be an ekcellent one for us all if her proposal can be moddified or made more clear on the following lines.

1. The Managing Director would not, I should think, be entitled to a vote on the Board of Directors.

2. He would have no power to dismiss or engage actors without permission from the Directors.

3. Fay should continue to produce — in the sense that he would derect actors as to their speaking, movements, gestures and positions etc. all DIALECT PLAYS. — (a better term than *peasants* plays as it would include work like the Canavans.)

4. Other plays should for the most part be produced by the Managing Director, but there could be no hard and fast rule which would compel us to give him, say, a play of Boyle's not quite in dialect, like the Eloquent Demsey, or possibly an historical play of mine[2] which I might think Fay would understand better, and lasty and most important of all, we must not *be bound* to give him the production of verse plays till we see that he is able to produce them according to our views, or as we may call them, The Samhain Principals.[3] Some of the most aggresively vulgar stage-management I have ever seen was in Irving's production of the Merchant of Venice,

so that the fact that the Managing Director is to [be] recommended by some one of known theatrical position, is no guarantee whatever on this point/ Therefore a certain freedom must be left to the Directors or their position will be a false and absurd one.[4]

5. Whatever arrangement is arrived at, it must be of such a kind that Fay will be able to cooperate in it cordially. We owe this to him, as he has in reality built up the company.

6 I trust Miss Horniman understands that there is no likelehood of our undertaking a large amount of touring, as we have seen so plainly that except in a few centres of culture our time and energy is thrown away.

I have written these notes on the proposal rapidly, and, except as to Fay, I am quite willing to discuss them with you if you are not in agreement with them.[5]

Yours sincerely

[*signed*] J. M. Synge

TS (MS emendations), Berg. *TB*, 185

[1] Still determined to wrest as much authority from Fay as possible, and to give Yeats further opportunities with his verse plays, Miss Horniman had written formally to Yeats on 17 Dec 1906 directing him to engage a managing director recommended by 'someone of known theatrical position' who 'would need to be able to stage manage anything and be competent to produce all plays except those treating of Irish peasant life' (TCD). Lady Gregory was uneasy about the offer, and appealed to JMS for support (*TB*, 183).

[2] Apparently JMS already had in mind the subject of his next play, *Deirdre of the Sorrows*.

[3] *Samhain*, December 1904, included 'First Principles', Yeats's philosophy of staging.

[4] An early draft of this letter is even more explicit: 'This is a vital point on which I — as far as my vote counts — will not give in — it would be better for us to come to find ourselves gradually driven into the sort of stage management that George Moore urged on us in his article in *Dana* [September 1904], which is after all the efficient stage management of the recognized London authority. There could be no better evidence that we have a sort of method of our own than George Moore's attack on Fay.' (TCD)

[5] Yeats replied immediately (?25 Dec 1906), 'I am altogether in agreement with you' (*TB*, 186).

To MOLLY ALLGOOD

[Glendalough House, Glenageary]

Xmas night/06

Dearest

This has been a long day without you, and, alas, there will be another like it tomorrow. I worked at the Playboy till half past one, and then we all went up to dine at my sister's. There were 10 of us in all and we had a pleasant dinner. My mind kept straying away to my little changeling and wishing she was there too. After that I went for a walk with one of my nephews and then back there for tea. Now at last I have come home with my mother and I have a moment to write to you. How have you passed the day Dear Heart and what presents have you got? I got two pair of stockings from my mother — in addition to the gloves, — a book from Florence Ross, a can of cigarettes from the nephews, a tie-pin from my little niece and two ties, so I am well made up. I gave Florence and the nephews and niece little books that I had, *and didn't want*! Isn't that a good way to give your relations presents.

You will say this is a dull letter but it cant be helped as I am stuffed up with plum pudding and cake, and have been doing gymnastic tricks for the boys into the bargain till my head is singing. Next Xmas I hope my heart will be singing too, with my little changeling to trot round. Dont the days seem long now when we are apart?

I hope your cold is well again, and that your spirits are tip-top.

With ten thousand blessings

Your old Tramp

I'll let you know *if I can* what time I'll be at the Abbey on *Thursday*

MS, TCD. *LM*, 80

To MOLLY ALLGOOD

[Glendalough House, Glenageary]
Thursday 27/XII/06

Dear One

I got your little note this morning. I am sorry mine did not reach you sooner I wrote it on Xmas and went out and posted it that evening in all the rain. I suppose it was delayed in the post — I went to the Abbey at 3 o'clock but I found nobody. I could not let you know before-hand as I did not know when I was going in. I have had two hard days at P.B. and I am very tired again. In the evenings now I am reading Petrarch's sonnets, with Miss Tobin's translations. I think I'll teach you Italian too so that you may be able to read the wonderful love-poetry of these Italian poets Dante, and Petrarch, and one or two others. You are more interested in the natural and human side of art than in the very exalted or poetical — you liked the Dutch pictures, the other day, for instance, better than the Italian ones, —.[1] That is as it should be, and I am the same I think.

Still we both have a poetical strain in us, and we should take care of it — as one takes care of some rare flower in one's garden, that dies easily and leaves one the poorer forever. You feel as fully as anyone can feel all the poetry and mystery of the nights we are out in — like that night a week ago when we came down from Rockbrook with the pale light of Dublin shining behind the naked trees till we seemed almost to come out of ourselves with the wonder and beauty of it all. Divine moments like that are infinitely precious to us both as people and as artists I with my writing and you with your acting, and by reading what is greatest in poetry or hearing what is greatest in Music — things like the Messiah — one trains one's soul, as a singer trains his voice, to respond to and understand the great moments of our own lives or of the outside world. I think people who feel these things — people like us — have a profound joy in love, that the ordinary run of people do not easily reach. They love with all their hearts — as we do — but their hearts perhaps, have not all the stops that you and I have found in ours. The worst of it is that we have the same openess to profound pain — of mind I mean — as we have to profound joy, but please Heaven we shall have a few years of divine love and life together and that is all I suppose any one need expect. I am growing sure of one thing and that is that we are not going to destroy this divine love that God has put between us by the wretched squabblings and fightings that seemed to threaten us at first. ——

I wonder will all that make you laugh I am in a dreamy sort of mood sitting over the fire by myself. So excuse me if I write like a fool —

I hope I shall see you tomorrow I shall be in I think, but I dont know when — I dare say in the evening.

Good night my priceless changeling

My heart's treasure
J.M.S.

MS, TCD. *LM*, 81

1 Probably on a visit to the National Gallery, a favourite haunt of JMS's.

To W. B. YEATS

Glendalough House | Kingstown
Dec. 31st/06

Dear Yeats

Thanks for your letter,[1] with which I am practically in agreement. I have not said anything to Fay as it would be better for Lady Gregory to speak to him if possible. I will do it of course if you and she think it advisable. Fay said to me on Saturday, that he was not going to make any further objections to anything that was proposed. We — or you — might appoint anyone we liked and if we got the whole place into a mess it would be our fault not his. Then he went on to say that he thought the time would come when we would find it necessary to have some independent person to manage the place, as we would find that a Board of Authors was nearly as unworkable as the old committee of actors. What he wants, I suppose, is some-one to have charge of the bills and put on plenty of Boyle. He is depressed, I think, and when he came home he took S. Allgood aside and advised her to save up some money as he thought the Abbey Company was in a very shaky state. All this of course IS PRIVATE between ourselves and Lady Gregory. I do not think he will oppose new proposal. If I am to break it to him I suppose I should tell him the salary that it is proposed to give.[2] Let me hear what I am to do.

Yours
J. M. Synge

£10 in house on Saturday. Both Fays got good round of applause on their entries in the Mineral Workers. The Hour Glass went well, except that F.J.F's cloak was too long and put him out a good deal.

MS, Berg. *TB*, 192

---

[1] Yeats had written on 28 Dec 1906 from London, where he had expected to see Willie Fay on holiday but had not, giving JMS lengthy reasons to use in persuading Fay to accept the new man. Lady Gregory wrote on the 29th from Coole, giving further reasons. (Both TCD.)

[2] The new appointee was to receive £500; Fay was to receive an additional £100.

PART SIX
January – June
1907

*

A Stormy Aftermath

A Stormy Aftermath

*

THE year 1907 began with yet one more reorganization of the theatre. In an attempt to be freed of managerial worries so that he might concentrate on the preparation of his collected works, Yeats had persuaded his reluctant co-directors to accept Miss Horniman's offer of a business manager for the Abbey. Worried about Molly's health and his own, and trying to complete his play, Synge found time to enter into a three-way correspondence over the problems of pacifying Willie Fay while acknowledging Yeats's needs. Eventually an English actor, Ben Iden Payne, was hired to produce the verse and classical plays, while W. G. Fay — at Synge's and Lady Gregory's insistence — retained control over the dialect plays.

Meanwhile Synge spent the whole of January rehearsing *The Playboy of the Western World*, in which Molly played Pegeen Mike. Although there had been disturbing rumours about the play, nobody was prepared for the anger which burst from the audience on opening night, Saturday, 26 January. By the third act it was no longer possible to hear the actors, pandemonium finally breaking loose at Christy Mahon's reply to the Widow Quin, 'It's Pegeen I'm seeking only and what'd I care if you brought me a drift of chosen females standing in their shifts itself, maybe, from this place to the Eastern World.' According to Joseph Holloway (NLI), a flustered Willie Fay made matters worse — and incidentally reinforced a more realistic interpretation of the play — by substituting 'Mayo girls' for 'chosen females'.

Lady Gregory ordered more cuts in the production and telegraphed for Yeats, who was lecturing in Aberdeen. He did not arrive until the Tuesday, but the serious troubles had already begun the night before when continual shouting from an organized audience forced the actors to perform in dumb show. Six police constables stationed themselves in the auditorium, but were asked by Synge and Lady Gregory to leave. After interviews with both directors were published the next day, the audience became more violent yet, causing an excited Yeats to call in even more policemen for Tuesday's performance. For the rest of the week the press delightedly divided its attention between the rows in the theatre each night and Yeats's performances in the courtroom during the day. By Thursday outbursts from the audience had become sporadic, and on Saturday both the matinée and evening performances were listened to attentively. Triumphant at this proof that, in Lady Gregory's words to the *Freeman's Journal*, 'it is the fiddler who chooses the tune', Yeats issued a general invitation to a public debate on the freedom of the theatre for Monday, 4 February.

But by then Synge was in bed with bronchitis brought on by the strain of rehearsing when suffering from a severe chest cold. His mother, who had worriedly consulted her daughter about John's new play ('not nice'), recorded his fluctuating health — and Molly's frequent visits — in her diary. At least twice he was tested for tuberculosis, but no one seemed aware that the recurring fevers, like the large swelling on his neck and perhaps even his frequent stomach ailments, were symptomatic of lymphatic sarcoma, Hodgkin's disease. He was not out until 14 March, and did not see the Wicklow mountains for almost two months.

Undeterred, he and Molly continued happily, if stormily, to plan a summer marriage and a holiday in the west. He contemplated a book on Wicklow, publishing 'At a Wicklow Fair' in the *Manchester Guardian* on 9 May 1907, and 'The People of the Glens' in the Spring 1907 issue of *The Shanachie*, and starting work on a series of articles on West Kerry for the same journal. Despite criticisms of *The Playboy* from Padraic Colum ('I think she should have stood by her man when he was attacked by a crowd. The play does not satisfy me') and even Frank Fay ('All the same, you must get more colours on to your palette; you paint too much in grey') (both TCD), he staunchly defended his play. Under a sketch by J. B. Yeats of himself at rehearsal, he wrote in W. A. Henderson's scrapbook of the riots (NLI),

> 'If Church and State reply
> Give Church and State the lie' (Raleigh)

and triumphantly signed it.

In April 1907, taking advantage of Payne's presence, Yeats and Lady Gregory went to Italy, once again leaving Synge to oversee Abbey affairs. On 11 May the company left on a tour of Glasgow, Birmingham, Oxford, Cambridge, and London, performing *The Playboy* with great critical success in the last three centres. But internal dissension increased, the players suffering conflicting loyalties between two producers, Payne torn between Miss Horniman's demands and the directors' requirements, Synge all too often in the middle. By the time the company arrived in London, Payne had announced his intention to resign and Synge had threatened to.

Convalescing too slowly to join the tour in its earlier stages,

Synge left for a quiet week with Jack Yeats in Devon on 30 May before meeting up with his colleagues in London on 8 June. With reviews of the published play confirming the favourable reception given *The Playboy* in England, and his book *The Aran Islands* at last published, in April, apprenticeship was definitely over. In spite of a persevering cough and quarrels with Molly, he enjoyed his meetings with John Masefield, Max Meyerfeld, and the Irish society of London.

When the company returned to Dublin on 17 June, Synge's doctor advised him to postpone an operation on his glands, and his marriage, until the autumn. Instead of their trip west he and Molly turned south, to Glencree in his beloved Wicklow, for what was to be their happiest time together.

To MOLLY ALLGOOD

Glendalough House [Glenageary]
January 1st 1907

Dearest Heart

This is the first letter I have written this year, and the first time I have written the new date — as it [is] right they are *for you*. My toe is rather better, but still so tender I think I had best keep it quiet tonight. Tomorrow I have a lot of things to do in town if I am well enough and of course I shall be in for the night shows but I do not see any way of getting you to meet me as I am so uncertain in my movements. Next week please God we'll manage better. I came home last night in wonderful good spirits. The air and moon were beautiful walking down from the train and New Year bells were ringing all round, and I remembered how good you had been and I was in great delight. The III Act is coming out all right and all will be well I hope. How did I ever live so long without a little changling? You are in every thought of my life now, and may it be so for ever! If I can give you happy New Years you'll have them as long as I am on this side of the grave. So good bye and a thousand blessings on you

Your Tramp.

MS, AS. *LM*, 84

To JAMES PATERSON[1]

Glendalough House | Glenageary | Kingstown | Co Dublin
Jan 1st/07

Dear Mr Paterson

Let me wish you the good wishes of the season and thank you — though it is so late in the day — for your kindness to us all in Edinburgh last summer. I have been very busy ever since on a new play, that is my only excuse for not writing to you sooner. Now I have handed over the MS to the company — rehearsals begin tomorrow — so I have a moment to breathe.

We have been very successful at our Abbey Theatre in Dublin since we opened again for our new season. Several times we have had the House quite full and people turned away from the doors. A most comforting sight!

Fay is married to Miss O'Demsey — the little lady whom you saw — for the rest the company remains as it was last year. We got in an Anglo–Irish actress — a Miss Darragh, for two plays of Yeats' in the autumn but the experiment was not altogether a success. Please remember me to Mrs Patterson and believe me

Cordially yours
J. M. Synge

MS copy, TCD

[1] James Paterson RSA (1854–1932), of Edinburgh, a long-time friend of Miss Horniman. He recalled years later, 'Few men have impressed me as vividly as Synge, both in his work and personality' (TCD). He made a crayon drawing of JMS (1906; cf. *MUJ*, frontispiece) on which he based a posthumous oil portrait, and took two photographs of him in 1908. Apparently Paterson sent copies of the letters JMS wrote him to JMS's nephew Edward Hutchinson Synge.

To H. J. C. GRIERSON[1]

Glendalough House | Glenageary | Kingstown | Co Dublin
Jan 1st/07

Dear Professor Grierson

May I wish you and Mrs Grierson the best compliments of the Season and thank you — although it is so long ago — for your kindness while we were at Aberdeen last summer. I have been very hard at work ever since at a new comedy — The Playboy of the Western World — which goes into rehearsal tomorrow, for production on the 26th of this month, so you can imagine that I am in an anxious state. My book on the Aran Islands was just late for Christmas so we are not bringing it out now till February.

We have had a very good season here since we opened again in September, but we have done no more touring since, and have no plans, though it is not unlikely that we may go to London before the summer. I do not know when there is any hope of our going to Scotland again. We were greatly interested in our trip but it was rather a great undertaking for such a small company. Do you ever come to Ireland?

Yours very sincerely
J. M. Synge

MS, Healy

[1] Herbert John Clifford Grierson (1866–1960), seventeenth-century scholar, first Professor of English Literature at the University of Aberdeen (1894–1915), later Professor of Rhetoric and English Literature (1915–35) and Rector (1936–9) at Edinburgh University; knighted in 1936. On the occasion of the company's 1906 visit to Aberdeen he wrote a letter of appreciation to the editor of the *Aberdeen Free Press* (13 June 1906), in which he implied that *Riders to the Sea* could be compared with Elizabethan tragedy.

To LADY GREGORY

> Glendalough House [Glenageary]
> Jan 2nd [1907]

Dear Lady Gregory

Thanks for note this morning. I will see Fay this afternoon and talk things over with him.

Yeats wrote to say he hoped *you* would speak to Fay, so I could not do so till I heard further. Your letter of Saturday was delayed somewhere and I did not get it till I came back from the Theatre on Monday night.

The House on Monday was the same to a penny as the Monday-night house of S. Waters and the Canavans.

I handed over two acts of Playboy on Monday, and am finishing 3rd this week I hope.

I was not in yesterday as I was laid up with a sore foot.

I will let you know result of talk with Fay as soon as I can.

> Yours sincerely
> J. M. Synge

Fay came home with a bad cough and had an attack of palpitation in the night after Saturday's show, bad enough to call in doctor in small hours, he seems fairly well again.

MS, Berg. *TB*, 194

To MOLLY ALLGOOD

> Glendalough [House, Glenageary]
> Jan 4th/ 07

Dear Heart

I have a little cold so I could not go in last night, and I will not go tonight — I think — or perhaps tomorrow. I am not at all bad but I do not want to be laid up again just as the rehearsals are beginning.

Write me a *very* nice letter when you get this to cheer me up. I am inclined to get very depressed when I think of my poor little changeling going home all by her little self. Be very good, and think about me a great deal. I am very much disgusted that I cant go in for the Playboy Rehearsal this morning. It is a great nuisance. However its well I'm not worse.

My cousin Florence Ross was at the Abbey last night with one of my nephews and another cousin.[1] They liked the shows very much indeed, and they tell me there was a fairly good House.

I am scribbling this in a great hurry as the servant is going out to the post in a few minutes, so do not be surprised that there is so little depth in it. You must be learning to understand all I mean now before I say it.

I will try and get in tomorrow.

With a thousand loves

Your old Tramp

Be careful with your cues etc and dont get into a row with Fay while we are all scattered.

I am writting about a *flat* I saw advertised in the paper today! Isn't time for me to make a move?

MS, TCD. *LM*, 84

[1] Mrs Synge's diary for 3 Jan 1907 records, 'Frank [Stephens], Ton [Traill, a South American cousin] and Florence went to the Abbey, not home till after 12. I lay awake a great deal.' (TCD)

To MOLLY ALLGOOD

[Glendalough House, Glenageary]

[7 January 1907]

Sweet Heart

I am so anxious to hear how you are. I had my ear cocked at the door all the morning till your note came to Fay. If I had known you were not coming I would have gone part of the way to the Hospital with you. Wasn't it curious how we met. I had just left my bicycle at Rudge's[1] (at the Grafton St. corner) to be mended and then I thought I'd walk as far as Dawson to see if I could see you, and pop out you come!

I hope you are resting well today, and that you will be in great form tomorrow. I shall be in tomorrow at eleven. If you aren't able to come out I'll go up and see you in the afternoon. I must know how you are.

We had a good rehearsal. This first act anyhow goes swimmingly. I am longing to hear you in Pegeen Mike with the others. If your eye doesn't get better soon[2] I'll have to go and teach you your part myself, so as not to tire you by reading it. No word from the Flat-man! I wonder why he advertises if he will not take the trouble to answer would-be tenants.[3] Take care yourself my treasure for my sake, and your sake, and the Abbey's sake.

Your old follower forever

J.M.S.

I have found my papers that were lost!!! Is that thanks to St. Antony? Do get well Dear Heart

MS, TCD. *LM*, 85

¹ Rudge, Whitworth Cycle Company Ltd. had a shop at No. 1 Stephens Green, just down the street from Park Chambers where Molly was staying with the Callenders.
² Molly was suffering from an eye infection which was to recur frequently.
³ On 7 Jan 1907 Mr Charles Henderson, 30 Eccles Street, replied (TCD) concerning flats available.

To MOLLY ALLGOOD

[Glendalough House, Glenageary]
Monday evening | 7/I/07.

Darling

I must write you another line so that you may have something to cheer you up when you awake tomorrow morning! I am troubled to think of you lying there all day with no one to cheer you up. I hope you wont go down to the Abbey tonight, you must have a rest to set you up.

My toe is very sore again tonight but I'm going off to the post in spite of it so that my little changeling may have her note tomorrow morning. I am taking in the 3rd Act of PlayB. tomorrow and I believe I am going to lunch with W.G. and then work at it all the afternoon with Frank, so that there may be no delay. I dont feel quite so sure of the third act as of the others. I have been a little hurried at the end of it. However it will play all the faster. Sweetheart be sure you do *everything* the doctor tells you so that you may get well *quickly*. If you are laid up for long what will become of your old Tramp. I hope you will have a long sound sleep tonight and be much better tomorrow. You have such a strong healthy constitution I am sure you will get well very fast once you begin.

With many blessings your old T.

MS, TCD. *LM*, 86

To W. B. YEATS

Glendalough House | Glenageary | Kingstown
Jan 9th/07

Dear Yeats

All things considered it is not surprising that Fay decided as he did. If he is unfair to his fellow workers, will not Miss Horniman be so to a far greater extent if she throws us over when we have carried out our side of the original bargain so rigourously?[1] Tunny[2] came round after one of the shows last week in the greatest enthusiasm over the proggress we had made since he saw us last about a year ago. Jimmy O'Brien — from the Queen's[3] — was in on Saturday and was immensely taken [with] the Hour Glass and Frank Fay. In the evening Mde Luzan — the prima donna of the Moody–Manners Opera Co now in the Royal[4] — came in, and went up to tea with them afterwards in the Green-Room. She told them she had never heard such beautiful speaking in her life, and was greatly pleased with the whole show. If Miss Horniman gives us up she cannot pretend to do so because we are an artistic failure.

The Playboy is going very well in rehearsal and — for the time — all is smooth. Please *do not* bring or send over new man till the playboy is over as it is *absolutely* essential that Fay should be undisturbed till he has got through this big part.

It will be well — I think — to impress on the new man that he is to co-oporate with — and help Fay in the friendliest way. A house divided against itself cannot stand, and if they do not get on I dont know where we shall be landed. I would take time if I were you and make sure you get the right man, it would be much better to wait a few months than to bring over a man who would make a mess of it. I am very much rushed getting MSS. of Playboy ready for the press, or I would have written sooner.

I suppose you heard what a middling week we have just had — financially.

Yours sincerely
J. M. Synge

MS, Yeats. *TB*, 200

[1] Fay was holding out for a better arrangement *vis-à-vis* the new man (not yet hired); Lady Gregory and JMS were both concerned about Miss Horniman's control over Yeats. (See *TB*, 196–9.)

[2] W. J. Tunney, an amateur actor in various Dublin productions; he appears to have performed with the company only during their tour to Oxford, Cambridge, and London the week of 23–8 Nov 1905.

[3] James O'Brien, a well-known actor of old-fashioned melodramas and popular pieces; a paragraph by JMS in the *Academy and Literature*, 11 June 1904, comments on his performance as Conn in a production of Boucicault's *The Shaughraun* at the Queen's Royal Theatre, Dublin (*Prose*, 397).

[4] Probably Mme Zélie de Lussan (1863–1949), an American soprano famous for her performance as Carmen, who regularly appeared at Covent Garden from 1888 to 1910; her name appears among the performers of one of the three Moody–Manners Opera Company troupes, who regularly visited the Theatre Royal, Dublin, from 1898 to 1916.

To W. B. YEATS

[Abbey Theatre, Dublin]
Jan 11th/07

Statement

Dear Yeats
    We[1] accept the new man at the following terms —
[1] £100 a year added to W. G. Fays present wages
2/ We — the authors — to be free to withdraw all our plays at the end of six months — in other words that the agreement we signed as to the Irish rights to be cancelled at the end of six months.
3/ You are if possible to talk out scheme of duties for new man with some one who knows and submit same to us.
4/ We take it for granted that my — (Synge's) — suggestions have been agreed to — or if not let us hear.
5/ Fay must have a written contract defining his duties and giving him control of dialect work.
6/ It is evident that new man will have more business than Stage-management and it is essential that he should be thorough theatrical *business* man, if possible an Irishman.

Yours sincerely
J. M. Synge

MS, Yeats. *TB*, 203

    [1] i.e. Lady Gregory and JMS, with W. G. Fay's agreement.

To LADY GREGORY

[Glendalough House, Glenageary]
Sunday [13 January 1907]

Dear Lady Gregory
    There was £12.10.0 in Matinée yesterday and I believe £20 in the evening Balcony filled from pit over flow.
    O'Mara[1] — the well known opera singer was in from Theatre Royal and told me our 'Make-up' is absolutely perfect!

Yours sincerely
J. M. Synge

MS, Berg. *TB*, 204

    [1] Joseph O'Mara (d. 1927), Irish-born tenor, formerly of Covent Garden, who after three successful years in the United States became leading tenor in the Moody–Manners Opera Company.

To JOSEPH HONE

[Glendalough House, Glenageary]
Jan 17th /07

Dear Hone

I cannot hit on any very brilliant title for the article[1] — I am doing. We might call it "Among the Glens of Wicklow," or if you think it better "The People of the Glens."

I hope to have it for you in a few days, — at least next week. As to terms I think two guineas an article is hardly sufficient, as the work takes me a long time and I could probably place it elsewhere if I took the trouble to send it round. I greatly prefer, however, working here for people I know, and I have no wish at all to press for a big price. Could you manage to give me 3 or 4 guineas, say, for each article according to length?

I find I have not enough material to do you a *Series* on the Blasquet Islands. I could however do you a series of several articles on the people of the South west Kerry coast — including an article or two on the Blasquet Islands. The places I would deal with are almost as little known and as interesting as the islands themselves. You can say in your prospectus that a great deal has been written (recently) about Achill and Aran and Connaght, but that the Blasquet Islands and the farther Kerry coast are quite unknown. Also that the people there differ greatly from the Donegal or Galway people and are in many ways peculiarly interesting.

I suppose publication in the Shanachie will *not* tend to disquality the stuff for publication by you in book-form afterwards?

Yours sincerely
J. M. Synge

MS, TCD

[1] 'The People of the Glens' (*Prose*, 216) appeared in the Spring (March) 1907 issue of *The Shanachie* (no. 3).

To MOLLY ALLGOOD

[Glendalough House, Glenageary]
Saturday Jan. 26th/07

My Heart's Delight

A thousand thanks for your little note. I was not, of course, angry with you last night but I felt queer and lonesome all the same on my way to the train. I am afraid it is not very likely that we shall get away together tonight, so I must send you all my blessings by post, or at least by letter.

I am not very bad, but, if anything, my cough is worse than it was yesterday so I do not know what to say about our Sunday walk. Unless I say something definite to you tonight you had better *not* come down tomorrow. It makes me sick to think of passing the long day without you, but it would be much worse if I got regularly laid up again, and did not see you for days like the last time. If it was not Sunday I would ask you to come out here, but that is not possible so many of my people will be here.

Fancy! I am thinking more about being without my little change-ling tomorrow than I am thinking about the P.B. All the same I most fervently hope it will go off well and be a credit to both of us.

With endless love
Your old Tramper

MS, TCD. *LM*, 86

To LADY GREGORY

Glendalough House [Glenageary]
Saturday afternoon [26 January 1907]

Dear Lady Gregory.

Thanks for your note. Yeats wired in favour of Riders so it goes on with Playboy though I think the Pot would have made a better bill.[1]

I do not know how things will go tonight, the day company are all very steady, but Power is in a most deplorable state of uncertainty. Miss O'Sullivan and [Craig] are very shaky also on the few words they have to speak[2]

Many thanks for your good wishes for P.Boy

I have a sort [of] second edition of influenza, and I am looking gloomily at everything. Fay has worked very hard all through and everything has gone smoothly.

Yours sincerely
J. M. Synge

MS, Berg. *TB*, 209

[1] According to Joseph Holloway (NLI), bills advertising *The Pot of Broth* as curtain-raiser with *The Playboy* had already been printed, but Lady Gregory objected strongly to Yeats, determined that 'Synge should not set fire to your house to roast his own pig' (*TB*, 205).

[2] Ambrose Power played Old Mahon; on 31 Jan 1907 he wrote to the newspapers denying reports that he had spoken anything obscene in the play. Alice O'Sullivan, who had previously appeared in *The Mineral Workers*, 20 Oct 1906, took the part of Susan Brady; Mary Craig (May Craig, *c.* 1889–1972) seems to have made her first appearance, as Honor Blake, in what was to be a long and distinguished career as an Abbey actress.

To MOLLY ALLGOOD

[Glendalough House, Glenageary]
Sunday | Jan. 27/07

My Treasure

I have been awake most of the night, so I am rather worn out and it is as well that we are not going out as we would be sure to tire ourselves. It is curious how much I have changed. Last year I would have been as happy as possible among my books for a long Sunday morning, but now I am so lonesome I dont know what to do with myself. I wonder how you feel today. You played wonderfully I thought last night, and everyone was delighted with you. Now for a secret. When you went over and sat down by the fire showing off the Mrs Siddons side — or Mrs Sheridan which was it[1] — I heard a man behind me saying "What a beautiful girl!" — Wasn't I telling you, and you a fine handsome young woman with a noble brow?

I wish I had you here to talk over the whole show last night. W.G. was pretty fluffy, and Power was very confused in places, then the crowd was wretched and Mrs W.G. missed the new cue we gave, though she can hardly be blamed for that.[2] I think with a better Mahon and crowd and a few slight cuts the play would be thoroughly sound. I feel like old Maura today "Its four fine plays I have though it was a hard birth I had with everyone of them and they coming to the world."[3]

It is better any day to have the row we had last night, than to have your play fizzling out in half-hearted applause. Now we'll be talked about. We're an event in the history of the Irish stage.

I have a splitting headache, and worse luck I have to go in and talk business with Lady Gregory half the day. She got an important wire from Yeats, so she came up in a hurry last night and we have to talk today. There is nothing new, only details of what we had on hand before. If I get an opportunity I think I'll tell her about *us*.

Dearest treasure you dont [know] how you have changed the world to me. Now that I have you I dont care twopence for what anyone else in the world may say or do. You are my whole world to me now, you that is, and the little shiny new moon, and the flowers of the earth. My little love how I am wrapped up in you! It went to my heart to desert you last night but I could not get away from Lady Gregory. There is the quarter to eleven bell ringing! That is usually my signal to put on my shoes and start for our walk. It goes through me. Perhaps we may get a walk tomorrow, or in any case on Tuesday. Now the P.B is off we are more our own masters, thank Heaven, though I have still an article to get written before Feb. 1st. I am starving, God help me. Now good bye my own soul, till tomorrow. I would take this and put it into your post box, but I dont know which it is. I suppose if I wire to you to-morrow morning you could come down the quarter to two to Bray and have a little walk. I may be too busy of course or too unwell.

Goodbye again

Your old Tramp

MS, (pp. 1 and 4) TCD; (pp. 2 and 3) AS. *LM*, 87

[1] Sarah Siddons (1755–1831), tragedienne and one of the greatest actresses of the English stage; the Mrs Sheridan meant may be R. B. Sheridan's mother (1724–66), author of both plays and novels, or his wife, Elizabeth Linley. Molly was frequently photographed in profile.

[2] *The Playboy* opened to an uneasy audience, and by the third act the reaction of the house had become so violent the noise drowned out the final speeches. Brigit O'Dempsey (Mrs Fay) played the village girl, Sara Tansey.

[3] A parody of the tragic speech by old Maurya in *Riders to the Sea*.

To THE EDITOR, *THE IRISH TIMES*

[Abbey Theatre, Dublin]

[30 January 1907]

Sir, —

As a rule the less a writer says about his own work the better, but as my views have been rather misunderstood in an interview which appeared in one of the evening papers,[1] and was alluded to in your leader to-day, I would like to say a word or two to put myself right. The interview took place in conditions that made it nearly impossible for me — in spite of the patience and courtesy of the interviewer — to give a clear account of my views about the play, and the lines I followed in writing it. "The Playboy of the Western World" is not a play with "a purpose" in the modern sense of the word, but although parts of it are, or are meant to be, extravagant comedy, still a great deal that is in it, and a great deal more that is behind it, is perfectly serious, when looked at in a certain light. That is often the case, I think, with comedy, and no one is quite sure to-day whether "Shylock" and "Alceste"[2] should be played seriously or not. There are, it may be hinted, several sides to "The Playboy." "Pat," I am glad to notice, has seen some of them in his own way.[3] There may be still others if anyone cares to look for them.

Yours, etc.,

J. M. Synge.

The Irish Times, 31 January 1907

[1] The interview published in the Dublin *Evening Mail*, 29 Jan 1907, included a quotation from JMS, 'I don't care a rap how the people take it. I never bother

whether my plots are typical Irish or not; but my methods are typical', and his hasty disclaimer, 'It is a comedy, an extravaganza, made to amuse —.'

² The controversial figures in *The Merchant of Venice* and Molière's *Le Misanthrope*.

³ P. D. Kenny ('Pat'; 1864–1944), author of *Economics for Irishmen* (1906) and *The Sorrows of Ireland* (1907), had favourably reviewed the play for the *Irish Times*, admiring its presentation of a realistic environment which he called 'more a psychological revelation than a dramatic process, but it is both'.

To MOLLY ALLGOOD

> [Glendalough House, Glenageary]
> Thursday | Jan [31st]/07[1]

Dear old Changeling

We see so little of each other now we'll have to begin to write letters to keep our spirits up, till we get a little peace again. Wont it be wonderful when we are out again in the twilight with ourselves only, and the little shiney new moon sinking on the hills? I have been lying half asleep all day trying to rest myself and my cough has been rather bad — it is getting worse bad cess to it — I am going in tonight but I wont go tomorrow, perhaps, if things are quieter. Then I'll have to lie up again on Sunday and keep myself for next week.

I have been longing to have you here with me today to pet me and make much of me. I hope you are feeling better today, you looked tired yesterday. This is a foolish empty note I fear, but I fancied you might like to see that I am thinking about my little changeling in spite of all the fuss.

I suppose you'll get this tomorrow morning

> Your old Tramp.

MS, TCD. *LM*, 89

1 Misdated 30 Jan 1907.

To MOLLY ALLGOOD

> [Glendalough House, Glenageary]
> [1 February 1907]

Dearest Heart.

I was delighted to get your envelope today. Cheer up, my little heart, the P.B. will soon be getting his rest I hope, and then, we'll be able to see a lot of each other till we get everything fixed up.

These two days I have had at home by myself I have been thinking about you a very great deal — I am always at it — and wishing I had your little voice to cheer me.

I hope we may be able to [get] a little walk on Sunday if I go on getting better but, of course, I will not be able to go far. I am sorry Peggy is bothering you, when you have so much to tire you without that. Did you fight about me?

I am getting a little better I think but I am sore all over from coughing. It gets very bad in the night sometimes. The mountains looked lovely today. I cannot tell you how much I longed to be away among them again with Pegeen Mike.

I suppose you will think this is as poor a note as the one I wrote last night. You mustn't mind if it is. It is my head that is heavy not my heart. I wonder shall we be able to get away for a supper together tomorrow if I am up for the matinee.

You dont know how much I admire the way you are playing P. Mike in spite of all the row

A thousand thousand blessings
Your Tramper

MS, TCD. *LM*, 89

To LADY GREGORY

[Glendalough House, Glenageary]
Tuesday [5 February 1907]

Dear Lady Gregory

I am lying up for a few days to try and shake off my cough. They got the doctor down to see me last night, and he told me to stay in bed for a couple of days as I have pretty sharp bronchitis. I daresay I shall be in town again by the end of the week.

Yours sincerely
J. M. Synge

MS, Berg. *TB*, 210

To MOLLY ALLGOOD

[Glendalough House, Glenageary]
[5 February 1907]

Dearest Life

I heard the post man's knock up the road today beyond this house and I was just beginning to curse etc like a gaudy officer when they came up with your note to my great joy. I am in bed still but

I may be up tomorrow I dont know yet, I would give the world to see you, but you had better not come tomorrow as I may not be up. Perhaps you might come on Thursday I will let you know again. I will tell them you are going to help me to type my article that I have to have this week!

I am thinking about you all the time, though even if I had you here I could not talk much I am so hoarse and wheesy. F Ross went away this morning and the other one[1] comes tomorrow Worse luck. It is a great plague to have semi-strangers here when one is ill. I laughed at the story of your attacking the poor orphan with a bottle I wish I had seen it! I think the debate was a mistake.[2] Yeats forgets that our opponents are low ruffians not men of intellect and honesty with whom one can reason. Good bye my treasure for another day or two. What hours are you free? Be sure you write to me again tomorrow. I'll worry myself ill if you dont.

YOUR OLD TRAMP

MS, TCD. *LM*, 90

[1] Another cousin, Mrs Frank Dobbs, and her little boy.
[2] On Monday, 4 Feb 1907, P. D. Kenny chaired a public debate on 'The Freedom of the Theatre', arranged by Yeats who rushed back to Dublin from a lecture tour of Scotland when telegraphed by JMS and Lady Gregory after the opening night of *The Playboy*.

To MOLLY ALLGOOD

[Glendalough House, Glenageary]
[6 February 1907]

Dearest Love

Many many thanks for all your little notes, they are the only comfort I have. I am afraid I am worse today instead of better, and I feel very down indeed. Did I tell you that we had the doctor out from Dublin to see me on Monday evening? He says there is nothing serious the matter but that I must lie up for a few days till I get over this cough. Oh what fools we were to go and sit in the Park that cold day, and then come back on top of the tram and bring on all this misery and separation. Unless I am much better than I am today there would be no use in your coming out tomorrow. If I am really better I may possibly wire to you before *one* tomorrow, asking you to come out in the afternoon. If I dont perhaps you will be able to come on Friday instead. It seems years since I saw you, my own little heart. I am delighted to hear about the rise in your salary. I knew there was talk of raising them sometime, but I did not know it would be done so soon.

I feel as 'blue' as F. Fay today. I got the three papers all right thanks and a letter from Lady G. also telling me about the evening. I am glad I was not there I would have got into a towering rage.

Go on writing to me, dear heart, as often as you can, every line you send is a joy to me

Your old Tramp.

MS, TCD. *LM*, 91

To MOLLY ALLGOOD

[Glendalough House, Glenageary]
Thursday [7 February 1907]

Dearest Life

You mustn't dream of being uneasy about me, there is not any thing serious the matter only a tedious bronchitis (i.e. chest cough) the sort of thing I've had scores of times in my day. I am up again for a while today but I am glad I did not ask you to come out, as talking makes me cough, and coughing hurts me as if I had ten scarlet divils twisting a crow-bar in the butt of my ribs.

Will you come and see me tomorrow (*Friday*) if you are free. Come down by the quarter to two or the quarter to three, and be prepared to see a poor sick man with a beard on him — God forgive him — and a wheesy chest. Of course if you are wanted for rehearsal dont come, but I dont suppose they can want you just then. Dont bother about your dream, I'm not going to die yet — with the help of God, and I am really not seriously ill. You have been very good with all your little letters, and I am very grateful. So goodbye till tomorrow

Now this must go
Your old Tramp.

MS, TCD. *LM*, 91

To MOLLY ALLGOOD

[Glendalough House, Glenageary]
Friday [8 February 1907]

Dear Heart

Instead of being downstairs today I am in bed again with feverish headache. It is too bad. I got your letter last night but none today. Of course I will lend you the money with a heart and a half,[1] but you'll have to wait for a few days till I can get it out of the Bank.

I hope to God I shall be well enough to be about by Sunday. I feel wretched today. Write me nice letters Dear Heart and keep me alive.

Your old Tramp.

MS, TCD. *LM*, 92

---

1 Molly and her sister Sally were perennially short of funds.

To MOLLY ALLGOOD

[Glendalough House, Glenageary]
[9 February 1907]

Dearest Heart

· I had a very bad night last night and I am staying in bed today to try and shake off my cough. I was delighted to get your note this morning. Be sure you write to me every day while I am ill. I think I am getting better now but I'm very shaky still, and I cannot write much to you, although I'm brimming over with things I would like to say. I will not, of course, be able to walk tomorrow. Write me long letters I cannot do more than this scrawl today.

A thousand blessings from
Your old Tramp.

I wish I had you here to read to me and look after me. I feel very flat after all the excitement   J.M.S.

MS, TCD. *LM*, 92

To LADY GREGORY

[Glendalough House, Glenageary]
Saturday Feb 9th [1907]

Dear Lady Gregory

Many thanks for your long letter, about the Monday evening. I hope you may have a reasonable house today and this evening. If we can hold our audiences now for a few weeks we shall be in a better position than ever.

I am getting on slowly, but not able to be up much or do anything yet. We had the doctor out again last night, he says I am going on all right, but that I must lie up, and keep quiet for a few days longer.

I hope by the end of next week I shall be on my feet again, as, though it is so tedious, I am not very bad.

Yours sincerely
J. M. Synge

MS, Berg. *TB*, 214

ʻ

To FRANK FAY

Glendalough House | Glenageary
Saturday | Feb. 9th [1907]

Dear Fay

Can you do a little job for me, (as it is very troublesome to do from here,). If it is at all inconvenient dont trouble about it, please, but if you can manage it I shall be very grateful.

I want 6 copies of Irish Times for Wednesday and Thursday (each) of Playboy week also 6 of the herald which had the columb of sketches and 6 Saturday (last Saturday) Telegraphs. It was Saturday I think that had the letter from Stephen Gwynne?[1] Also one Claimheam Soluis[2] of current week and one copy of anything else you have come across that you think I *really ought* to have — if there is any such. I want to have some record myself of the week and I want the extra numbers for Musek, Meyerfeld, Lebeau etc. The ones I have chosen are I think the most characteristic, and are safe to send about without annotation.

I have had a nasty turn but I am better though not getting up much yet, or doing anything. If you could come out and see me, say Tuesday afternoon I would be delighted and I hope by then I shall be well enough to talk. Remember if the papers are any bother dont trouble about them, I can order them when I am well Also of course there is no hurry about them.

I hope you may have good luck today with your houses I wish I could go in.

Yours sincerely
J. M. Synge

MS, NLI

[1] Stephen Gwynn's letter to the editor of the *Freeman's Journal*, in support of *The Playboy*, appeared on 2 Feb 1907.

[2] In *An Claidheamh Soluis*, one of the official newspapers of the Gaelic League, the editor Pádraic Pearse on 9 Feb 1907 denounced the entire Anglo-Irish dramatic movement for 'the spoiling of a noble poet in Mr Yeats, and the generation of a sort of Evil Spirit in the shape of Mr J. M. Synge'. (In *Irish Freedom*, June 1913, Pearse made an indirect apology: 'When a man like Synge, a man in whose sad heart there glowed a true love of Ireland, one of the two

or three men who have in our time made Ireland considerable in the eyes of the world, uses strange symbols which we do not understand, we cry out that he has blasphemed and we proceed to crucify him.')

To MOLLY ALLGOOD

[Glendalough House, Glenageary]
Monday 3 P.M. [11 February 1907]

Dearest Love

Your note has come by the midday post. I hope you are not getting my cough, that would be too bad! I was a little tired yesterday, and I got very depressed after you had gone — I felt so lonesome — then I picked up heart again, and I was saying to myself all the evening, what a little god-send you were, so pretty, and so kindly, and so clever, and so sensible, and such a baby, and so fond of the world, and so fond of an old T---p [*deletion*], — and I got very happy again. I'd like to thank God for giving me such a soul's treasure as you are to me, and I kept wondering last night how I had lived so long without you. I couldn't live without you now, not for a month. It is funny about what you made me think by holding these terrible secrets over my head! Of course you were right to tell me what you did yesterday, and it would be best — if [it] is worth while — to tell me anymore little troubles you have of the same kind. Why shouldn't I know everything that has to do with you? I dont like being kept out in the cold. However we wont bother ourselves about trifles we've had enough of that.

This is a badly written and disjointed sort of letter. I am not much better yet I am afraid, it is apallingly slow. F Ross has just been up paying me a visit, but I feel very sad at having to pass the day without my own little changling. I wish you weren't so far away so that you could look in at me very often — three or four times a day — wouldn't that be better. I have an overwhelming thirst to be out with you again in the quiet glens, and a warm sun in it and the spring birds. Well in a week or two please Heaven we'll be off again. The thought of it keeps me up through the weary day. You dont know what it is to be shut up like this day after day when I am so used to tramping on the hills. Write me a nice letter next time, my soul's light, and cheer me up. I wish it was Wednesday.

Your Tramp

MS, TCD. *LM*, 100

To MOLLY ALLGOOD

[Glendalough House, Glenageary]
Tuesday [12 February 1907]

Dearest Life

God reward you for all your notes! I live on them. F. Fay hasn't turned up yet, I hope he wont come tomorrow, you must come in any case and we'll have to chance it. Come by the quarter to three.

I dont know how I am I feel very wretched and my breathing is very bad. I fear we'll have the doctor out again. Miss Horniman wrote to say the Playboy was 'splendid', and I am to make haste and write another play. She wants to make peace, I suppose. I have written to thank her a little dryly. I wish I could get better, day after day with no change is fearfully depressing. Be sure you come tomorrow. I cant get on another day without you. I think of nothing but my little changling.

Your old Tramp

MS, TCD. *LM*, 96

To MOLLY ALLGOOD

[Glendalough House, Glenageary]
Thursday [14 February 1907]

Dearest Life

Thanks for notes and dream — I wonder who the grey mare was!

I had a bad night, and I am staying in bed the whole day today, the doctor did not come yesterday, but is coming tonight instead. The turn I had yesterday has passed off — more or less — , but it has weakened me very much, and made my cough worse again.

I feel terribly wretched today, and inclined to blaspheme creation, and all that is in it except a Changling. I am afraid there is no use in bringing you down tomorrow, it would be better, I think, if you would come on Saturday, when there is some chance of my being a little better. I suppose you are free on Saturday afternoon. A thousand blessings Dear Heart, on you, and your kind eyes, and your little notes, and your love that is such a joy to me. How did I live without you?

Excuse this scrawl I cant write easily in bed. Good bye sweet Heart, I'll write to you of course tomorrow, and you'll come on Saturday.

Your old Tramp.

MS, TCD. *LM*, 96

To MOLLY ALLGOOD

[Glendalough House, Glenageary]
[?16 February 1907]

Dearest Love

I am better today, and the pain in stomach has stopped at last. You know this last turn I have had I brought on myself by taking too many pills and too many oranges, I hope it is over now. You mustn't be uneasy. I have a little bronchitis and a little laryngites — a dryness in my throat — brought on by being out and talking so much, the P.B. week when I was ill already. The laryngites is a very slow thing, the doctor says, so I must have patience a little longer. If my stomach will get well now, I hope I shall get better steadily now. It has nothing whatever to say to my neck. W.G. is a little ass very fond of talking wisely about things he knows nothing about. It is a very simple operation getting these lumps out. The last time, when they were much bigger than they are, now, I was perfectly well in ten days. So you see you needn't mind him.

The doctor says that on account of my throat I should talk as little as possible for a few days so you had better not come and see me — I fear — for a day or two yet. I doubt that I shall be up tomorrow, I am afraid of upsetting my stomach again. Take care of *yourself*. Goodbye, dont be anxious.

Your old Tramp.

MS, TCD. *LM*, 97

To MOLLY ALLGOOD

[Glendalough House, Glenageary]
[17 February 1907]

Dearest Heart

I am a great deal better I think today, but I am staying in bed still, and possibly tomorrow also. I felt very gay this morning for a while but now, I am infinitely depressed and infinitely weary, lying here day after day. I half wish I had asked you to come down today, but if you had I'd have talked, and made my throat worse, so perhaps it is better as it is. This day four weeks was the day we had our last walk. Do you remember in Glen Cullen, where we sat on the top of the bank?

I wonder when I'll be about again, it is 20 years since I have had such a bout of it as I am having now so you must not think that this is a usual occurence. When — at what hour? — do you have your verse classes with F.J.F.? I want to know what afternoons you are free next week, none at all I suppose between the rehearsals and classes, but perhaps you could come down after your class, or on Tuesday evening. I may be up then. I could have written you a nice letter if I had had a pen this morning, but now I am too wretched, so excuse this dreary scrawl. I think of you a great deal and I dont like the thought [of] America.[1] I hope it wont come off just yet. W.B.Y. came yesterday but I did not see him. Goodbye Dearest

Your old Tramp.

MS, TCD. *LM*, 93

[1] The directors were making various enquiries, through John Quinn and others, about the possibility of an American tour.

To MOLLY ALLGOOD

[Glendalough House, Glenageary]
Monday [18 February 1907]

Dearest

I got no letter this morning and I felt very upset. It seemed strange that you should pass the whole day without writing a line. A letter has come now by the 2 'oclock post, to say that you dont want to come and see me. I dont understand it at all. I was going to ask you to come on Wednesday — my mother suggested the same thing — but of course if you dont want to come I wont press you. As I say it seems very strange — I am up now in the little front room. It is pouring rain and I feel very lonely and weak, sitting here by myself.

I wrote to you yesterday as usual and had it sent to the post. I am sorry it has not reached you.

In a week, I hope, I shall be about again.

Your old Tramp

P.S. Why wont you come and see me? You'll make me as ill as ever, if you upset me like this.

P.S. This is a nasty sort of production I am afraid. Forgive it I am very weak and I suppose very foolish. I am sure you will come! I am a good deal better I think if it will only last. How are you dear Heart? What hour is your class on Wednesday.

P.S. You'll be able *to pull my beard* next time!

MS, TCD. *LM*, 94

To M. J. NOLAN[1]

Glendalough House | Glenageary | Kingstown
Feb.19.07

Mr M. J. Nolan

Dear Sir

I must ask you to excuse me for delaying so long before returning your interesting essay and thanking you for it. During the week of the play I had influenza rather severely, and as soon as it was over, I had to take to my bed where I have been ever since. Otherwise you should have heard from me long ago.

With a great deal of what you say I am most heartily in agreement — as where you see that I wrote the P.B. directly as a piece of life, without thinking, or caring to think, whether it was a comedy tragedy, or extravaganza, or whether it would be held to have, or not to have, a purpose, — also where you speak very accurately and rightly about Shakespere's 'mirror'. In the same way you see, — what is seems so impossible to get our Dublin people to see, obvious as it is — that the wildness and, if you will, vices of the Irish peasantry are due, like their extraordinary good points of all kinds, to the *richness* of their nature — a thing that is priceless beyond words.

I fancy when you read the play — or see it performed in more possible conditions — you will find Christy Mahon more interesting than you are inclined to do now. Remember on the first production of a play the most suttle characters always tend to come out less strongly than the simple characters, because those who act the suttle parts can do no more than feel their way till they have acted the whole play a number of times. Whether or not I agree with your final interpretation of the whole play is my secret. I follow Goethe's rule to tell no one what one means in one's writings, I am sure you will agree that the rule is a good one.

Thanking you very cordially for letting me see your interesting and clear headed essay I remain

faithfully yours
J. M. Synge

MS, TCD

[1] Little is known of this correspondent beyond the information he gives JMS in a letter of 6 Feb 1907 and subsequent letters (TCD), each of which was accompanied by a piece of original writing; he was a salesman in the wholesale fruit market, and his only published work appears to be a series of articles for the *Cork Examiner* on fruit marketing. JMS returned all his submissions.

To MOLLY ALLGOOD

[Glendalough House, Glenageary]
Tuesday | 12 o'c. [19 February 1907]

Dearest Pet

I am sorry I wrote you a 'grumpy' letter yesterday, I am so worn out, a little thing upsets me. This morning I have been in terrible pain, — with the ailment I had in Kerry, — since four o'clock. At eight I thought I heard the post pass without coming here, and I gave myself up for lost, and ⟨I⟩ broke out into a cold sweat of misery all over; I thought you had only written me one line in two days instead of two letters every day as you did, and I was in dispair. Then the servant brought a letter and I went wild with delight. The second time I read it I found it was written on Sunday, so your Monday letters are due still.

If you could have seen me raging this morning when I thought you had forgotten me you would not ask if I am tired of you or your notes. Poor Heart, dont you know they are the one joy I have? That I live on them? Perhaps you think my letters have been cold, but remember I have been almost too ill to write them at all. I think you make very few slips in spelling now, I daresay not more than I do, and your notes are charming always, like your own little self. Isn't that a nice compliment? Alas St Antony I am afraid doesn't like the job of curing me. I dont think I ever in my life had such pain as this morning. Otherwise, the cough and all, are much the same, not really better to any extent. It is heart-breaking. I dont know what to say about tomorrow, perhaps I shall hear from you at two o'c.

Later

Your letter has come. Yes I was a silly ass to kick up such a row about nothing, but you know my folly, so you should have told me *why* at once.

I am up again now a little stronger than yesterday, but, God knows, wretched enough. ⟨I am afraid, my life, it would be better after all to put off your visit to Friday, I am bitterly sorry but with my [throat] still so bad I should not talk at all, and with this turn of my Kerry ailment⟩ on me I do not know how I may be tomorrow. — (My mother has been in and we have talked your visit over) the verdict is *you are* TO COME, and if I am not up to much I'll send you off in an hour — (of course I wont) or we'll wire to you, to the Green before one o'clock. So come along and God speed you, by the quarter to three as usual. That is something to look forward to — !!

So goodbye for 24 hours from now your train is just passing up —

Your old Tramper —

MS, Texas. *LM*, 94

To LADY GREGORY

[Glendalough House, Glenageary]
Thursday [21 February 1907]

Dear Lady Gregory

Thanks for your note, yes, I hope I am mending definitely now. It has been extraordinarily tedeous, first bronchitis, then laryngites, and then worse of all a sort of dissentry, which was very bad. Please thank Yeats for his visit, I was very sorry not to see him, but that was one of my worst days, and while my larynx is affected the Doctor does not want me to talk. If there is a matinée next week I hope I may get in to see the Jackdaw[1] and Cockade, it will depend I daresay on the weather. I am sorry to hear that you have a cough too, I hope it will pass off before next week. Do not do the way I did.

It is very exciting about Frohman,[2] I wonder what will come of it. My feeling is all against rushing things, however there is also always a tide in one's affairs that must be taken. Understudies I fear will be a great difficulty. The understudying last tour was an utter farce — though I did not admit it to Miss H. I am glad to hear that Payne[3] seems a 'likely man'.

I hope I shall be in town next week and see you then.

Yours sincerely
J. M. Synge

MS, Berg. *TB*, 215

[1] *The Jackdaw*, Lady Gregory's new comedy, first produced on 23 Feb 1907.

[2] Charles Frohman (1860–1915), American manager and producer, had expressed through Agnes Tobin an interest in promoting the company on an American tour. In the event, however, it was only the Fays who performed under his management, as The Irish Players, in February 1908 and caused further trouble with the directors. Frohman was drowned on the *Lusitania*.

[3] Ben Iden Payne (1881–1976), English actor and director, later well known in both England and America, chiefly for his productions of Shakespeare at Stratford-upon-Avon. On the recommendation of John E. Vedrenne, Granville-Barker's partner at the Court Theatre, London, Yeats wrote on 16 Jan 1907 (NYPL) offering Payne the position of manager; he was at the time with the Keightley company in Waterford. His interview with Lady Gregory and JMS took place on the day of the first performance of *The Playboy*; he took up his duties about the middle of February.

To MOLLY ALLGOOD

[Glendalough House, Glenageary]
Friday [22 February 1907]

Beloved

Thanks for your two letters, a nice one this morning, and your answer to my sermon, not altogether a reassuring answer by the way. It is a healthy sign enough to be eager for adventures, so long as one has the precaution to have the right sort of adventures, and so long as one does not get flighty.

I am getting on slowly I think in the right direction, but very slowly. My mother has knocked up now and is in bed too, so we are a dreary household. I have been trying to work today at the wretched article for the Shanac⟨h⟩ie, but I am hardly able for it, and I have got very depressed. Thanks very much for the books and papers. They came last night about eight o'c, and I have finished one of them already, the Master of Ballantrae. I should think Sunday would be the best day for you to come down to see me again. You asked twice whether you should ⟨have⟩ come today, but of course there was no time to answer. I think Sunday will do best, if I [am] not ill again which Heaven forbid.

Your old Tramp.

MS, Texas. *LM*, 97

To MOLLY ALLGOOD

[Glendalough House, Glenageary]
Friday Night [22 February 1907]

My little Pigeen

Your little midday note has come. Please, it was *I* who was the '*hurt*' one, by rights, this time. You didn't say a word about coming down today till, it was too late, obviously, to arrange it! So we're both hurt — ingeniously enough — we're clever at it — and we're therefore quits! I am glad your little note came, it has cheered me up somehow again, and we'll look forward to Sunday, with the help of God. Of course you were right to tell me what was in your little scatter-brain, and I'd be much more hurt, profoundly hurt, if I thought you didn't tell me all you think of.

I, and some other people of *genius* I have known, in my youth nearly always got a wild impulse to wander off and tramp the world in the spring and autumn, the time the birds migrate, so as you're a genius too it's right and proper that you should have the impulse. We're all wild geese, at bottom, all we players, artists, and writers, and there is no keeping us in a back yard like a barndoor fowl. The one point is that when we fly it should be to the North Sea or the Islands of the Blessed, not to some sooty ornamental water in some filthy town. Now my geniusette are you satisfied?

Saturday [23 February 1907]

Dearest

I wrote the enclosed[1] last night. Your other note and card have just come! You should know by this time that I write to you every day and that my letters sometimes catch the 4 o'c post here, so that they reach you in the evening, and sometimes — more often — miss it and do not reach you till the next morning. I hope you will come and see me tomorrow by the quarter to three train. My mother is in bed still and will be in bed tomorrow so ask for me.

I am a little better but not much. It is very depressing, and instead of being sorry for me, and writing me cheerful letters you go as you have been doing. It is too foolish to annoy me.

Dont miss your train tomorrow

Yours as always

J. M. Synge

MSS, TCD. *LM*, 98, 99

1   i.e. the letter of 22 Feb 1907 printed above.

To MOLLY ALLGOOD

[Glendalough House, Glenageary]
Monday [25 February 1907]

Dearest Pigeenette

I got your note all right this morning, I have been in great spirits too since your visit yesterday. I am getting on well still, and I am hard at work on my Shanacie article today. I typed three pages this morning, and I am going to do three more now, so that I hope to finish it tomorrow. Hone has kept back the Shanacie a whole month on my account. Isn't that a compliment? If I wasn't in too good a humour I'd scold you *fiersely* for throwing aside 'the Master and Man,'[1] and reading instead that commonplace trash you were at yesterday. It makes me sad to think that you find more pleasure in such stuff.

I think now the cold is gone I'll very soon be well, we'll hardly know ourselves when I'm about again, and we can go off to see how Glencullen is, and Miss Fluke,[2] and Bray Head. My mother is in bed still, but she is getting better. I want you, please, to send me ·

tomorrow's (Tuesday's) Freeman, they have a lecture on the Western Peasant at the I.N. Literary tonight, and I know that means abuse of me, which I always enjoy.[3] I feel very happy and very wicket, I wish you were coming today. Goodbye my best one, be good,

Your old Tramp.

P.S. I enjoyed your visit last night to no end. It is a blessing that all last week's nonsense has blown away. Let us keep it off in God's name

Amen.

MS, TCD. *LM*, 99

[1] The story by Tolstoy, which had been published separately several times since its first English translation in 1895.

[2] Possibly Mrs Flude of The Cottage, Kilbride Road, Bray, listed in the Dublin Post Office Directory.

[3] The *Freeman's Journal and National Press*, edited by William Brayden, had attacked *The Playboy* as a 'squalid, offensive production'. At the meeting of the Irish National Literary Society on 25 Feb 1907, the president, Dr George Sigerson (1838–1925), Professor of Botany and Zoology at University College, Dublin, and translator of Gaelic poetry, read a paper on 'The Peasants of the West'. JMS was attacked during the discussion afterwards.

To MOLLY ALLGOOD

[Glendalough House, Glenageary]
Tuesday 2 o'c. [26 February 1907]

Dear Heart

No letter today! and I am disappointed. However I got your note last night so I must not complain, you have been very good to me. The books haven't turned up either. I suppose they hadn't them in stock. There is a post-knock just as I had given him up! I have read your note twice, and I am happy again — I was just beginning to go down, down — down.

I worked too hard at my article yesterday and I had a visit from Roberts and between the two I gave myself a headache which I have still, so I do not feel so gay as I did yesterday.

I would not bother about your parts. You have played lead in the biggest play of the season, so that ought to satisfy you for the time being. We have to try and get something out of Mrs [W.G.] F[ay] as we have to pay her. She will never do much but with practise she may improve for the small parts she has to get. Work hard as you say and sooner or later you will get the position you deserve whatever that may be. You have made your place in the peasant plays, and you may I dare say do the same in verse. But you will never reach the very top in either unless you read plenty of what is best and train your natural instincts. There is a sermon!!

I hope to finish my article today or tomorrow in spite of my head. They have sold 200 P.B.s in a week, i e £20 worth of which my share is £3. That is not bad. My mother is better but in bed still. Come tomorrow, quarter to 3 as usual. I shall be on the lookout for you.

Your old T.

MS, AS. *LM*, 101

To MOLLY ALLGOOD

[Glendalough House, Glenageary]
Thursday [28 February 1907]

Dearest

Your letter has just come, thanks. The Doctor came soon after you went last night. He said I was much better and that if I wasn't feverish I was to go down stairs today and *out* on Friday. Unluckily I *am* more feverish today, so I am in *our* room still. I shall be down stairs tomorrow however so I am afraid we wouldn't enjoy ourselves if you came out. I shall make some excuse for sitting up here on Sunday so that will be a better day for you to come. I felt worlds better for your visit yesterday. Now I hope I shall be all right very soon indeed, and then we must see each other every day.

Your dreams are funny indeed! I dont remember mine now except very occasionally. Sweetheart I wish you were here today, the afternoon here over the fire is so different, when I have you to make much of me. I told the Doctor there was some talk of the Co. going to America soon and he said that would be just the thing for me, and that if I got the glands out of my neck and then had a sea voyage and change I would be a[s] strong as a horse! I wonder if there is any chance of it — I fear not. If I could lecture it would be another thing, but unfortunately that is not in my line.

Write a lot, my dearest life, and let us live on letters till Sunday. I wish you could have seen me through the key-hole yesterday when I found you hadn't come by that train. I nearly got a fit with despair. I think we should soon be married, we are too long this way already. Dont you think so?

Now goodbye for this time I wonder will this reach you tonight or tomorrow morning. I hope I shall have another note tonight. Ever and Ever

Your old Tramp.

MS, TCD. *LM*, 105

To MOLLY ALLGOOD

[Glendalough House, Glenageary]
Saturday [2 March 1907]

Dearest Life

Another disappointment! I am very feverish still so I cannot get up tomorrow. I hope I shall be able to see you by *Monday* or *Tuesday*. The Doctor is coming out again today to have a look at me. I dont think I am quite so bad as I was yesterday. Thanks for your letters, my sweet life. Dont be uneasy about me. It is only influenza I think. I cant write any more. With infinite love

Your old Tramp.

Read Milton tomorrow and be cheerful my cough is nearly gone so I will soon be well now.

Later Your morning's letter has just come. You needn't be uneasy Dear Heart, this will pass off in turn. I am intensely sorry not to have you tomorrow, but it is quite out of the question I fear. It is too, too bad.   T.

Write me a good letter tomorrow and post it yourself.

MS, TCD. *LM*, 102

To MOLLY ALLGOOD

[Glendalough House, Glenageary]
[3 March 1907]

My dear Life

I am *very decidedly* better today, thank Heaven, but I am very weak after all the fever. I hope I shall be able to see you in a day or two

Your old Tramp

I am afraid to write much for fear of bringing on the fever again.

MS, TCD. *LM*, 103

To MOLLY ALLGOOD

[Glendalough House, Glenageary]
Monday morning [4 March 1907]

My dear Love

I think it you who [is] the cruel one! You must know I would give anything to see you, but I have been too ill, the excitement of a visit from you — it is bound to excite — would have made me much worse. It would be different of course if you were staying here. I dont wonder you were uneasy — we were all uneasy — but that is not my fault. You might have pity on me instead of scolding me. However, dearest Heart, we wont fight. Today thank Heaven the *fever* is *entirely gone*, so I hope I shall be up tomorrow. I am dreadfully weak, I have a sharp headache and the sweat is runing down my face with the exertion of writing these few lines. That is only natural of course, as I have had no solid food since Friday. I feel otherwise wonderfully better. Perhaps I shall write to you again today. I am sending this early to let you know I am so much better

Your Tramp

MS, TCD. *LM*, 103

To MOLLY ALLGOOD

[Glendalough House, Glenageary]
Tuesday [5 March 1907]

Dearest

I am a little doubtful whether or not to write to you to day as you seem to say you are coming down for F. Fay['s] book. However I will write a line in case you do not come, I am getting on very well now, and I am to get up tomorrow I hope, I was not allowed to do so today by the Doctor. He says it is of the GREATEST IMPOR-TANCE that I should not get a return of the fever, so that I must stay very quiet indeed for a few days. He examined me very carefully on Saturday from Head to Foot and could find nothing really the matter with me, but the fever was terrible on Saturday night, the highest I have ever had. So you will understand, sweetheart that it is as much as my life is worth to tire myself or worry myself in any way. So let us be careful. You ask if you may come down today, with your usual blind indifference to the fact that it is impossible to answer you in time. Do use your little head! Tomorrow I fear would not be a good day to come as I shall be getting up for the first time and I shall be very shaky and wretched, besides my brother[1] has to telephone to the doctor about me tomorrow afternoon, about 3 or 4, and he will be in and out all the afternoon. You will not mind waiting a day or two longer now you know I am going on well. Words could not tell you what I suffer in the way of dullness and impatience at having to lie here all day by myself, without my little changling, that is, but that makes it all the more important that I should stay quiet and get well this time. I wonder when you'll get this.

You can see by my writing how much stronger I am today, Thank Heaven. What has St Antony been at these days?

Ever your old
Tramp.

MS, TCD. *LM*, 103

¹ Robert Synge had visited regularly during his brother's and mother's illnesses.

To MOLLY ALLGOOD

[Glendalough House, Glenageary]
Wednesday [6 March 1907]

My dearest old Heart

I have now three letters to answer — as I wrote to you yesterday before the 2 o'cl letter came. I seem to have quite a lot to say. First [of] all I am up and dying to see you, and I suppose I am better though I am very shaky. I am very sorry about your eye. I wish you would go to Swanzie,¹ I am sure it wont get well by itself, and if you take it at once it will get well much faster, — perhaps after one visit. Do be wise!

If you *did* use your little head, — [*deletion*] — your little head is little use!!! You wrote late on Monday and I got it on Tuesday at nine o'clock, I might have wired for you, but could not get a letter written and posted before ten in my present state. You might have guessed that!!! Of course, dear Heart, you should go to Glen Dhu with the others on Sunday if your eye is well enough. I would be a brute indeed if I objected to your going. I know you wont let them walk arm-in-arm with you or anything of that kind, and I hope when you are coming back you will keep with the crowd. It would give me pain to think of you walking through OUR ROADS in the twilight with anyone else! If your eye isn't better come to me instead. When I came to the part in your letter where you spoke about our last walk up there, and the beauty of the mountains yesterday, a wave of anguish came over me, I got a lump in my throat, and the next thing I had tears streaming down like a baby. There in my bed I cannot even see a bit of sky or a cloud. That [is] what comes when you are as weak as I am, and as wretched. Will you come and see me, Dear Heart, I cant live any longer without you. Come tomorrow or Friday only let me know, by posting before eleven. Tomorrow you ought to go to Swanzie I am sure.

I am very sorry I forgot to thank you at once and properly for the Ireland.² It slipped out of my poor weary head when I was writing.

I was very glad to get it indeed, though I'd like to strangle the wretch who took that photo of you Goodbye dearest Love

Your Tramp

MS, TCD. *LM*, 104

¹ Henry R. Swanzy (later Sir Henry), MG, FRCSI, surgeon at the Royal Victoria Eye and Ear Hospital; his office was at 23 Merrion Square North.
² *Ireland*, vol. VI, no. 8 (March 1907), 385-7, included a photographic essay by Julian Grande, 'The Playboy of the Western World: "Much Ado about Nothing" ', which included a photograph of Molly, crouching, in the role of Cathleen in *Riders to the Sea.*

To MOLLY ALLGOOD

[Glendalough House, Glenageary]
Friday [8]¹ March [1907]

Dearest Heart

I am as happy as the Lord God today. Do you remember the plaintive way I talked about getting consumption yesterday? Well the reason was — I may as well tell you the whole story — the doctor in order to see if he could find out the cause of my fever last week, was examining the stuff I coughed up to see if there were the tubercular microbes in it, and he was so long letting me know that I was getting uneasy. I heard this morning, however, that none could be found, so I am all right, and in ten days, please Heaven, I shall be trotting you about as usual. This is the third time they have tried to find the tubercular microbes in me and they have always failed utterly so if Peggy says again that I am tubercular you may tell her to HOLD HER GOB!

I am in great form today but I am not going out till tomorrow as a precaution. I delight in the memory of seeing you yesterday sitting among my books. Be sure and let me know about Sunday, though of course you can come even if I dont expect you, for instance if the morning turned out too wild for your walk. I hope the Sunday after you will be out with your Tramp again. How we will enjoy it!! Dont leave me with too few letters whatever you do or I'll get ill again. I have a whole lot of books of poetry out of my press this morning and I am delighted to be able to read them again; when I am ill I have not the energy. Do read the good books I lend you instead of that dressmaker's trash!² Write me a good cheering letter to put me finally in Heaven. I wish I could see you today!

with blessings
Your old
Tramp

MS, TCD. *LM*, 106

    ² The heroine of George Fitzmaurice's play *The Country Dressmaker* had a
fondness, like Molly, for romantic novels.

To FRANK FAY

> Glendalough House | Adelaide Road [Glenageary]
> March 8th/07

Dear Fay

I have had a terribl time as you have no doubt heard, but I am
much better now and I hope my troubles are over. I have been very
thoughly examined by my doctor and there is apparently nothing
really the matter with me. I am much obliged for the loan of your
'cutting' book, which I sent back to you yesterday.¹ I am also
grateful for the papers you sent and I enclose stamps with thanks
for the amount.

Did you see Roleston's article in the Indepenent?² It is the best
I have had yet I think. I have had a letter from George Moore ap-
proving highly of play, but as usual wanting me to rewrite some of
it according to an idea of his — one by the way, which I tried myself
a year ago and rejected as too common place.³ Any evening after
eight that you are free I would be delighted to see you if you have
nothing better to do.

Remember the handle of gate *pulls back* does not turn.

> Ever yours
> J. M. Synge

MS, NLI

    ¹ JMS sent back Fay's scrapbook concerning the theatre via Molly; see
p. 305.
    ² Thomas William Rolleston (1857–1920), poet, translator, journalist, and
biographer; founder and editor (May 1885–December 1886) of the *Dublin
University Review* which published the early work of W. B. Yeats, he was first
honorary secretary (1892–3) of the Irish Literary Society, London, before
returning to Dublin in 1894 as secretary to the Irish Industries' Association,
later organizer to the Department of Agriculture (1900–5). His appreciation of
the published *Playboy* in the *Irish Independent*, 6 Mar 1907, took the form of
a lengthy letter to the editor.
    ³ Moore's letter of 6 Mar 1907 suggested that an acceptable ending would
be 'that at some moment the old man Mahon discovers that his son is about to
marry a very rich girl; the peasant's instinct for money overtakes him, causes
him to forget his wounds, and he begins to boast like his son' (TCD).

To AGNES TOBIN[1]

Glendalough House | Glenageary | Kingstown | Dublin
8/III/07

Dear Miss Tobin

I hope you have heard how ill I have been since 'Playboy' show —
I have four weeks and a half without getting down stairs! — and so
exused me for not an[swering your letter][2]

MS fragment, TCD

---

[1] Agnes Tobin (1864–1939), poet and translator of Petrarch. Daughter of
a prominent San Francisco banker, she spent much of her time in Britain, where
she became a friend of many artists and writers of the time, including Joseph
Conrad (who dedicated *Under Western Eyes* to her and her 'genius for friendship'). She and JMS apparently corresponded regularly and he advised her on
the punctuating and proofreading of her translations from the Italian. The
directors considered producing her translation of Racine's *Phèdre* at the Abbey.

[2] This fragment is on the back of an early draft of JMS's poem 'Queens';
in her letter of 20 Jan 1907 Miss Tobin had written of *The Playboy*, 'What a
blessing you did not go to Version L, if Version K has had such a disastrous
effect! I hope you will write verse, now, as I want you to — and take a rest from
play-writing.' (TCD)

To MOLLY ALLGOOD

[Glendalough House, Glenageary]
Saturday March 9th/07

My dearest Love

I have four letters to answer this time. You are very very good to
me, and I am very grateful! The tour is a surprise, I dont think it
can be settled, as you seemed to say in your letter of last night, or
I should have heard something of it. I knew London was being
negociated about, but I had not heard of the others. A good deal
of it, you may be sure, is W. G. Fay! I should go with you most
likely to Oxford and London but not further, I think, not certainly
if Miss Horniman is going.

Today I am writing with a sharp pen and it feels horrible I cant get
on at all with it. As to your head this time you wrote YESTERDAY of
Sunday — as tomorrow! and hoped it would rain. I dont think you
ought to go to the Glens tomorrow after all this rain, at this time of
the year they do not dry up after rain, and even if it is a fine day
Glen Dhu will be like a wet sponge. So that if you go you may
expect to have your shoulder in your ear on Monday! If you dont
walk out there come down by the quarter to three. I hope it will be

too wet for your expedition partly because I want to see you here, partly because I dont like the thoughts of your going to the glens without me. Do you understand that feeling? cant you get a pain in your stomach or something tomorrow? However it doesn't really matter much one way or other. I have not got out yet as it was too wet today, and yesterday I wasn't let, but I am getting on well and feeling more myself. Tell W.G. I would be glad to see him any evening after eight, but that the afternoon is uncertain. I hope I shall often be out now. I fully agree that the third Act wants pulling together. I hope if they go on tour Power wont be able to go, so that we may get a decent Old Mahon. It would make all the difference in the world.

My mother was talking the other day about our marriage, and how we intended to get on. She is still rather frightened at our poverty, but she is much more rational about it than she was. You must have charmed her! By the way I've a compliment for you. The last Sunday that you came I happened to see you passing from my top window, and you *walked* very prettily indeed. Quite charmingly. Keep to your low heels now, and dont spoil it, there is nothing so charming in a woman as an easy and graceful walk, and there is nothing more rare! So my dear old love you may be proud of yourself. I wonder if this will seem a nice letter to you? I am in too good spirits to write anything very deep, but, dear Heart, the depth is there, and it is filled with happy thoughts of you. I hope I shall see you to-morrow, but do whatever is best.

Your old Tramp.

P.S. I think you should date your letters. They are all in a jumble now and I dont know which is which.

Thanks for the stamps.

MS, TCD. *LM*, 107

To JOSEPH HONE

[Glendalough House, Glenageary]
Monday March 11th/07

Dear Hone

At last I send remainder of copy and proof. I should see the new piece[1] in galley sheets also if possible. I find that I have more stuff than I had calculated on I suppose it is not too much. I also return MS. of a sonnet that had got in with my stuff. I am better now and I hope soon to be all right.

Yours sincerely
J. M. Synge

MS, Langmuir

¹ Probably the first of his series of articles, 'In West Kerry' (*Prose*, 237), which appeared in three succeeding numbers of *The Shanachie*, nos. 4–6 (Summer, Autumn, and Winter 1907).

To MOLLY ALLGOOD

[Glendalough House, Glenageary]
March 11th [1907]

Dearest Life

I have had no letter from you today so far. I have been working at my article nearly all day and I am dog tired I hope I shall not be the worse. It is finished now and going to the post. How did you get on last night with the Fays? You must excuse this scrawl I am really too tired to write. I had a nice little walk this morning for ¾ of an hour the air felt beautiful and spring like I was wishing I had you with me, now good bye till tomorrow I['ll] try and write you a nice letter then

Your old Tramp¹

MS, TCD. *LM*, 108

¹ At the foot of this letter Molly has scribbled 'appalling' twice.

To MOLLY ALLGOOD

Glendalough [House, Glenageary]
March 12th [1907]

Dear Heart

Your note has just come at two o'clock, with the proofs,¹ thanks. I like the serious one best, I will show you which it is when you come down again. I am not at all the worse for my day's work yesterday. I was out for nearly an hour this morning, and I was going out again after dinner, but it came on to rain just as I was going out on the steps. I did not work at my article for the sake of Roberts and Co., but for the sake of the two good guineas that it will bring in to me. Still I admit I was a fool yesterday, and I worked too hard. Will you come down and see me tomorrow by the quarter to three? If you can and will, let me know by the early post that you are coming. I expect F.J.F. down this evening after supper to have a talk. I heard from him last night, in answer to my letter. I am not in a good letter-writing humour to-day, I suppose because I am diss-appointed at not getting my second walk. I have a horrid lot of letters to write and I keep putting them [off] in the most hopeless way. I shall never get them done at this rate. I wish you were here this afternoon I am dejected and heavy, and I want someone to cheer me. The birds are singing a great deal all round here now, it makes me sad when I cannot be out along with them enjoying the showers as much as they do. Perhaps we shall be able to have a little walk on Sunday, but it will only be a little one. I have a nasty cough still and till it is gone I cannot do very much. This will not be a very fat note but there is a mighty lot in it I have [written] so closely with this small pen. I am thinking about you a great deal. There is the cook going to the post this must go. Hope to see you tomorrow

Your old Tramp

MS, TCD. *LM*, 109

¹ Of one or perhaps both of the photographs of Molly reproduced in *LM*, 83 and 235.

To JAMES PATERSON

Glendalough House | Glenageary | Kingstown
March 12th/07

My dear Paterson,

I am very much obliged for your two letters which I would have answered long ago if I had been able, but I have had a sort of complicated influenza for the last five weeks that has made me good for nothing. I am out again now, for a little every day, and I hope soon to be on my feet again as usual. I am afraid I cannot claim the thanks you give me for sending you the 'Playboy' and the 'Economics',¹ it must have been some of your other friends, as, though I meant to send you a 'playboy', I have not been well enough to send any copies out yet. I am extremely glad to hear that the play interested you. As to the point you raise as to a possible want of contrast in the moral attitude of my people,² I am doubtful myself. I feel the want, and yet my instinct when I am working is always towards keeping my characters bound together as far as possible in one mood. One gains perhaps as much as one loses. The storm has quite blown over here now, but I do not know what reception the play will get when we revive it. There have been several very intelligent and favourable articles in the papers recently, so the Dublin public may come round to understand it better by degrees. I do not at all know when I shall be in Edinburgh again, but I hope as you say

that you will come over to Ireland before long. I hope Mrs. Patterson
is keeping well. Please give her my compliments and believe me

cordially yours

J. M. Synge

MS copy, TCD

1 *Economics for Irishmen*, by 'Pat' (P. D. Kenny).
2 Paterson had written on 26 Feb 1907, 'To me it is strange beyond words
and profoundly convincing as a picture of a life unknown till now. Perhaps . . .
it suffers as drama from the want of contrast in the moral outlook of the characters. And though there is no room in the play itself would it not have been well
in a prefatory note to indicate the genesis of what to us seems unnatural perver-
sion of feeling on the part of everybody concerned.' (TCD)

To MOLLY ALLGOOD

[Glendalough House, Glenageary]

March 14th [1907]

Dearest Heart

I am better today and I am thinking of going out for a turn.
Had you very long to wait for your train last night? I did not see
your train going up, I suppose I missed it as I was walking about
the house. I shall have a long dull afternoon today with no one
to talk to. I feel woefully stupid with nothing to say. I am writing
to Combridge[1] for 5s/0 worth of books, is not that extravagant?
I suppose I wont get them till after the bankholiday on Monday.

I had a kind letter from Miss Tobin this morning. She is very
keen about Frohman and seems to think it will come off. It is very
hard luck that he is not to see the 'Well of the Saints', so if there is
any money made out of the tour I shant get much of it. I dont think
I'll go out after all I've got a headache, and I dont feel very gay. I
haven't heard from you yet but the post will soon come now I suppose unless it has passed. I'll wait to finish this till I know —— ——.
No letter! I feel disappointed and uneasy. I hope you are not unwell.
Even if you are dont leave me without news of you. I cannot get on
without hearing from you. Now I shall be in low spirits — or in
lower spirits, they were not very high! — all the afternoon. Perhaps
I shall hear at six o'clock

Good bye my dearest love

YOUR OLD TRAMP

MS, TCD. *LM*, 110

1 Combridge & Co. Ltd., a bookshop at 18 Grafton Street, Dublin, which
later also provided books for James Joyce in Trieste and Paris.

To MOLLY ALLGOOD

Glendalough [House, Glenageary]
March 15 [1907]

Dearest Heart

Your letter came yesterday by the 6 o'clock post, and the second one this morning. I half hoped I would get one today at two to say that you were coming down this afternoon to see me, but the post man just sailed by on his bicycle and made my heart sink within me. So now we must wait till Sunday! For my sake – I was going to say for Heaven's sake but I think you mind me more – be careful with that flaming cauldron tomorrow in Baile's Strand.[1] If you burned yourself and got laid up now what would become of us. I am sorry to hear that your sister is so unwell, but as you are not accustomed to illness perhaps she is not so bad as you fear. I hope she will soon get better. I am not making much way, in fact I have felt (and feel) very poorly. I went out yesterday after all, and again this morning, and possibly I shall take another turn this afternoon, though I am inclined to be feverish again. Did I tell you that I heard from Henderson acknowledging the cheques. He says that five years ago he got into bad health something the way I am, and that the doctor made him take a sea voyage with the result that he has been quite well ever since! He added at the end "What fine times we had with the Playboy!" Little hypocrite!![2]

I am doing my all and utmost to make this a *corpulent* letter for you, and with the Help of God I'm getting on wonderfully. I got a wire from George Moore last night asking me to dine with him on Saturday, but of course I wont be able. Can you read that last word? I am beginning not to be able 'to stick' your writing. Today for instance you say, apparently, that as Mrs P[ayne] is ill *Dancy* has asked Sally to understudy?[3] What does that mean? I wont be able to go in tomorrow for the show as I half hoped. If W.B.Y. is over and you hear that he is coming to see me let him know that I am visable in the evenings, but in the afternoon I am *often* out walking! Poor old love I wish you were coming down today, I dread these long afternoon, I keep going from book to book seeking rest and finding none. This morning I have been reading Walter Scott's Diary[4] during the last 9 years of his life, when he was getting old and had lost immense sums of money. It is wonderful stuff full of humour and cheerfulness. Now it is your turn to write me a fat letter. You should have all the news instead of

Your old Tramp till death
us do part.

MS, TCD. *LM*, 110

¹ Payne's production of Maeterlinck's *Interior* in translation and a revised version of Yeats's *On Baile's Strand* (in which Molly played one of the three Women who carry and tend a bowl of fire) opened 16 Mar 1907.

² According to Joseph Holloway (NLI), W. A. Henderson did not approve of JMS's plays, although he kept a scrapbook on *The Playboy* (see p. 188).

³ Mrs Payne, née Mary Charlotte Louise Gadney (*c.* 1882–1968), who performed as 'Mona Limerick', was to play the lead in the revivals of Yeats's plays this season. She later created the role of Sarah Casey in the first production of *The Tinker's Wedding*, in London on 11 Nov 1909, but performed with the Abbey only during her husband's brief tenure as manager. 'Dancy' is probably Dossie Wright, the stage manager.

⁴ 'Once in his illness,' wrote Lady Gregory, 'Yeats found him reading Lockhart's *Life of Scott*, and he said that in reading it he was often reminded of me, writing and keeping power of invention in the midst of so many activities' (*Seventy Years*, 388).

To MOLLY ALLGOOD

Glendalough House [Glenageary]
March 16th/07

Dearest Heart

I was very glad to get your letter this morning, and I will expect you tomorrow at three as usual. I feel in a bad humour this afternoon because it has come on to rain so that I cannot get my little walk as I hoped. I wasn't very flourishing last night, but I am better again today, although I dont feel that I have made much progress since last Saturday. It is slow work. I dont think I need write you a 'fat' note today as I shall see you tomorrow, and I dont get any very fat ones from you. I would like to work at something or other today but I suppose I had better not till I am stronger. It is a dreary time. I never had such an experience in my life before. It is well I have you to come down and see me sometimes. This is a miserable dismal scrawl I am afraid, well what can you expect from a poor fellow shut up here looking out back and front at wet roofs and dank drizzling rain? Thank Heaven I'll have you to cheer me tomorrow.

Your old woe-begone Tramper

MS, TCD. *LM*, 112

To JOSEPH HONE

Glendalough House [Glenageary]
March 17th [1907]

Dear Hone

I return Proof.¹ The last page was carelessly set up, and I am nearly sure the omission of 'too courteous' which will entail some resetting is the printers fault, though as you did not send me my MS. I cannot be certain. I am getting on well but my convalescense is so uncertain that I do not know when I shall be going about town again. You can always see me here in the evening (after eight) or in the morning if you will send me a card to say you are coming so that I may not be out. I am well enough to stroll about now on fine days.

In Haste   sincerely yours
J. M. Synge

MS, TCD

1 Of 'The People of the Glens', *The Shanachie*, Spring 1907; his original TSS are in TCD.

To MOLLY ALLGOOD

Glendalough Ho [Glenageary]
March 18th/07

Dearest

You were not five minutes gone last night when W.G. and Mrs. F. turned up. We had a long chat and I heard all the inner news which do not definitely reach you. Nothing is settled — as I thought — about the tours. I hear however that they are showing Frohman ONE play of mine 'Riders', five or six of L G's and several of Yeats. I am raging about it, though of course you must not breath a word about it. I suppose after the P.B fuss they are afraid of stirring up the Irish Americans if they take me. However I am going to find out what is at the bottom of it and if I am not getting fair play I'll withdraw my plays from both tours English and American altogether. It is getting past a joke the way they are treating me. I am going to write to "My dear Friend"[1] again to tell her how I am getting on, and let her know incidentally what is going on here. I dont think she will be pleased. She, I imagine, does not worship Lady G. I have no letter from you today as there are no posts owing to Bank Holiday. I do not know whether I shall get to the doctor or not tomorrow so there is no use asking you to meet me. I am getting on well but my cough is very bad still.

"Yours affectionately"
Your old T.

MS, AS. *LM*, 112

1 Agnes Tobin.

To MOLLY ALLGOOD

Glendalough House [Glenageary]
March 19th [1907]

Dearest Treasure

I congratulate you about Fand[1] though I wish it was a better play and more 'actable' verse. Still it shows that you are rising in the estimation of every one. You should read the story about Fand, on which the play is founded in "Cuchulin". It is called "The Only Jealousy of Emer", I think, there are beautiful passages in it, which you should delight in, but as a story it is rather incoherent. I cannot of course go to the doctor today as the weather is so bad, so I must go tomorrow. If it is fine I shall go up by the train that gets to Westland Row at *two minutes past two*. If you are quite free then you might meet me and walk up with me, but dont miss your dinner or anything. I will not wait for you, of course, so it will not matter if you do not come.

I did not mind your 'huff' it was too utterly silly. The Fays went away at 9.30, and of course I was tired, however as I told you I was glad to see Fay and to hear all the news. You mustn't be foolish like that it is too ridiculous. I haven't written to Miss Tobin yet, but I am going to. If Frohman is genuinely afraid of taking my work for fear of making a row with the Irish Americans then, of course I have no cause to be annoyed with the directors. But if as I understand the tour is going largely for the cultivated University audiences in America it is a very different matter. My cough was very bad last night, and my head feels shaken and weary so I cannot write much Good bye dear Heart

Your old Tramp

MS, TCD. *LM*, 113

[1] Molly had been given the title role in *Fand* by W. S. Blunt, to be performed 20 Apr 1907.

To MOLLY ALLGOOD

[Glendalough House, Glenageary]
March 21st [1907]

Dearest Heart

It was well I did not ask you to wait yesterday. When I had been in the waiting room about ten minutes the doctor telephoned down from I dont know where to say that he had been called away to Lucan and would not be back till 3.30. So I had to sit it out. It was nearly a quarter to four when I got in to him at last. He says I am going on well and as the cough leaves me I may gradually get back to my ordinary ways. I am as deaf as a post in one of my ears today, I dont know whether it is cold or a lump of wax. It is a nuisance and makes me feel lopsided, and wretched.

I have written to F.J.F. for a list of how many times 'Spreading the News', 'The Shadow', "Kathleen" and "Riders" and 'Baile's Strand' have been played in the Abbey since we opened.[1] I expect their pieces have been done at least three times as often as mine. If that is so there'll be a row. I am tied to the company now by your own good self otherwise I would be inclined to clear away to Paris and let them make it a Yeats-Gregory show in name as well as in deed. However it is best not to do anything rash. They have both been very kind to me at times and I owe them a great deal.

I could have written you a very pretty letter last night but I was too tired and lazy, and now, alas, I am in a bad temper with my ear! My mother was enquiring about your temper today, she says my temper is so bad, it would be a terrible thing to marry a bad-tempered wife!! If she only knew! Your letter has just come. You told me you would not come till FRIDAY, and I believed you. So it is well you did not come today without letting me know as I should have been *out*, and what would you have said then?

I wonder if Glasgow is real! The doctor advises me to have my operation[2] early in May, so that would fit in while you are away. I must go in some time and see them at the Nassau. I dare say I could get in on Saturday but I am not very keen to, except for the 'Interior' which would interest me of course. I must go out now dear Heart and post this so that you may get it tonight. I *may* meet you *to-morrow* in the station or in the little lane outside. I suppose you will come by the quarter to three if *you are not coming let me know* by the early post. We shall have Sunday in any case I haven't written to Miss Tobin yet, I am so lazy

Your old Tramp

I am glad they are fining you, you DESERVE IT SO RICHLY![3]

MS, TCD. *LM*, 114

[1] 'Synge also wrote me a letter (which, *at his request*, I burnt) in which he said a Yeats-Gregory Theatre would be no use to anybody' (Frank J. Fay to W. J. Lawrence, 27 Oct 1912, reprinted in *Joseph Holloway's Abbey Theatre*, ed. Robert Hogan and Michael J. O'Neill [Carbondale, Ill., 1967], 156).

[2] On the swollen glands in his neck.

[3] In an attempt to discipline the company, Willie Fay imposed a system of fines for unpunctuality at rehearsals; JMS has underlined the last four words ten times.

To MOLLY ALLGOOD

[Glendalough House, Glenageary]
Saturday [23 March 1907]

Dearest Heart

No letter has come from you today so I really dont know where to write to you. I suppose I better try Mary St,[1] but I wont put anything priceless into my letter for fear it should not find you. You will come of course tomorrow whether you get it or not, at least so I hope. I am better and stronger today I think than I have been yet, though I am still deaf and coughing badly.

I heard from F.J.F last night[2] and got the list of plays put on. I have not come off so badly — largely no doubt because I was always there to fight my own battle and did so — as I thought, and I have decided to make no row for the present at least. This American tour is of course very important, and I dont want any one to be able to say I wrecked it by forcing on my unpopular plays. I dont think it is wise to leave me out the way they have done, but let them take the responsibility, my plays will get their chance in the long run. Now I'm going out for another walk and I'll keep all sorts of nice things to say to you tomorrow.

Good luck
Your old Tramp

MS, AS. *LM*, 115

1 Molly's widowed mother lived at 37 Mary Street with her six other unmarried children.

2 Fay had replied on 22 Mar 1907,

Of course the answer will be, We have staged Riders to the Sea very frequently and when you write uncontroversial pieces you will get plenty of show . . . . There is a strong feeling in the company against The Playboy and I doubt if they will agree to take it to the other side, but I may be wrong here and they may raise no objection. One thing is certain, no crowd of professional actors would have gone thro' what the company went thro' during The Playboy week and if we go to London, there will *probably* be a storm . . . . You have doubtless thought the thing out well, but so long as you write plays like The Playboy, the other Directors will always have an excellent answer.   (TCD)

To MOLLY ALLGOOD

Glendalough [House, Glenageary]
March 25 [1907]

Dearest

This is just a 'how-do-you-do' as nothing new has happened since last night. I have written a lovely curse on the 'flighty one'[1] but I'm half-afraid to send it to you. How did you get on last night I wonder.

I was thinking about you. I am getting on all right and had quite a longish walk this morning, still my cough is damnable at times. I went over a back part of Killiney Hill or rather Ballybrack Hill this morning and had a wonderful view of the mountains, and our chimney, and the Sugar Loaves, it made my heart jump within me. I wonder when we shall get away to them again!

I thought a lot more over my play last night, and got some new ideas. I think I'll make the old woman be the mother of the man the saints killed, instead of his own mother, she might be a heathen and keep up a sort of jeering chorus through it all.[2] However I cannot decide anything yet. You'll say this is the dullest letter you ever got from me, and — for once — you'll be perfectly right. Letter-writing seems flat work after yesterday!

Your old Tramp

MS, TCD. *LM*, 116

---

[1] Molly's sister Mrs Callender, who disapproved of *The Playboy*.
[2] No scenario resembling this plot has been found; but on 13 Mar 1907 Agnes Tobin wrote from London, 'It is good news about the Miracle Play — if only Frohman could have it for America, so that you might be well represented there! ' (TCD).

To MOLLY ALLGOOD

[Glendalough House, Glenageary]
March. Twentysomething [26th 1907]

Dearest Heart

I got no letter yesterday and no letter on Saturday so I hardly think you deserve one every day. However the one I got this morning was very nice so I'll forgive you. I'm amused but not surprised to hear that you and Mrs Callender are as good friends as ever. I haven't finished her curse yet, so it'll be a rich one. I have written ⟨a⟩ another little poem about you and your troubles, that promises well. You'll have to try and do something poetical every week to keep up my stock in trade. It is — the poem — a little obscure and I dont know yet if it is any good; small affairs like it always seem pure gold when you do them first and then a week later you find they're poor stuff after all. I'm too lazy to type it so here it is

> May one sorrow every day
> Your festivity waylay,
> May seven tears in every week
> From your well of pleasure⟨s⟩ leak,

That I signed with such a dew
May for my full pittance sue
Of the Love forever curled
Round the Maypole of the world, ——

Heavy riddles lie in this
Sorrow's sauce for every kiss!

That'll want seeing to but there's a poem in it or I'm the more mistaken.[1] I wish you'd read a lot of verse I want some one who can tell me when — if ever — my verses are good. That is a thing I cannot do for myself and I've got to find out. Treasure I love you like the dew of Heaven. God be with you, come down tomorrow as usual.

                 Your old Tramp.

MS, Texas, *LM*, 117

[1] The final version was published in the Cuala edition of his poems two years later (see *Poems*, 51).

To MOLLY ALLGOOD

                Glendalough House [Glenageary]
                    Thursday [28 March 1907]

Dearest Heart

I hope you got home all right. I fancy I am a little better today, but I'm not sure it is so terribly slow. I am writing this in rather a hurry as I am going out for a walk again this afternoon, and I dont want to be too late. I am re-writing my curse[1] and making it much better, I wish I dared to make it thoroughly wicket then it would be lovely. I must write to Yeats this evening to tell him I cannot go to their meeting on Saturday. I hate this sort of cloudless east wind weather, there is so little colour or life about anything. I suppose you hardly know the world well enough yet to know the difference between an east wind and a west wind! I'll soon teach you when I have you in my care. I am sending this to Molly Street[2] I suppose you'll get it tonight. I expect a letter from you this evening. I hope it'll be a nice one and better than this.

                 Forever your old
                       Tramp

MS, Texas. *LM*, 118

[1] 'To a sister of an enemy of the author's who disapproved of "The Playboy" ' (*Poems*, 49).
[2] i.e. Mary Street.

To MOLLY ALLGOOD

Glendalough House [Glenageary]
March 29th [1907]

Dearest Love

I got your note last night and I hope you got mine. I did not think of asking you to come down today. I am sorry not to see you, but I am not feeling very flourishing and perhaps it is as well for me to be quiet today.

Dear Heart your letter last night upset me very much — I know you did not mean it to — and I did not go to sleep till nearly 3 o'clock this morning. It is a long way to Glendalough three or four hours each way,[1] and you would not get back till late at night, it is of course *impossible* that you should go off that way with those four louts. Mac would certainly be drunk coming home, and you know how Power goes on — with Mrs Callender for instance! It is a disgusting excursion on Sunday as everyone gets drunk. Surely you must have known that I would not be able to tolerate the idea of your going off that way with four men!

I am very wretched and very unwell, I may go up to the doctor tomorrow — I am not sure — in any case come to me on Sunday as usual, dearest love, and comfort me again. I wonder if I shall ever get well

Your old Tramp

MS, TCD. *LM*, 118

[1] Glendalough, the ruined monastic city in Co. Wicklow, is 32 miles from Dublin.

To MOLLY ALLGOOD

[Glendalough House, Glenageary]
March 30th [1907]

Sweetest Heart

I am just going out for my little walk so I had better send you a line, though it must be a very short one. I am not worse today, but my throat is very hoarse again. If I had been as much better as I hoped a week ago I would have got you to come down early tomorrow and take my walk with me and spend the day, but as I am not able to talk much with my throat you had better come, please, in the afternoon as usual. I cannot tell you how overjoyed I was to see you coming down the road yesterday! It was so good of you to come. I wasn't feverish last night!

Some one sent me a paper from the Abbey with a favourable notice of the Playboy. They are mounting up. It must be very dull in Dublin today it is black enough out here. This will not be good weather for Glendalough, it is probably raining out there.

> Till tomorrow
> with infinite blessings
> Your old
> Tramp

MS, TCD. *LM*, 119

To MOLLY ALLGOOD

> [Glendalough House, Glenageary]
> Afternoon [30 March 1907]

Dearest

Your letter has just come. *I* cannot decide whether you are to go or not!

If you think you promised to go, and they want you to go, and you want to go, you had better go, though you are not bound to go and you can so badly afford it. I wont be hurt.

I have just heard from Lady G. that Yeats wants to come and see me *tomorrow afternoon.* I am asking him *to come*, so I shall not be alone. I would not be surprised if she comes too. Of course if you had been coming I would have put them off.

Dear Heart you are utterly mistaken in thinking that I do not trust you. I trust your little heart and soul utterly, but I do not trust your *judgement* and your knowledge of the world, that is all and that is not your fault. If you go for God's sake take care of yourself if you go on the lakes, or into St. Kevin's bed.[1] I dont know when I shall see you now, I suppose on Wednesday. I feel a queer sad feeling that you are going to see the Wicklow lakes for the first time without me. That is selfish and foolish I suppose

> Your old Tramp.

MS, TCD. *LM*, 120

[1] A hole or excavation in the rocky face of the cliff about 30 feet above the Upper Lake at Glendalough.

To MOLLY ALLGOOD

Glendalough House [Glenageary]
March 31st [1907]

Dear Heart

Thanks for your letters. I am a little less well today and I am not going out. I feel profoundly miserable, you promised to come and comfort me today when everyone is away holiday making[1] and then! However that is foolish talk. I was very tired after F.J.F's visit last night, and I slept very badly. Now I have to face W.B.Y. today and I am quite unfit for it.

I am going to the doctor on Tuesday so do not come and see me till Wednesday I must try and go away some where I will never get well at this rate. I suppose I shall not hear from you now till Tuesday as tomorrow is a holiday. I hope you are having a good time. Oh God I wish Yeats wasn't coming today I am so utterly wretched.

Those lines of that poem I showed you in my book have stuck in my head. They seem to fit me!

"Oh have my grave in readiness
Fain would I die to end this stress."[2]

Forgive this contemptible sort of whinging. I am so lonely and miserable I cant help it, if I am to write at all.

Your old Tramp

Dont let this rubbish upset you I suppose it is because I am so ill that I am such an unreasonable ass. You are quite right to amuse yourself I dare say. Be good sweetheart.

MS, TCD. *LM*, 120

[1] On the Easter weekend.
[2] 'Of Misery' by T. Howell, first published in *The Arbour of Amity* (1568).

To MOLLY ALLGOOD

Glendalough House [Glenageary]
April 1st [1907]

Dearest Heart

Your letter last night has made me very uneasy. You must see a doctor that is all about it. You should not have gone to the Fays when you were tired, it is getting past a joke when you cannot even say 'No' to an invitation to tea. I hope you went to Swanzy today you must get your eyes *cured* this time, or you will have endless trouble. I am much better, only that I am so distressed about my poor little changeling. Send me a note by return when you get this to say how you are. If you became an invalid now what would become of us? I blame myself terribly for taking you those long walks in the summer, you should not have let me when you were not well.[1]

We had better not walk tomorrow as you have two rehearsals, so come *here* by the quarter to three as usual. Perhaps I shall meet you in the little lane beside the station and take you for a little turn if you are well, if you dont see me come on here straight away.

I do hope my dearest love you are better again. I am so unhappy about you.

Your old Tramp.

P.S. Your letter of this morning has just come. I am so glad you are better. However you had better be very quiet for a day or two. I wonder if you make too much of your pains. I dont understand the way you go up and down! However I am glad you aren't so bad as I feared. I wrote half my next Shanachie article this morning and didn't feel much the worse so my strength is coming back all right. Take care Sally doesn't tell our affairs to the company. It is better to keep quiet.   T.

MS, TCD. *LM*, 121

[1] Molly began to menstruate unusually late and suffered considerable pain with her periods.

To LADY GREGORY

Glendalough House [Glenageary]
April 1st [1907]

I will not be able to call at the Nassau tomorrow — as I hoped, — but if possible I shall do so later in the week. I will let you know.

J.M.S.

MS postcard, Berg. *TB*, 218

To LADY GREGORY

Glendalough House [Glenageary]
April [3rd][1] [1907]

Dear Lady Gregory

I will call at the Nassau on Friday morning about a quarter to twelve — if it is convenient for you and Yeats to be in then. There are a good many little things I would like to talk over before you go off for your tour,[2] and of course I am very curious to hear what Frohman thought of the shows.[3] I hope also to get to the Matinée on Saturday to see the Jackdaw and Rising of the Moon.

If Friday morning will suit you please do not trouble to write but expect me then.

Yours sincerely
J. M. Synge

P.S. I am sorry to hear of the nasty row between the Fays.[4]

MS, Berg. *TB*, 219

[1] The letter is dated 'April 2nd', but the envelope is postmarked 4 p.m. on 3 Apr 1907.

[2] Lady Gregory and her son Robert left the following week for a tour of northern Italy, where they were later joined by Yeats.

[3] No one at the Abbey was aware until afterwards of Charles Frohman's visit on Easter Monday, 1 Apr 1907, with J. M. Barrie, whose *Peter Pan* was on in Dublin.

[4] The Fays apparently quarrelled over *The Playboy* and the state of the company on the evening of Frohman's visit, just before the evening performance of Lady Gregory's *The Rising of the Moon* and a new play, *The Eyes of the Blind*, by Winifred Letts.

To MOLLY ALLGOOD

Glendalough [House, Glenageary]
April [3rd][1] [1907]

Dearest Heart

I was very glad to find your letter waiting for me when I got home. It was a nice one.

I would like to wring Boyle's neck. The last time I saw him he was all cordiality, inviting me to stay with him, and Heaven knows what, and now he turns on me and attacks me scurrilously in the papers.[2] I'll roast him yet.

The doctor says I am getting on well, and that I am not to take my temperature any more at present or bother myself whether I am a little feverish or not! He advises me to go away for a week to Lucan or Rostrevor, which I may do. I am going to see Lady Gregory on Friday morning, so if you can come down and see me *tomorrow Thursday* afternoon as usual. Let me know by morning post if you are coming. I am coughing away like the mischief today, but I do not feel worse. My cousin has given me *one* of his pictures in the Academy will you go in and see which of them you like best![3]

P.S. I forgot you are not free these evenings next week will be time enough.

Your old TRAMP

MS, TCD. *LM*, 122

¹ Misdated 2 Apr.

² Having withdrawn his three plays from the theatre repertoire during the *Playboy* row, Boyle now reiterated his stand on the occasion of Frohman's visit to Dublin, attacking JMS's play in an article for the *Catholic Herald* (London), which was reprinted in the Dublin *Evening Telegraph*.

³ Molly chose an etching by Edward Synge entitled *A Courtyard, Venice*, one of two works shown in the annual exhibition of the Royal Hibernian Academy in Dublin. This was the first time any of his works had been selected for the exhibition.

To MOLLY ALLGOOD

Glendalough House | Glenageary | Kingstown
6th April/07

Dearest

I did not get home from town yesterday till four o'clock and it came on so wet then I wasn't able to send out a letter for you. I will not go in to town today the weather is so bad. They want me to make up the number for a meeting of the old I.N.T. Society, but I'm not going to risk knocking myself up again for all the Societies in Europe. Isn't that right? I was very glad to get your letter last night and the verses which I rewrote *at once*. I will try and post this to the Theatre before 4 so that you may get it tonight. Will you come down tomorrow by the *quarter to two*, I will meet you at the station and take you to Bray, if it is fine, if not come on here. If you cannot do that will you send me a line *tonight* please. I will take *your* ticket *from Glenageary*, so please dont miss your train. We will have a lot to talk over tomorrow, as I heard a great deal yesterday. I counted up my money last night, and if all goes well I think we shall have £150 for our first year, if we get married soon, that is £3 a week.

Goodbye till tomorrow

Your old Scamp.

[*Enclosure*]

> Is it a month or a years' pain since I
> Watched with my chosen how red twilights die,
> When her soft fingers, neck, soft arms, and chin
> Made all the bars that fence God's glory in,
> And her young voice, tempered to twilight's key,

Brought back my spirit it's lost liberty,
Till the stars' vault, half-shrinking, seemed to crush
Our boundless joy, who went in lanes of slush
Kissing from ear to ear, from throat to brow,
Losing the past and present in one radiant NOW.
Till we went silent to the spattered train,
That lead us to the city, and mere life again.[1]

MSS, letter (photo) NLI; encl. TCD. *LM*, 123

[1] See *Poems*, 52 and Appendix A.

To JOSEPH HONE

Glendalough House [Glenageary]
April 6th/07

Dear Hone

Many thanks for cheque for which I enclose receipt.

Excuse delay in answering your former letter — I imagined you were away still. I am much better now, and I hope to begin the first Kerry article on Monday, so that if all goes well it will be ready for you by the 25th. As my health is still rather uncertain, however, you had better have something else to hand as you suggest so that you may be able to go on without me if I am not ready.

The terms you suggest, — three guineas up to 8 pages in 'Shanachie', and more for longer articles, will suit me all right.

Your last number was a very strong and good one I think, I hope it has sold well.

Yours sincerely
J. M. Synge

P.S. Please give enclosed to Roberts.[1]

MS, Kansas

[1] On the same day, 6 Apr 1907, George Roberts wrote to JMS (TCD), sending 100 sheets of the half-title page of the large-paper issue of *The Aran Islands* for signature, and announcing that he expected to reprint a small-paper edition of *The Playboy of the Western World* 'next week'.

To MOLLY ALLGOOD

Glendalough House [Glenageary]
8th/iv/07

Dearest

I hope you are not the worse for our walk and that you have been to Swanzy this morning. I felt a lot better last night than

I have done yet, the little trips seem to do me good. If it is fine today I may go to Bray again, but I think it looks rather doubtful.

I got an invitation from Madame Esposito this morning to dine there on Thursday evening but I will not go as I am not well enough yet I think to be out at night.

I began fiddling with my Kerry article this morning I shall easily get it done I think, but I have got uncommonly lazy I have been off work so long.

I wonder shall I hear from you today. I have written the verses again, your criticism is useful!

Your old Scamp

MS, TCD. *LM*, 124

To STEPHEN MacKENNA

Glendalough House | Glenageary | Kingstown
April 9th/07

Dear MacKenna

Forgive an unfortunate poor devil who has been ill for two months — four weeks not even downstairs — for not answering your letter long ago, and for not thanking you for your invitation which my poor bowels — they've had disentry — yearned to accept. I am much better now, but I'm to have an operation on my neck in about a month, so there is no chance of getting to Paris at present. Have you heard of the 'Playboy' Row? I am sending you a copy and a few cuttings I have not got most of the richest as I have given up getting or keeping cuttings, they are too great a nuisance. Did you hear that we had to have 57 peelers in to keep the stage from being rushed, and that for four nights not a word could be heard for booing? A number of young men however were on our side and on the whole I think — we all think — we have gained ground in Dublin but in the country and in America (where one side only can be heard,) we have come off badly. Lady Gregory and Yeats thus suffer more than I do. I wonder did you hear that Dublin and the Freeman were chiefly outraged because I used the word 'shift,' instead of 'chemise' for an article of fine linen, or perhaps named it at all. Lady G. asked our charwoman — the Theatre charwoman what she thought of it. The charwoman said she wouldn't mention the garment at all if it could be helped, but if she did she hoped she would always say 'chemise,' even if she was alone! Then she went down on the stage and met the stage carpenter. "Ah", *says she*, "isn't Mr Synge a bloody old snot to write such a play!" There's Dublin delicasy! Did you hear that ⟨?O'Donoghue⟩ wrote a ⟨?letter to the *Freeman's*

Journal)[1] to prove that I didn't know anything about the Irish peasant, which makes me convinced, MacKenna, that you can never trust a man who spits upon your carpet.

I hear you have met my friend Lebeau, I think you will like him. He is full of sympathy for Ireland and knows it intelligently — as you know a rare thing with the French. I sometimes wish I had never left my garret in the rue d'Assas — it seems funny to write the words again — the scurility, and ignorance and treachery of some of the attacks upon me have rather disgusted me with the middle class Irish Catholic. As you know I have the wildest admiration for the Irish Peasants, and for Irish men of known or unknown genius — do you bow? — but between the two there's an ungodly ruck of fat-faced, sweaty-headed, swine. They are in Dublin, and Kingstown, and alas in all the country towns ⟨, — they stink of porter on every board of Guardians.⟩ Do you ⟨   ⟩[2] Do you know that the Bs of Guardians all over the west and south have been passing resolutions condemning me and the French Government? Irish humour is dead, MacKenna, and I've got influenza.

I don't know when I'll get to Paris again, as I'm thinking of ⟨getting married⟩ [keep] ⟨this⟩ please strictly private — [*obliterated*][3] We play the Playboy in London about the 9th of June. You ought to slip over and see us having our heads broken. I hope you will be on our side, by the way, about the Playboy. How goes Madame? Please remember me very kindly to her. I never hear any music now. Write to me some day though letters are a codd. Get Lebeau to lend some articles on Wicklow that I am sending him — he wants to write on me I believe —

Yours cordially
J. M. Synge

MS (mutilated), TCD

[1] MacKenna cut out the name and heavily scored out the second passage, but the reference is probably to a letter written by D. J. O'Donoghue to the *Freeman's Journal*, 4 Feb 1907, in reply to a letter from Stephen Gwynn supporting *The Playboy* (see p. 292) and criticizing Boyle for withdrawing his plays. O'Donoghue praised Boyle's knowledge of the peasants in comparison to what he considered JMS's calumny of them.

[2] Struck out by JMS.

[3] MacKenna has here inked out an entire page, commenting 'Some highly personal criticism of harmless and obscure people.'

To MOLLY ALLGOOD

[Glendalough House, Glenageary]
Saturday | 13.IV.07

Dearest

What a day! Of course I cant go in, so Payne will have to decide about Power.[1] I am just as glad. I hope you were not tired last night, we had a good little time on Killiney Hill, hadn't we? There is no use getting up anything 'out of the way', for tomorrow the weather will be so uncertain, and everything will be so wet. Come down by the quarter to two, — you had better come second, to Glenageary — if it is fine I'll meet you with tickets to Bray and we'll go on. If I am not there come on down to the House. If it is wet come by either the quarter to two or to three which ever suits you the best. Excuse this bit of paper I've run out so that I haven't enough to go on with my article. You must get me some on Monday morning, I'll give you the money tomorrow. I've been thinking I'll have a book for my birthday present, there is one that I want badly

I had a card from Payne this morning urging me to go in today about the 'Hour Glass' but the weather is quite impossible. I've ⟨have⟩ been working at my verses all the morning, it is a waste of time but it amuses me. I must have this ready in case anyone goes to the post. Be sure to be *in* the quarter to two if it is fine.

A thousand blessings,
Your old Tramp
J. M. Synge

MS, Texas. *LM*, 125

[1] Ambrose Power was involved in the quarrel with W. G. Fay which led to his temporary resignation from the company.

To MOLLY ALLGOOD

Glendalough Ho. [Glenageary]
16/IV/07

Dearest

I expected you down today so I did not write to you yesterday. Didn't you say just before I got out of the train on Sunday that you would come down on *Tuesday*? I waited about for you half the afternoon, and met the three train but there was no sign of you. Did I mistake Tuesday for Thursday or the the other way round?

This is my birthday, where shall we be the next one? Eh? I think my mother forgets it she has not said anything about it.

I got the paper all right thanks, and I thank you in anticipation for the book. I may be going to town tomorrow but it is quite uncertain, and so is the time so I cannot arrange to see you, — besides I have too many things to do. — Come down by the quarter to *two* on *Thursday* and we'll go to the Dargle if it is a fine day! Let me know if you will come.

Yes we had a great time on Sunday. Yesterday I went to Killiney in the train and walked up through the Brides Glen a bit towards the — (our) — chimney and then back again. It was nice but lonesome.

I have only six pages more of my article to do now. I hope to finish it on Thursday morning. I am afraid you wont get this till tomorrow morning, as I say I expected you today so I did not write.

Your old Tramp.

MS, TCD. *LM*, 126

To MOLLY ALLGOOD

Glendalough Ho. [Glenageary]
April 17 [1907]

Dearest Love

Your letter came last night — it was a foolish bungle that we made about yesterday. Was your fault or mine? The book came last night, it is charming inside and out, many thanks dear Heart. So I shall meet you at the quarter to two tomorrow with tickets for Bray. If by any chance I'm not there of course you are to come on here. I am just off to town now to *shop*. It is a nuisance, but it must be done. I had a hateful dream last night about you and Dossy. You are unwise to encourage him the way you do when you know I dislike it. I haven't anything very much to say today, but to send you my love and blessings. I am getting on all right but still coughing. I'll shave now and see if a letter comes from you by the two post before I go out. — No letter so goodbye till tomorrow come here if it is wet, will you?

Your old Tramp

MS, TCD. *LM*, 127

To STEPHEN MacKENNA

[Glendalough House, Glenageary]
Wednesday morning [?17 April 1907]

Dear MacKenna

I cant let ⟨Gwynne's⟩ bloody rot[1] fester in your mind. Of course Playboy is serious. Extravanza theory is partly my fault — an interviewer — whom the devil hang by his own guts — ran up and down stairs after me for two hours on the Monday night when there was the first *riot* and I was in charge as Yeats was away. He — the interviewer got in my way — may the divil bung a cesspool with his scull — and said, "Do you really think Mr Synge, that if a man did this in Mayo girls would bring him a poulet?" The next time it was "do you think Mr Synge they'd bring him eggs?" I lost my poor temper (God forgive me, that I didn't wring his neck,) and I said, "Oh well, if you like, its improbable, its extravagant, its extravzanca (how's it spelt?) so is Don Quixote!" He hashed up what I said a great worse than I expected, but I wrote next day *politely* backing out of all that was in the interview. That's the whole myth. It isn't quite accurate to say, I think, that the thing is a generalization from a single case. *If* the idea had occured to me I could and would just as readily [have] written the thing, as it stands, without the Lynchehaun case or the Aran case.[2] The story — in its ESSENCE[3] — is probable, given the psychic state of the locality. I used the cases afterwards to controvert critics who said it was *impossible*. Amen. Go brath[4]

Yours
J. M. Synge

MS (mutilated), TCD

[1] Stephen Gwynn's letter (MacKenna struck out the name with green ink) to the editor of the *Freeman's Journal* on 2 Feb 1907, in response to William Boyle's letter the previous day withdrawing his plays, read in part,

he [JMS] has undoubtedly put his admirers into a very difficult position ... because Mr Synge has taken an unfair advantage of certain notorious facts.... the facts out of which his exaggeration springs exist unquestionable, and no good critic will take his play as a social document, a literal impeachment, of Irish country people. But practically I recognise that if the play succeeded it would be held as justifying the view which represents Ireland as peopled by a murderous race of savages. For that reason, when Mr Synge invents a community without any natural repugnance to the idea of homicide, and brings into it a young man much oppressed by fear and by conscience after killing his father, in order to show the comic effect of surroundings upon character, it seems to me our best course is to say that we know very well Mr Synge is joking, but that we do not like his turn of humour.

MacKenna's lengthy letter of April 1907 from Paris, praising the play, had lamented that not even Gwynn had 'yell[ed], even in a fury of rage, his admiration for the startling genius of the play' (TCD).

[2] James Lynchehaun, who had assaulted a woman on Achill Island, was hidden by peasant women and eventually escaped to America, where Irish patriotic organizations influenced the American courts to refuse extradition; Yeats was fond of quoting an old man of Aran who had said solemnly to him in 1896, 'If any gentleman has done a crime we'll hide him. There was a gentleman that killed his father, and I had him in my house six months till he got away to America.' ('The Bounty of Sweden', *Autobiographies* [1955], 569)

[3] Underlined four times.   [4] In Gaelic.

To MOLLY ALLGOOD

Glendalough House [Glenageary]
April 25 [1907]

My sweet Pet

How is your eye. Be sure to go Swanzie tomorrow, or I'll roar and rage.

I got a tram last night down Brunswick Street and caught my train by about a quarter of a minute, so I was here in good time for supper. The evening was beautiful when I got out of the train, colours, like what we saw on Sunday, over the trees and blackbirds singing every-where. I pitied my poor changeling shut up with a lot of — in a fusty theatre. I sometimes wish you weren't an actress! I found my new suit here when I came home — I haven't opened it yet, and some of the Aran Books from Roberts.[1] By the way if you have really ordered those pictures of Jack B Y's we must keep them,[2] dont mind my little burst of temper — I am very grateful to you for thinking of getting them for me, but I have been getting a little bit scary about your extravagance lately that is why I blew up. Dont mind it — that is dont mind it this time, but be very economical in future.

I have just finished my article and I am posting it with this. I hope it will be a success. Remember to talk about the Aran Book a lot so that people may buy it. If it fails financialy it will be a serious matter.

Your old Scamp.

I found the enclosed photo in an envelope. Do you know who it belongs to? If it is yours you cant value it much as you never missed all this time. I'm wounded etc.

MS, TCD. *LM*, 128

[1] There is some bibliographical confusion about the date of first printing of *The Aran Islands*, since a few copies bear the date 1906; these were probably advance copies sent to Elkin Mathews, since the earliest signed presentation copies are dated by JMS 28 Apr 1907.
[2] No pictures by Jack Yeats were among JMS's possessions when he died.

To MOLLY ALLGOOD

Glendalough House [Glenageary]
Saturday [27 April 1907]

Dearest

I have just got your letter. I was in town today till nearly 3 o'clock, and then I came home and worked. As you dont want to walk tomorrow you had better come down by the *quarter to four* and come here to house, and then *stay the whole evening* with me over the fire. My mother says you are to stay for supper Isn't that fun?

I am sending this to post now in a hurry.

Here is a GREAT SECRET the Playboy is to be done in Edinburgh[1] on your tour. *Not a word to anyone.*

Till four tomorrow
Your old Tramp

MS, TCD. *LM*, 129

[1] Apparently a mistake for Birmingham.

To MOLLY ALLGOOD

Glendalough Ho. [Glenageary]
May 3rd [1907]

My Dearest

I got your note at two o'clock today, and now I dont know whether I shall be able to post this tonight, or not, as the weather is so bad. I hope you are feeling better again by this time. My throat is better but my cough is rather worse than it was last week so I must be careful. I dont know what to say about tomorrow. There is no use going to the Dargle as there would be *too* many people there if it fine — there always are on Saturdays, — and I dont think you should walk far yet. On the other hand if it is very fine it would be a pity not to meet, so if the day is *realy fine* meet me at Tara St at five minutes *past two*. If the weather is not good I wont go ⟨so you need not wait if I dont come in that train.⟩ You will not have very far to go back if I am not there. If you dont feel well enough for a walk send me a wire in the morning.

I have just got a good review of the Playboy written by H. Jackson,[1] one of the men who had supper with us in Leeds — the night you were so depressed! I also got a letter from a man in Bohemia — not Musek — who wants to translate the Playboy into Bohemian.[2] So you see Christy is making his way —

I have just got a card from Payne to say that he is coming to see me tomorrow morning. IF he runs me late for my train I shall go by the next that gets to Tara St at *20* minutes to *3* so meet that *too* if fine.

Your old Tramp.

This is a dull note that's because I'm trying to think a better plan about our trains but there is none. We are both lonesome these times, but I hope it wont be for long now.   T.

MS, TCD. *LM*, 129

   [1] Holbrook Jackson (see below), whose review appeared in the *New Age* for 2 May 1907.

   [2] J. J. David (see p. 340).

To HOLBROOK JACKSON[1]

> Glendalough House | Glenageary | Kingstown | Dublin
> May 4th [1907]

Dear Mr Jackson

Many thanks for your excellent review in the New Age.[2] I hope you and Mr Orage will have good luck with your venture.[3] There ought to be a good opening, I ⟨thi⟩ should think, for such a paper.

We hope to play the "Playboy" in London in June and if I can get over then I hope I shall have the pleasure of seeing you and Mr Orage again. Please remember me to him and believe me

> Sincerely yours
> J. M. Synge

MS, AS

   [1] Holbrook Jackson (1874–1948), essayist, biographer, editor, and bibliophile; he later included a perceptive, critically balanced chapter on JMS in his book of literary studies, *All Manner of Folk* (1912), in which he recalled their first meeting after a performance of *Riders to the Sea* 'in a provincial city'. With A. R. Orage, Jackson edited the *New Age*, 'An Independent Socialist Review of Politics, Literature and Art', 1907–8.

   [2] Jackson's review in the *New Age* for 2 May 1907, under 'The Book of the Week', praised *The Playboy* for its language and psychological truth, 'force yielding to force and not a peculiarity of Western Ireland . . . . Mr Singe [*sic*] has achieved a masterpiece by simply collaborating with nature. He and the Irish are to be congratulated.'

   [3] Arthur Richard Orage (1873–1934) had just given up school-teaching in Leeds for free-lance journalism when JMS met him in 1906. After Jackson dropped out in 1908, Orage ran the *New Age* until 1922, encouraging many young writers. Author of two pioneer books on Nietzsche, he was strongly committed to guild socialism along Gurdjieff's lines, and in 1931 founded the *New English Weekly*, dedicated to social credit theory.

To MAX MEYERFELD

> Glendalough House | Glenageary | Kingstown | Dublin
> May 4th/07

Dear Dr. Meyerfeld

I must ask you to excuse me for not writing to you for so long. I got very ill after the shows of the Playboy in January, and I am only just beginning to pick up with my correspondence again. I hope you were interested in my new play. It is certainly a much stronger *stage-play* than the 'Well-of-the Saints' or any of my other work. If it was translated for the German — or any foreign stage — a few incidents such as the talk of the "bona fides" would of course have to be adapted in some way to make them comprehensible, but the main line of the story I imagine would be clear enough anywhere. We hope to play it in London in about a month — about the 11th of June — so perhaps you will be able to see it, as I think you generally come to England about that time. If I am well enough I shall go over myself also and I would be greatly pleased if I could make your acquaintance personally. My book on the Aran Islands has just come out, and I hope to have the pleasure of sending you a copy in a day or two.

With best compliments
yours sincerely
J. M. Synge

MS, NLI

To KAREL MUŠEK

Glendalough House | Glenageary | Kingstown | Dublin
May 4th/07

Dear Mr Musek.

I hope you received the copy of my new play which I sent you a few weeks ago. We had a great row over the performance here — I forget whether I sent you papers about it so I am sending you some now, — but by this time things are quite quiet again. I was very unwell during the week of the show (at the end of January) and when it was over I became extremely ill with influenza and was not able to come downstairs for more than a month. I am much better now and about as usual, but I am not well yet. That is why I have been so long without writing to you.

Do you think you are likely to translate the 'Playboy' into Bohemian? I ask you now because a gentleman has written to me from Königräz for permission to translate it, and I would much rather, of course, that you should do it, if you are at all inclined to do so. Please let me know what you think about it when quite convenient.

Was the 'Shadow of the Glen' played at your National Theatre in March, as you told me you thought it would be? My book on the Aran Islands has just been published I will send you a copy in a few days.

Yours sincerely
J. M. Synge

MS, Berg

To MOLLY ALLGOOD

[Glendalough House, Glenageary]
Saturday Night [4 May 1907]

Dearest

My old aunt[1] is still here so if it *is wet* tomorrow *do not come.* Of course if you come and for any reason I am not at the station come on here. If you are not in the quarter to *two* train I will go on to Bray and wait for you there till the next train. But I hope you wont miss your *quarter to two.*

I think we eat too many chockolats today, I felt very queer on my way home. What a tussle we had!

I had a letter from Lebeau tonight.[2] He is delighted with the Playboy. I will show you his letter tomorrow. By the way it looks as if tomorrow would be fine so I hope we shall have a good walk. Take a good rest in the morning.

These fights make me feel intollerably wretched.

Goodbye my dear old Heart

Your old
Tramp

MS, Texas. *LM*, 130

[1] Harriet Traill Dobbs, who was visiting her sister Mrs Synge from 1 to 6 May 1907.

[2] Henri Lebeau's letter of 3 May 1907 from Paris (TCD) thanking JMS for 'the beautiful Playboy, and the various articles or newspaper slips' continues, 'as you say yourself of your play, the subject is too big for a letter' and reminds him that JMS once told him there was no logic in Irish affairs.

To LADY GREGORY and W. B. YEATS

Glendalough House | Glenageary | Kingstown
May 7th [1907]

⎰ Dear Lady Gregory
⎱ Dear Yeats

I am not sure whether this will reach you, but I am sending it on the chance.[1]

Payne showed me a letter from Miss Darragh claiming to be 'starred' in Oxford and London. I do not think that it should be done, or if it is W. G. Fay, and Miss Sarah Allgood should be starred equally. We go to the cultured people of these places to show them something that is new to them — our plays and the emsemble acting of our little company. If however we placard Miss Darragh, a very ordinary if clever actress, — as the atraction, we put ourselves on a very different, and, I think, a very ridiculous footing. I am vehemently against it. I talked it over at length with Payne. He is against it definitely. He says it could do Miss Darragh no professional injury to play without being starred, although obviously, to be starred on a large scale would be an excellent advertisement for her. It would be better to double or treble the salary she is to get than to do so.

The first show of Fand was deplorable, it came out as a bastard literary pantomime, put on with many of the worst tricks of the English stage That is the end of all the Samhain principals and this new tradition that we were to lay down!! I felt inclined to walk out of the Abbey and go back no more. The second Saturday was much less offensive. Payne is doing his best obviously and consciensiously and he may come to understand our methods perhaps in time. I am getting on well but still coughing so that nothing has been settled about the operation

Yours sincerely
J. M. Synge

MS, Berg. *TB*, 220

[1] Yeats had left London on 10 Apr 1907 to join Lady Gregory and her son Robert in Venice; they returned to London on 22 May.

To KAREL MUŠEK

Glendalough House | Glenageary | Kingstown
May 9th [1907]

Dear Herr Musek

I am much obliged for your letter, and very pleased to hear that that there is a likelihood of the 'Well of Saints' being produced in Bohemian.[1]

I need not say that I am delighted to hear that you intend to translate the 'Playboy' also, and, of course, I will very gladly reserve the right of translation for you. When ever you begin to work at it I shall be glad to explain any local words etc. that you may find obscure. I am sending you my Aran Book with this, and also a magazine which may interest you as it contains an article by myself on the people of Wicklow, and an article also on the 'Playboy.'[2]

Thanking you again for your long letter and all the news it contained I remain

sincerely yours
J. M. Synge

MS, TCD

¹ Mušek does not appear to have translated *The Well of the Saints*. His letter of 7 May 1907 (TCD) thanks JMS for a copy of *The Playboy*, to which he wishes translation rights, and informs him that the Prague production of *The Shadow of the Glen* had been postponed until autumn.

² The Spring 1907 issue of *The Shanachie* (no. 3) included 'The People of the Glens' by JMS and an article by George Roberts praising *The Playboy* and JMS as 'A National Dramatist'.

To J. J. DAVID¹

Glendalough House | Glenageary | Kingstown | Dublin
May 10th/07

To Mr J. J. David.

Dear Sir

Please excuse delay in answering your kind letter of April 30th.

I am much obliged for your proposal to translate my play — The Playboy of the Western World — into Bohemian, but I have already a translator Herr Karel Musek of Prague, who has translated ⟨the Shadow of the Glen and⟩ several of my plays into Bohemian, and I have given him the authorization to translate the Playboy also, I am sorry

copy of letter to J. J. David²

Dear Sir

Please excuse delay in answering your letter of April 30th.

I am very much obliged for your proposal to translate my play, but I have already authorised a writer in ⟨Bra⟩ Prague — who has translated several of my other plays — to do it, so obviously I cannot let you have it.

I am much pleased by the interest you seem to take in our Irish work and if by any chance you should come to Ireland I should be very pleased to see you.

Yours very truly
J. M. Synge

MSS (drafts), TCD

¹ Probably Josef Julius David (b. 1871), a translator of English literature, author of a three-volume textbook and editor of an anthology of English short stories; at this time he was Professor of English at the Commercial Academy in Königgrätz and principal of a high school. Apparently he did not translate any of JMS's works.

² Second draft on the other side of the page.

To FRANK FAY

Glendalough House | Glenageary
May 12th [1907]

Dear Fay

I hope I explained the matter of Birmingham satisfactorily the other day. I am as excitable as you are so that when we take to arguing in public its the Divil!

I have just heard from Musek that the Shadow of Glen had to be put off till autumn as the Court came to Prague and they had to change all their bills and stick in a lot of Operas for the grandees. He also tells me that the Director of the Urania Theatre[1] — I suppose a theatre in Prague — is going to bring out the 'Well of the Saints' some time. Musek says he will translate the Playboy also and hopes to get it done next winter.

Let me know how things get on with you in Glasgow, I feel very lonesome here by myself.[2]

Yours sincerely
J. M. Synge

MS, NLI

[1] A private, nonsubsidized theatre in Prague.
[2] The players had left on 11 May 1907 for a five-week tour of Glasgow, Cambridge, Birmingham, Oxford, and London.

To MOLLY ALLGOOD

[Glendalough House, Glenageary]
May 12th [1907]

My own dearest Heart

I got your two little notes yesterday, and they brought tears into my gizzard! I have been going about since yesterday morning feeling as if I had one of those iron balls we saw in the convict ship tied to each of my legs and another hanging on my heart.

Last night I got into such a dead abyss of melancholly I got scared so I am trying to be cheerful — but not succeeding very well. This is a desperately wet foggy day so I shall be sitting here now for hours and hours by myself, it's horrible. I wonder how you got across, it must have been calm enough, but I fear you must have had fog, and perhaps been delayed. I was thinking about you whenever I woke in the night, and almost wishing I had an old pal, of a St Antony I could ask to take care of you. I stuck up five photos of you along the table in front of my bed so I had quite a little picture-gallery of changlings to look at this morning. Yesterday afternoon I took the first bicycle ride I have had for months — since I was ill — up through Carrickmines and Kilternan — do you remember Kilternan? — and then down through the Bride's Glen, and past the little house in Loughlinstown where we had tea and jamroll. It was a beautiful evening and I kept saying to myself whenever I heard a blackbird or a thrush or a yellow Hammer, "How Molly'd enjoy this." What would become of us if you had to go to America? And yet you were longing for it, you little scamp!

I remind myself today of Darley writing his long letters last year on tour, I rather dispised him then for writing so much but I'm wiser now, God help me. I am going to the doctor tomorrow and then I'll either have the operation, or go away to Jack Yeats,[1] I cannot stick on here doing nothing in particular for a long weary month. I wrote to Oxford yesterday to say I would *not* go there. If my neck is as bad as it is now I would not care to go and stay with strangers — I mean — I feel rather queer with this unsightly lump in my lug — and if I have the operation done now of course I would have no chance of being well enough to get to Oxford at the beginning of June.

My dear heart you dont know how much I love you. Do be good to me and come back soon as nice and natural and simple as when you went away. I will send you a bundle of books tomorrow, you have Ivanhoe to start with so I did not send them yesterday. I will write again as soon as I hear of your arrival in Glasgow. I have written to F.J.F. this morning also to patch up our fight the other day. I dont want him to be nursing his wrath against me all through the tour.

My God how shall I get through this long lonely day! I'm a fool, at my age, amn't I? Goodbye my own dearest love.

Your old Tramp.

MS, TCD. *LM*, 131

[1] Jack Yeats, whom JMS saw on his frequent visits to Ireland, had invited him to stay with him at his home near Dartmouth, South Devon.

To THOMAS B. RUDMOSE BROWN[1]

Glendalough House | Glenageary | Kingstown
May 13th/07

Dear Mr Rudmose Brown

I do not know how to excuse myself for having kept your book so long, I now return it with very many thanks. I think the writer[2] is certainly remarkable in many ways, and likely to do excellent work. It is a pity he has so many of the curious mannerisms of his school.

I suppose you have heard about our Row here over my last play? The company are on tour again now. They open tonight in Glasgow, then they go to Cambridge, Birmingham, Oxford, and London I hope to join them in London to see how the Playboy gets on there. They are not doing it in G[l]asgow or Cambridge, but it is to be done at the other towns.

I have just brought out my book on the Aran Islands. It is nearly time as I wrote the first part of it in 1898, and the whole thing was finished five years ago.

Please remember me to Mrs Rudmose Brown and believe me

very sincerely yours

J. M. Synge

MS, Langmuir

1 Thomas Brown Rudmose Brown (1878-1942), a friend of Stephen Mac-Kenna, had recently moved from Aberdeen to the University of Leeds, where he lectured in French Language and Romance Philosophy until taking up the position of Professor of French in Trinity College, Dublin, in 1909. He was especially interested in metrics, and later published a volume of poetry in addition to essays and critical editions of the works of Racine and Corneille.

2 Paul Claudel (1868-1955), French poet–dramatist and disciple of Rimbaud and Mallarmé.

To MOLLY ALLGOOD

[Glendalough House] Kingstown
Monday May 13th/07

My dearest Love

No letter today, I am greatly dissappointed! I made sure of having one today as you promised to write yesterday.

I went for a long lonely walk yesterday — (it cleared in the afternoon) up along the lane that runs beneath *our* chimney and then down to Killiney station and home by train. I enjoyed myself for a while as the day was beautiful and the birds were singing but then I got very lonely and dejected on my way home. In the evening I read Shelley's Epipsychidion — a curious love poem, and thought about you

Today I went to see Mrs Payne after dinner but found the house locked up, so I went on to the Exhibition[1] for a while. I didn't enjoy it very much as I was lonesome again, but there are good things in it. The Somali village especially is curious. A bit of the war-song the niggers were singing was exactly like some of the keens on Aran.

This evening after supper I have been for a little walk up towards Killiney hill as it is a lovely evening, but there is a cloud on me and I could not enjoy it. It is curious how your going has upset me altogether; I hope I wont be like this all the time you're away!

I heard from the Manchester Guardian this evening asking for more articles,[2] which is a good sign! I suppose now (it is nine o'clock) you are in the thick of your first evening's bill I wonder how things are going.

I wont write any more to you tonight and I hope I shall hear from you tomorrow morning. I hope you got the letter all right that I sent off yesterday.

Tuesday

Dearest Heart

Your little note came this morning and did me a world of good. *Be sure* to write to me so that I shall get a letter every day. Please go on being "awfully good", if you possibly can.

I am so glad that you had a good journey over but you must be careful not to smoke too much if your hand is shaking it is very bad for you, your heart will begin to shake next, and that, I can tell you by sad experience. is a most horrible sensation.

It is twelve o'clock now and I have been hard at work all the morning so I am too tired to write very much. I am going to the doctor this afternoon or tomorrow to settle my programme, and then we'll know what we can do. I dont see why I shouldn't leave the operation over till the autumn. I think that would be the best way and then our coast would be clear. I am counting the days till I see you again. Half a week is gone now, and four weeks will bring us together again. It is hard to be parted from you, when I have been so much alone. Take care by the way that you dont let grease paint into your eyes. If they got sore now you might loose your sight or Goodness knows what before the tour was over

Good bye my Dear love write often and fully to your old

T.

MS, TCD. *LM*, 132

[1] The International Exhibition, held at Herbert Park, Ballsbridge, from 4 May to 9 Nov 1907.

[2] 'At a Wicklow Fair' was published in the *Manchester Guardian*, 9 May 1907 (*Prose*, 225).

To MOLLY ALLGOOD

[Glendalough House, Glenageary]
Tuesday evening May 14th 1907

My dearest Love

To my great surprise and delight a second letter came from you at two o'clock (I posted a letter to you at 12 o'clock today) just as I was getting ready to go out for a bicycle ride. I went up through the Bride's Glen into the Scalp, and then I sat down and ate one of your oranges (can you read that?) and read your two letters again. My good little heart! Then I went on to Enniskerry and up past the church, and then along the upper road — you remember where we heard the thrush singing so beautifully — and down into Bray and home again through Ballybrack. The weather was perfect. All the trees in fresh green and a wonderful blue on the mountains — a summer blue that looks as if you could take it up in your arms. I was only trundling along on the roads so I could not enjoy it, as WE might have done. That is not much news to tell you; Do you care to hear where I ride to every day?

I am glad to hear that you like your 'digs'. I hope Sally wasn't *rude* to Payne, *you* ought to invite him in to tea another time to make up. It is much better to be polite 'always and ever', even if it is a little inconvenient. Told shortly in a letter the story of turning him out looked queer! Dont be offended, my old heart I'm not scolding. If I dont comment on what you tell me, and, vice versa, we wont have stuff always for our letters.

Did I tell you that I heard from Lady G? There was not much in it. I have put up three novels for you and I'll send them off tomorrow. 'Tess' is the most interesting. Have you read any of Ivanhoe? Do you like it? I hope I'll have another letter from you tomorrow morning. Then I'll finish this. It is nearly bedtime.

I sent off the books today

Wednesday (afternoon)

Dearest Love

I have just come back from town — the doctors — and found your letter waiting for me. I suppose it came at two after I had gone out.

The doctor seems to think well of me on the whole and he has given me some medicine to take for my neck. He says if it goes on well there might be no harm in leaving the operation over till *after* my summer holiday, in any case although I could hardly get it done now and be ready to face London, I would be well enough after a fortnight he thinks to go to the West. So we might have three of your five weeks. I haven't made up my mind yet about Jack Yeats! Perhaps I'll go perhaps not.

I enclose a little poem[1] to you I began last night, and part of my letter I wrote then.[2] Why dont you tell me all you do morning and afternoon, that would help you if you find it hard to fill up your letters!

I dont think my picture can be on view now, it was in a special show of Paterson's pictures which was probably only for a week or two. I heard from F.J.F. this morning he said he had been looking at a Rossetti picture in Sauchiehall street. Have you seen it? I am writing this in a hurry as I am going to post it now. I saw Roberts today and he says Aran Book is going very well. That is good. I told the doctor I was going to be married. He laughed and said "Well you're a great sportsman to go and get married before you've made your name!" He meant I would be hard up. Goodbye now sweet Heart

YOUR OLD SCAMP[3]

MSS, (14 May) Texas; (Wednesday) TCD. *LM*, 134

---

[1] Probably the following (and not the poem referred to in *LM*, 135):

> You're herewith summoned, for the longest day (ie June 21st)
> To come back, changling, while the woods are gay,
> To Wicklow, and the Dargle, and Glen Cree,
> And all the little nooks you've loved with me . . . .
> I think the furze will be half-faded then
> But I know many a far off hilly glen
> Where we may catch the summer's last full hour
> And smell again the primrose, violet and cuckoo flower . . . .
>
> And wont you love to stretch in fresh, green grass
> and watch the little clouds and showers pass
> And show your new-found wisdom of the wrens'
> And swallows' songs . . . (the rest is not written yet) —

(TS, TCD)

[2] i.e. the letter of 14 May 1907, printed above.
[3] Underlined eight times.

To FRANK FAY

[Glendalough House, Glenageary]
May 15th [1907]

Dear Fay

Thanks for your letter, and cuttings. Miss K's review[1] will be useful to the book, but from a reviewer's point of view there is far too much quotation, and what there is is not very tackfully chosen. The other article shows independence of thought, but is, of course, jouralistically amateurish — inexperienced is perhaps a kinder word. She is evidently clever.

I agreed to Riders going on first; as we are supposed always to end with a comedy there was no way to get out of it. Where there is a reason for it, I let my work take its chance. (Excuse eliptical sentence)

It is not Payne's work or fault, I think, that Baile's Strand is being done in Glasgow. Lady G. protested very strongly after last tour against, our ever going to important towns without some of Yeats' verse plays, the production of which she considers the most important part of our work. She was very strong on this point, and I agreed that we should show this side of our work whenever possible. If they told Payne to play B. Strand in Glasgow — as I imagine they did — he had no choice. I am writing this to show you that he is not over-riding us. I do not expect to get to Oxford, I think the London week will be enough for me this hot weather.

There is an interesting little picture of Millets in the permanent picture gallery in Glasgow² which is worth seeing.

Yours sincerely

J. M. Synge

MS, NLI

¹ Possibly the unsigned review of *The Aran Islands*, 'Primitive Ireland', featured on the literature page of the *Glasgow News*, Thursday, 9 May 1907 (4). 'Miss K' and the second article are unidentified.

² The Glasgow Art Gallery in 1905 received two works by Jean François Millet (1814–75), *The Sheepfold* (charcoal and pastel) and *Going to Work* (oil on canvas).

To MOLLY ALLGOOD

Glendalough House [Glenageary]

Thursday evening. 16-5-07

My dearest Love

I got your nice little letter all right today (2 o'clock) before I went out for my cycle ride. I have posted no letter to you today, as I wrote pretty late yesterday, and I think it is better to keep this and post it to you pretty early tomorrow so that you will be sure to get it on Saturday — your last day in Glasgow. I am much more cheerful now and I have got over my depression though I am lonesome of course. This was a beautiful grey day and I had a pleasant ride up through Kilternan and then up a hill (that we have not been on together) which joins the lane where we saw the little tinker camp on our first walk. The furze all down the lane was magnificently golden and the mountains very blue and beautiful behind it. I got home about five, had some tea, and then worked for a while on a Wicklow article for the Guardian first of all, and for a Wicklow book afterwards. I have written in all about 1300 words today, that is, typing out stuff from my notes taken on the spot. That is a good day's work isn't [it]? Do you know what? I've an idea! Go out when you get this and buy a good thick square note-book with a strong cover and begin to keep a journal of your tour writing down everything as it comes helter-skelter, especially the small things. Say what sort of landlady you have and what she says to you, if it is funny, what you have for dinner, what your dressing rooms are like and your journeys etc. Will you do it? At the least you will find it intensely interesting and amusing reading ten years hence – and later (if not now) when you are touring in Ireland, and you have caught the knack, you will write stuff about places like the Wexford Theatre that, *with my help*, you will be able to sell. Wouldn't that be fun! The public are very ignorant about the inner side of the smaller theatrical life, and very curious about it, so such articles would be sure to go, if you put enough little details in them to make the thing individual. I mean thousands of people travel from Glasgow to Cambridge (we know all about that), but no one knows what you are having for dinner tomorrow, so to start with you have an unknown fact, and unknown facts are interesting. ──

You will say this is a dull letter, will you? This is my fourth to Glasgow so I dont think I have done badly. You have been very good. I will not write again now till I hear of your arrival in Cambridge and get your address. Be sure to send it. Then Monday is a holiday so there may be a delay. My dear Heart dont forget to be very dignified and good on your long Sunday journey! You dont mind my reminding you, do you? You know what a little madcap you are!

Friday 12.30 P.M. I have been working all the morning at a ballad for two voices for you and F J [Fay] to recite if it comes off. I got your photo this morning in S. the News,[1] many thanks. I am so glad to have it to add to my *changling gallery*. I showed it to my mother she was greatly amused by it.

You dont tell me enough what you do all day and every day. Do you go out much? Who do you go with? What do you do? You know everything that I have done since you went and I only know that you were out once before breakfast – a very Wonderful thing! – and that you went once to a gallery. I am not asking, of course, because I am uneasy but simply because I want to be able to follow my little changling along and know what she is doing. I wont post this till I see if I am to have a letter by the 2 o'clock post. I am sending you an unfinished copy of the verses I quoted to you on our wet walk[2] please be very careful not to lose them. Did you like the other.

Friday
2 o'clock

Dearest

Your letter has come and it is a very nice one. Yes you are telling me every thing this time. Are the whole company in your house or how do they know what you have for dinner? I am glad to hear that the houses are not so bad.

Let me know your address in Cambridge as soon as you can, and I'll write to you my poor pet. I am glad you seem lonesome, so am I. This will be a *fat* letter.

Your old
TRAMP[3]

P.S. I hope YOU wont take to card playing. *Please dont*!

[*Enclosure*]

Irish Stage-Land
by Miss Maire O'Neill

(or — by J. M. Synge   (N.B. if we write this we can
and Another)   get it into Manchester Guardian)
Journey to a southern town (Wexford but you dont name it) the gathering in Harcourt Street, the excitement of starting, the clear winter's morning, as you pass down through Carrickmines, Bray and Greystones. The bewildered old woman who sells us apples in Wicklow. Then the company gets tired looking out of the window and they sing songs —

(give Molly McGuirk \ and any other
You gay old Turk / quaint ones

You pass on and arrive in Wexford. Dinner. Visit to little theatre describe Wexford Theatre, entry etc. Rest and hurried tea before the theatre. Describe dressing room, the feeling of the audience, the striking matches in the gallery, describe how you come out go up the shaky stairs into the balcony and what you see there. The turmoil of packing after the show.

Then take some other tour and run all the other interesting experiences you have had engine driver etc into it. In this you can end by the late supper in Dundalk the long wait for the train at three o'clock, the dancing in the dim light, the going out into the grey dawn the sun rises as you get into the deserted station; you walk up and down; then train comes; you have glimpses of magnificent bright morning; you go to sleep and wake in Dublin.[4]

MSS, TCD. *LM*, 136

[1] Picture postcards with scenes from various plays in the repertoire were used for advertising future shows.

[2] Probably the following poem preserved by Molly, and reproduced in Coxhead, *Daughters of Erin*, 186–7:

> With one long kiss
> Were you near by,
> You'd break the dismal cloud that is
> On all my sky.
>
> With one long kiss
> If you were near
> You'd sweeten days I take amiss
> When lonely here.
>
> With one long kiss
> You'd make for me
> A golden paradise of this
> Day's beggary.

[3] Underlined five times.

[4] Although Molly did not make use of this scenario, JMS included it in a list of articles intended for his Wicklow book (TCD).

To MOLLY ALLGOOD

Glendalough House.Kingstown.Dublin
Wednesday morning | May 22nd/07

Dearest

I got your long and interesting letter last night (Tuesday night) and was very glad to hear that you were safe in Cambridge. What a journey you had. I meant to warn you before you started not to go out from your lodgings without making sure you knew the name and address — as you did in Newcastle dont you remember? — and now you have done it again! I suppose experience will teach you. There is nothing new here. It is very cold and I am rather worse in consequence. I rode too far on my cycle before I was used to it, and hurt my leg so I stayed at home all day on Sunday, and to make things worse my eyes have got sore — nearly as bad as yours so I was not very gay. On Monday I went — walked — to Killiney and back by train. Then yesterday I went to Bray by the quarter-to-two — it seemed strange not to find you in the train waiting for me — and walked up the road we went on our last walk, then down to the lower road and up the hill into the lane where the old cross is and so back to Bray for the five train. It was cold and wretched and I did not enjoy it at all.

You have not told me yet who was sharing your digs in Glasgow? You say in your last (from there) that you sat up talking after Sally went to bed, but you do not say with whom so I am puzzled. You told me before you went that the men were not going with you. *Please explain fully*. This kind of mystery troubles me, *more than I can say*.

I had two friendly letters from Miss Horniman yesterday. A great deal depends — as to future tours — on the impression she gets of the acting and what she calls the *'discipline'* of the company — *this is strictly between ourselves* — the acting in our peasant plays is all right, I hope the discipline, the orderliness, of the company is the same. How are W.G. and Mrs F[ay] behaving themselves this tour? You had best be steadily polite — I dont mean effusive — to Miss Horniman if you come in contact with her. It is the only way to keep oneself right. One gets into the way of wearing a sort of masque after a while, which is a rather needful trick.

It will be a fortnight in two days since we saw the last of each other. It seems — to me at least — unconscionably long. This is the dullest letter I have sent you yet, but I am heavy and unwell so you must not mind. Remember to take care of yourself at the end of this week.

I am writing to Jack Yeats today to see if he can have me for a week or so before I go to London. I want a change badly. I forgot to tell you of my doings on Saturday. My leg was a little sore before dinner so I thought I would take great care of myself I dodged up on my bicycle just above Shankill — a place between Bray and Loughlinstown — then I sat in a sunny ditch and read for an hour in the East wind — it was then I got cold in my eyes — and at last set off home. My leg was very stiff so I was going very slowly when pop my back tyre blew up with a bang. I had only 35 minutes then to get to Killiney station to catch the 4 train so I rushed along in spite of my leg packing my bicycle and just got in, in time. That is why I was laid up on Sunday. My leg is all right again now.

I must write to Jack Y. now so goodbye my poor little changling be good and write often — I expected a letter this morning but didn't get one —

Your old Tramp

P.S. How much money did *you* clear out of your Glasgow salary?

MS, TCD. *LM*, 139

To MAX MEYERFELD

> Glendalough House | Kingstown. Dublin
> May 22nd 1907

Dear Dr. Meyerfeld

It is practically settled now that I shall be in London about June 10th and week following so I hope I shall see you then. If you will kindly let me know your London address as soon as you arrive there I will send you my Aran Book. There is no use sending it to Berlin as you may have started.

> Yours   J. M. Synge

MS postcard, NLI

To MOLLY ALLGOOD

> [Glendalough House, Glenageary]
> Wednesday night [22 May 1907]

Dearest Heart

You DIDN'T give me your address in your Glasgow letter so I couldn't have written any sooner. *I* was very dissapointed at not hearing of you till Tuesday night. This is a mere line to make up for all the long time you have been without a letter. *I told you long ago* that I had been to the Exposition and how I liked it. I'm afraid you dont pay much attention to my letters!!! Be very civil to Miss Gildea[1] if you come across her it is the best way of showing you dont care a *"wag"* about her or her talk. Nothing has happened today I wrote to you this morning and then dodged about. I have got fresh cold or something and I dont feel well. Be sure to tell me *in time* what day you leave Cambridge and to give your address in advance this time. If you would post earlier if possible and convenient I ought to get your letter in the morning instead of evening, it seems slow

> Your old Tramper

You'll have got no letter today either so you wont know what's happened. It is your own little fault however as you didn't *give me an address*

MS, TCD. *LM*, 140

[1] Ida Gildea (later Mrs Hargreaves Heap), a close friend of Miss Horniman, had volunteered to help the company on tour by selling copies of the plays.

To MOLLY ALLGOOD

[Glendalough House, Glenageary]
Wednesday evening (late) | 22.5.07

Dearest Heart

This is no less than *my third* letter to you today. What do you say to me now?

It is a wonderfully still beautiful evening and I feel as if I ought to write verses but I haven't the energy. There is nearly a half moon, and I have been picturing in my mind how all our nooks and glens and rivers would look, if we were out among them as we should be! Do you ever think of them? Ever think of them I mean not as places that you've been to, but as places that are there still, with the little moon shining, and the rivers running, and the thrushes singing, while you and I, God help us, are far away from them. I used to sit over my sparks of fire long ago in Paris picturing glen after glen in my mind, and river after river — there are rivers like the Annamoe that I fished in till I knew every stone and eddy — and then one goes on to see a time when the rivers will be there and the thrushes, and we'll be dead surely. It makes one grudge every evening one spends dully in a town, what wouldn't I give to be out with you now in this rich twilight coming down from Rockbrook or Enniskerry with strange smells and sounds, and the first stars, and the wonderful air of Wicklow? Is there anything in the world to equal the joy of it? And you, my poor changling, have to go to Birmingham next week, and I, poor divil, amn't well enough to go out to far-away places for even solitary walks. Write a nice *intimate* letter the next time and tell me how your little mind is feeling in its wandering.

I wrote to Jack Yeats today to ask if I might go there. I wonder shall I like it, if I go. I'll leave this now to see if there is anything new in the morning.

Thursday morning

Nothing new except an American Magazine with an account of the Irish writers — poor stuff enough. I am to go to the dentist today and see what he can do for me before I go away.

Write me a nice letter

Your old
Tramp

MS, TCD. *LM*, 141

To MOLLY ALLGOOD

Glendalough House | Kingstown
23rd/5/07 | Thursday night

My dearest Pet

I have just got your poor little Wednesday note. I tired of you indeed!! What a thing to say. Now I'm going to lecture you. If you'd brought a sheet of paper with you in the train and written three lines to say you were safe in Cambridge and to give me your address, and posted them when you arrived there, I would have got it on Monday and you'd have had an answer on *Tuesday*. If you couldn't do that you might have asked someone on Monday what time you had to post to catch the *Irish* Mail and posted your letter in time for it. Then I would have got it on Tuesday morning and you'd have had an answer on Wednesday! But you went and missed the Monday mail so I didn't hear till Tuesday night, and I wasn't able to write to you till Wednesday. Will you be wiser next time? I hardly know now whether to post this to you tomorrow (Friday) or not as I do not know what time you leave Cambridge, on Saturday, or whether it is not till Sunday that you go, and I'm quite sure you do not leave your next address in your digs in case anything comes after you are gone! That would be a bit of Wisdom far beyond you. Well that's lecture enough.

I was at the dentist's today and got my teeth settled up for the time being. They are not so bad as I feared. This is a most gloomy, dismal and dark evening — more like October than the end of May — and I feel wretched enough. I'd like to be away on some warm sunny hill — like the purple grapes hill — and to be warm, and well, and sun-burnt, and dressed in summer clothes, and to have you with me dressed in nice light summer clothes too, and a big hat so that we might be as happy as the day was long, instead of being boxed up here in this accursed place. Well I hope good times are coming.

Friday morning

Dearest

Your letter came this morning, and I was glad to get it. I thought when I began to read it that you had not got my letter but then I found you had.

I am more pained than I can possibly tell you about your Glasgow 'digs', not the fact of your lodging together — though that is not desirable from many points of view — but that you should have deceived me, after all your promises. I find it hard to believe that you did not know all the last week in Dublin that you were going to lodge with the men. In fact you told me in the Park that you were going to do so, and then when I did not like it you said it was only a joke. Besides you promised to tell me everything, and then to keep me in the dark on this important point all that week —— I cannot write about it, it is too painful. Cannot you see that you have cut away the very foundation of our happiness. Now when you are in America or God knows where I will never know whether you are not deceiving me or not in some matter that I have a right to know. ⟨Great Christ⟩ the thought of your writing so kindly last week when you were deceiving me all the time makes me sick with anguish. You said ⟨what is the use of talking to you. What is⟩ I am not scolding you, my poor pet, I do not think you understood what you were doing. Now even when you read this you will not understand why I feel ten years older than I did last week, and ⟨that⟩ why my whole life seems frozen up inside me, [*deletion*] Oh Why, why, why, do you torture me?

You know that I tell lies like anyone in small trivial matters to outside people, but you know, I think, that I would not deceive you on any matter. I lay awake nearly all night on Sunday brooding over this, then I thought it could not be true, my poor little changling, I am sure you did not mean to distress me the way you have done. I shall see you I suppose in a fortnight, the thought is not a joy to me now. I read some of your letters the other day that you wrote to me last summer. It is extraordinary how you have 'come on' in the whole turn and ease of letter-writing, I say to myself that perhaps you will learn to be open and be true with me also, when you get more used to my way of ⟨life and⟩ looking at things. I wrote a poem on you last night but I have not the heart to send it to you. Perhaps you will smile when I tell you that there are tears on the back of my eyes. I had begun to trust you so completly and ——

I see you are spending all your money, but I thought you were looking forward to our getting married in July? How do you spend it? It is impossible to tell you how utterly broken and dejected I am feeling today

                                  Your old Tramp.
Write to me soon and write lovingly if you want to cheer me. It is only because I *love you so deeply* that I feel all this so much.

MSS, (Thursday night) TCD; (Friday morning) AS. *LM*, 142

To ANNIE E. F. HORNIMAN[1]

Glendalough House | Kingstown
May 24th [1907]

Dear Miss Horniman

Many thanks for your long letter, I am glad things are going well. I have not yet settled anything about my visit to Jack Yeats, if I go I sháll let you know so that you can wire for me if I am wanted for anything.

During the weeks you speak of — as to 'fit up'[2] — I was — as I told you entirely taken up with the 'Playboy' and was seldom in Dublin. I thought Mr Robert Gregory had settled about the 'fit up' — if I remember rightly. *Certainly* I never understood that I was supposed to over-see its' construction, during the time that I stayed here to have my time free to work at my play. As you know it has never been a part of my work, in connection with the Abbey, to

MS fragment (draft), TCD

[1] Miss Horniman (see p. 89), was becoming increasingly disillusioned by the 'unbusinesslike' manner in which the directors, and, in her eyes, JMS especially, were managing the theatre she had helped to establish, and she made various attempts to pressure the directors into running the company as she felt it should be.

[2] On 16 May 1907 (TCD) Miss Horniman queried the rental of scenery for Cambridge when she had paid £50 for travelling scenery to be built for touring, during the previous June.

To MOLLY ALLGOOD

Stoneview Kingstown 25 May 1907 10.05 A.M.
Miss M Allgood c/o Petit 34 City Rd Cambridge
All right dont worry good luck for journey send next address

Synge

Telegram, TCD. *LM*, 144

To MOLLY ALLGOOD

Glendalough House | Kingstown
Sunday | May 26th/07

My own darling Changling

I got your little note this morning, and the sad ending you wrote to it disstresses me. I did not mean to hurt you, but I could not write anything else if I wrote to you at all. I sent my telegram to cheer you up when I got your letter yesterday morning. I thought you would get it just after my letter and that it would brighten you up. You mustn't worry yourself my poor little pet, I know you did not mean to do anything, but that sort of thing has a dreadful effect on me. Love so strong as ours is, is a dangerous comodity and I think it will kill us if we do not get married soon. I am very unwell. All the anxiety and distress during this last week has had a very bad effect on me, I am afraid. I have not been able to walk or go about much so I have just been sitting here brooding all day, and I have had some terrible fits of depression. Write me a nice loving letter when you get this, that is the only thing that is the only thing that does me any good now. I meant this to be a bright cheerful letter to make you happy again, but I fear you will not think it so.

I have heard nothing of Jack Yeats so I think that visit is 'off'. I shall go to London (DONT SPEAK OF THIS) probably about Tuesday week, — I am not well enough for Oxford — and stay there till you come back, I do not know what day you will come. There are only three nights in Oxford so I suppose you will come back on Thursday. So — if I am well enough to go over at all — we shall meet now in about ten days. That is one comfort at any rate. It is of course an *immense joy to me* to think of seeing you again. I wish you weren't on the stage, the continual separations it will entail are not good for either of us. I was dreaming about you last night, but nothing very tangible that I can remember.

I wonder shall we be able to get married in the early summer. You, apparently, are throwing away your money as if you did not wish it anymore. What did you save in Cambridge? But I must not begin to scold you again. I feel very broken down, and I have a pain in my knee so I wont be able to have a walk today either.

I do not think the story you heard about 'Playboy' in Birmingham was quite true. It was withdrawn for *political* reasons I believe. I am not satisfied with the way things are going in the company, (— Miss H. is 'at' me again, so far in a friendly way, about some 'fit-up' that was to have been made last summer, and that I know nothing of —) and I wrote to Yeats yesterday proposing to resign my directorship.[1] It does not do me or any one else anyone else any good, that I can see, and it is an endless worry to me. I will not do anything in a hurry, however, and please dont speak of this to *anyone*. I do not think things can go on much longer as they are, and I think I would have a freer hand to ask for what ⟨terms⟩ arrangements I want made for the working of the company if I was *outside it*. I will not desert W.G.F. if he wants me to stay on, so I must consult him.

My poor pet I love you more than I know myself my life I think is in your hands, as I told you before. How I wish you were coming to ·

see me this afternoon. I feel so down. I suppose you are travelling to Birmingham today. I wonder how you will do there. Are you all lodging together again?

I went to see Frou-Frou played by Jane Hading[2] at the Royal on Friday. I went to the gallery and sat with Conally, Starkie, Steward,[3] and Holloway. It was not very gay, I disliked the play very much and I didn't greatly care for J. Hading. I think the fashionable 'passionate' actress is a fraud. There is nothing inherently interesting or artistic in these violent scenes. I caught myself in the middle of a dismal yawn while the poor lady was flinging chairs about the stage. I found the French a little hard to follow for the first five minutes, then I got on all right.

Now be good and dont worry and we'll meet in ten days and be very happy again. Write me nice letters and write very often. I am sending you my last verses[4] they are not good but they are sincere now I hope you feel all right my sweet love. When you come home you must go to some doctor here and get yourself seen to. You cannot be well. With a million blessings

Your old Tramp

MS, Texas. *LM*, 144

1 JMS's letter is not extant. Yeats replied on 27 May 1907 confirming that the decision to withdraw *The Playboy* from the Birmingham bill was out of fear that a row there would cause the censor to withdraw his licence; he concluded with, 'While we are fighting your battles is hardly the moment to talk of resignation' (TCD; see *TB*, 222).

2 Jeanette Hadingue (1859–1933), a French actress with a popular following in Great Britain; *Frou-Frou*, by André Meilhac, was also a favourite vehicle for Sarah Bernhardt.

3 Probably Seamus O'Connolly, James Starkey, and perhaps C. T. Stewart (see p. 220).

4 Not preserved with the letter.

To MOLLY ALLGOOD

Glendalough House [Glenageary]
Monday May 27th/07

My own dearest Love

I got your letter this [morning], and it upset me so much, that I sat on my chair trembling all over, and I could hardly eat my breakfast. I have wired to you now to know how you are. It is a miserable business. You seem to have thought it a slight matter to tell me a lie, I, as I have often told you, and as you must see now feel it very differently. We will get to understand each other better by degrees

I hope and believe so I think we need not be depressed. I dont think any good will come of discussing this affair any more in our letters. Let us drop it, and try and build up our old confidence again. When I said it would be no joy to see you in London I meant merely that I was so unspeakably hurt by the way you had treated me that for the moment I had lost the *joy* of our love, not, (I need not say), the love itself. Further, what I meant about cutting away the foundations of our happiness was, of course, that without perfect, absolute confidence and openess ⟨that is the only thing⟩ all sorts of misunderstandings and doubts were sure to arise, and that you had made this confidence difficult. However do not let us discuss it unless you wish to. Oh my poor love if you know how I have suffered and am suffering still. Do not talk as if you thought we should separate. How could we do it? Dont you remember those evenings when we came down from our walks so perfectly happy in each other? Isn't it some peace to you to think that we shall have that again in three or four weeks now. Dont you look forward to lying up in the heather again and eating purple grapes? My poor sweet little heart I am sorry I have hurt you, but I have been hurt as badly or *worse* myself so you must not blame me. I am sure that when we are together we will understand each other better, and not have these fearful troubles. It seems so simple for you to tell me straight out all that [you] are are going to do, and to let us talk it over together, then we would never have any trouble, but you will not do it.

Remember I am very nervous, very highly-strung, as they call it, — if I was not I couldn't be a writer — and the only way to keep things clear is to tell me everything at the beginning, not to keep me in miserable doubt for days till I find out what has happened. My dear love we have to learn by pain and trouble how to live our life together. We both have the deep true love, I am quite sure, that will bring everything all right in the end. Do be good to me, my sweet little pet, and tell me *everything* as you have promised so often. I heard from Jack Yeats at last this morning. He wants me to go over at the end of this week, for a week before I go to London. I dont know whether I shall be well enough now. I am going to the doctor today. There would be no use going to Yeats if I couldn't walk about with him, and see the country. I do not know yet how I shall go it is a very troublesome journey. If I go by long sea[1] I shall leave Dublin on Wednesday and not get to his place till Friday, but I dont think I shall go that way. *Go on* writing here till I send you the new address I will write to you very often of course. My knee feels very bad today I doubt that I shall be able to go at all. Perhaps I wont be able to go to London even. That would be too bad. Now promise me, my little life, that you wont worry and make yourself ill. The thought of it makes me ill too. I wonder the answer doesn't come to my wire. I hope I have read your address right it was rather hard to read what you wrote. I wrote you a long letter yesterday. It wasn't a very cheerful one I am afraid still it was better than the last. I wish I could put my two arms round you and give you a good long squeese, and then I know we would both be all right again. Wouldn't we? Write to me cheerfully. Your old

Tramp

MS, AS. *LM*, 146

[1] The Dublin–Liverpool route is almost double the sailing time of the Rosslare–Fishguard route.

To MOLLY ALLGOOD

Glendalough House [Glenageary]
May 28th/07

My dearest Love

Your letter has come this morning and it has rolled the stone off my grave at last. Your letter yesterday moved me in the morning, because you seemed so ill, but when I read it again (after I had written to you) I felt that it was very strange and unreasonable, and I got angry again. However I'll burn it today as you suggest. I was going to write you a very nice letter this morning, but I have just been answering a rather nasty letter from Yeats so I am not in a good humour for the moment.

I am as over-strung as y¬u are, and when I got the wire yesterday tears of relief came into my eyes. It made me laugh this morning when I heard Sally had sent it. Dont tell her. I went to the doctor again yesterday he says I am to go away at once. He was astonished at the muscles of my legs, he said I must be as strong as a horse! So take care not to make me kick you!! After the doctor I went to Old Yeats and he drew me again. We began to talk about Maire Walker and then Sally whom he now admires very much. Then he went on to Sally's *sister* "Oh" he said "isn't she wonderful! I declare I think she is better than Sarah, though I always feel jealeous when I see a younger sister beating an older one."!

I am going to Jack Yeats after all, I think, I shall leave here on Thursday evening and get there some time on Friday. So you may write here once more after you get this, and then I will send you his address so that you may write there. I shall stay with him for about a week and then go to London. If you get 'dig' address near Russell's Square or Russell's Street try and take them because I shall be somewhere about there. Be sure you get a 'decent' address as thousands of bad characters live in that neighbourhood. The man who translated the 'Well of Saints' into German is to be there and I shall have to see a good deal of him but I will have some time to spare I suppose.

I feel indescribably sick of the continual worries of this company, worries with F.J.F. Miss Horniman, Lady G. Yeats, you never know where it will break out next.

Of course if you gave W.G. £1 that accounts for your Glasgow salary. I was sure you would not find it so easy to pay off that great debt as you thought. It is a pity. I am afraid this tour round by Jack Yeats will cost a good deal but I must get a change or I dont know what mayn't happen to me.

Did I tell you that Florence Ross has come to stay here for a few days? She has been painting a lot and is getting on well.

I dont seem to have much to say this morning so good bye my dear love, it wont be long now till we meet again. You will like Oxford I think, it is a beautiful place.

Your old
Tramp

MS, TCD. *LM*, 148

To ISABELLA SYNGE[1]

Glendalough House | Kingstown
May 29th. 07

Dear Isabel

Many thanks for the paper — it is curious indeed to see how the news of the Playboy has traveled — and for your letter. I have been intending for years to call at Vanburgh Park Road to make, or re-make, all your acquaintances but my visits to London are so short and so filled up that I have never managed to do it. I shall certainly go, however, before long. I was glad to see Percy at Bertha's in the winter when I was over I had not seen him for years.

I hope you will be interested in my book on the Aran Islands. As you will see in it Uncle Alexander is very well remembered there. I think — I hope — you are wrong in saying that the Island people attacked him, I have always heard both from the islanders, and Aunt Jane, long ago, that it was the Claddagh fishermen in Galway who did so. They thought his trawl was destroying the spawn of the fish, and it seems they were not altogether mistaken as trawling is not allowed now within three miles of the shore. The old people on Aran who remember Uncle Alec so well are of course dying off, but I heard a great deal about him when I went there first, and I was shown fruit trees in the parsons garden that he had I think brought from Glanmore. They say he was extraordinarily powerful and could pull in the yard of his boat single-handed — a job that usually took two men. He made an sort of avenue also down to the parson's house and carted away the earth himself in a sort of wheel barrow that he used to yoke himself into with a leather strap.

Excuse this hurried line I am off to Devonshire (to stay with Jack Yeats) in six hours

Your affec cousin
J. M. Synge

MS, Farrington

¹ Isabella Hamilton Synge, daughter of the Revd Alexander Hamilton Synge (see p. 67); her father's brother, Percy Hamilton Synge, and sister Jane (for whom JMS wrote his first poem), had frequently stayed with Mrs Synge during JMS's childhood.

To MOLLY ALLGOOD

[Glendalough House, Glenageary]
Wednesday night [29 May 1907]

Dearest

I got your letter this evening at six o'clock. I hope you will post today's letter in better time or I *wont get* it before I start tomorrow. As I got no letter this morning I did not write to you, so — I have just remembered — you will have no address to write to me tomorrow (Thursday). I hope you are taking care of yourself.

I have been in town and packing, and generally putting up my books and things for the summer, today, so I am too tired to write much. I was at the Abbey today getting some things. It looked very deserted and queer. My knee is better. I am going over by the new route Rosslare and Fishguard so I shall start off through Bray

MS fragment, Texas. *LM*, 150

To MOLLY ALLGOOD

Glendalough House [Glenageary]
Thursday [30 May 1907]

Dearest

I have just got your letter I am writing this in a great hurry as I have a good deal of packing etc. to do and I am off at three o'clock.

I sail tonight from Rosslare just outside Wexford so I shall go down the whole line where we went, on our first tour together and under the old castle that we sat under so confidentially. It will seem strange. I wish you had sent me a nicer letter to read and think over on my long lonely journey; I do not reach Jack Y. till 1.15 tomorrow afternoon. When you said that I should write to you every day to keep you 'good' I got a "qualm of dread"! You little —— do you find it so hard as that to keep yourself 'good'? N.B. I'm writing this with a grin, so dont be offended.

I'm sorry to hear of bad business and rows in Birm. I knew the place would be a failure. If I resigned my directorship, I would stay on in the company and leave my plays just the same. It would make little difference except that I would be rid of all the endless worry with Miss Horniman F.J.F. and and the rest of them. However it is not likely that I shall do it at present. When I said that things could not go on much longer as they are, I meant that with the two managers, F.J.F., W.B.Y. and myself and Miss Horniman, there are so many possible points for friction that one never knows when a bad row may break out. What part did the paper attack you for? You said you had been attacked. I am not surprised that Baile's Strand failed in Birm. We knew it would.

My address will be for the next week·

      c/o Jack B. Yeats Esq
      Cashlauna Shelmiddy
      Strete
      Near Dartmouth
      South Devon

Give me your Oxford address as *soon as you can* and write it *very distinctly*. I could hardly read this last one you gave me. I shall try and write you a line on the journey and post it somewhere on Friday. Then I shall not be able to write again till I get the Oxford address as a letter from Devon on Saturday would probably miss you in Birm. Try and see as many of the Colleges etc as you can in Oxford it is a wonderful place. Dont be alarmed or worried if you are some time without hearing from me. I shall do my best to write often but away there on a visit in such an outofthe way place, it is not always easy to manage. Now Goodbye my poor changling I have not given up the idea of being married in the summer. But we shall have to see how our money stands. I have not got my Doctor's bill yet. Good bye tomorrow anyhow we shall be in the same country.

           Your old T.

MS, TCD. *LM*, 150

To MOLLY ALLGOOD

[30 May 1907]

Dearest

I've started, out through our little tunnel past Kiliney Strand past our *little lighthouse* then into Bray and on round the Head where we found the *puppy dog*! How it is all mixed up with you now. I am below Wicklow and the rain has stopped. The country is beautifully green under the clouds. I can hardly write the train is shaking so much. I wonder what I'll do with myself the three hours in Wexford before I sail. I feel lonesome and sad, here all by myself. The half lifted cloud is very beautiful and I'm seeing great sights all the same.

Arklow. My spirits are going *UP*. The country is wonderful, masses of bluebells, and wet green trees and ferns everywhere. It's wonderful after the long imprisonment I've had. I wonder could *we* come home by

WHITE'S HOTEL | WEXFORD.
Thursday night

(*continuation*)

I am in Wexford now as you see trying to pass my evening I have two hours more to get through. I wish I could write to you for two hours I dont know what else I am to do. I have just had tea and plaice at the end of a big table, and there are three men at a table near discussing the world. I thought at first they were commercials but they seem to have too much information and knowledge for that noble calling. One of them has just told a ⟨fearful⟩ fearsome tale on the effects of hypnotism — or mesmerism as you call it — I'll tell it to you by and by when we meet. Now they are on the Rebellion and they seem to know a lot about it.

It seems funny to me to be on the road again I have been so long shut up. Certainly there is nothing like travelling. I feel better already. It is one of the wettest nights I have ever come across, it is coming down in bucket-fulls so I cant walk about any where. This is like writing when you are hypnotised because I'm scribbling away as hard as I can and all the time I'm listening to the talk at the table behind me. I dont know how much this trip will cost, I like this route it has something out of the common. Did I tell you I am not to get to Jack Yeats' till a quarter past one tomorrow. Isn't that a good trot? By the way I had a funy incident today. You know my old breeches are in bits. 'Well' — as you say — I bought a new pair ready made yesterday to wear on my journey with my old coat and waistcoat I ⟨have⟩ hadn't time to try them on till ⟨I was just⟩ an hour before I was to start. I put them on then and found them — I thought — mighty elegant. Then I sat down plump, to put on my shoes, and I heard a rend. The seam in the gable end had split right down and there I was! Fancy if I that had happened when I was getting into the train after I had started. I dragged them off and got the cook to sew them up as best she could. Now I [am] walking about in great trepidation for fear they'll go again! — I have had a long talk with the waiter, he says they dont half know the bay yet on this line and they have run aground two or three times. I hope we wont be wrecked. If you get this you'll know I'm safe as it's going over with me!

MSS, (30 May) TCD; (Thursday night) Texas. *LM*, 151

To MOLLY ALLGOOD

c/o Jack Yeats etc [Strete, Devon]
Monday morning 6.A.M. [3 June 1907]

Dearest

I hope you got my letter all right that I sent from Cardiff — did you see the postmark? — I got two of yours on Saturday one from Birmingham in the morning and the other in the evening sent on from Kingstown. You do not give me your Oxford address so I must send this to the Theatre. I dont feel very sure that it will find you, — or you it, so I wont put in any thing confidential. Let me know as soon as you can what day you go on to London so that I may write to you there, in case I am not able to write again in time to catch you in Oxford. The post is difficult here, it only goes out once or twice in the day and we are a long way from the village. Besides on a visit like this it is not easy to find time to write. I shall go up to London on Saturday most likely. I dont know where I shall stay.

This is a charming place, my room looks out across a little creen vally, with a little water mill at the bottom, and the birds sing so loud they seem to waken me at 4 o'clock every morning. I went for a long walk along by the sea with J.B.Y. on Saturday, so that we were out all day from 11. till 7. Yesterday we puttered about, and today we are going for another long expedition after Breakfast. He is a charming fellow. I dont feel much better for the change yet, my cough is bad still, and I'm not sleeping well, or in good spirits. J.B.Y. and his wife seem a very happy couple after eleven years of it, and they must be comfortably off as everything is very nice in a simple way. I wonder how the Playboy will go in Oxford. How often was he rehearsed in Birmingham?

I'll leave this now till the post comes.

Later

No letter from you today. Please let me hear soon. I could write you a lot of nice things if I knew your address for certain. So now in four or five days we shall meet again! That will be *good* anyhow! It seems a long weary time since you went off do write me a nice letter I am afraid I shall be very busy in London but of course I shall be able to see you. I'm off now for a long country walk with Jack Yeats so I cannot write much. Dont mind dullness of enclosed note I was lying awake and in low spirits I hope you are all right again. Be good and cheerful

Your old Tramp

MS, TCD. *LM*, 153

To MOLLY ALLGOOD

[c/o Jack Yeats, Strete, Devon]
[4 June 1907]

Dearest Heart

Many thanks for your two letters which I got this morning. I hope you are better I am uneasy at all these bad accounts of your health. I am not very well myself either I am sorry to say. My cough is troublesome. I do not go to London till Saturday and I dont know yet what my address will be. Send me your London address as soon as you can as this will be the last time I can write to you at Oxford. Excuse my little scrawls from here, it isn't possible to write much. They are delightful people to be with here, but I am out of spirits rather as I am not well. I hope the second change to London will do me good. Write as often as you can I wrote *you* yesterday to the *New Theatre* I hope you will get it all right

Ever your old Tramp

MS, TCD. *LM*, 154

To MOLLY ALLGOOD

c/o Mrs Ward | 4 Handel Street | Brunswick Square | W.C.
[11 June 1907]

My dearest Life

It's too bad I have nothing to do this afternoon, but write letters, so I might have had you out to tea with me if I had arranged it. It's too late now as if I went round I would not find you. You were CAPITAL[1] last night in almost all of it, and everyone is speaking well of you. Yeats especially. He says also that you are excellent in the 'Shadow of the Glen' and that he withdraws all his former criticisms of you.

My poor pet I am sick of being shut away from you like this, and I fear it will get worse as the week goes on as I am being asked to go to all sorts of teas and things. Last night Yeats and I had supper with a Mrs Meakin and Lord Dunraven and his daughter.[2] All the time I was wishing I was away walking the world with my little fresh madcap of a changling! I wonder shall I get a sight of you tonight. There isn't much use going behind the scenes the place is so cramped and crowded. Tomorrow you have the two shows so there is no chance, on Thursday we are all going to the House of Commons to see Stephen Gwynn I met him this morning, and he asked [me] to go with the company so I shall get a word with you then at any rate I hope. Anyhow we haven't much more of it. In four more days the tour will be over. Be good and dont think that I am neglecting you I'd give the world and all to be with you but it is hard to arrange and it isn't very satisfactory in any case to go dragging about in the hot streets Ten thousand blessings on my little heart and soul.

Your old T.

MS, TCD. *LM*, 154

[1] Underlined seven times.
[2] Windham Thomas Wyndham-Quin, Earl of Dunraven and Mount-Earl (1841-1926), had been chairman of the Irish Land Conference (1902-3), and president of the Irish Reform Association. His daughter, Lady Ardee, was married to the Earl of Meath. The other guest was Annette Meakin (d. 1959), the first Englishwoman to cross Siberia by the Great Siberian Railway in 1900; a musician, travel writer, and translator of the classics, she published *Women in Transition* in 1907.

To MOLLY ALLGOOD

4 Handel Street | Brunswick Sq. | W.C.
Friday [14 June 1907]

Dearest

I have had a terrible night and I feel very ill. I want you to let me know at once, if you can, by what train and what day you go back to Ireland. If it is on Monday I will try and go with you — I suppose you would like me to do so?

Will you meet me tomorrow at *12 o'clock* sharp (Saturday) along the side of Brunswick Square that I showed you, and dine with me. I must talk to you and I will not say anything to upset you before your shows.

I nearly fainted yesterday when I got back to my room, my dispair was so intense. ⟨God⟩

I feel very ill indeed. Today I have to go to Greenwich to see Masefield.

Oh Christ what will become of me if you go on like this

Your T.

Write at once for Heaven's sake.

MS, TCD. *LM*, 155

To MOLLY ALLGOOD

Glendalough House [Glenageary]
Wednesday [19 June 1907]

My own dearest

I have been to the doctor and he says that there is nothing the matter with my lungs, that they are stronger in fact than they were a few years ago. He thinks however that I ought to get the glands out and recover myself a bit before I get married. That is reasonable enough as it would be wretched to knock up again after that affair. Meet me tomorrow at *2 o'clock at Westland Row* if it is fine and we'll go up towards the glens for a change we haven't been there for an age now. *If I am not there* or if it *is wet come down here — to the House —* by the *quarter* to *three*. That way we cannot miss each other. It seems very hard to have to put off our wedding again, but it will only be I hope till the autumn or early winter. I will take a 'digs', 'our digs'! when I come home from my summer outings and then it will be ready for us as soon as we are ready for it. What Heaven that will be, my sweetest little heart, it seems almost too beautiful to be possible but we'll make it possible all the same.

The Holidays are a great problem. Would Sally come with us if F J F. came?[1] I dont know about your coming here yet. I'll find out tonight, and tell you tomorrow.

Excuse these tags of paper I cant find anything better for the moment. Till tomorrow my dear love, good bye

Your old Tramp

MS, TCD. *LM*, 125

[1] JMS and Molly were planning to spend her holiday from the theatre in Glencree, west of Enniskerry, Co. Wicklow, a rugged valley stretching between the mountains near the base of the Great Sugar Loaf to the foot of Glendhu Mountain.

To ELKIN MATHEWS

Glendalough House | Kingstown | Ireland
June 20th [1907]

Dear Mr Mathews

Will you kindly let me have an account of my volume of Plays, and a cheque for the royalties that are due to me. I am settling up various accounts before I go away for the summer so I would be greatly obliged if you would be good enough to settle this little matter as soon as convenient. I hear the Plays are out of print I suppose you are bringing out another edition?[1]

Yours very truly
J. M. Synge

MS, TCD

[1] Mathews replied on 21 June 1907 (TCD) with a cheque for £3.11.3, being the royalty on the sale of 855 copies; he immediately set about preparing another edition.

To MOLLY ALLGOOD

Glendalough House [Glenageary]
Saturday [22 June 1907]

Dearest Heart

I feel lonesome these two long days without you, and I feel a little hurt, I think, that you did not choose to be with me, instead of with the crowd, when we have just been separated for so long, and are going to be separated again, in a few days, for a couple of months more. Have you heard about Glen Cree? If you go there I will try and find lodgings in the neighbourhood, I think, for the fortnight you are there, wouldn't that be great? I expected a letter from you last night and this morning but none has come. F.J.F. came out to see me last night in low spirits as usual, poor man, he seems to have no way of spending his holidays. I had a long letter from Lady G. last night with important news,[1] I will tell you some of it when I see you tomorrow.

Will you come down by the quarter to eleven tomorrow, if it is *fine*. I will meet you in the station lane and take you for a little walk, and then back *here* to lunch and to Bray afterwards. If it is wet come by the quarter *to two* and *come* here to the House. I wish it was tomorrow I have to go for another long lonely walk today God help me, when you're off amusing yourself — !!

Your old Tramp

MS, TCD. *LM*, 127

¹ Payne's relationship with the Abbey players and directors had remained uneasy, and Lady Gregory wrote from London on 20 June 1907 (TCD) that he had now resigned, at the end of the tour, and was to become manager of a new theatre Miss Horniman planned to open in Manchester. Yeats had rejected an offer to transfer his plays there, and Miss Horniman then made it clear that after 1910 she would withdraw all support from the Abbey; until that time she would honour her commitment to provide a rent-free theatre, but refused to have anything to do with Ireland, JMS, or Lady Gregory again. (See *TB*, 223–6).

To MOLLY ALLGOOD

[Glendalough House, Glenageary]
[?25 June 1907]

The post has passed I half hoped there'd be a line from you asking me to go in today, however I am sure it is better for you to stay quiet. A thousand loves and blessings on you my dear treasure.

T

MS fragment, Texas. *LM*, 157

To MOLLY ALLGOOD

Glendalough Ho. [Glenageary]   26.VI.07

Dearest Love

Thanks for your note, excuse this paper I have no other.¹ Dont forget that you have to tell me *when* and *where* I'm to meet you tomorrow. I'll bring in the bag with me and leave it a[t] Westland Row for you, if you really want it.

Remember to ask the doctor every thing I told you, ask him also how much of his medicine you are to take, and if you are to take it again when you get a turn. Ask him if cycling is better for you than walking, and anything else you can think of.² I am ready to kill myself for having let you walk so much last autumn. I thought you were old enough to manage yourself — God help us!!!!! However I hope there's no harm done. Isnt the weather awful. It is making my cough worse again.

Forever ever your old Tramp

Did you order my Guardians last night? If you didn't you had better not as you wouldn't have time to get them before you go.

MS, TCD. *LM*, 157

¹ Scribbled on the back of the first page of a draft of 'In a Landlord's Garden'.

2 Among Molly's papers is a reassuring letter to her concerning her menstrual difficulties from Arthur P. Barry (1879–1938), gynaecologist of the National Maternity Hospital, Holles Street, Dublin, 26 June 1907, and a draft of a letter in JMS's hand, evidently for Molly to copy, addressed to the doctor:

Mr Synge brought me your kind letter last week, and I am extremely glad to know what you tell me. I fancied things were much more serious and something I said frightened Mr S also. I feel quite easy in my mind now and I am able to enjoy my holiday . . . . I dont know how to thank you for all your kindness, but I hope you will believe that I am grateful to you indeed. (TCD)

Apparently JMS himself had written to the doctor on 26 June 1907.

To MOLLY ALLGOOD

> Glendalough Ho. [Glenageary]
> Wednesday [26 June 1907]

My little Heart's Core

I want you to find this in your little paw when you awake to-morrow morning to drive away your depressions I have had a long talk about you with my mother, and I feel cheered-up some how. She seems to have known a lot of cases like yours Mrs X. Mrs Z. and Miss Y and so on and they all got well and lived happily ever afterwards.[1] I think it's only fair that you should have a turn at being ill too, if you were too well you wouldn't be able to sympathise with your poor old Tramp when he gets put up on the shelf. Now be very good and very cheerful and take care of yourself.

My mother — on second thoughts — seemed to think it would be rather improper for me to stay in the same cottage with you and Sally. So enquire about other places near by, when you get there. I shall go up on Friday — if it is fine and stay the one night anyhow and see how it suits me and then I can look round.[2] Now be sure and be happy you'll find your poor little illness will only draw us closer together, and make us realize how much we love each other — if that is possible — . I mean I dont think we'll ever really know how dear we are to each other.

For ever and ever my own poor darling

> Your old Tramp.

MS, TCD. *LM*, 156

1 On 26 June 1907 Mrs Synge wrote to Samuel Synge, 'Johnnie is rather distressed just now as he hears Mollie is not in good health, those long walks she used to take with him every Sunday for so many months were too much for her . . . . I am not telling anyone about this delicacy of Mollie's but you, it is best to say nothing about it.' (TCD)

2 They eventually settled in neighbouring cottages close by Lough Bray, on the old Military Road between Enniskerry and Glencree.

To FRANK FAY

> Glendalough House [Glenageary]
> June 27 [1907]

Dear Fay

I am much obliged for the cuttings and your letter.[1] I have been going to write to you all the week, but have let the time go by as usual.

The books of Elizabethan lyrics we were looking at here one evening were A Sixteenth Century Anthology, and a Seventeenth Century Anthology, both in *Red Letter Library* series. It is hard to say which is the best one wants both to complet the Elizabeth[an] series. It is the 16th cent. volume that is edited by A. Symons.[2]

I will write you out Meyerfeld's opinion as nearly as I can one of these days — I haven't time tonight — and send it to you.

My plans are still very uncertain but I shall be here off and on for some time still, and I hope we may have a walk when the weather takes up if it ever does so. My cough is still dragging on so I am rather anxious to avoid getting too much rain.

> Yours sincerely
> J. M. Synge

MS, Lilly

1 With his request on 22 June 1907 (TCD) for Meyerfeld's comments on the plays when he saw them in London and his enquiry, Fay had sent a copy of *The Peasant and Irish Ireland*, 9 Feb 1907, with two articles about the Abbey rows, and *The Planet*, 22 June 1907, with an article praising *Riders to the Sea* in London.

2 Arthur Symons (1865–1945), poet, critic, and translator, editor of the *Savoy* and author of *The Symbolist Movement in Literature* (1899), was a long-time friend of Yeats. He had written to Lady Gregory on 11 Feb 1903 recommending that JMS, whom he had met the evening before, send *Riders to the Sea* to the *Fortnightly* (but without success; see *TB*, 39). Among the many anthologies he edited was *A Sixteenth Century Anthology* (1905) in the Red Letter Library series established by Blaikie and Son of London in 1902. The *Seventeenth Century Anthology* (1904) was edited by Alice Meynell.

To W. B. YEATS

> Glendalough House | Kingstown
> June 27th/07

Dear Yeats

I have seen Henderson today. At first he seemed rather sad, and inclined to think he was being very badly treated, but he rather cheered up. He says that it would be impossible for him to get anything to do at present, so that he thinks we should give him three months notice or its equivalent. We shall want him I suppose for two months, so it would probably be better to give him the extra month's salary and let him feel that he is being well treated by us. As to statement of accounts he says that if a mere statement of how we stand is needed he can make it out easily himself, but if we want a ballance sheet we should have to get Swayne as you suggested.[1] I am not sure from your letter which you want so I have told him to ask you. I do not feel sure that we are wise to get rid of Henderson altogether as he was certainly of use in bringing us in audiences. From one reason or another we are all unpopular and it was a good thing to have one man in the place who was definitely popular in Dublin. However we could not keep him at his present salary or in his present position, and I suppose it would only make complications if we tried to keep him on in any sort of minor position as Master of the Ceremonies.

Yours
J. M. Synge

MS, Berg. *TB*, 228

[1] With the probability of Miss Horniman's stopping her subsidy, the directors had decided to cut back expenses by stopping W. A. Henderson's position (cf. *TB*, 227 ff.). Swayne Little was the theatre's accountant.

INDEX OF RECIPIENTS

GENERAL INDEX

JMS = J. M. Synge